Left-Handed Bass Chord Picture Book

© 2017 BY MEL BAY PUBLICATIONS, INC., PACIFIC, MO 63069.
ALL RIGHTS RESERVED. INTERNATIONAL COPYRIGHT SECURED. MADE AND PRINTED IN U.S.A.
No part of this publication may be reproduced in whole or in part, or stored in a retrieval system, or transmitted in any form or by any means, electronic, mechanical, photocopy, recording, or otherwise, without written permission of the publisher.

Visit us on the Web at www.melbay.com — E-mail us at email@melbay.com

Tuning the Bass

The four opens strings of the bass guitar will be of the same pitch as the four notes shown in the illustration of the piano keyboard. Note that all of the strings are below the middle C of the piano keyboard.

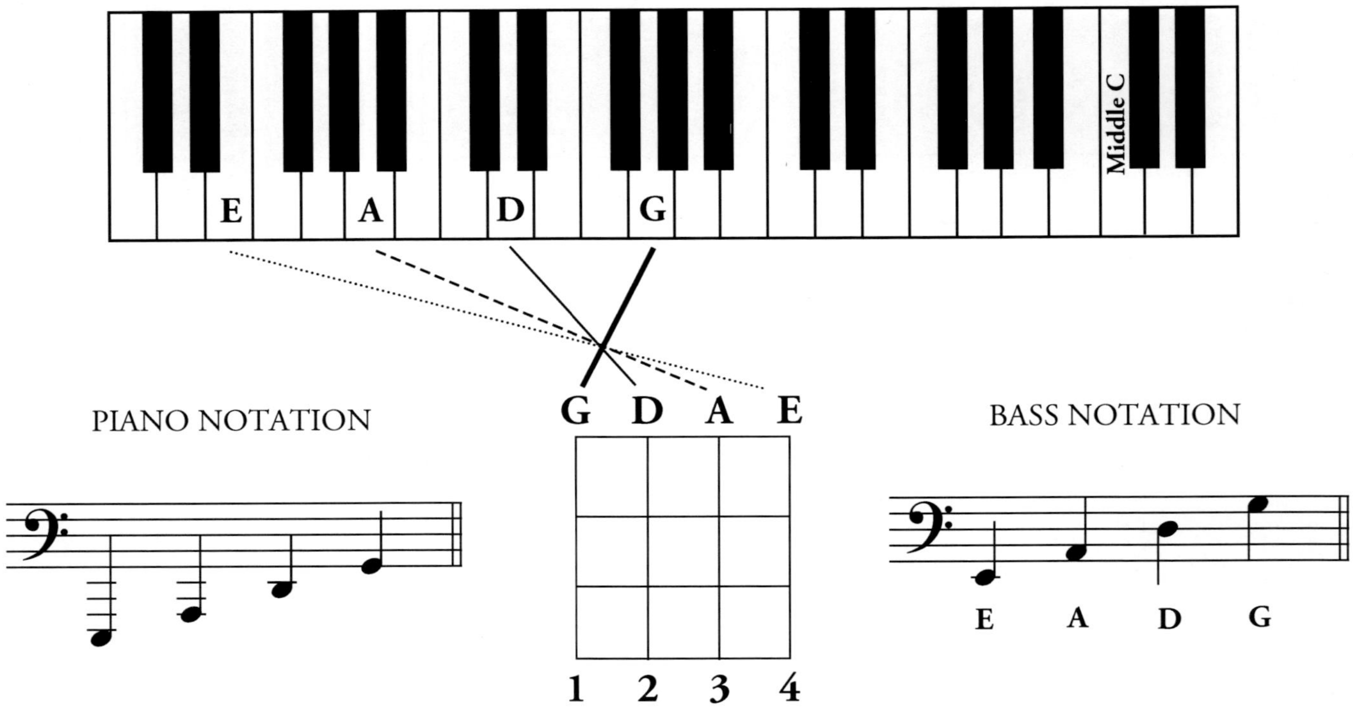

Another Method of Tuning

1. Tune the 4th string in unison with the E or 19th white key to the LEFT of MIDDLE C on the piano.
2. Place the finger behind the fifth fret of the 4th string. This will give you the tone or pitch of the 3rd string (A).
3. Place finger behind the fifth fret of the 3rd string to get the pitch of the 2nd string (D).
4. Repeat same procedure to obtain the pitch of the 1st string (G).

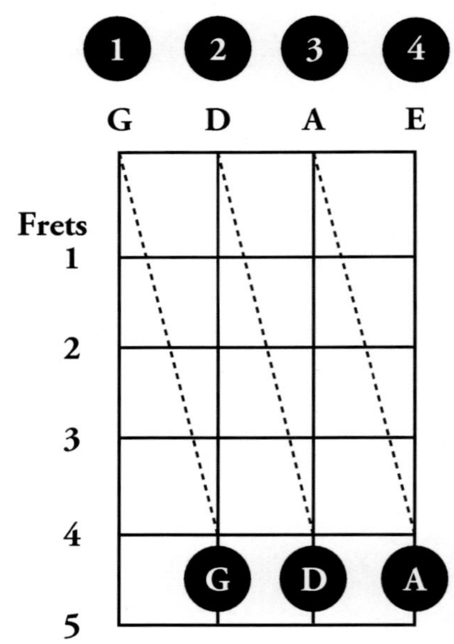

Electronic Guitar Tuner

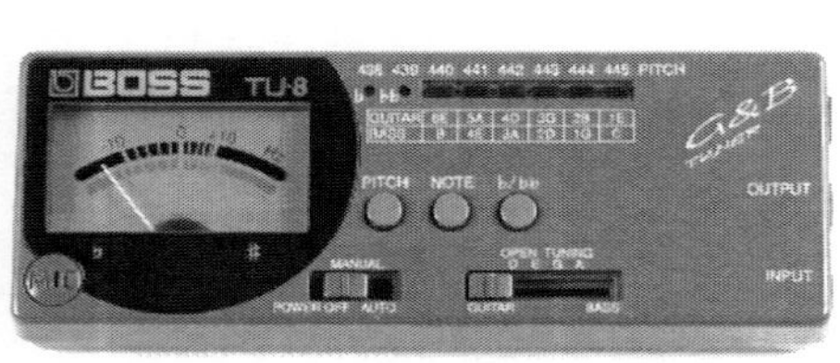

Electronic Guitar Tuners are available at your music store. They are a handy device and highly recommended.

Contents

Key of C

CMaj

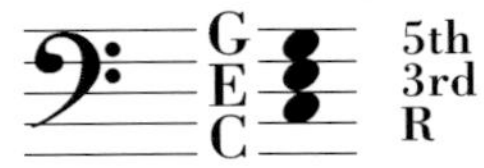

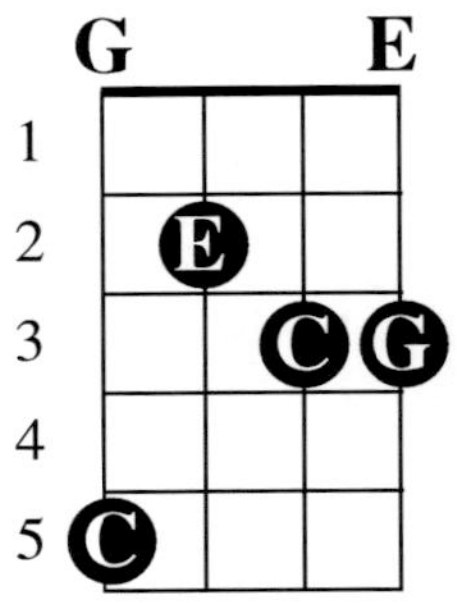

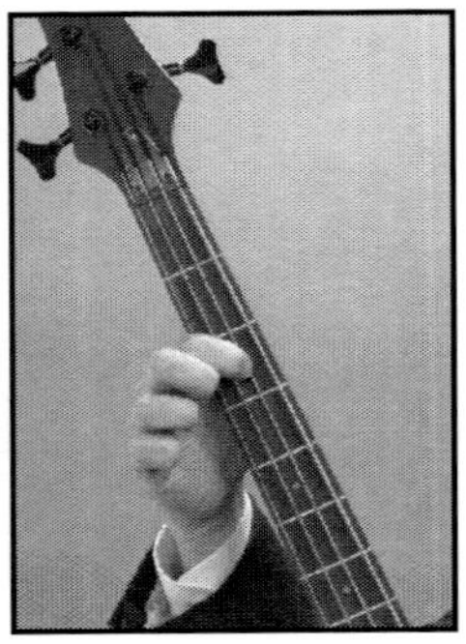

Root – C

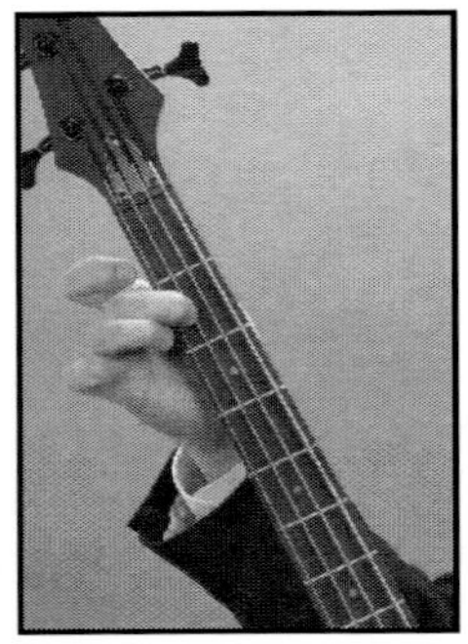

3rd – E

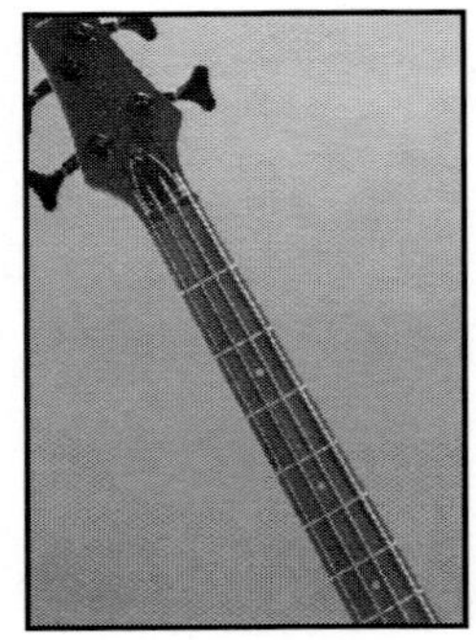

5th – G

Cmin

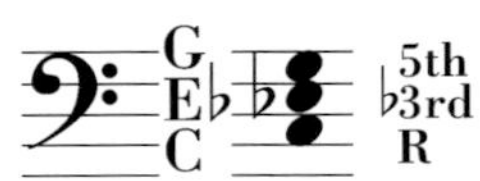

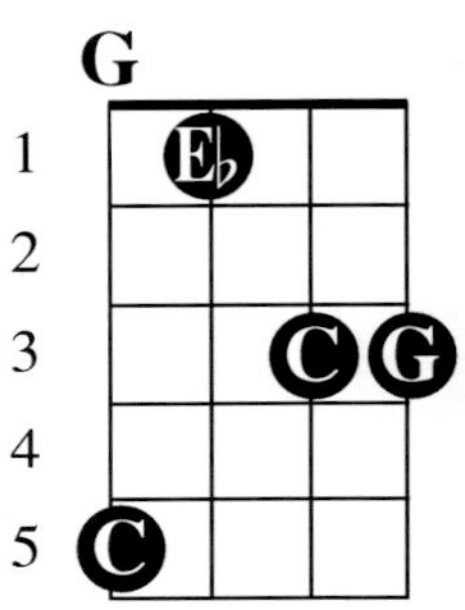

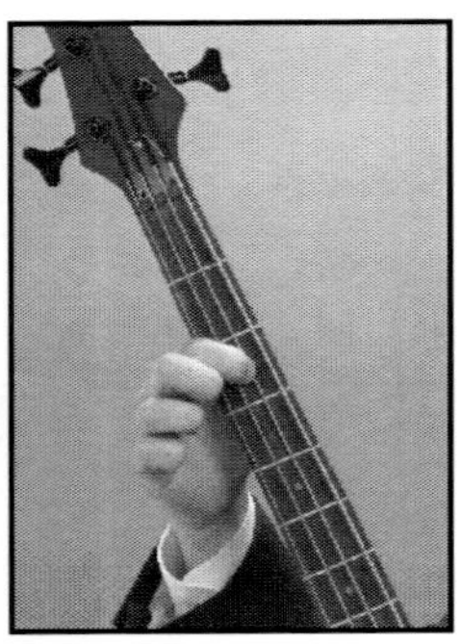

Root – C

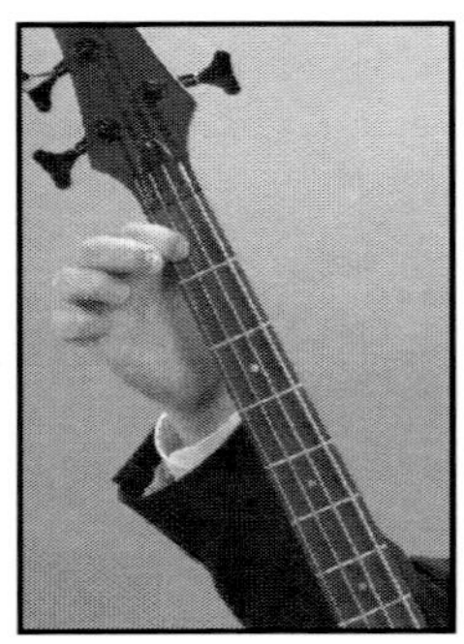

♭3rd – E♭

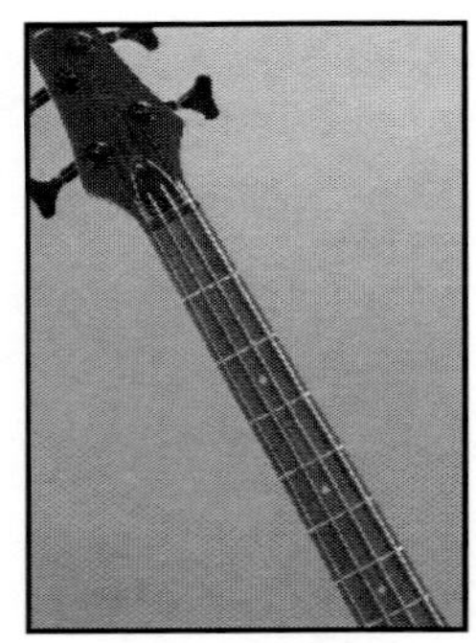

5th – G

C7

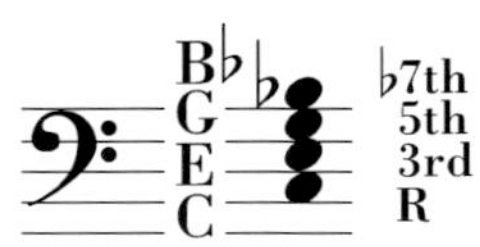

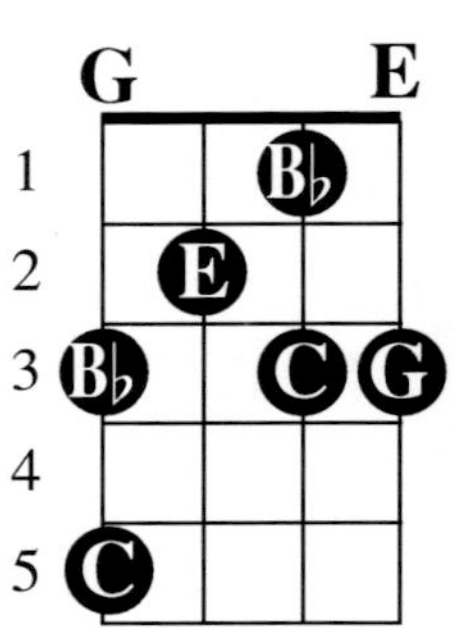

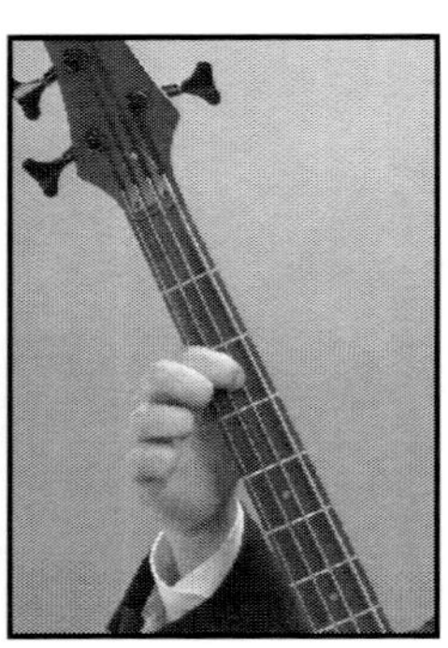

Root – C

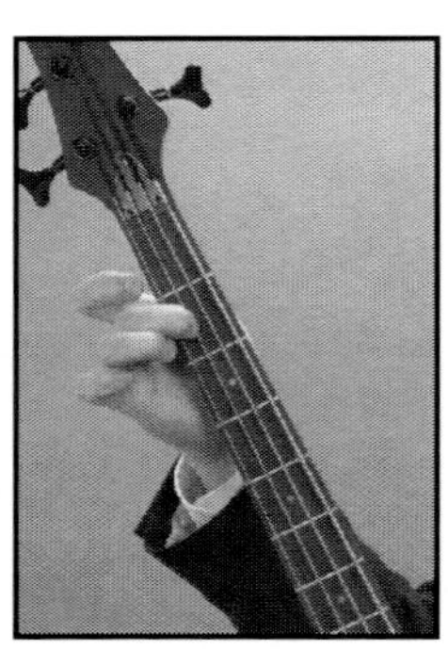

3rd – E

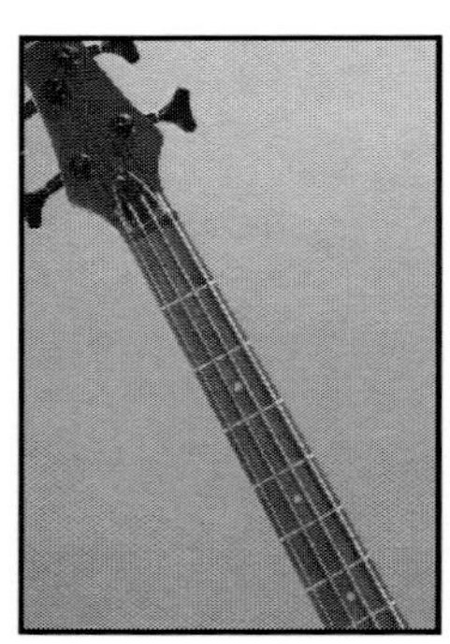

5th – G

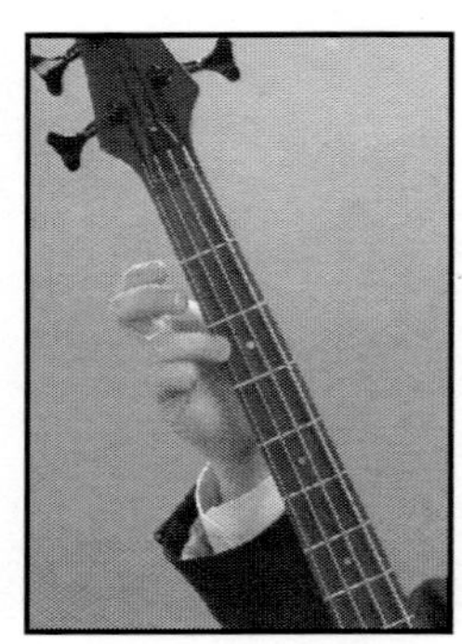

♭7th – B♭

Key of C (cont.)

C7sus

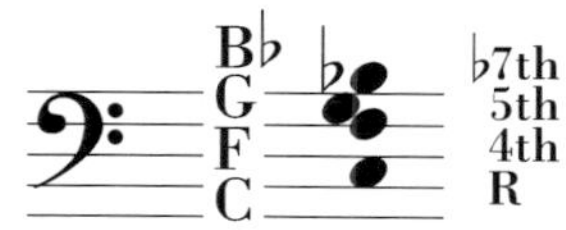

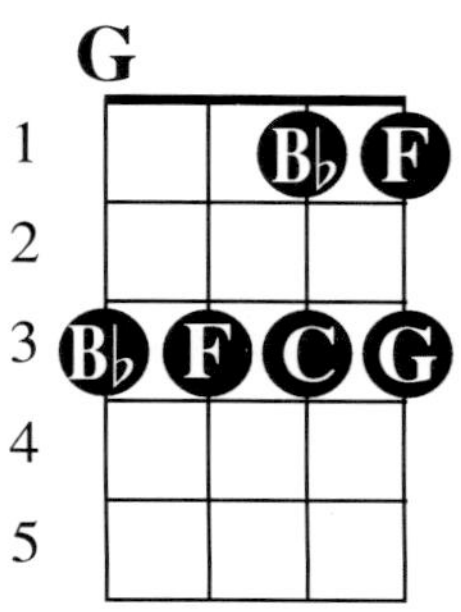

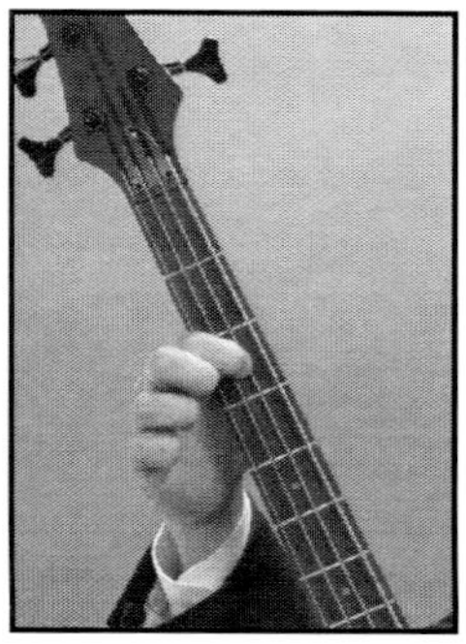

Root – C

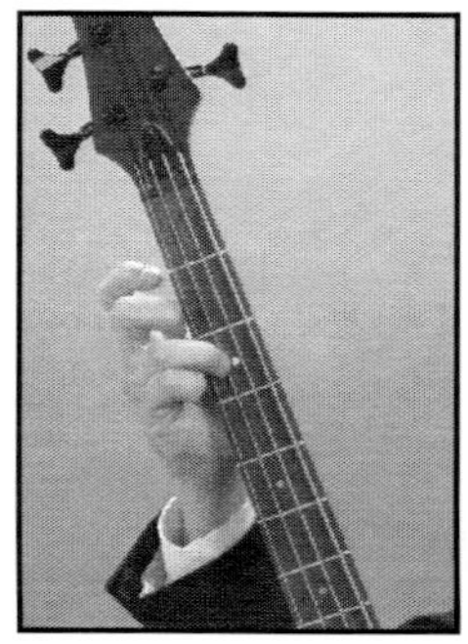

4th – F

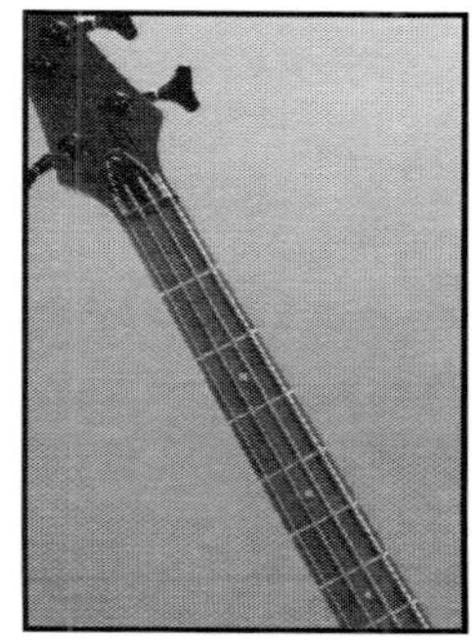

5th – G

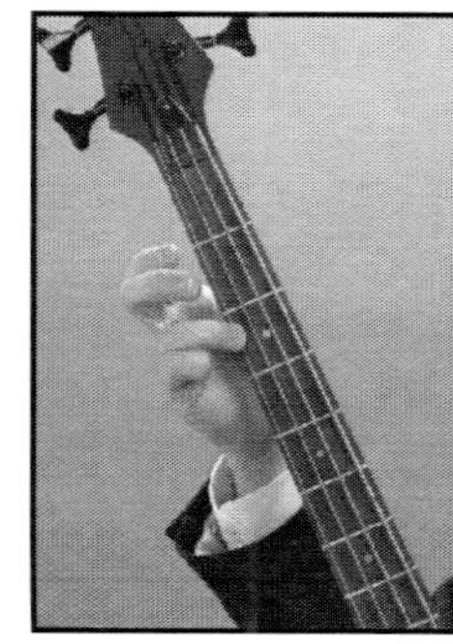

♭7th – B♭

Cm7

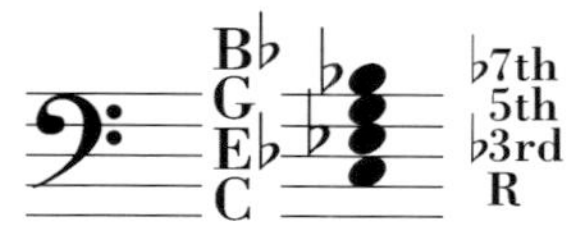

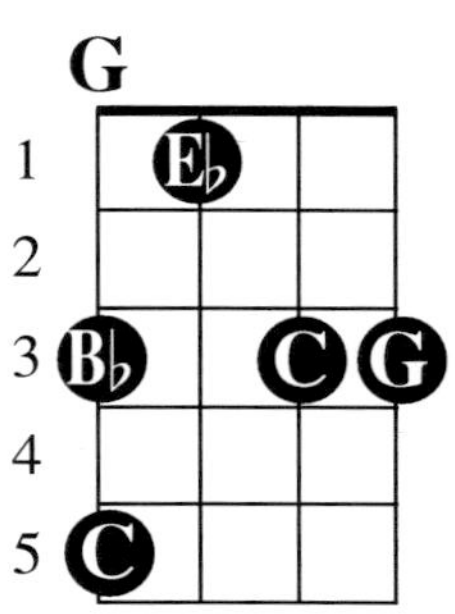

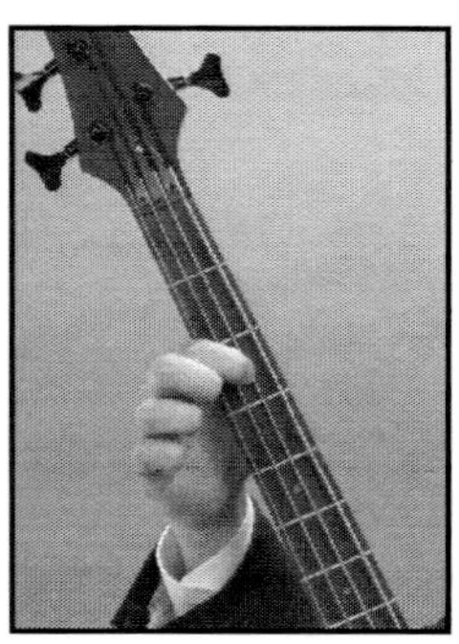

Root – C

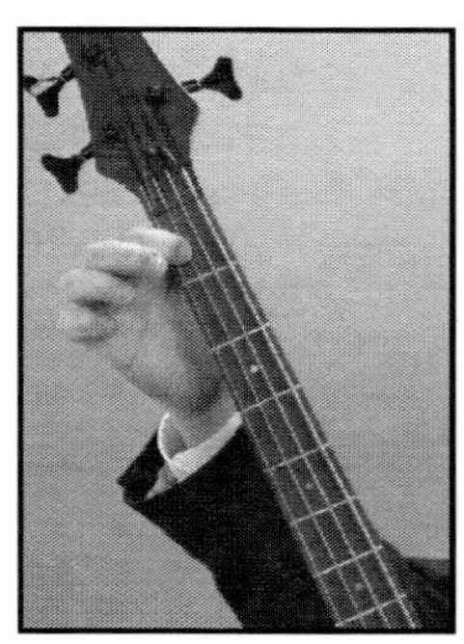

♭3rd – E♭

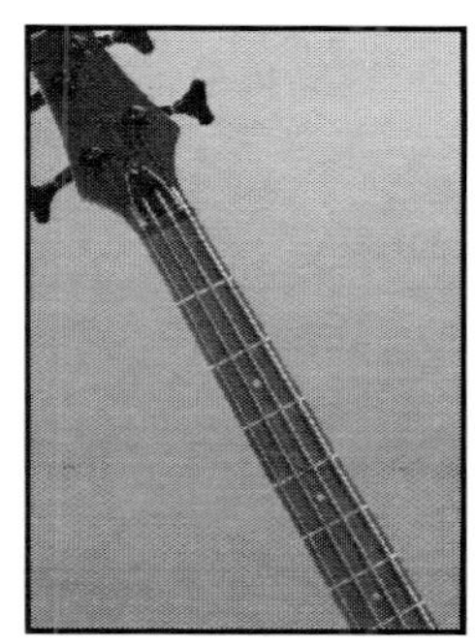

5th – G

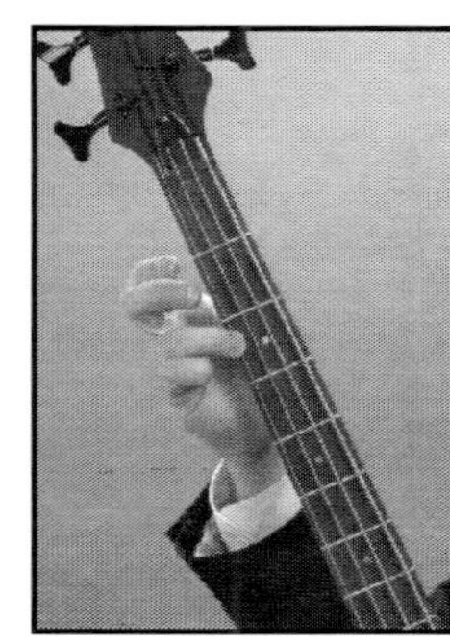

♭7th – B♭

CMa7

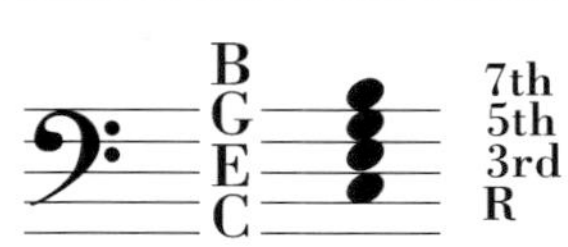

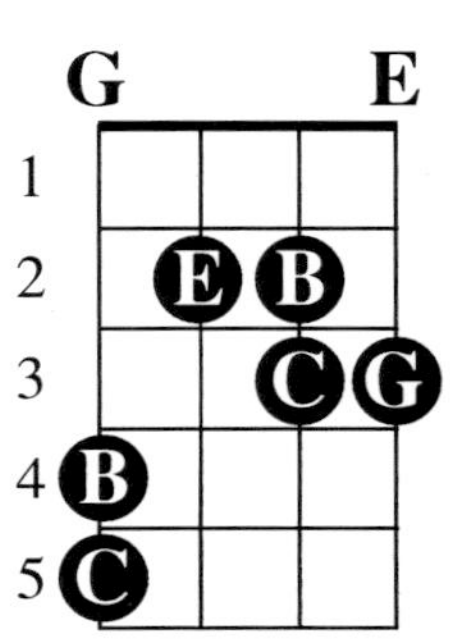

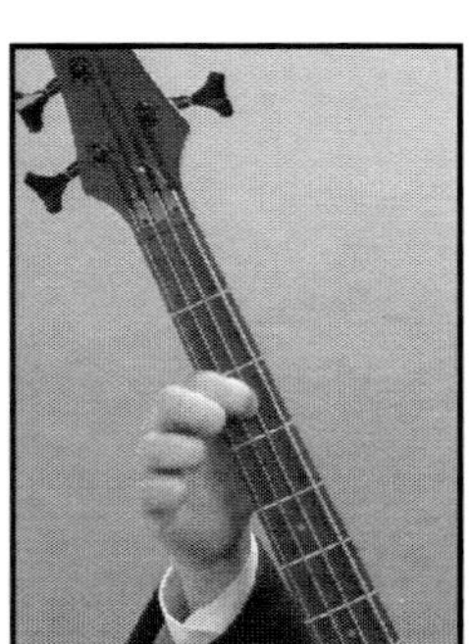

Root – C

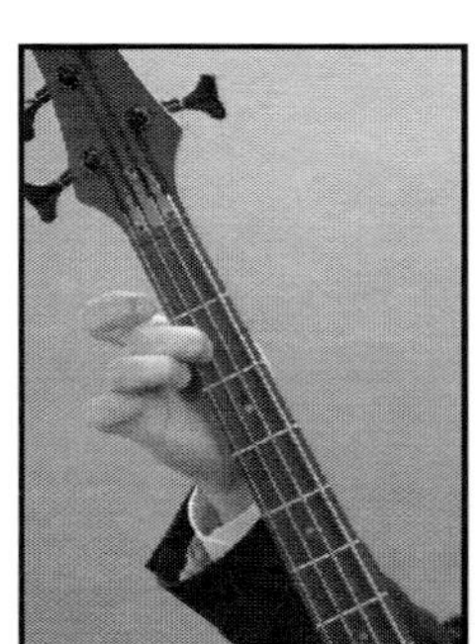

3rd – E

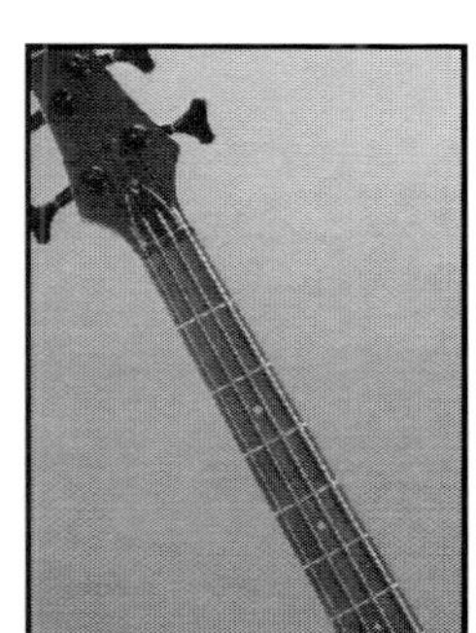

5th – G

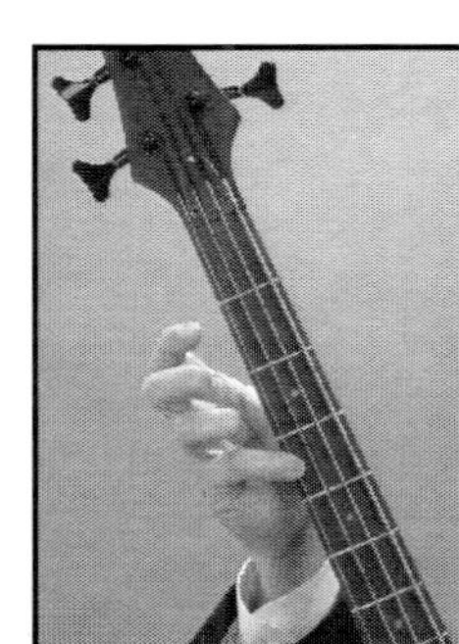

7th – B

Key of C (cont.)

Cdim

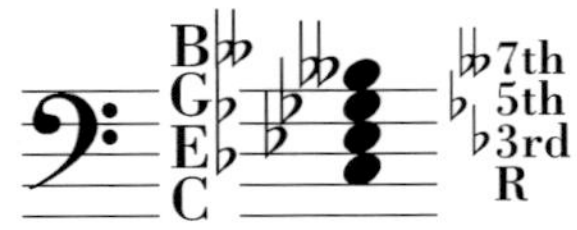

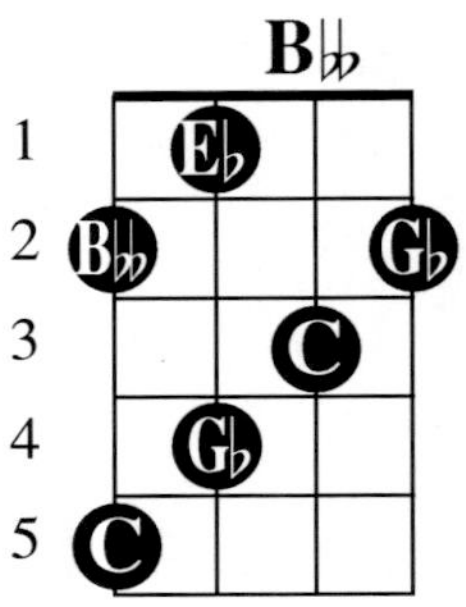

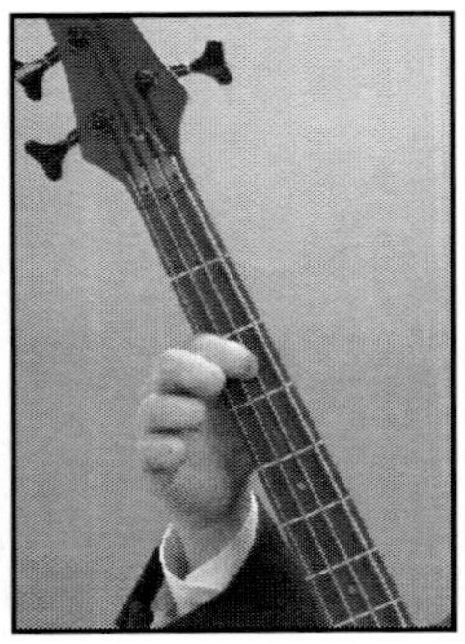

Root – C

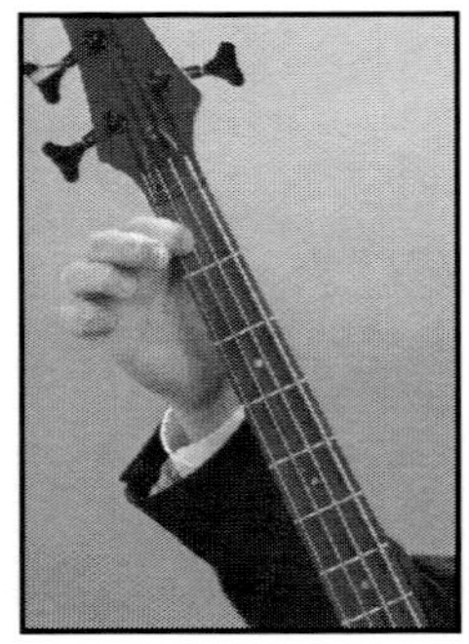

♭3rd – E♭

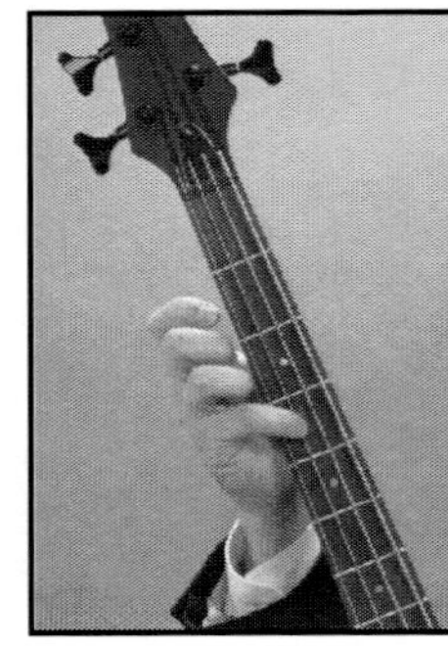

♭5th – G♭

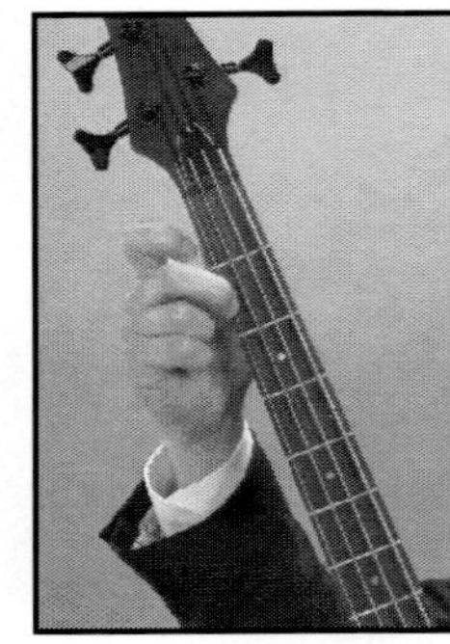

♭♭7th – B♭♭

Caug

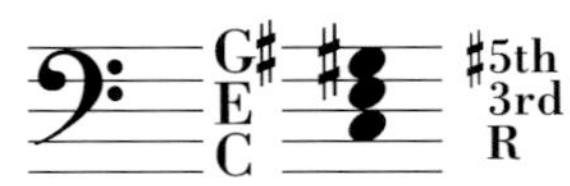

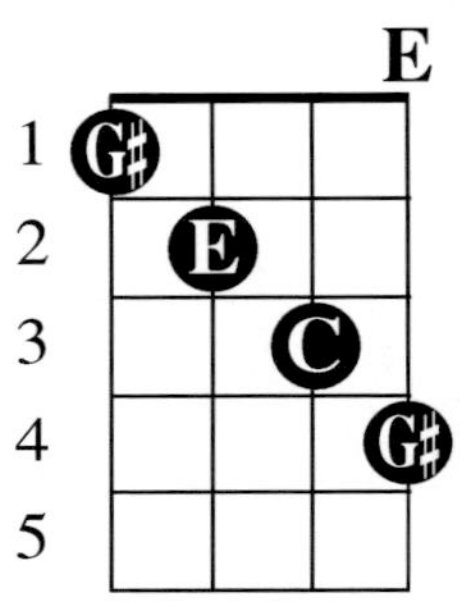

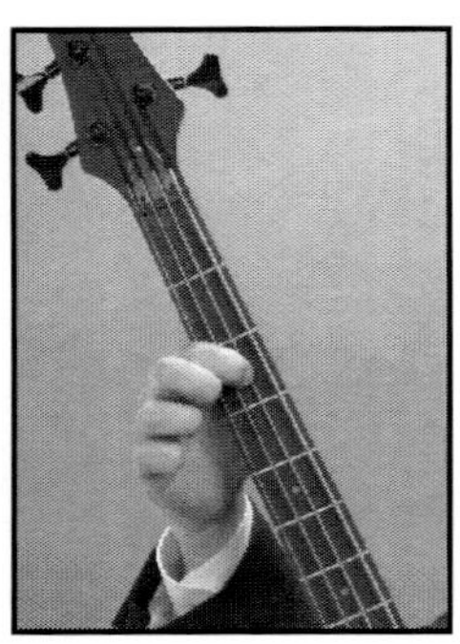

Root – C

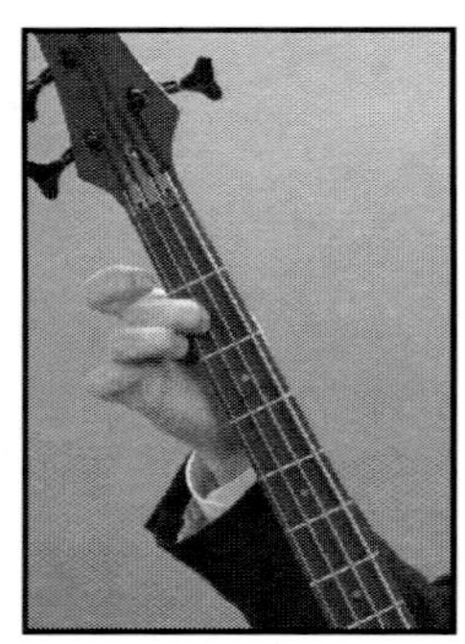

3rd – E

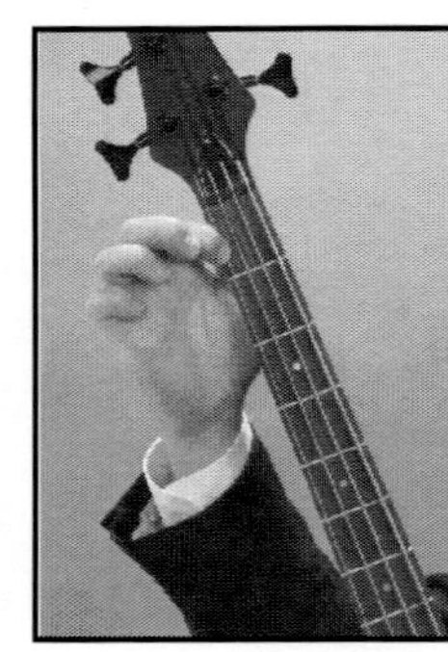

♯5th – G♯

C6

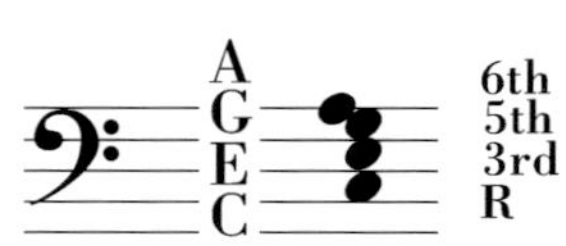

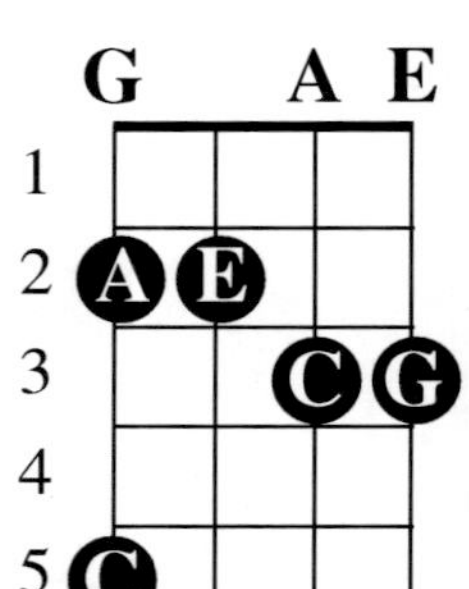

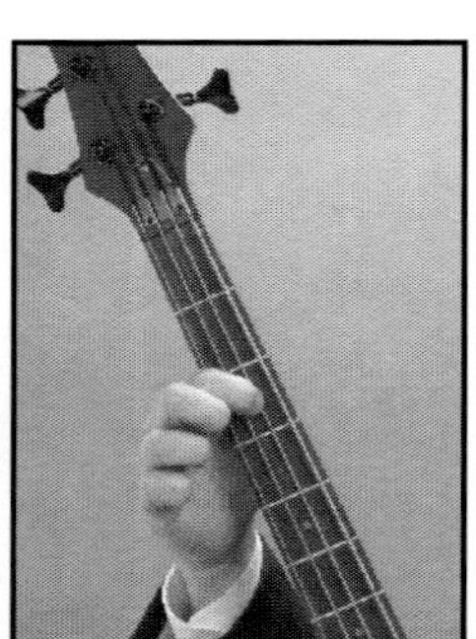

Root – C

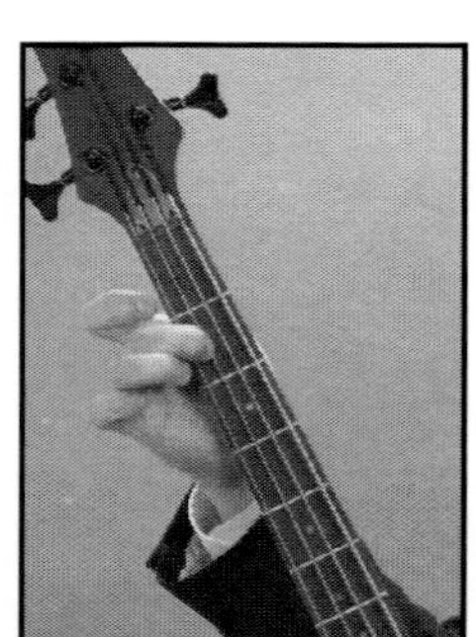

3rd – E

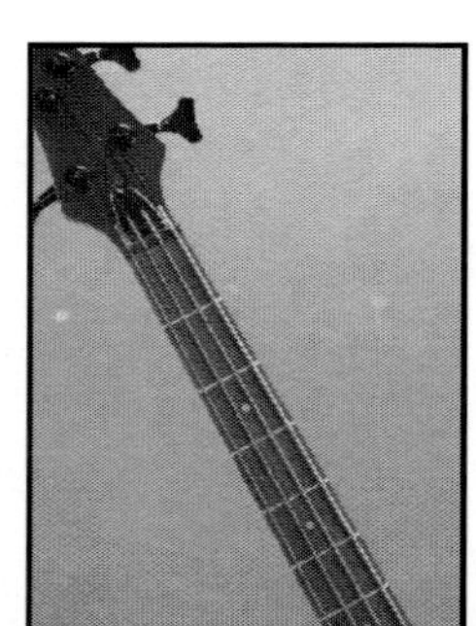

5th – G

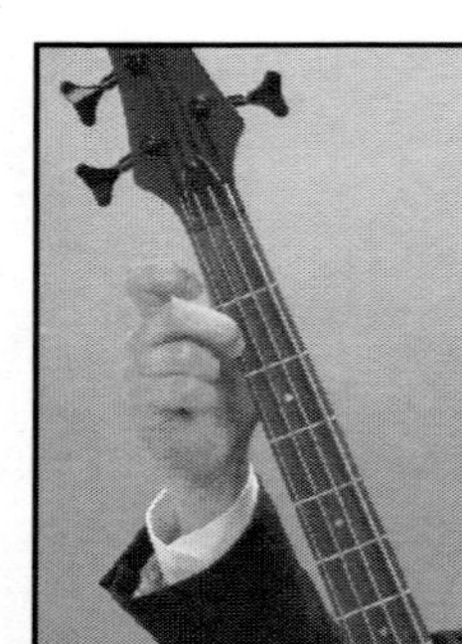

6th – A

Key of C (cont.)

Cm6

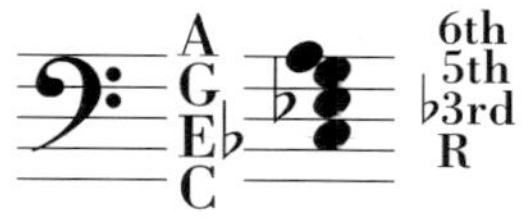

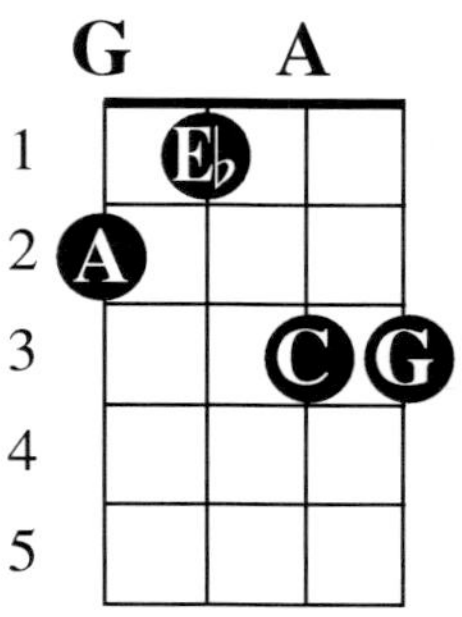

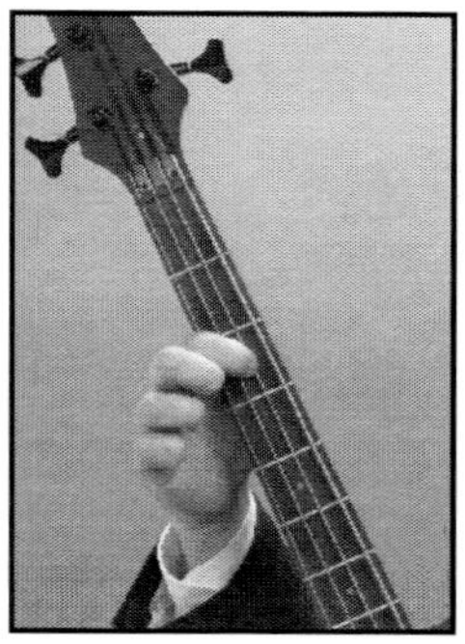

Root – C

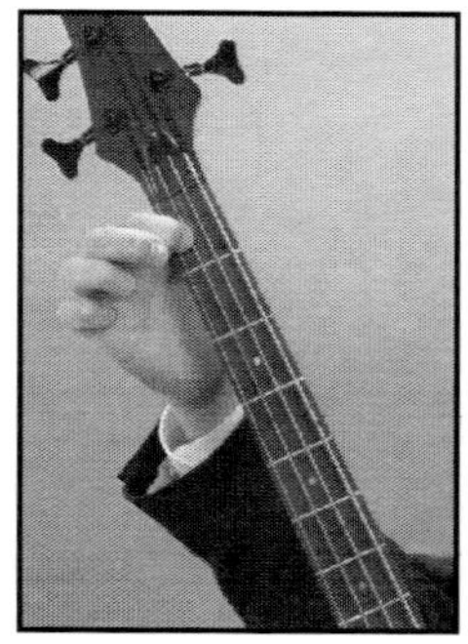

♭3rd – E♭

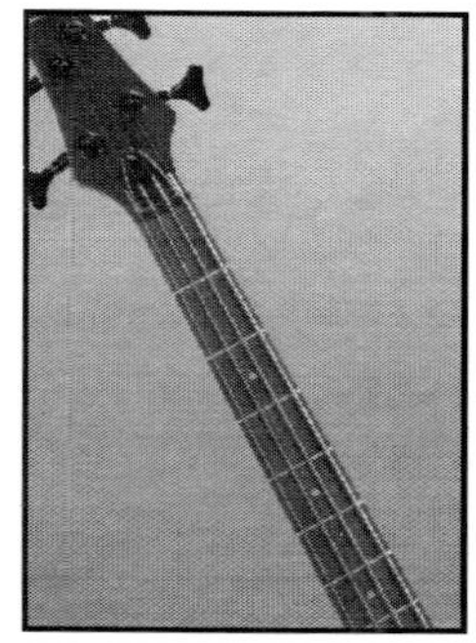

5th – G

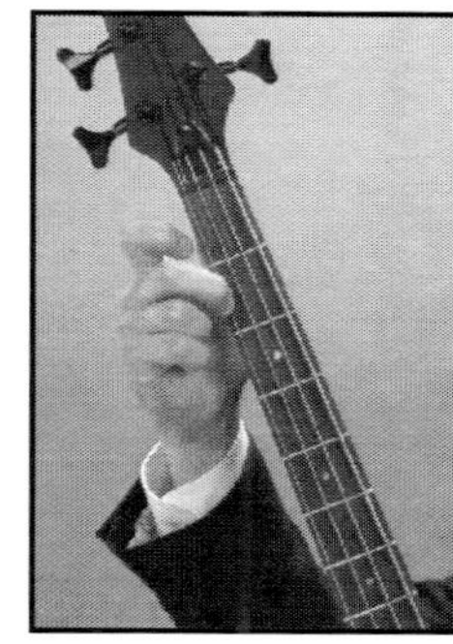

6th – A

C7♯5

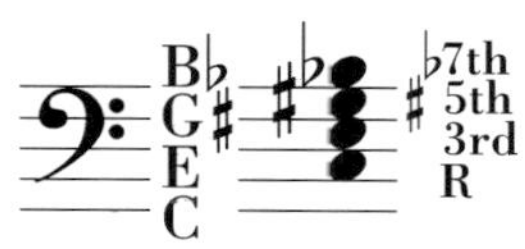

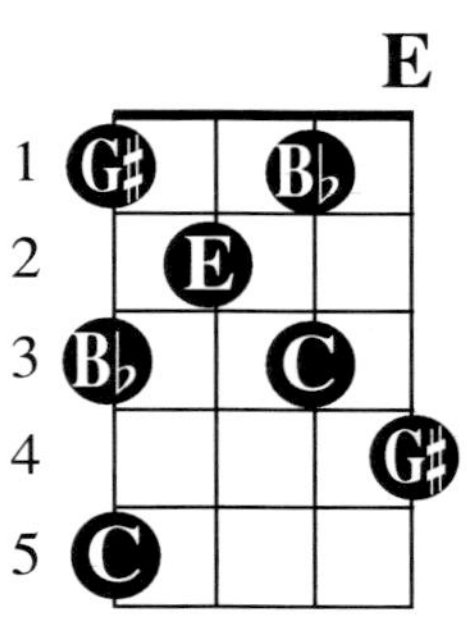

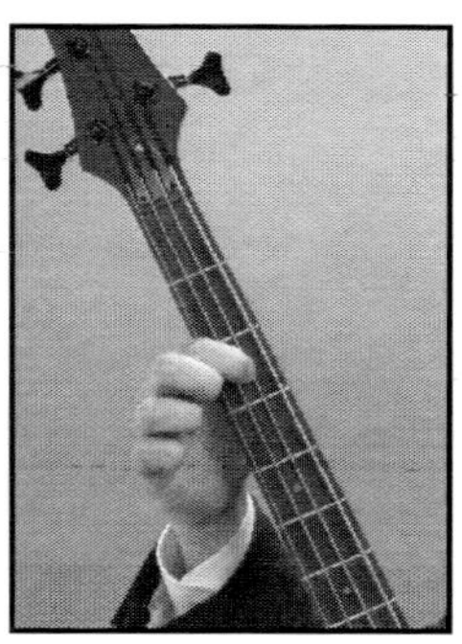

Root – C

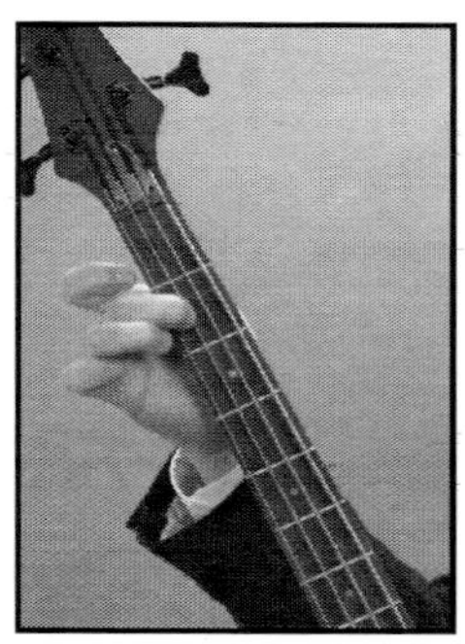

3rd – E

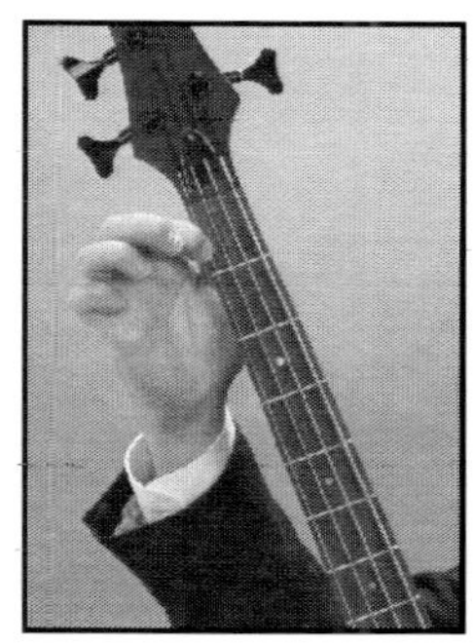

♯5th – G♯

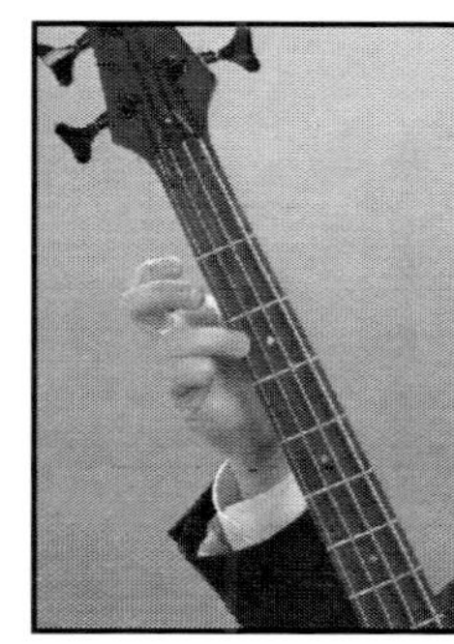

♭7th – B♭

C7♭5

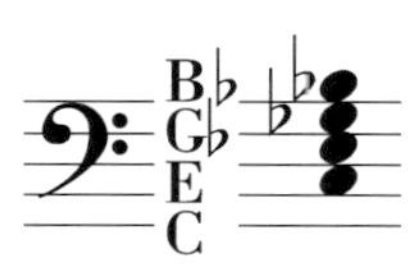

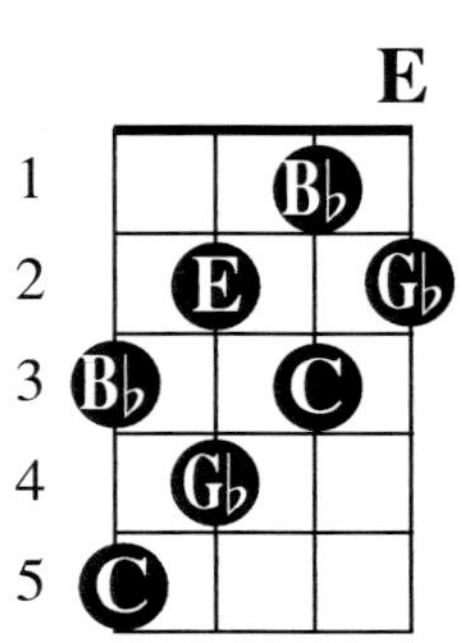

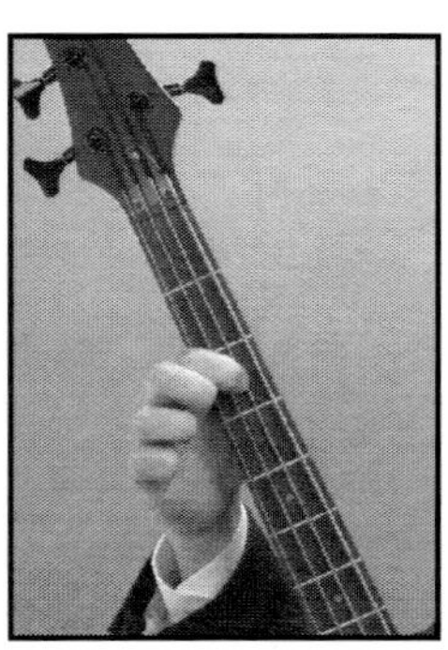

Root – C

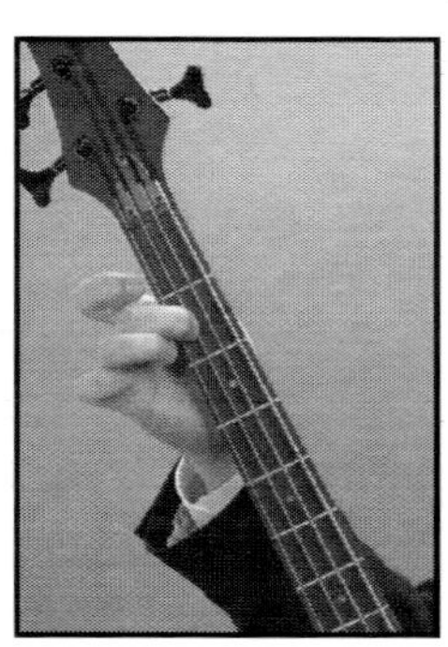

3rd – E

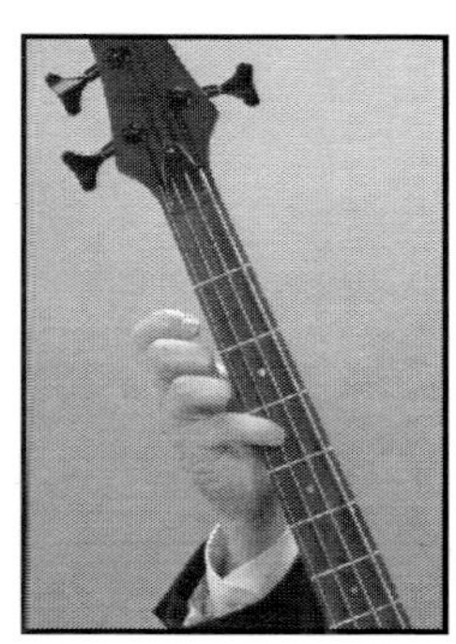

♭5th – G♭

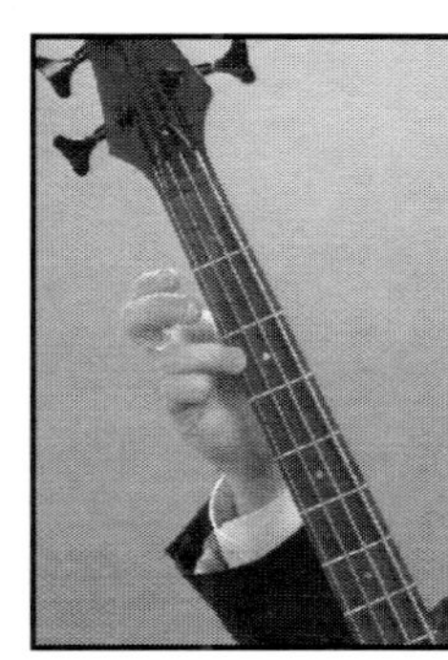

♭7th – B♭

Key of C♯/D♭

D♭Major

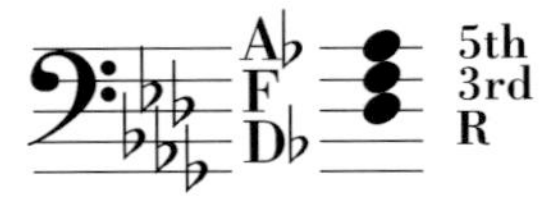

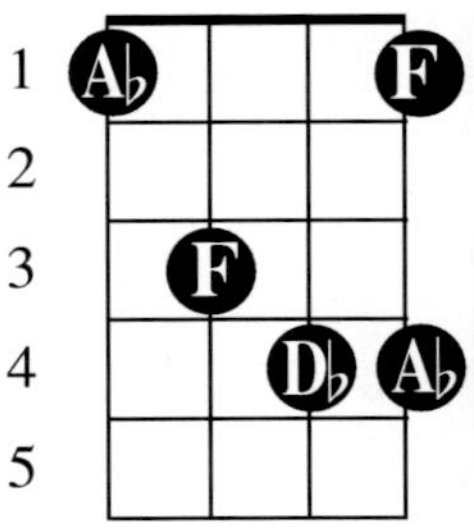

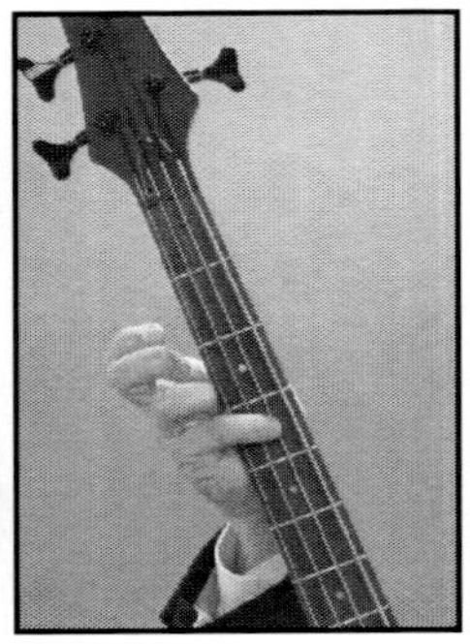

Root – D♭

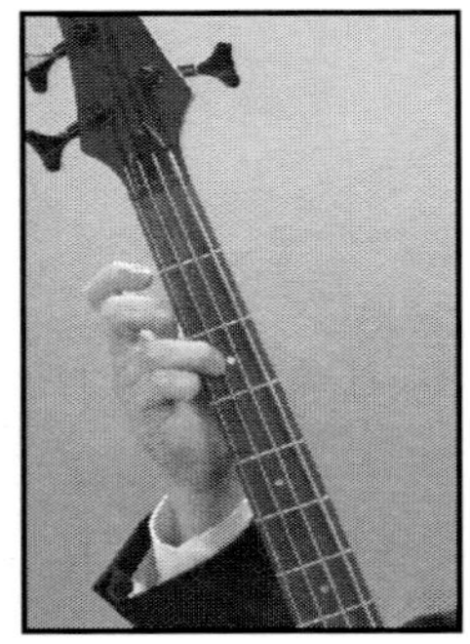

3rd – F

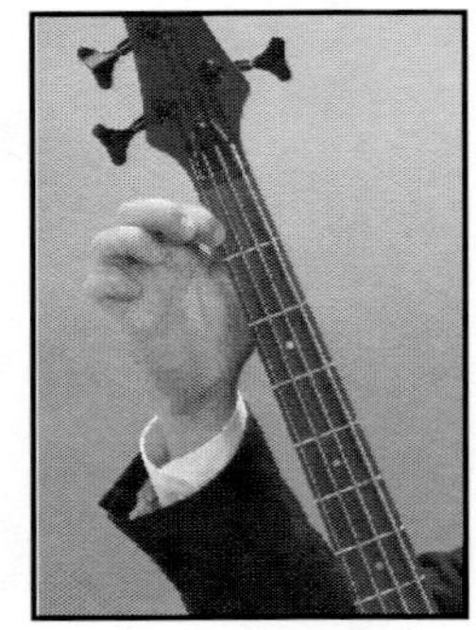

5th – A♭

D♭minor

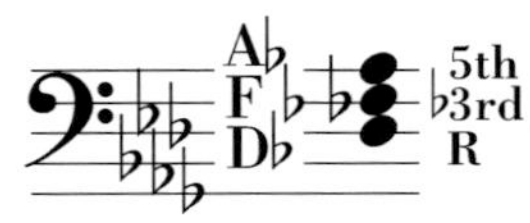

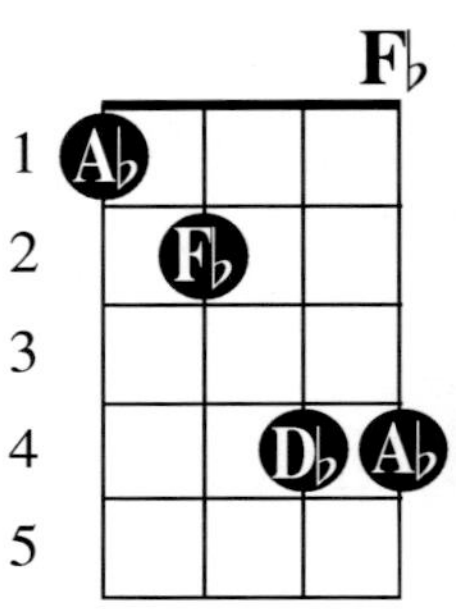

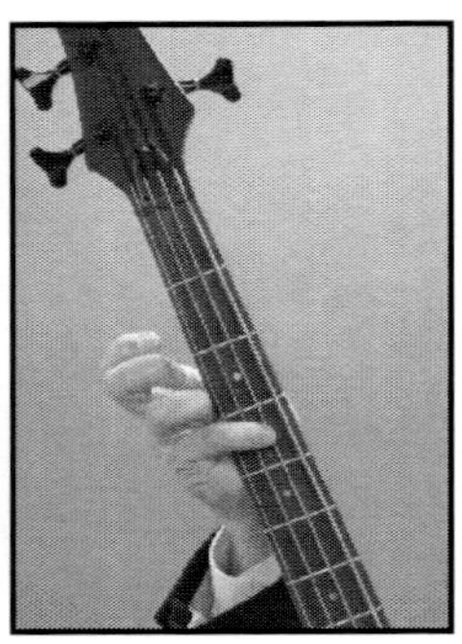

Root – D♭

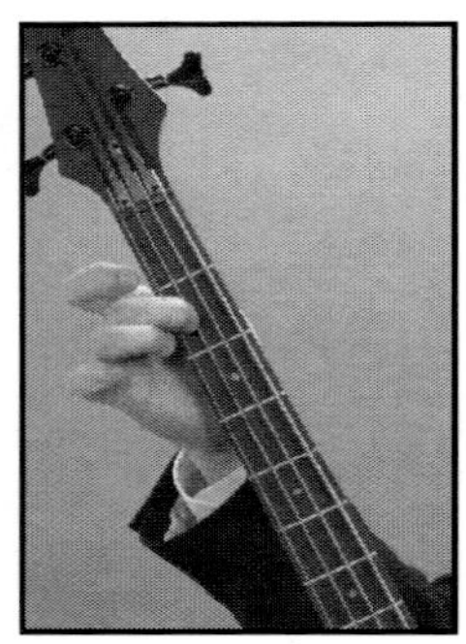

♭3rd – F♭ or E

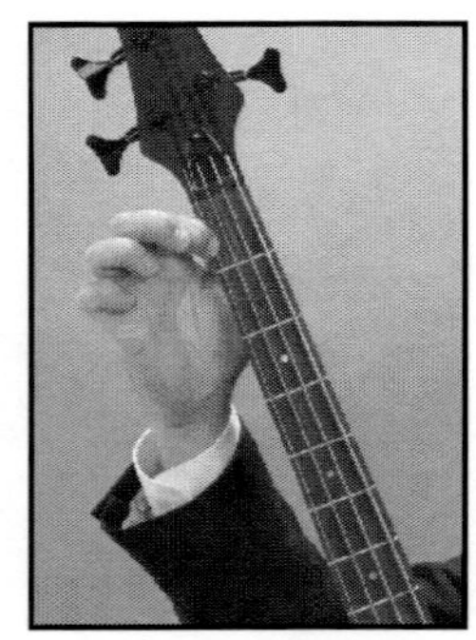

5th – A♭

D♭7

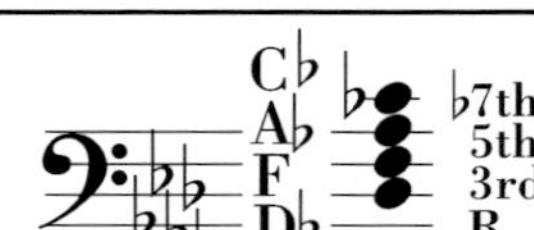

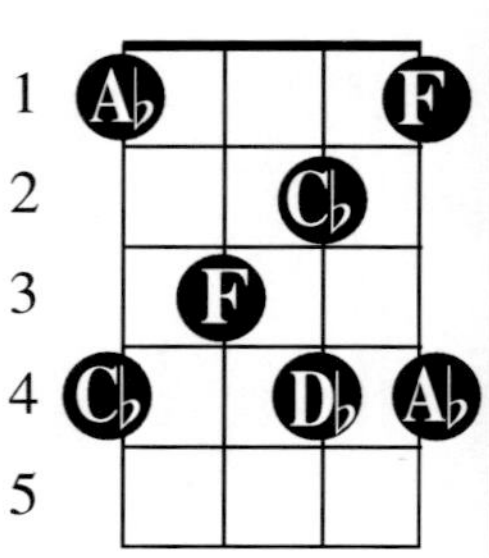

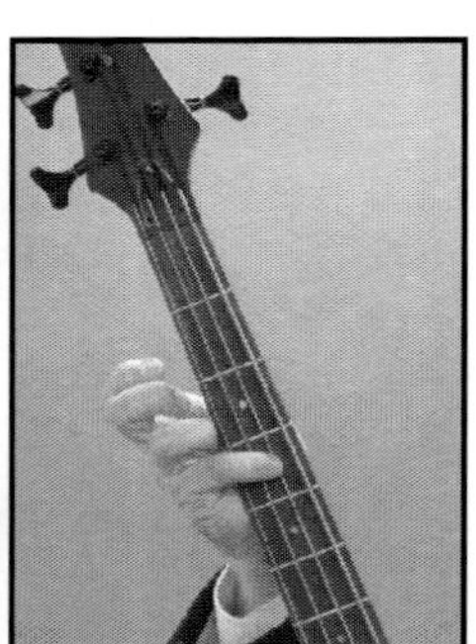

Root – D♭

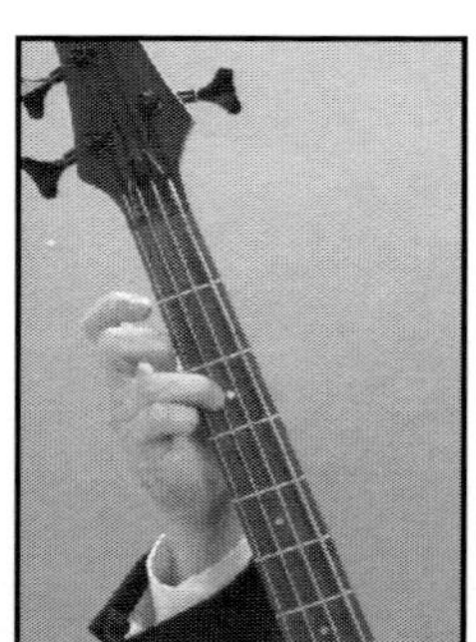

3rd – F

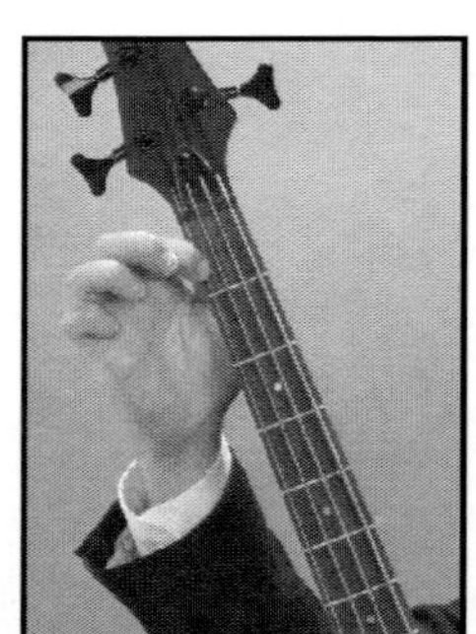

5th – A♭

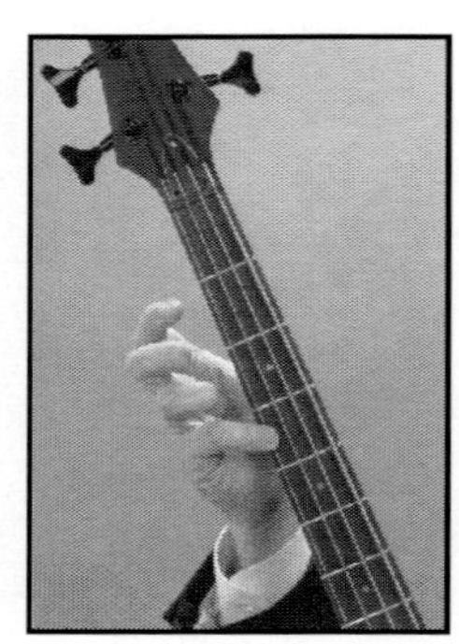

♭7th – C♭ or B

Key of C♯/D♭ (cont.)

D♭7sus

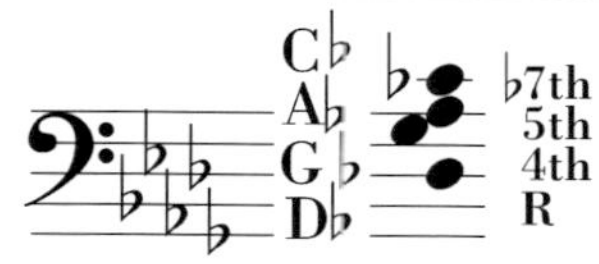

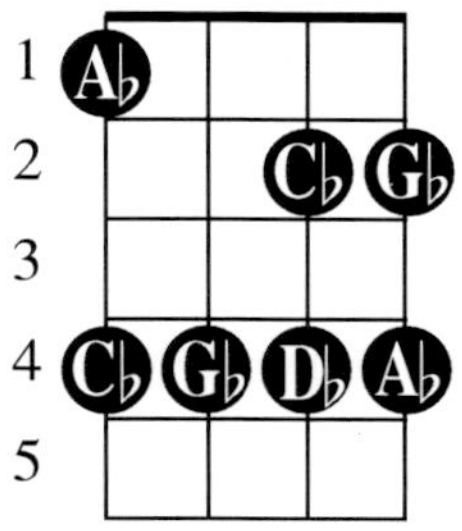

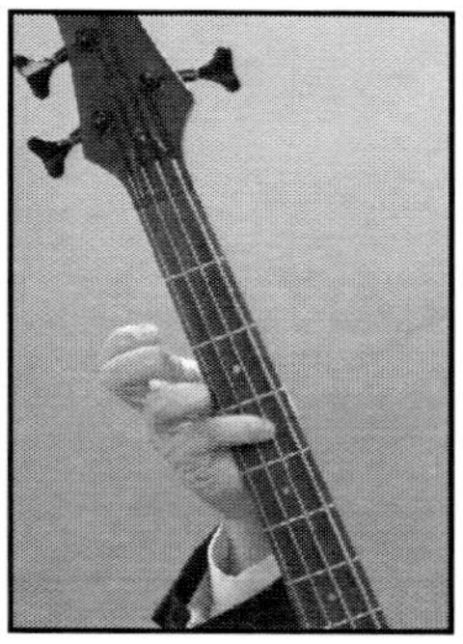

Root – D♭

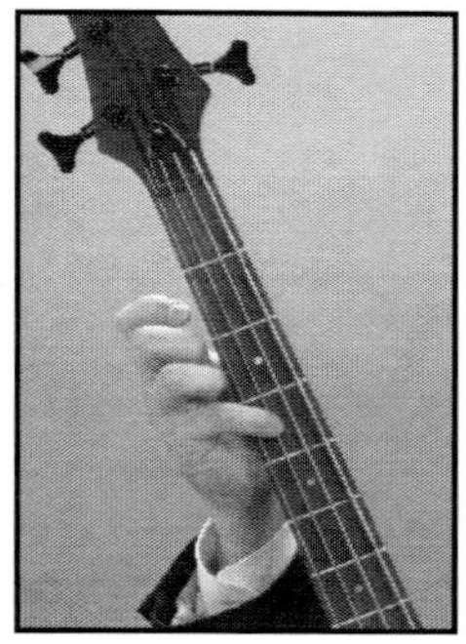

4th – G♭

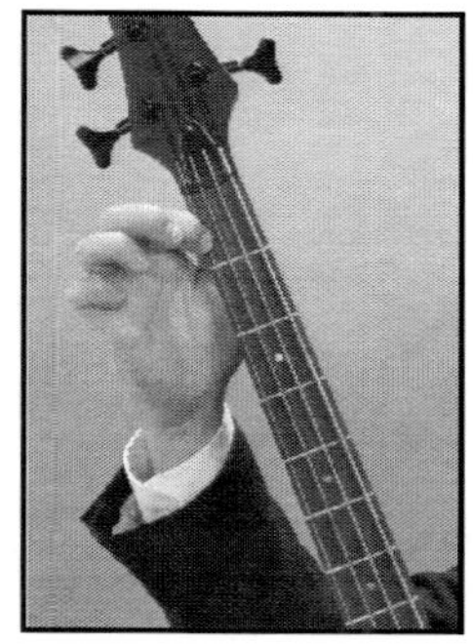

5th – A♭

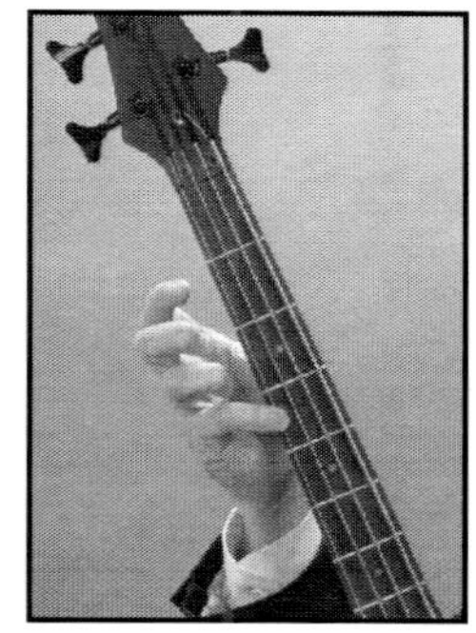

♭7th – C♭

D♭m7

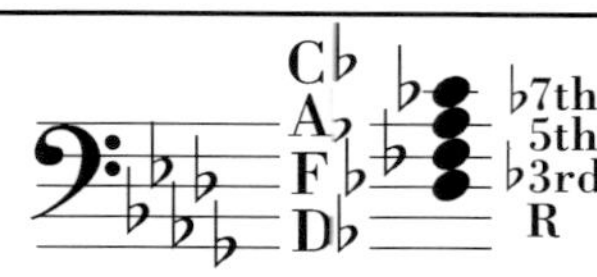

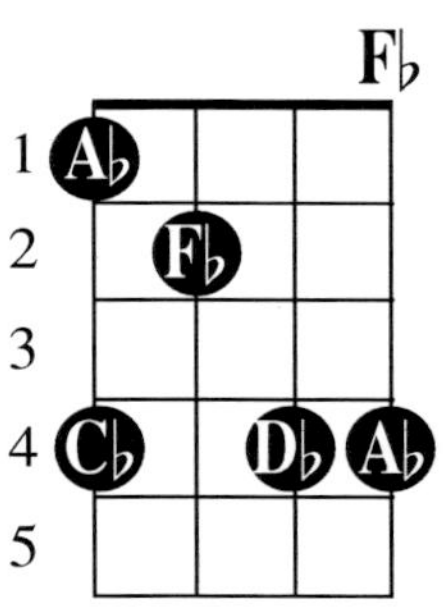

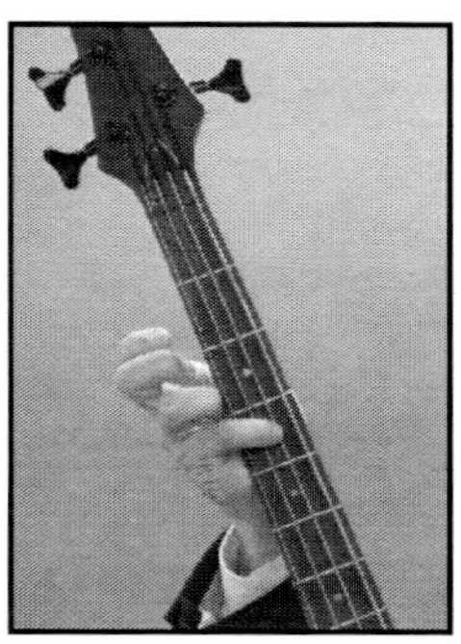

Root – D♭

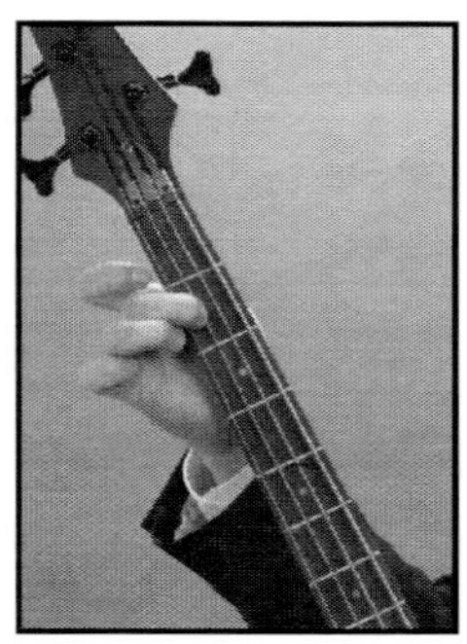

♭3rd – F♭ or E

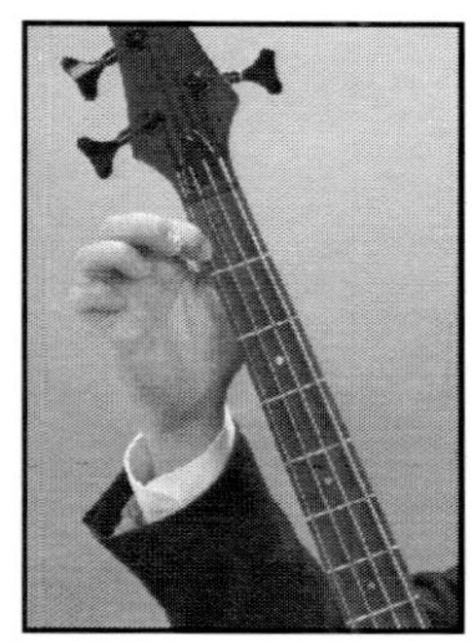

5th – A♭

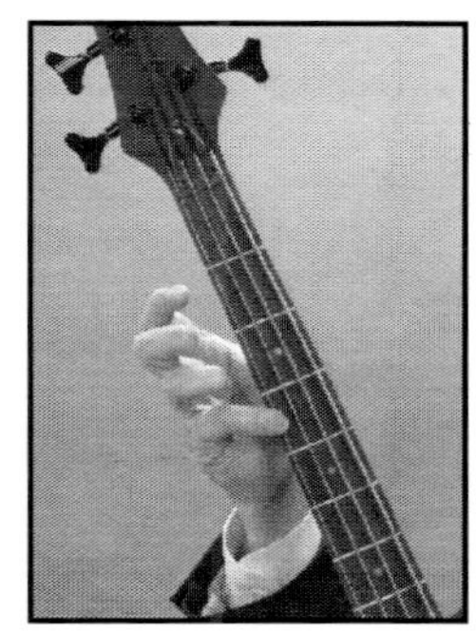

♭7th – C♭

D♭Ma7

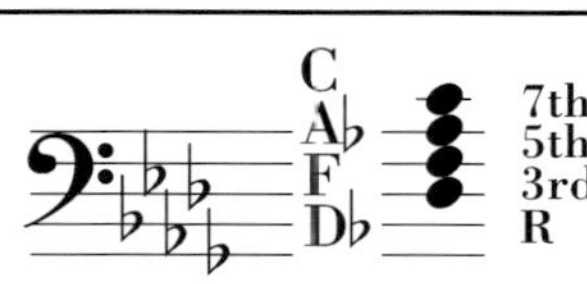

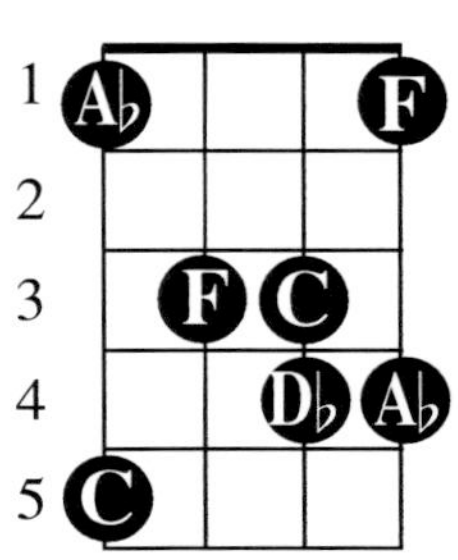

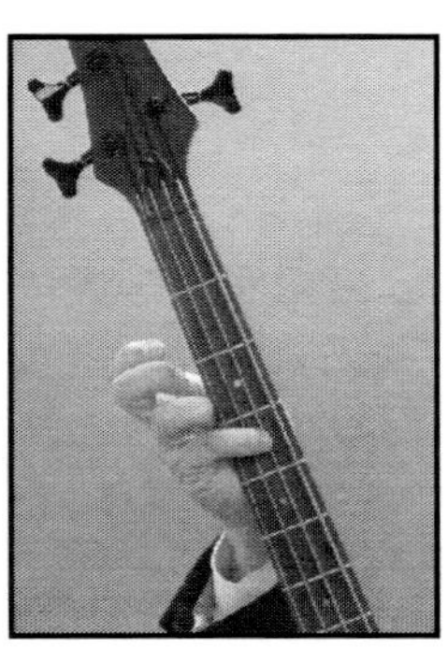

Root – D♭

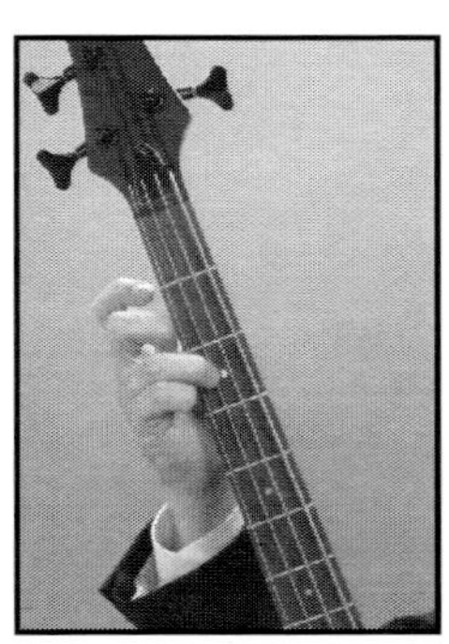

3rd – F

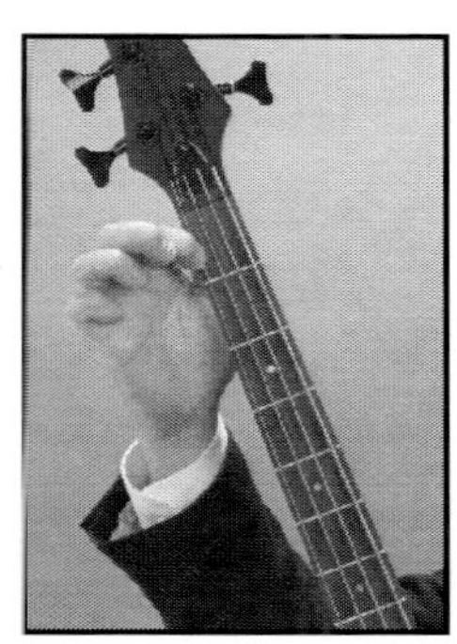

5th – A♭

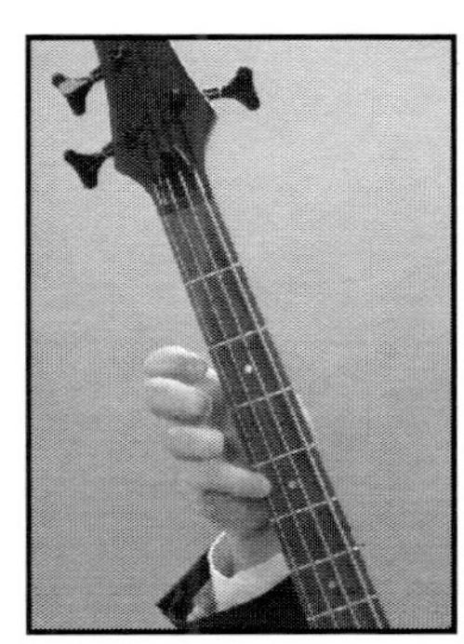

7th – C

Key of C♯/D♭ (cont.)

D♭dim

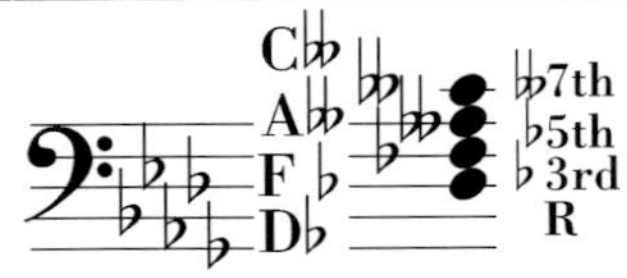

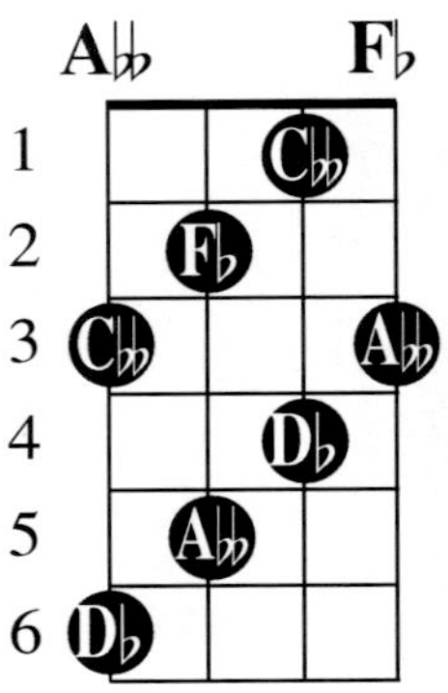

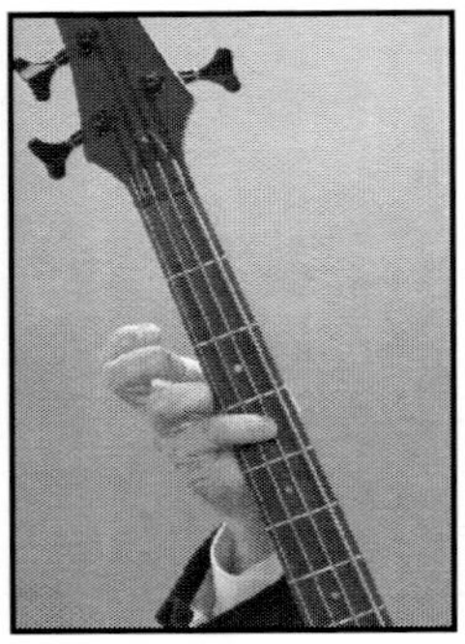

Root – D♭

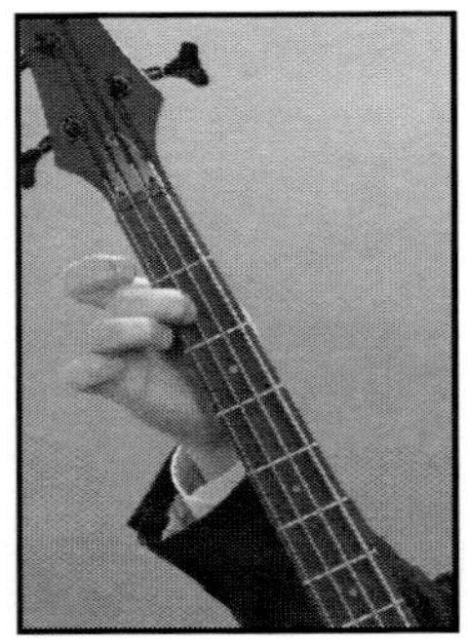

♭3rd – F♭

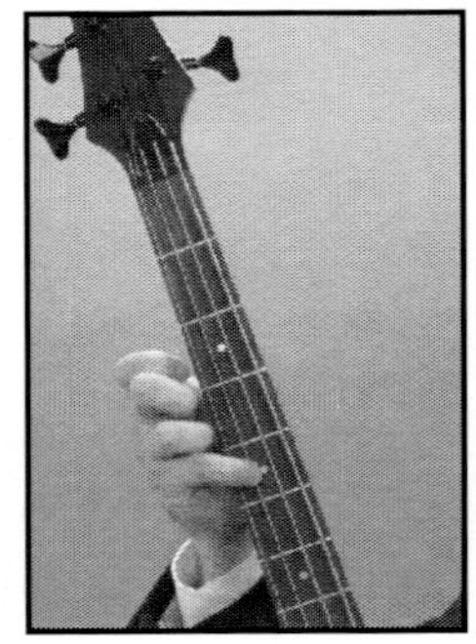

♭5th – A𝄫

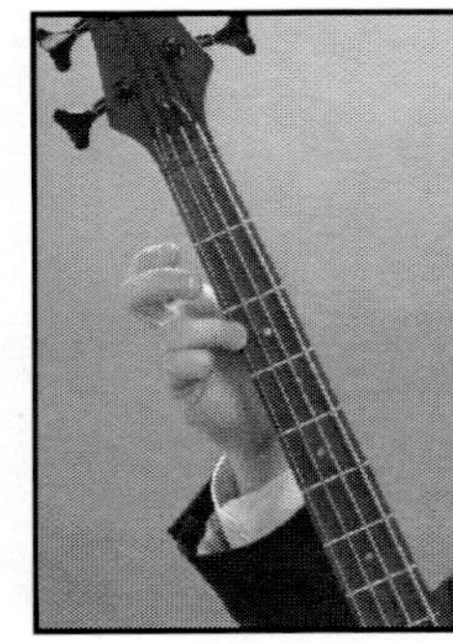

𝄫7th – C𝄫

D♭aug

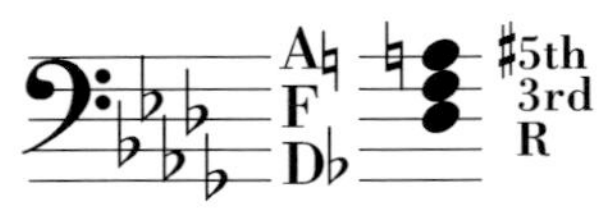

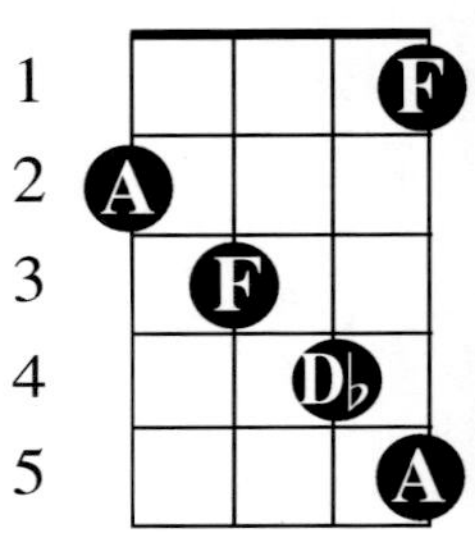

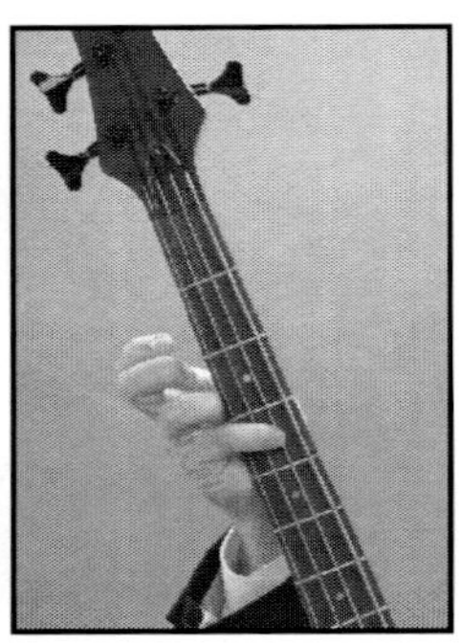

Root – D♭

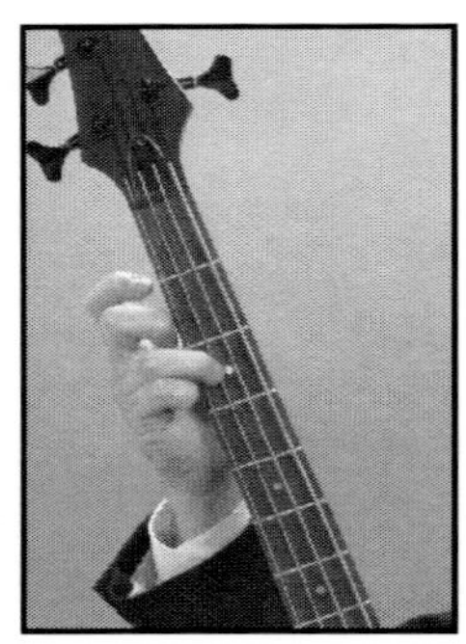

3rd – F

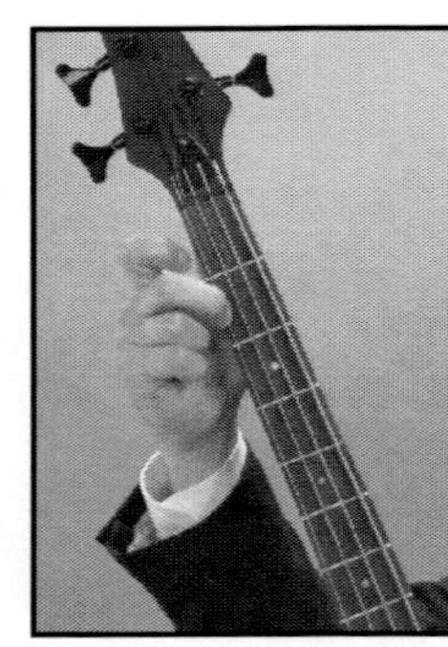

♯5th – A♮

D♭6

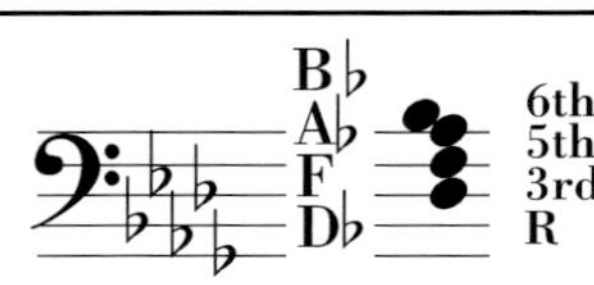

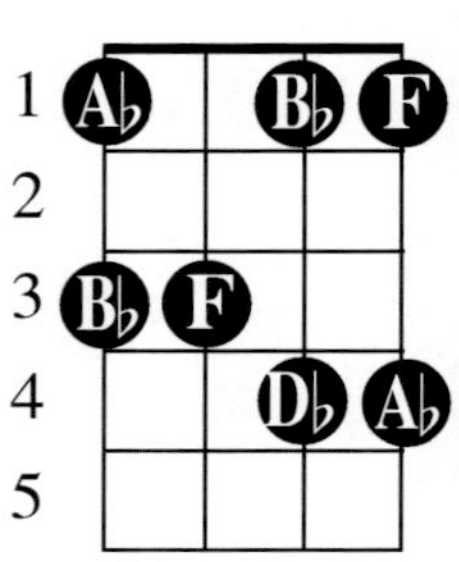

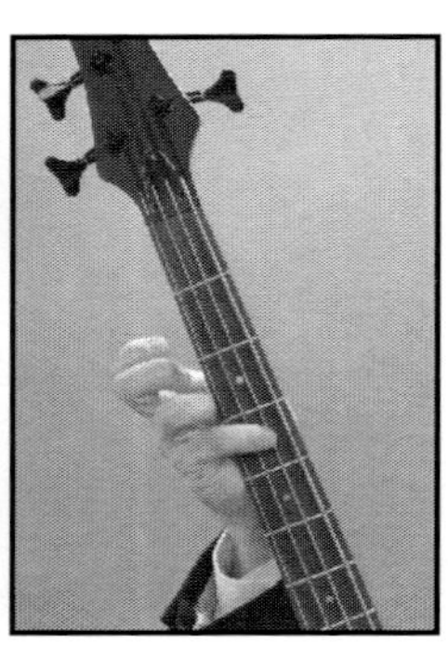

Root – D♭

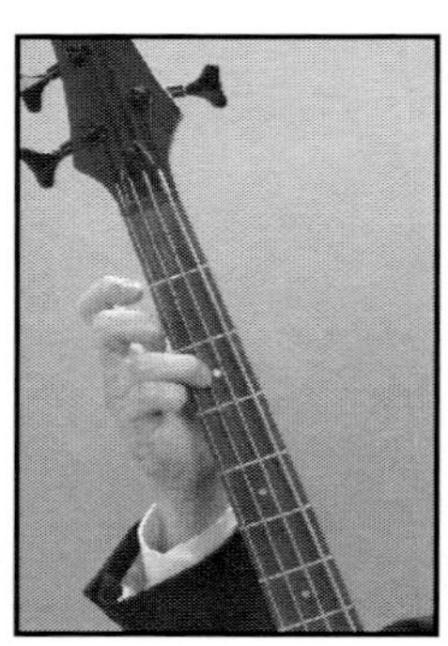

3rd – F

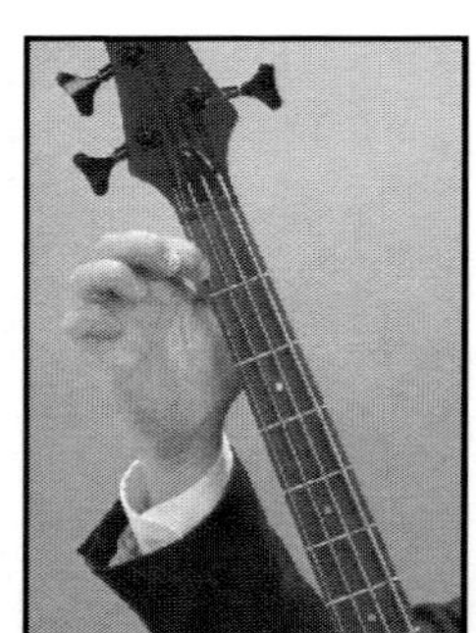

5th – A♭

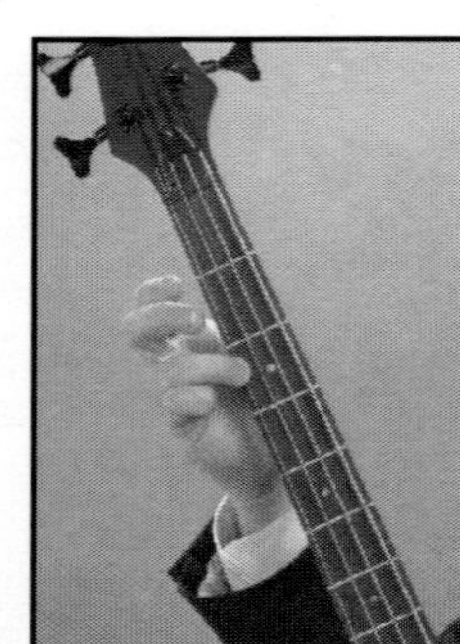

6th – B♭

Key of C♯/D♭ (cont.)

D♭m6

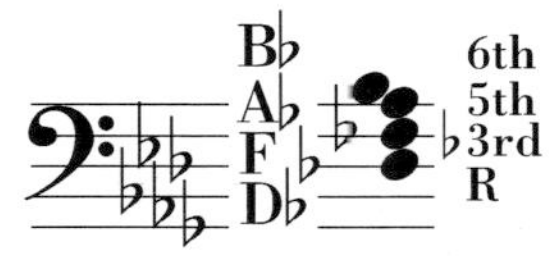

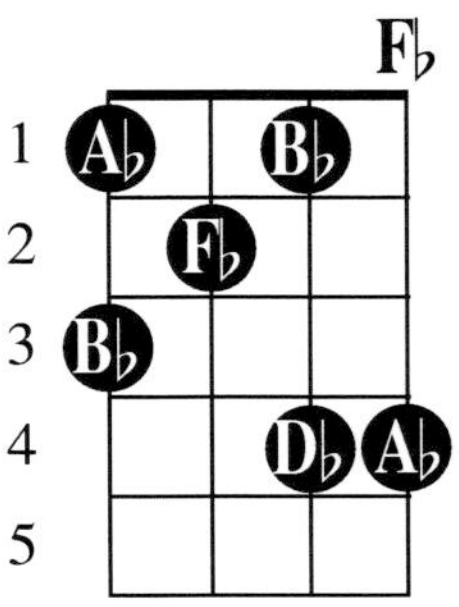

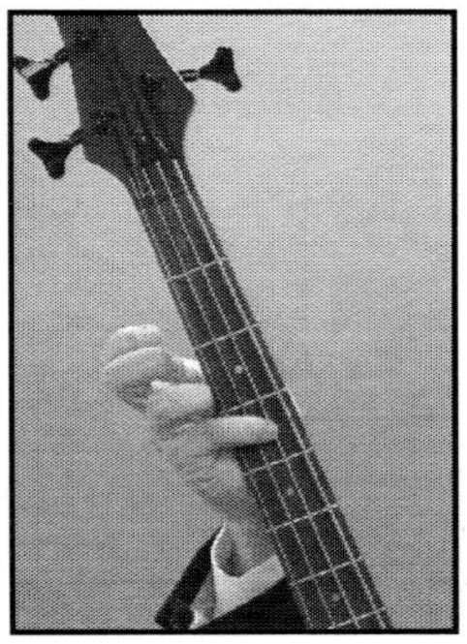
Root – D♭

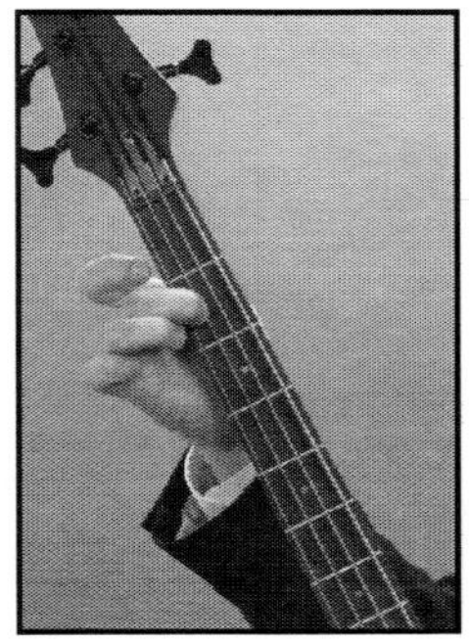
♭3rd – F♭

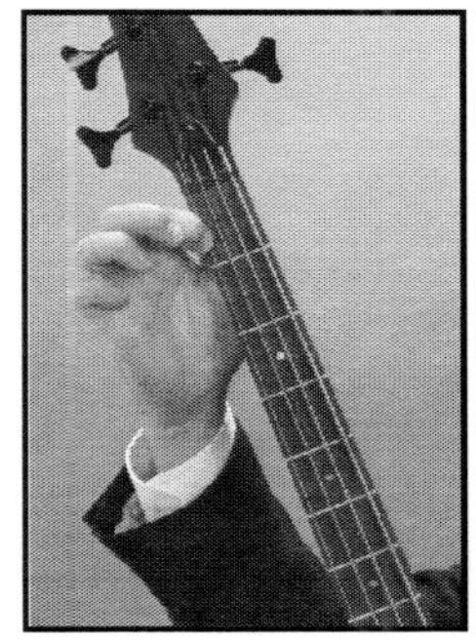
5th – A♭

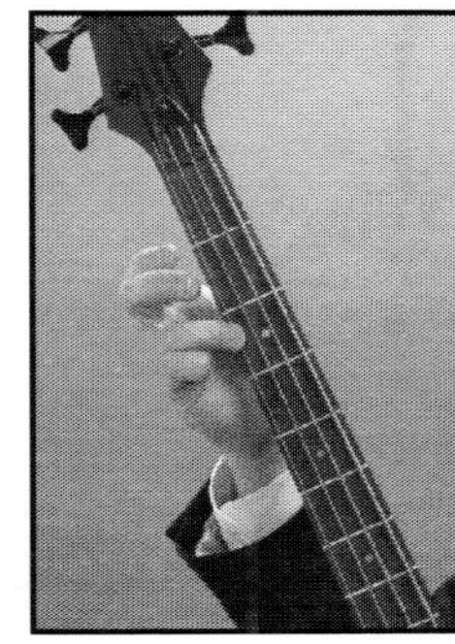
6th – B♭

D♭7♯5

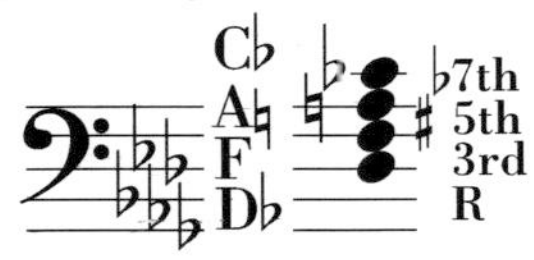

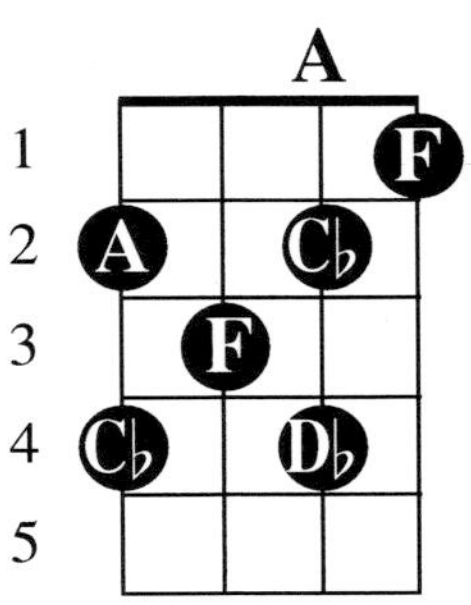

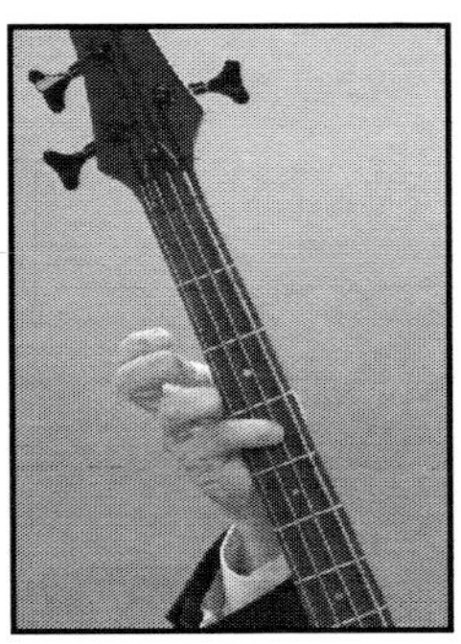
Root – D♭

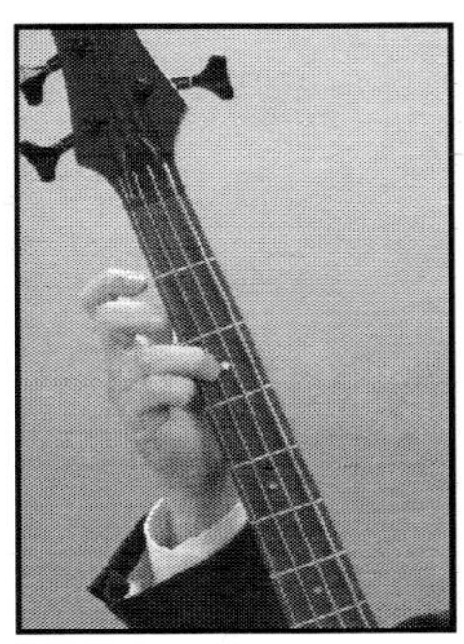
3rd – F

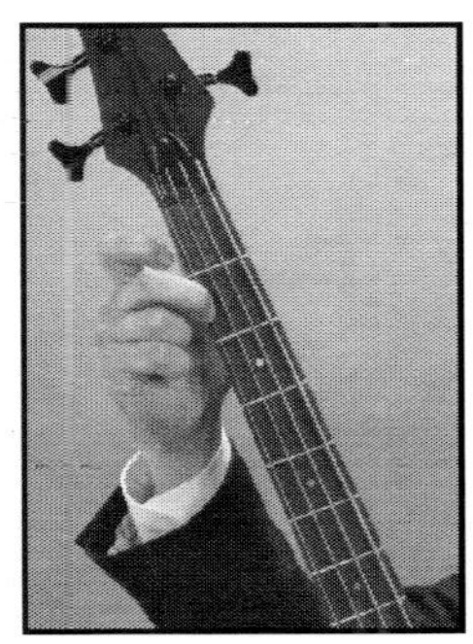
♯5th – A♮

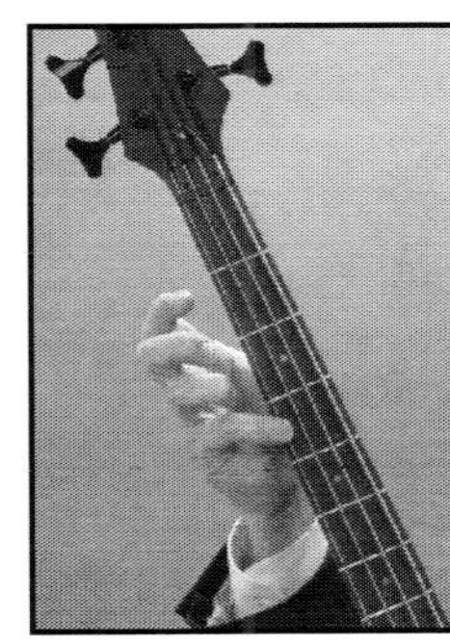
♭7th – C♭

D♭7♭5

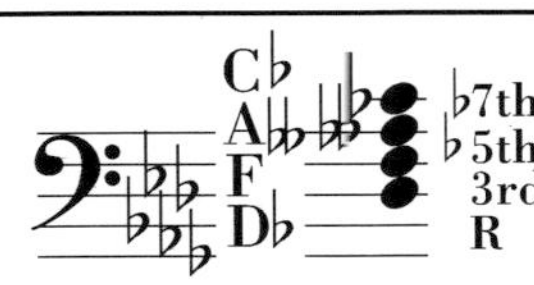

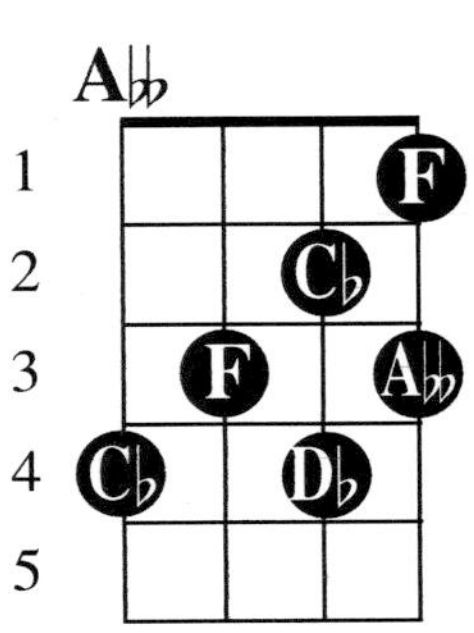

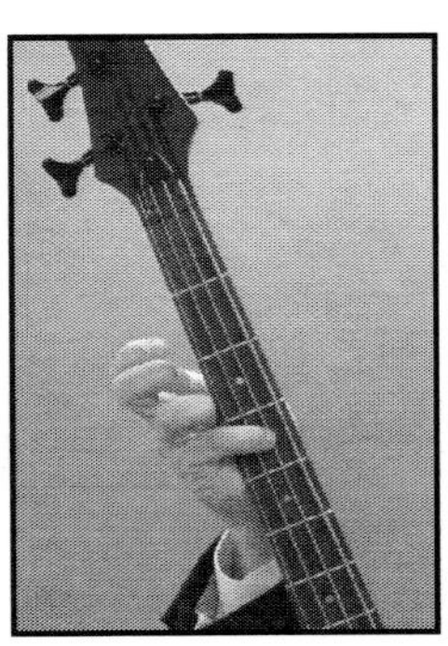
Root – D♭

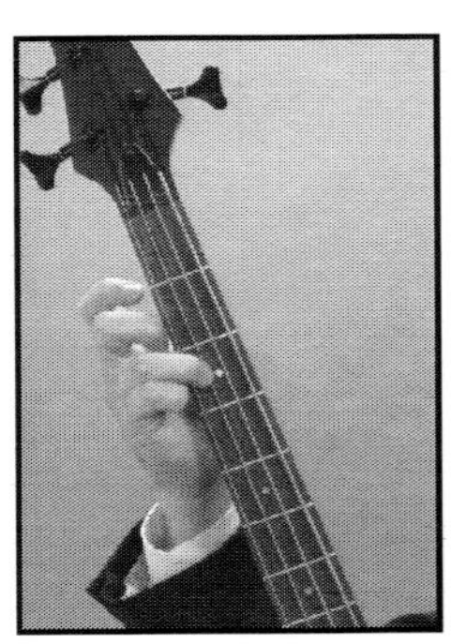
3rd – F

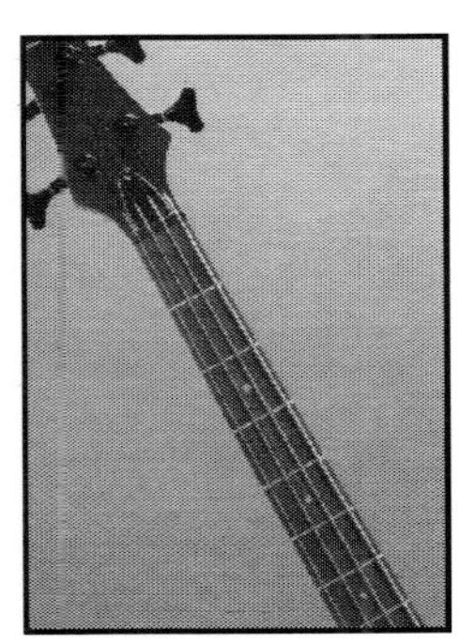
♭5th – A♭♭ or G

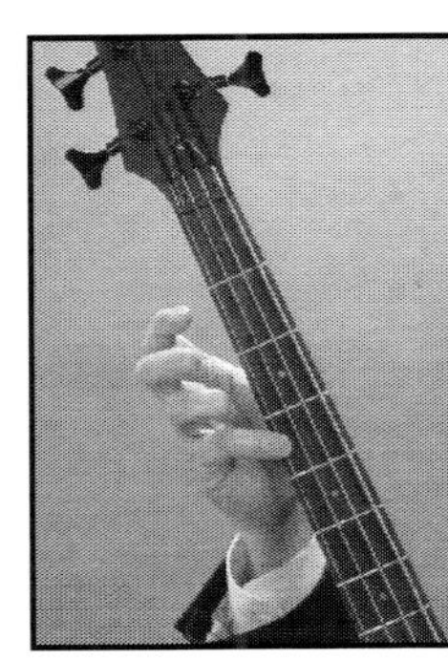
♭7th – C♭

Key of D

DMajor

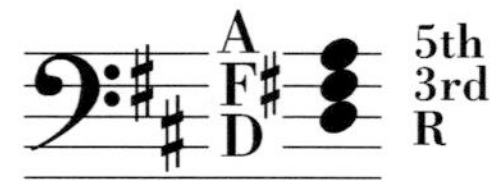

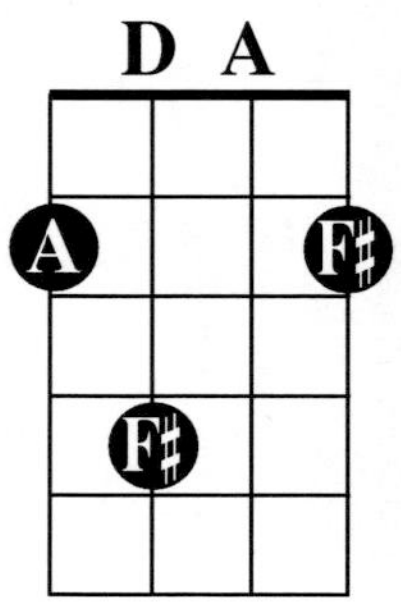

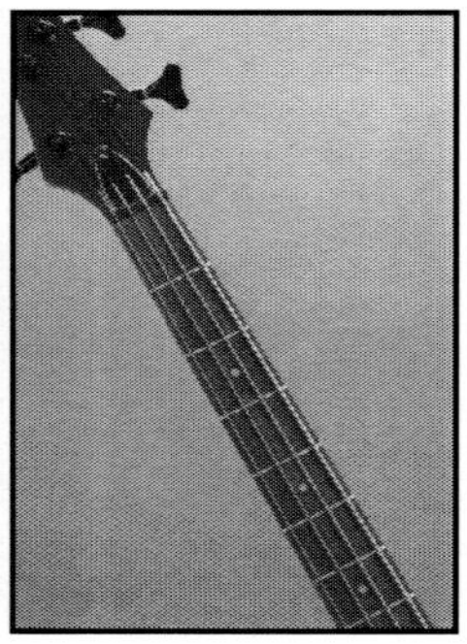

Root – D

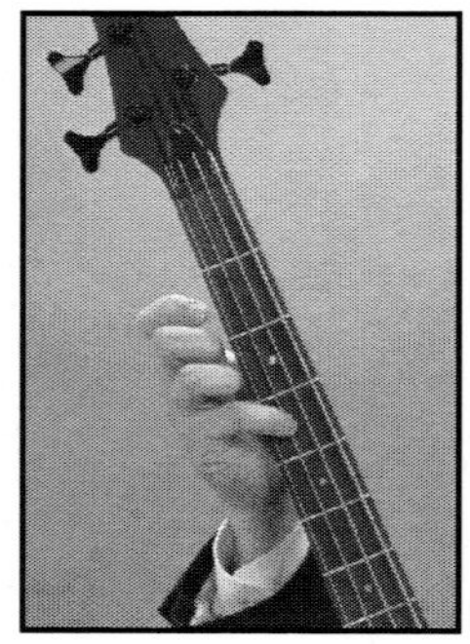

3rd – F♯

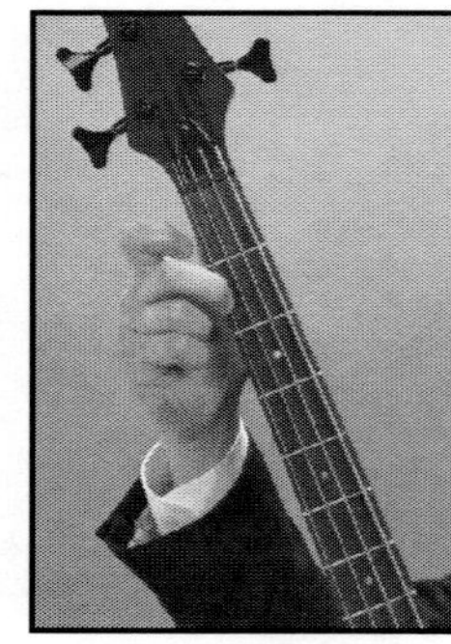

5th – A

Dminor

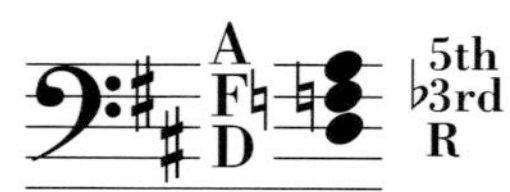

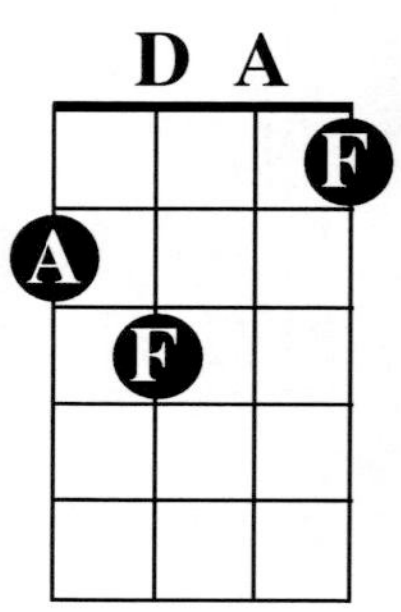

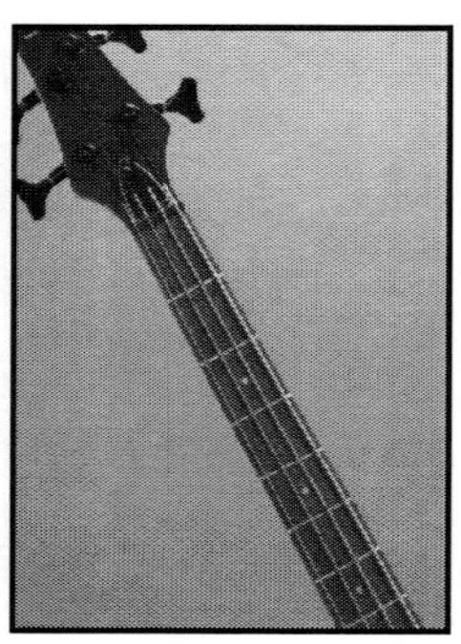

Root – D

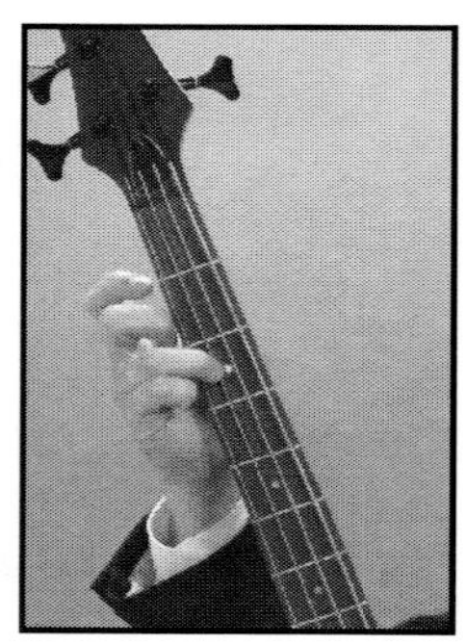

♭3rd – F♮

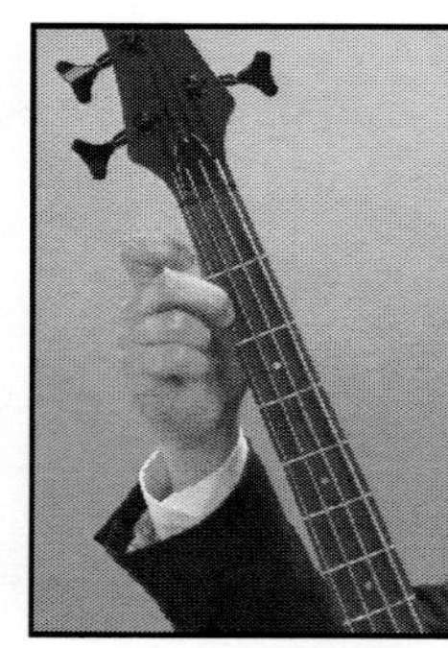

5th – A

D7

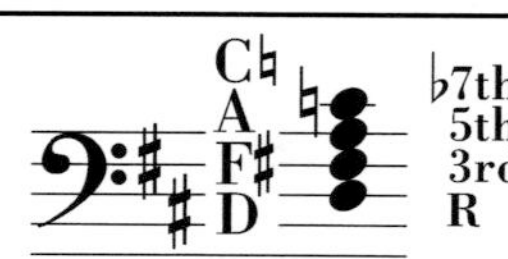

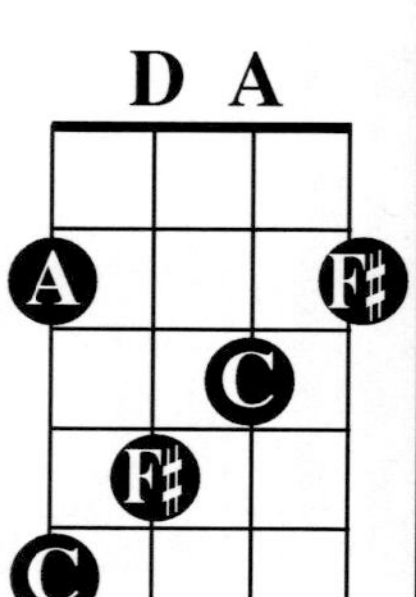

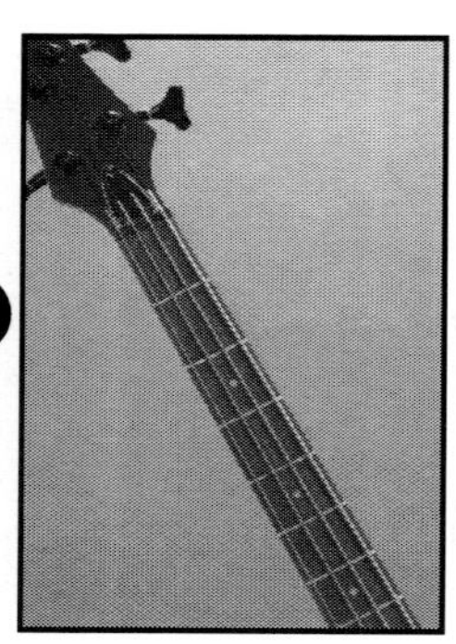

Root – D

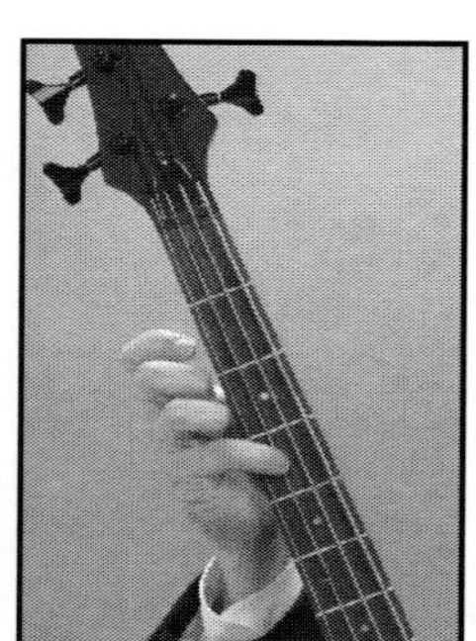

3rd – F♯

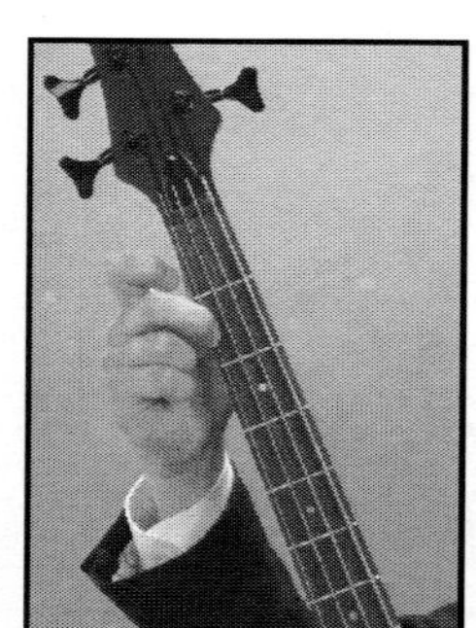

5th – A

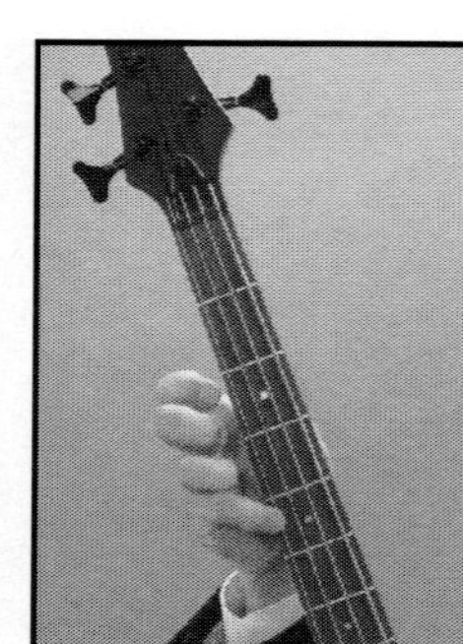

♭7th – C♮

Key of D (cont.)

D7sus

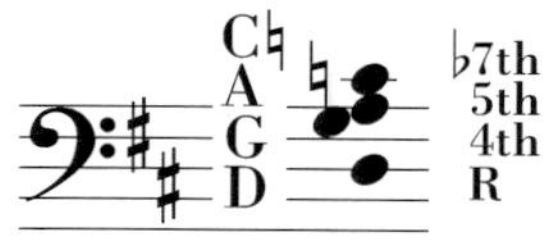

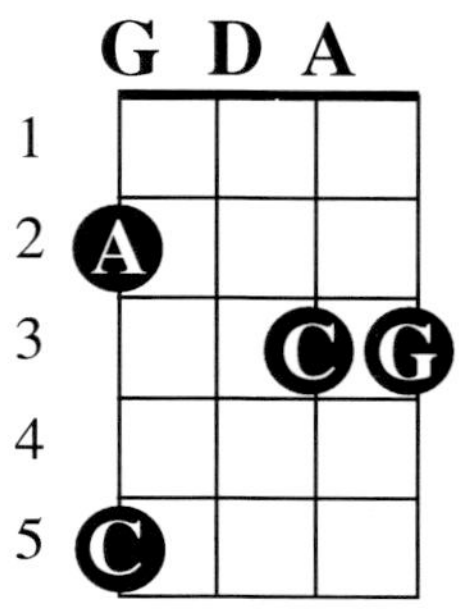

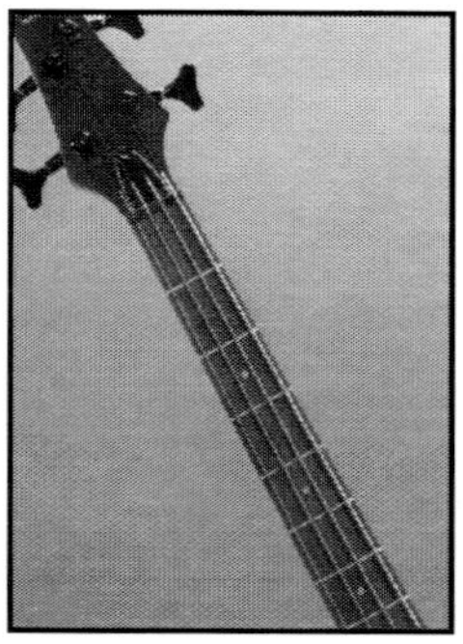

Root – D

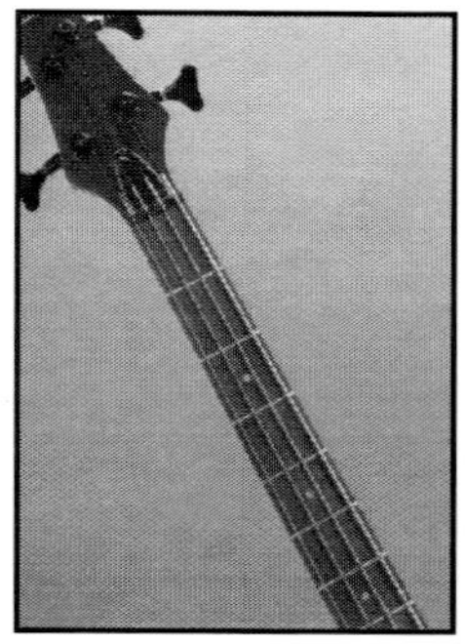

4th – G

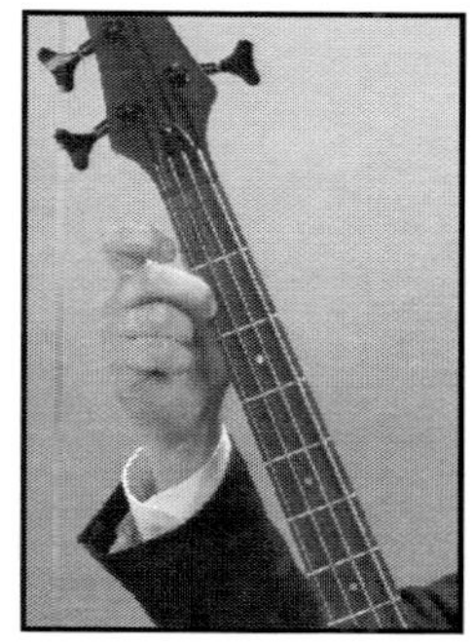

5th – A

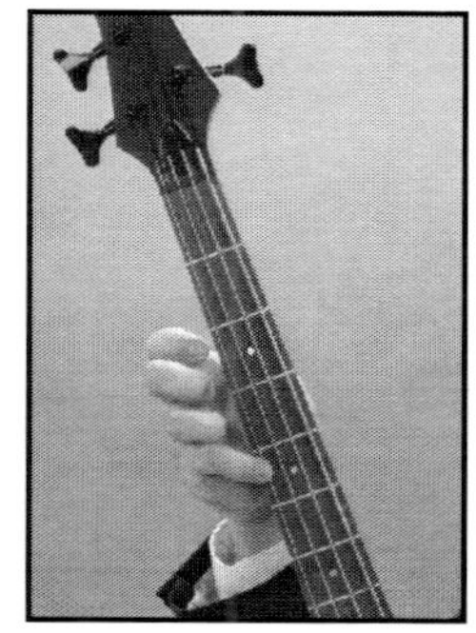

♭7th – C♮

Dm7

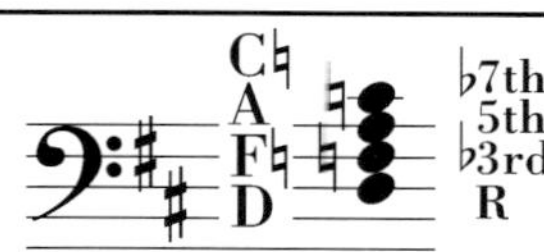

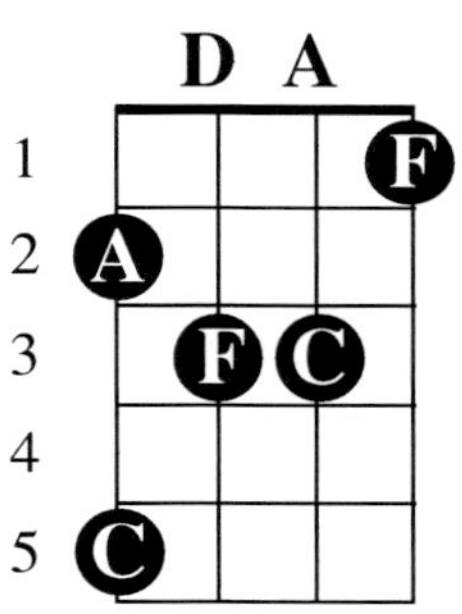

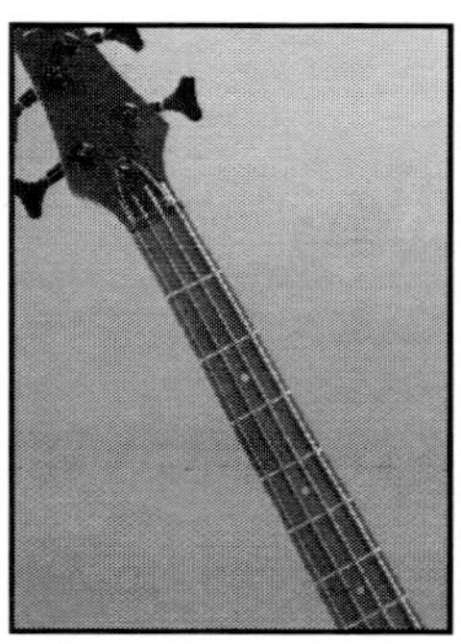

Root – D

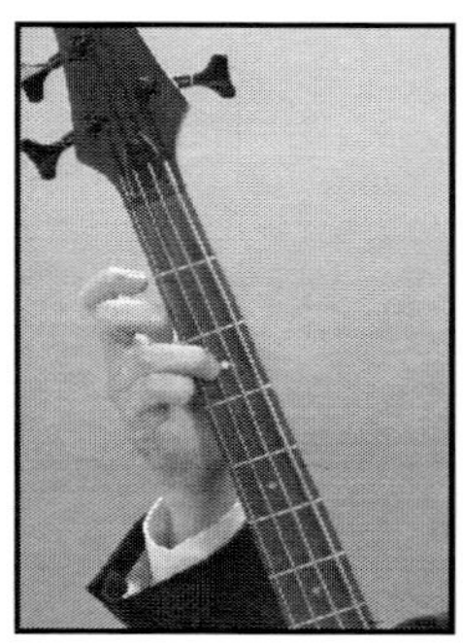

♭3rd – F♮

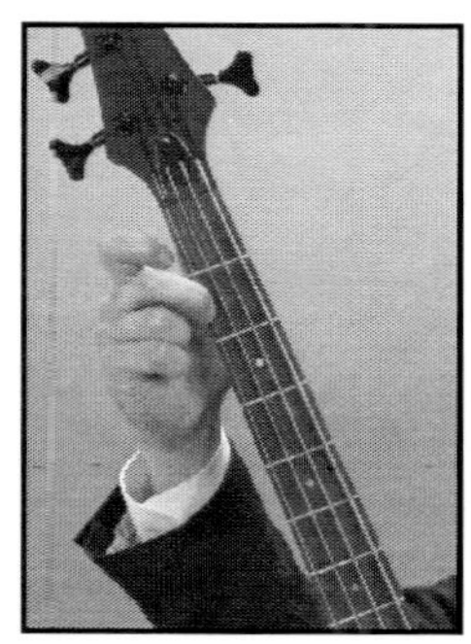

5th – A

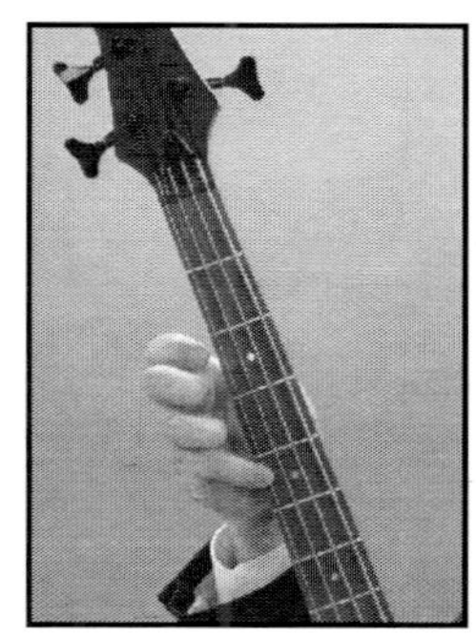

♭7th – C♮

DMa7

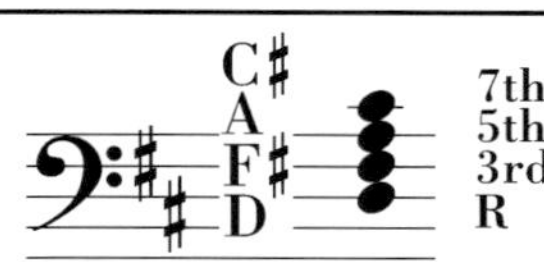

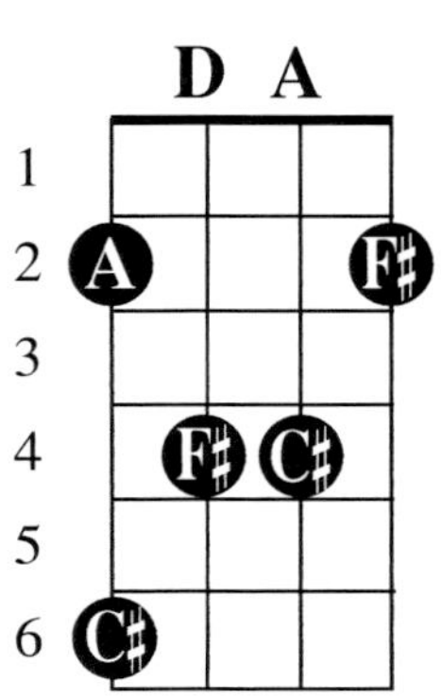

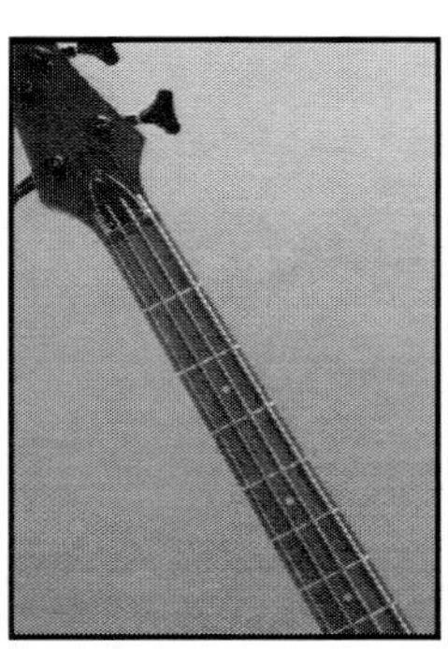

Root – D

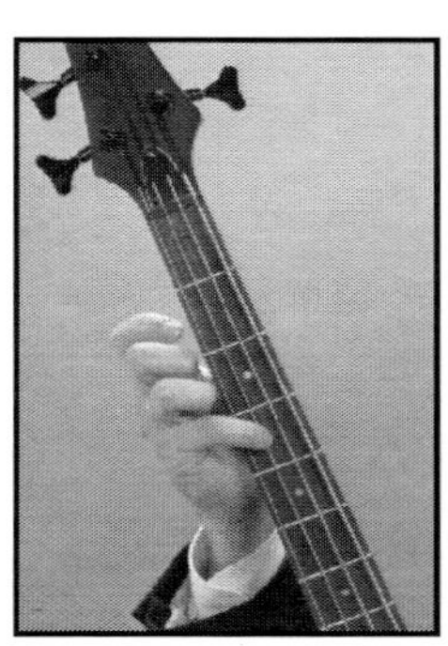

3rd – F♯

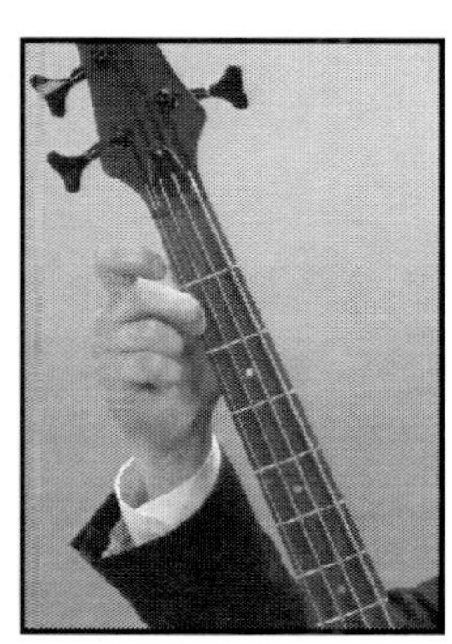

5th – A

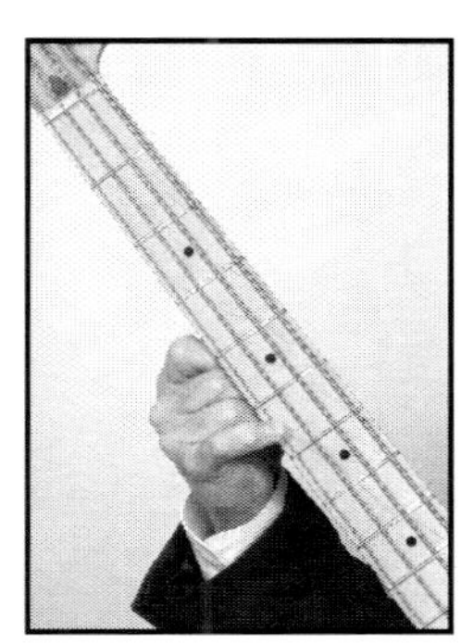

7th – C♯

Key of D (cont.)

Ddim

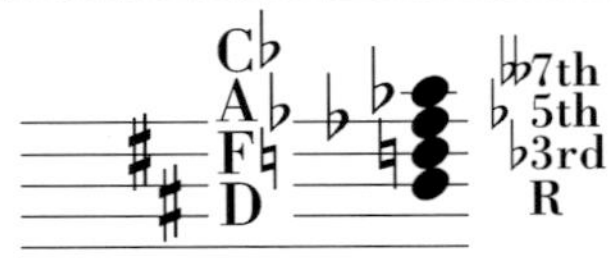

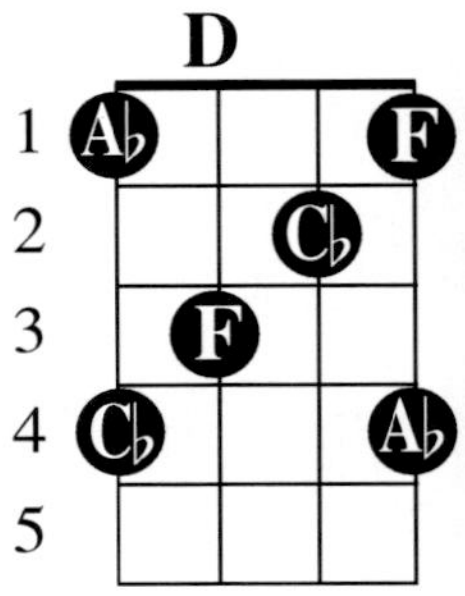

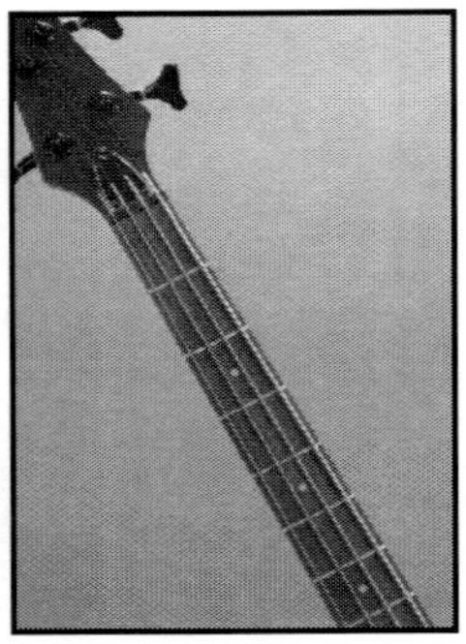

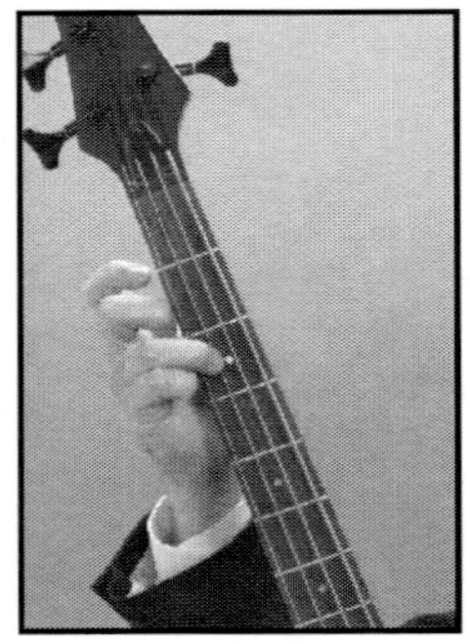

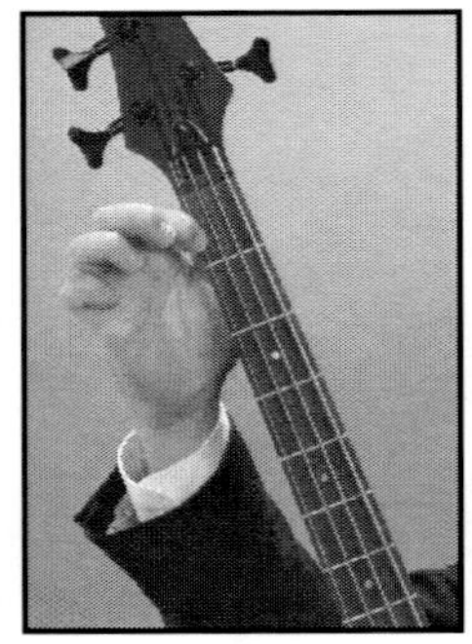

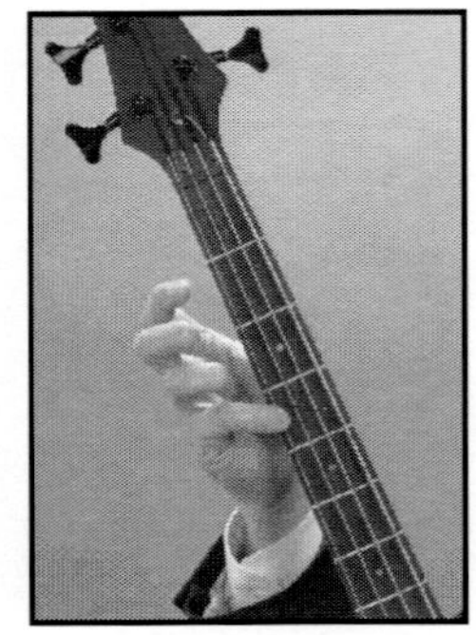

Root – D **♭3rd – F♮** **♭5th – A♭** **♭♭7th – C♭**

Daug

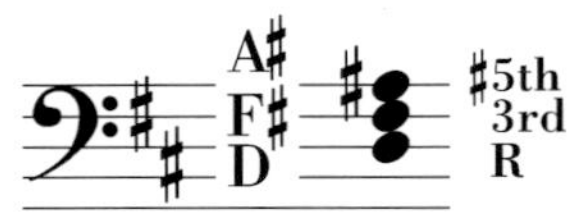

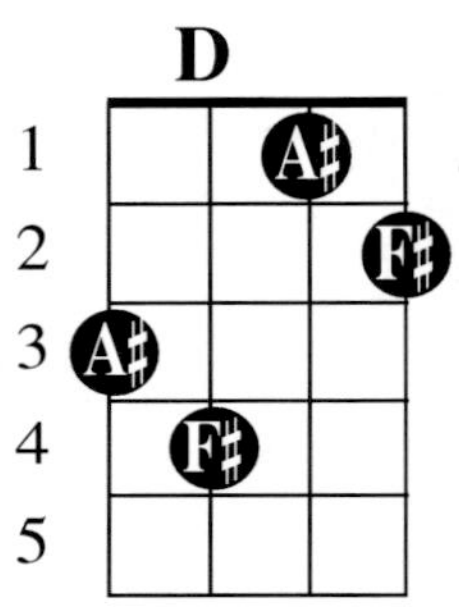

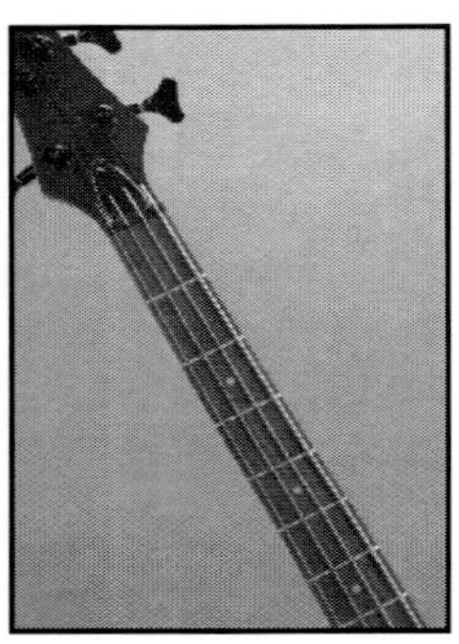

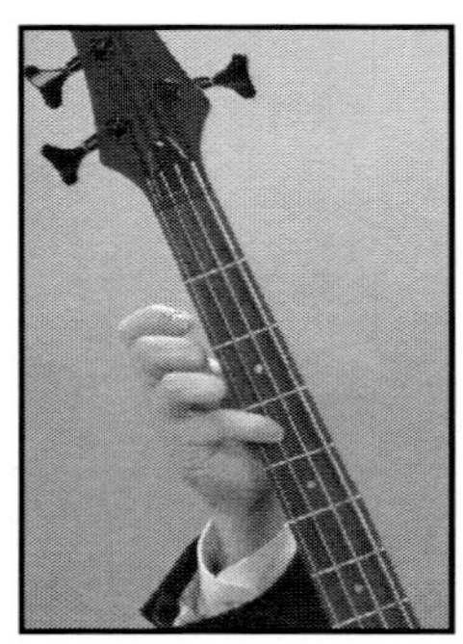

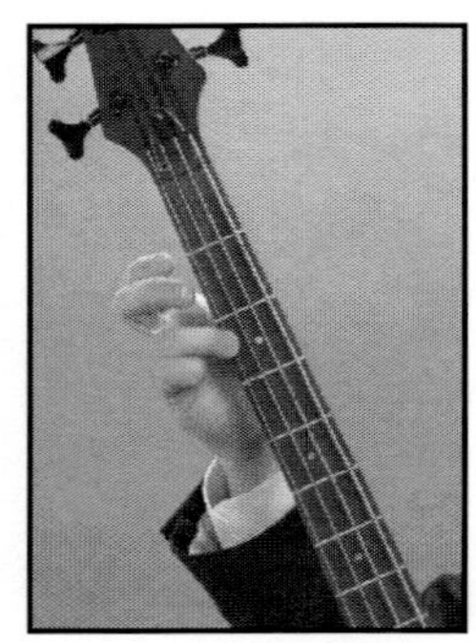

Root – D **3rd – F♯** **♯5th – A♯**

D6

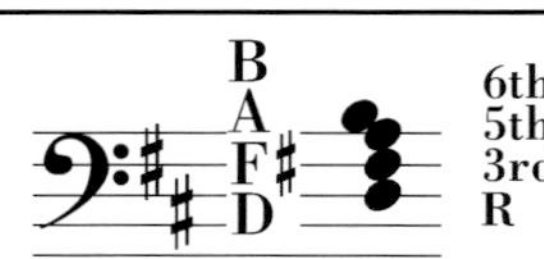

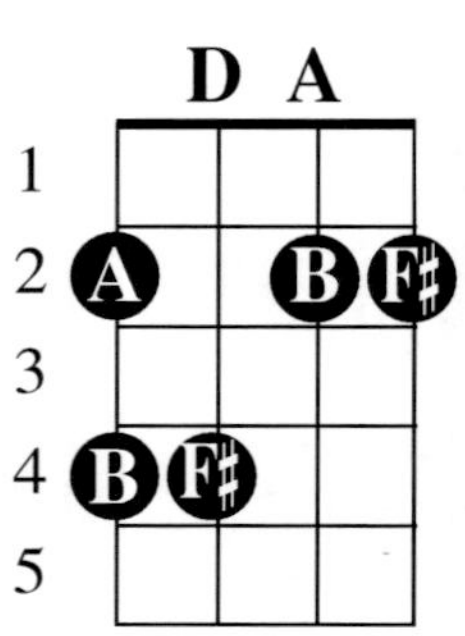

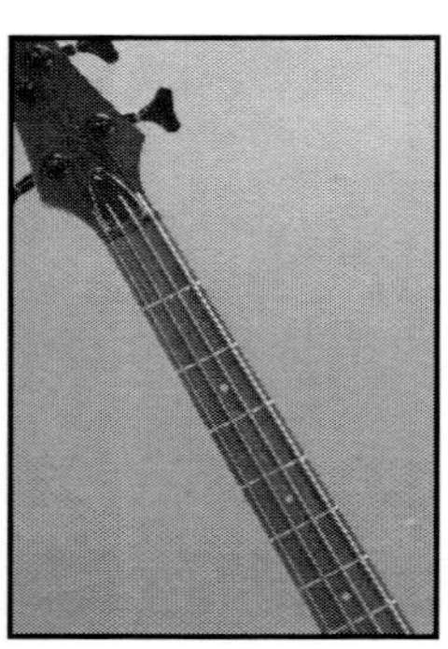

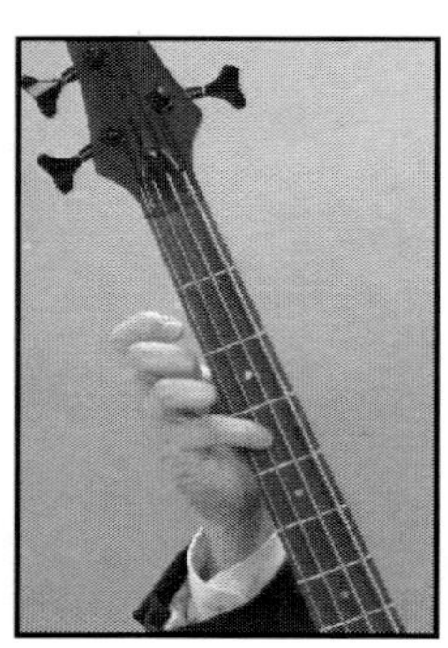

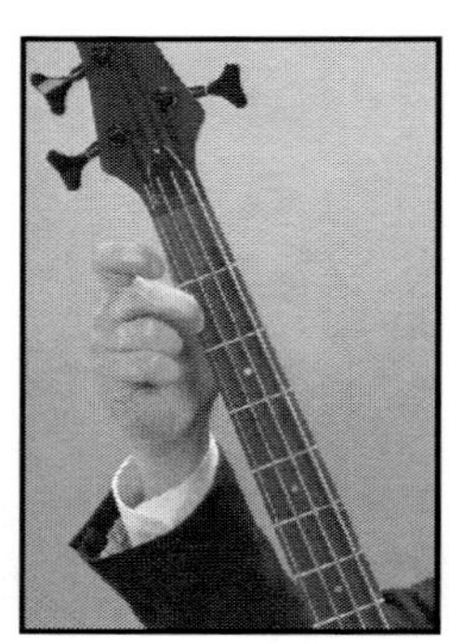

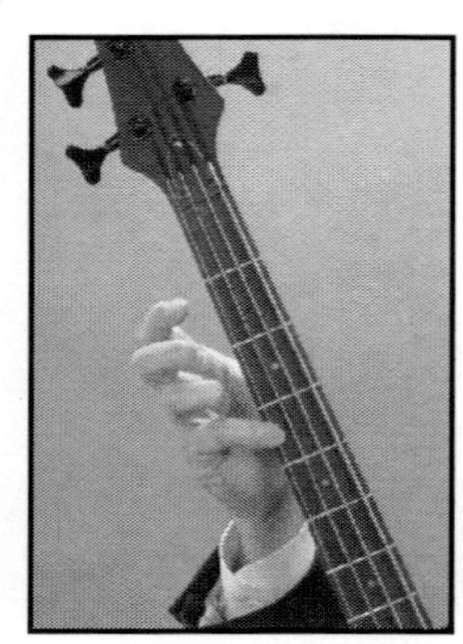

Root – D **3rd – F♯** **5th – A** **6th – B**

Key of D (cont.)

Dm6

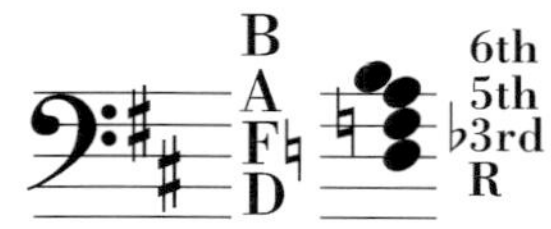

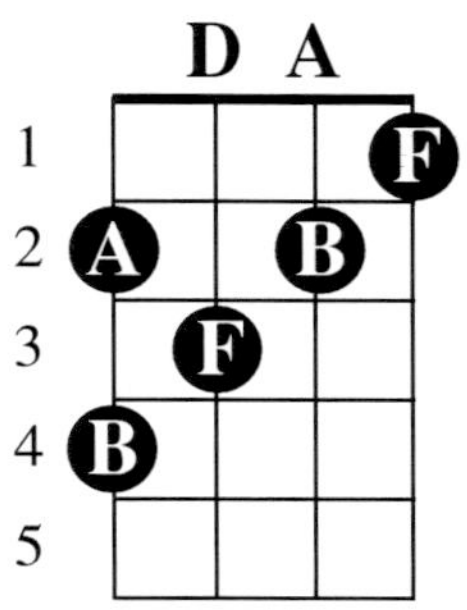

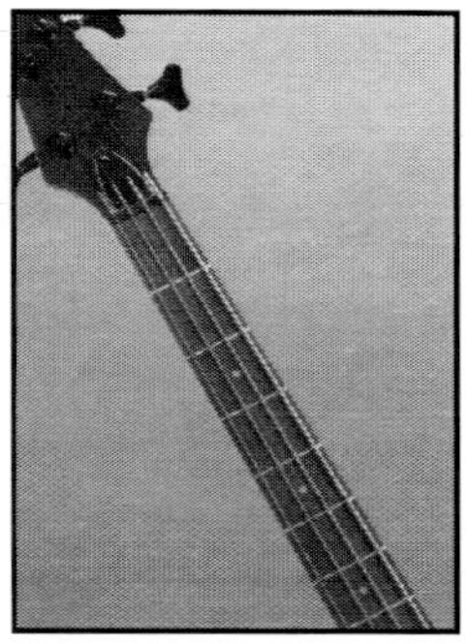

Root – D

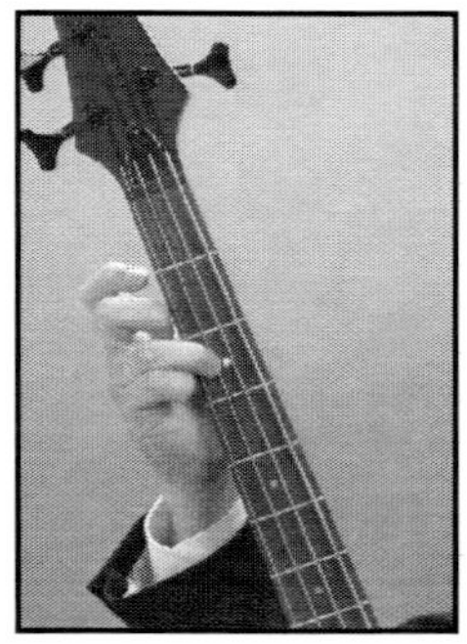

♭3rd – F♮

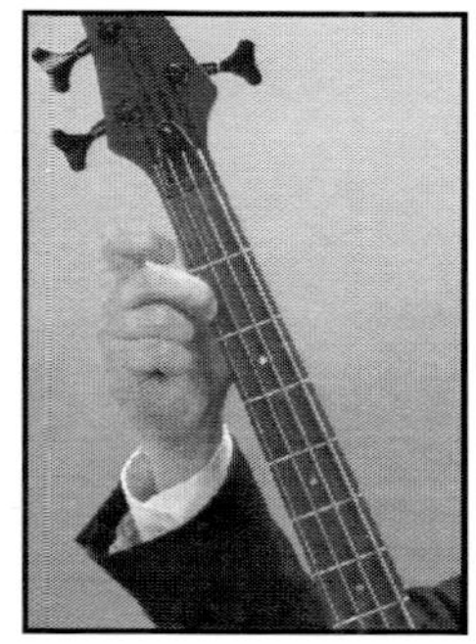

5th – A

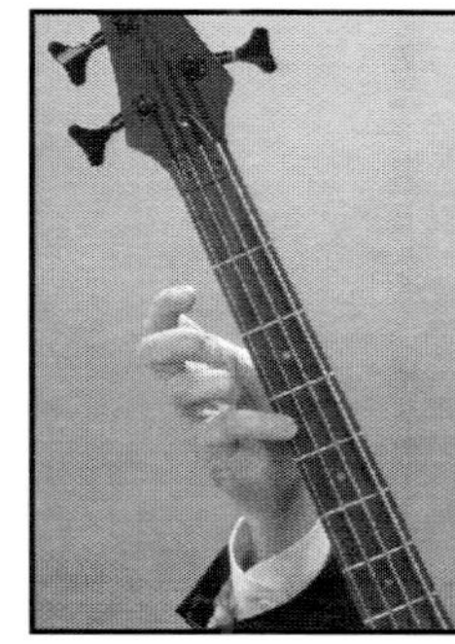

6th – B

D7♯5

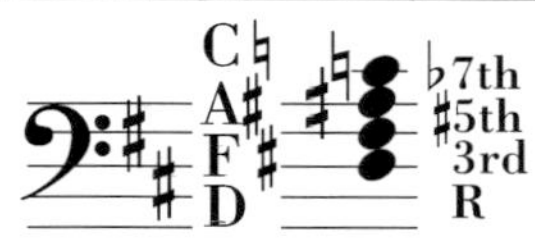

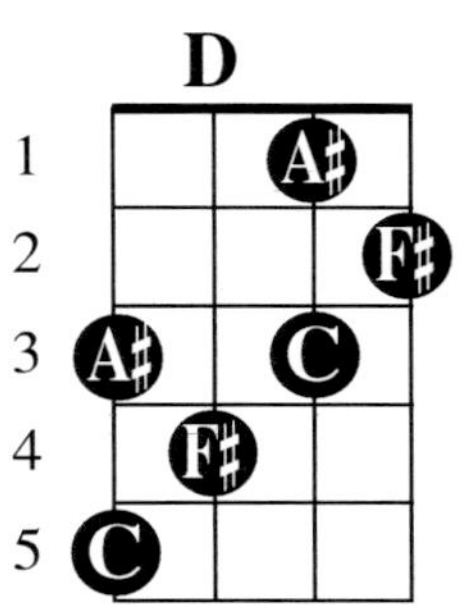

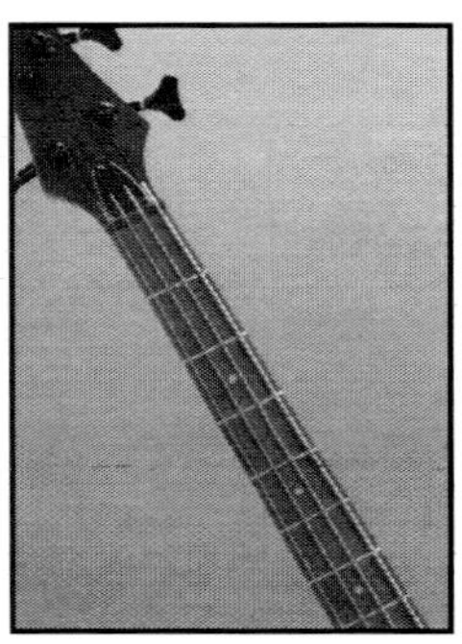

Root – D

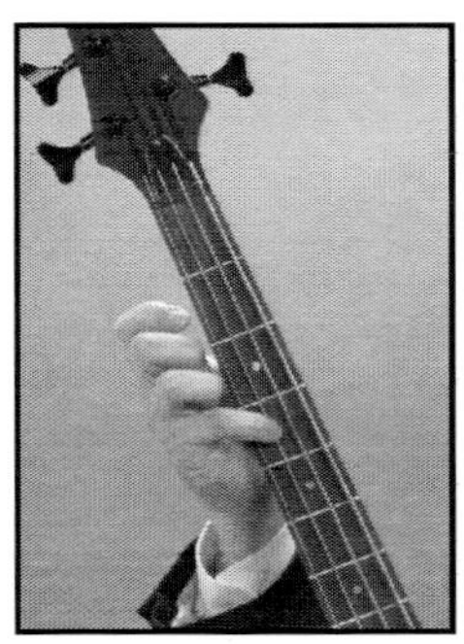

3rd – F♯

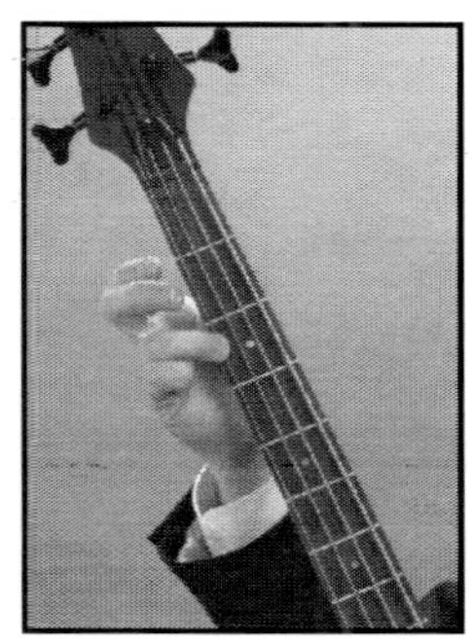

♯5th – A♯

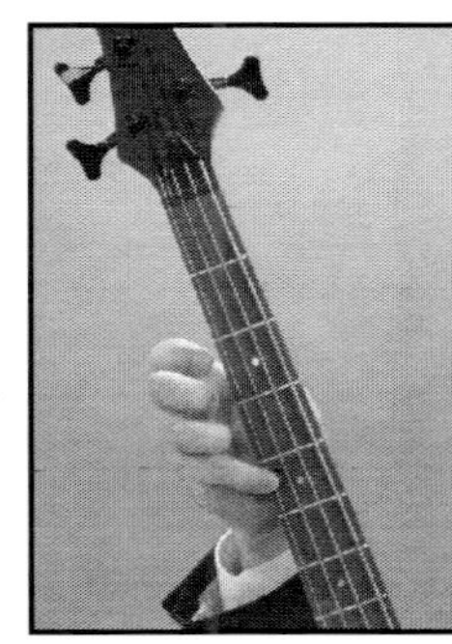

♭7th – C♮

D7♭5

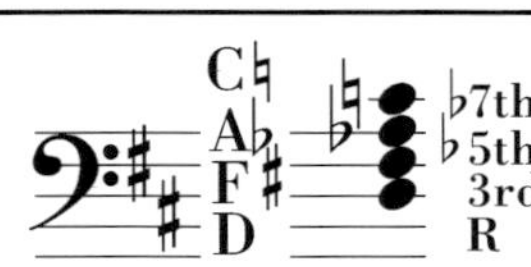

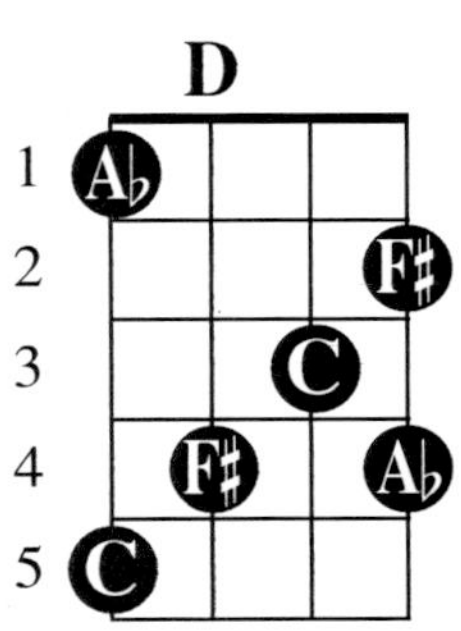

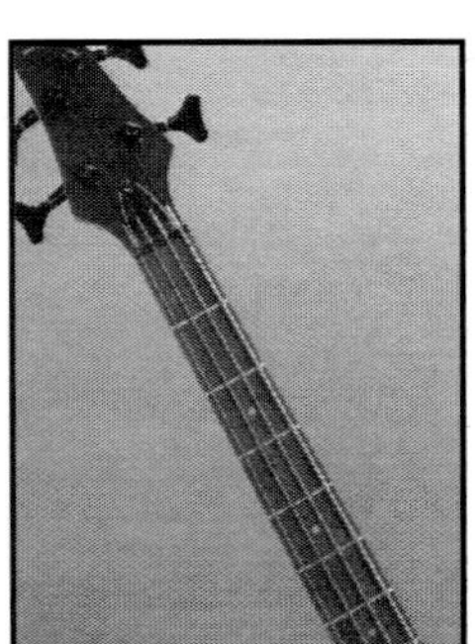

Root – D

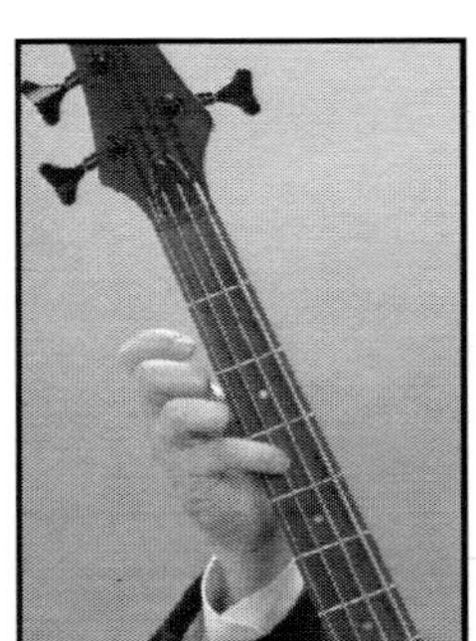

3rd – F♯

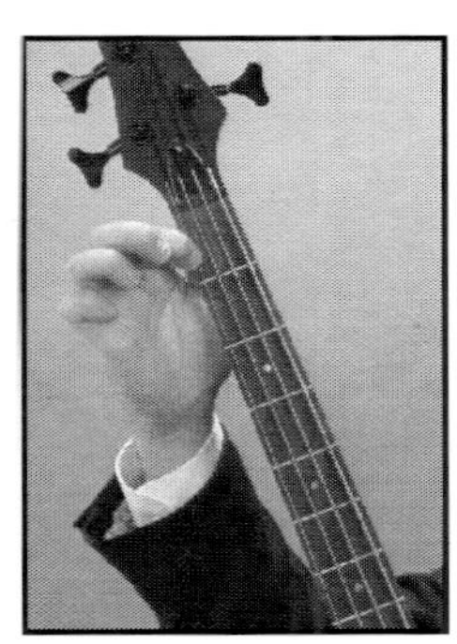

♭5th – A♭

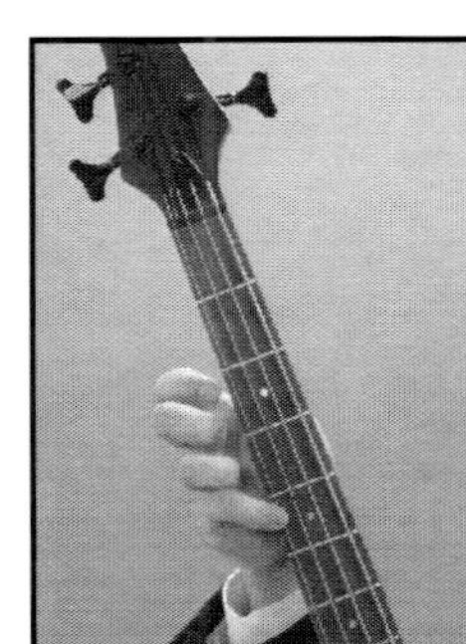

♭7th – C♮

Key of E♭

E♭Major

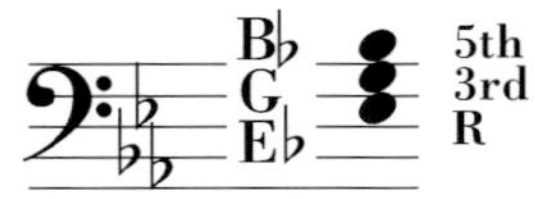

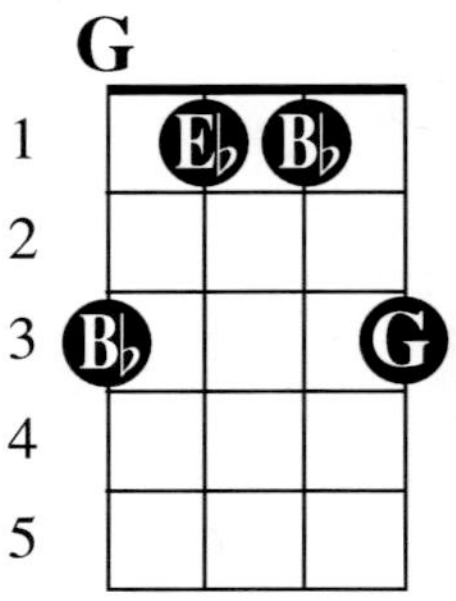

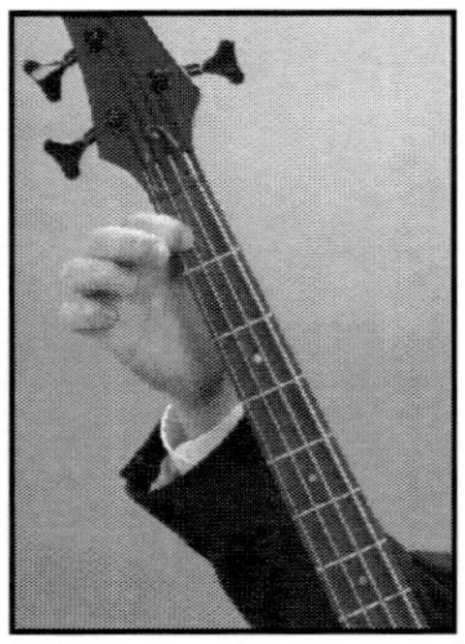

Root – E♭

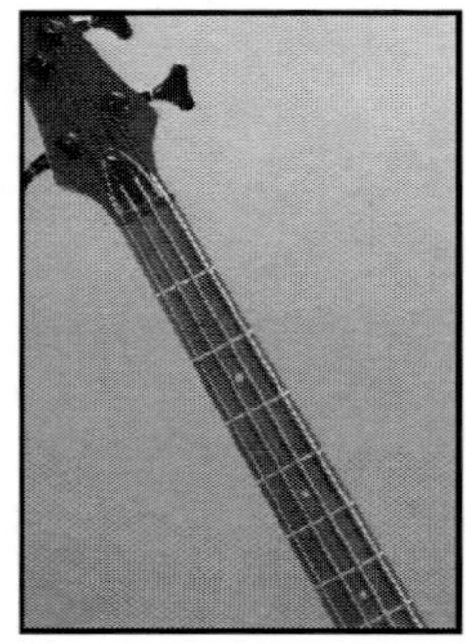

3rd – G

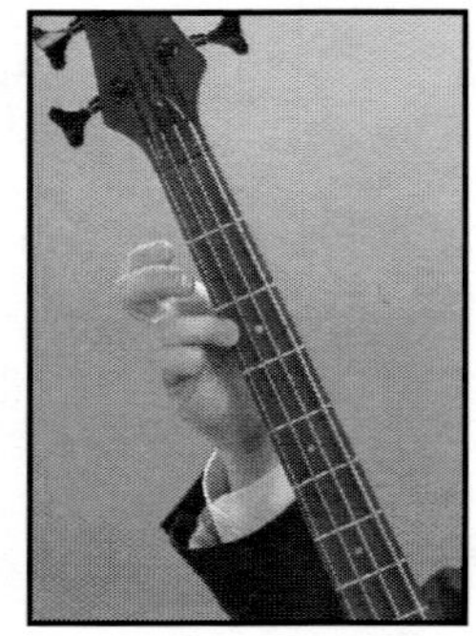

5th – B♭

E♭minor

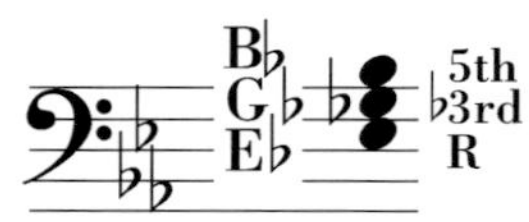

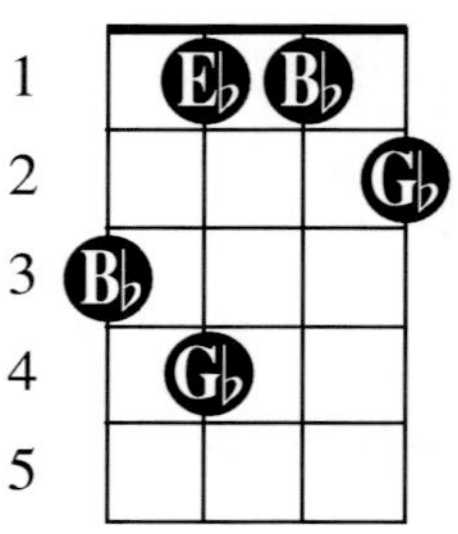

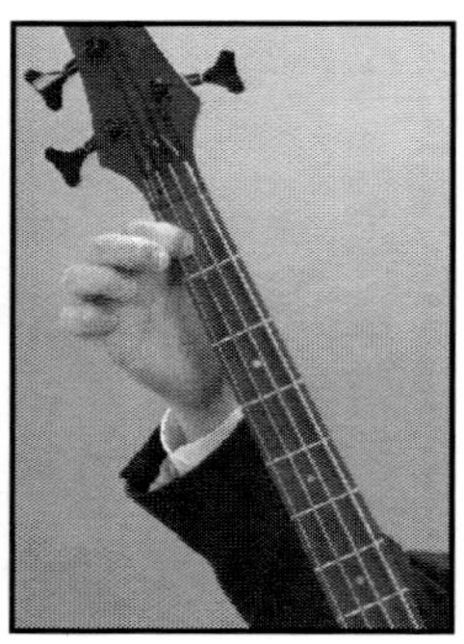

Root – E♭

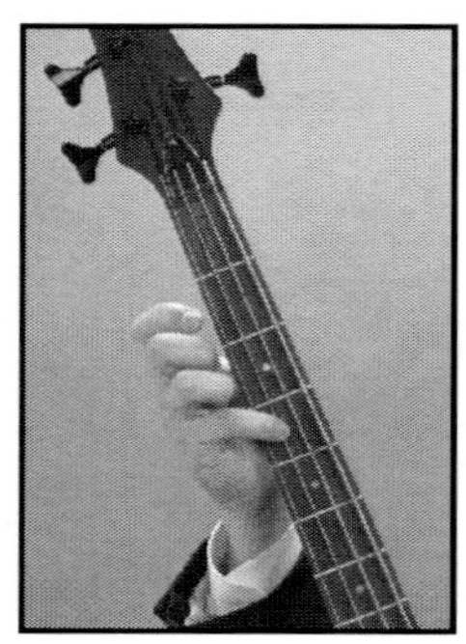

♭3rd – G♭

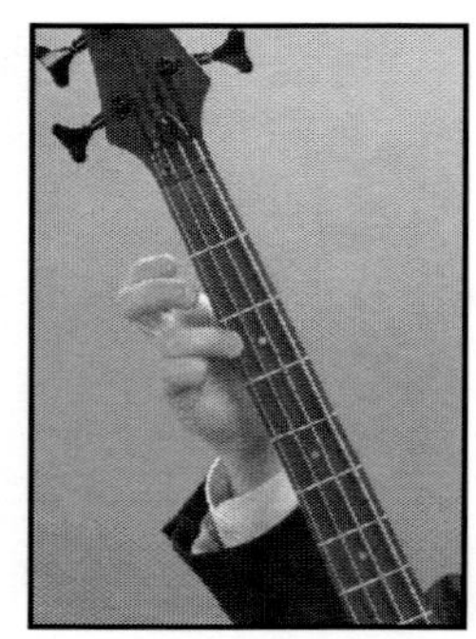

5th – B♭

E♭7

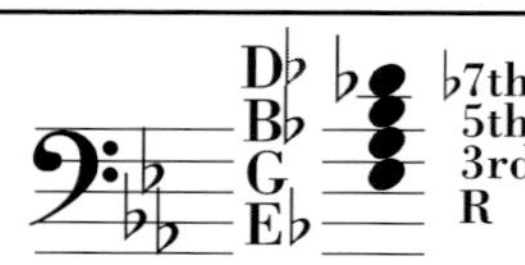

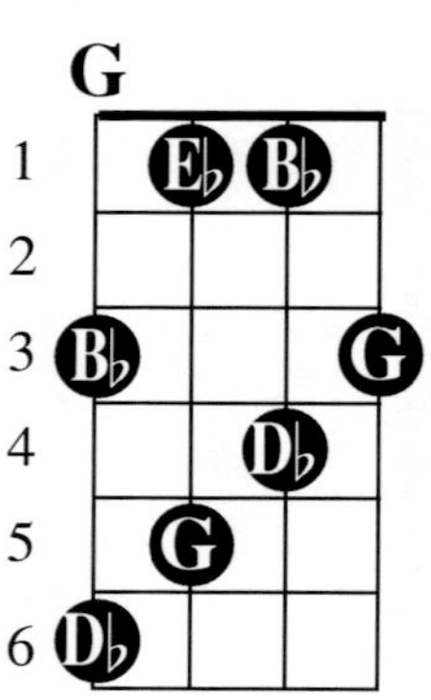

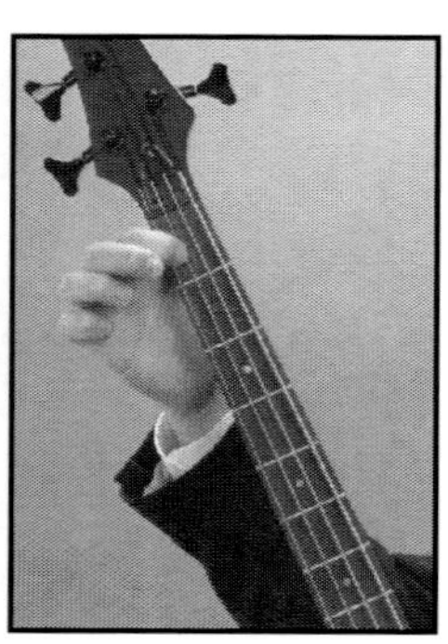

Root – E♭

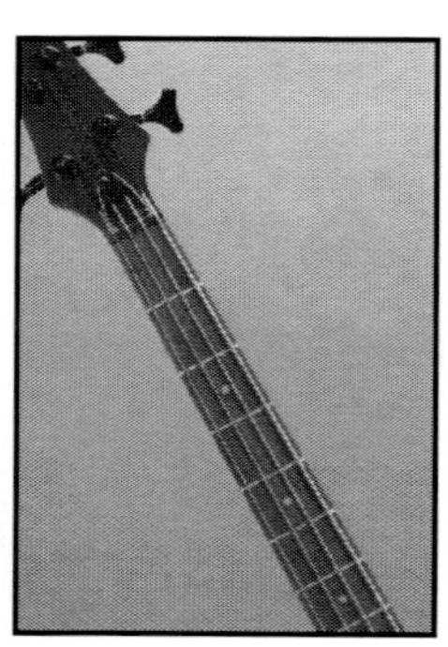

3rd – G

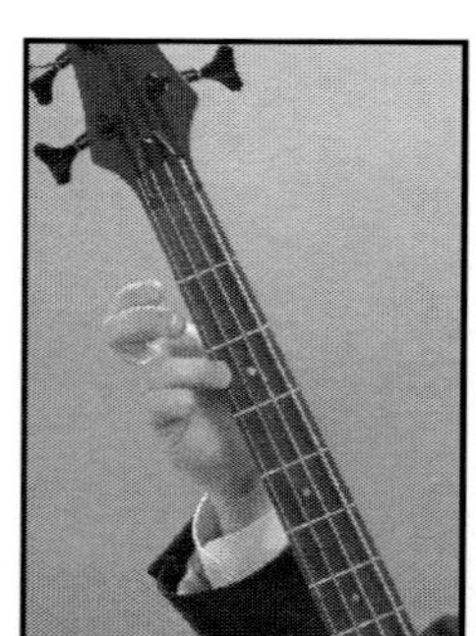

5th – B♭

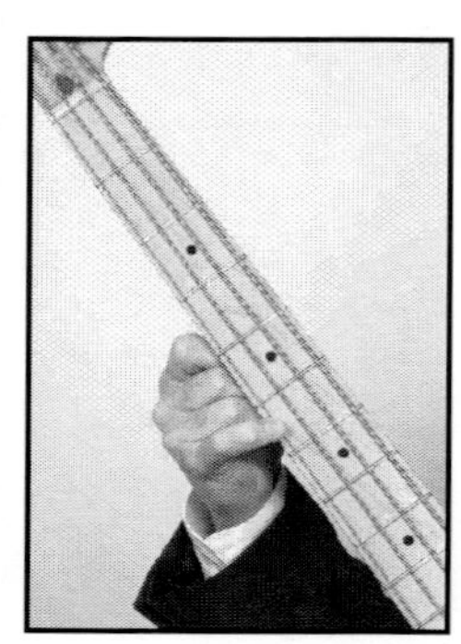

♭7th – D♭

Key of E♭ (cont.)

E♭7sus

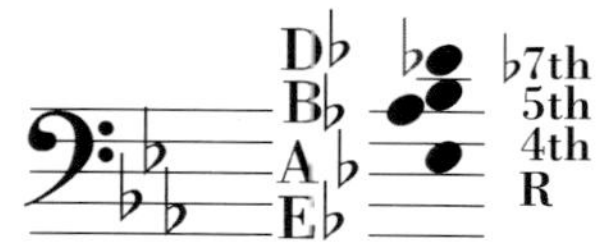

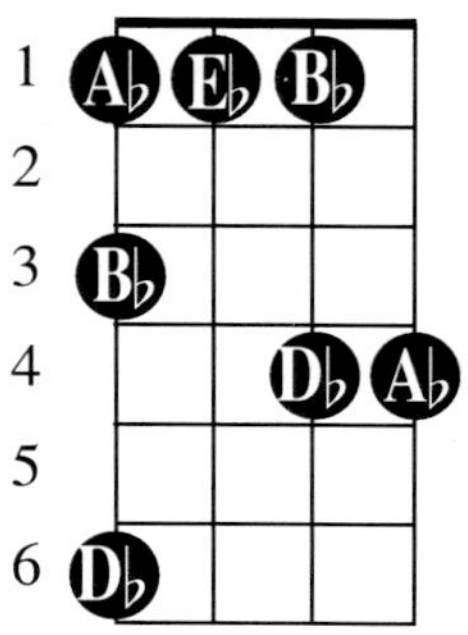

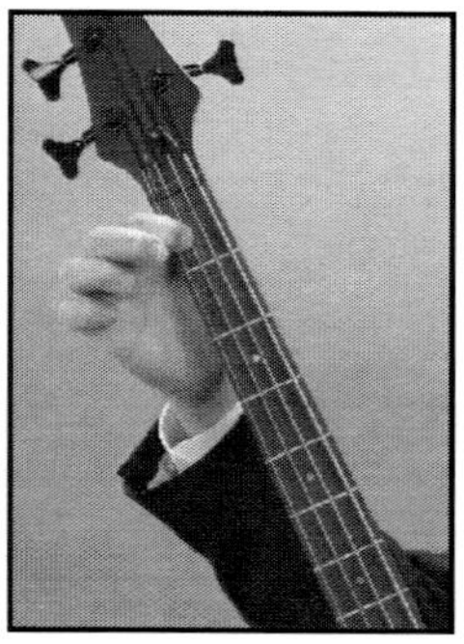

Root – E♭

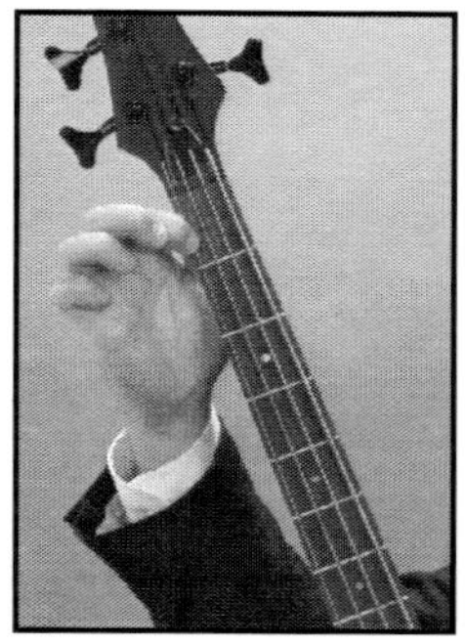

4th – A♭

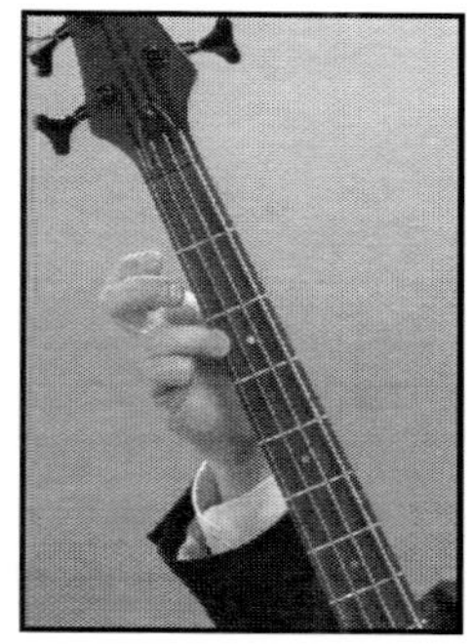

5th – B♭

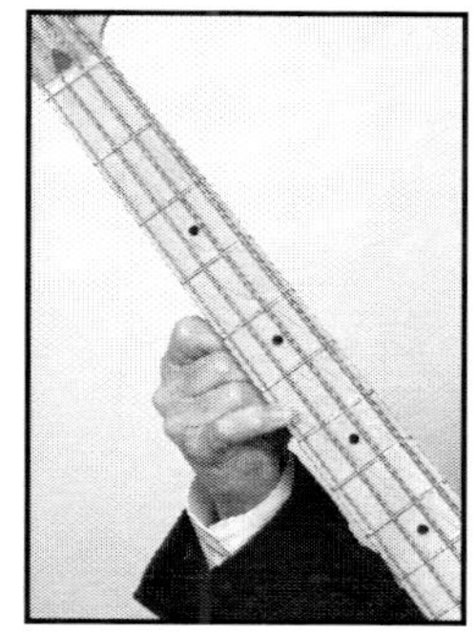

♭7th – D♭

E♭m7

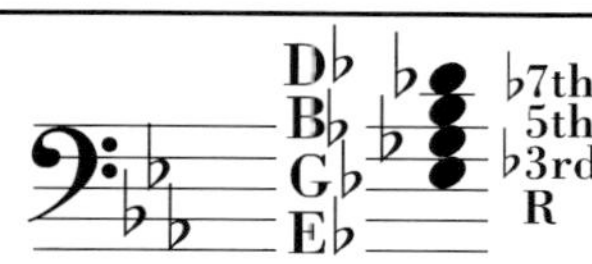

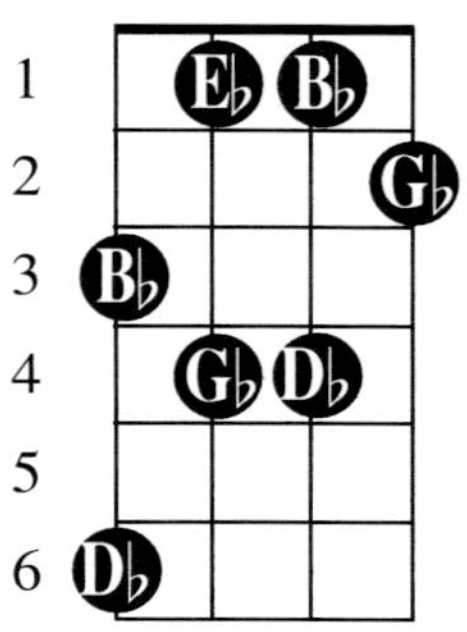

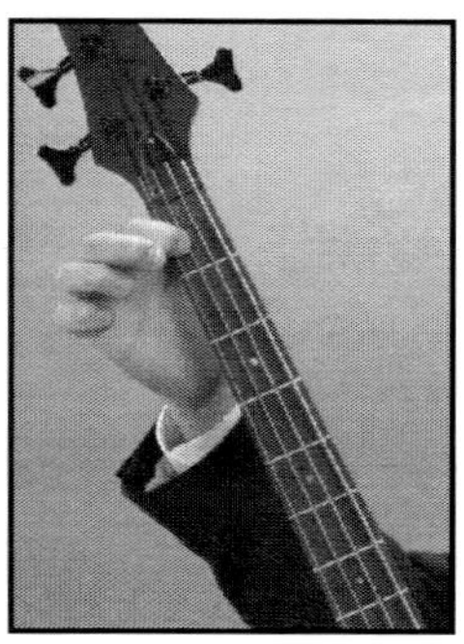

Root – E♭

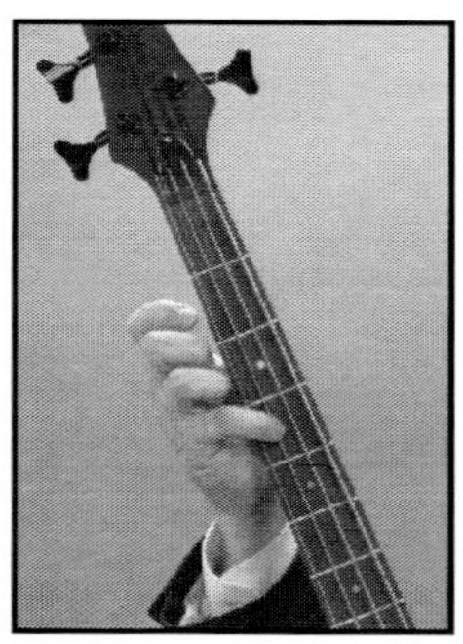

♭3rd – G♭

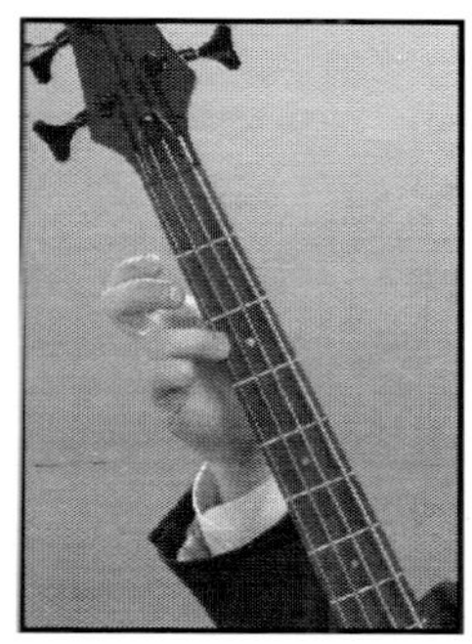

5th – B♭

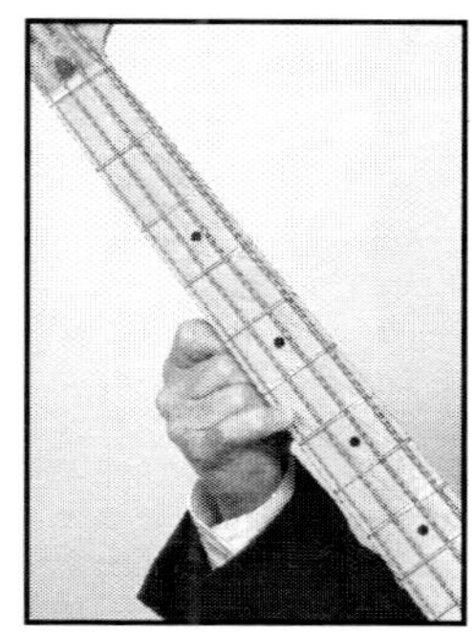

♭7th – D♭

E♭Ma7

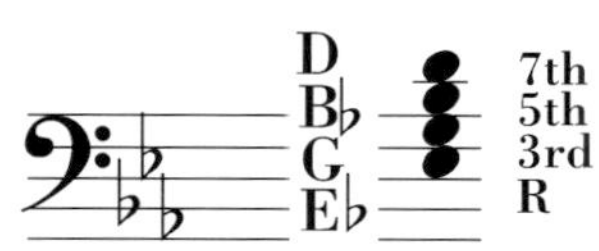

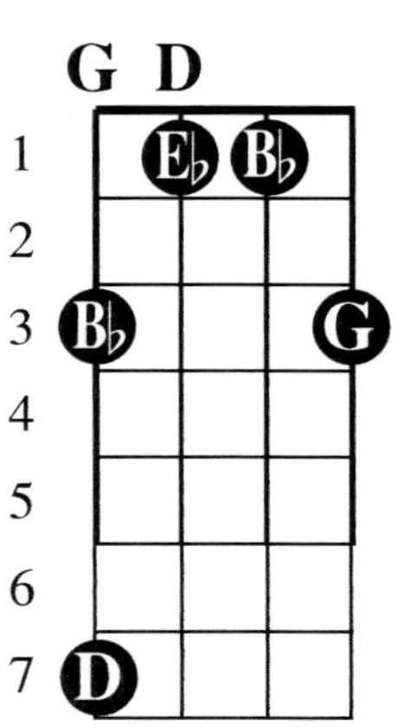

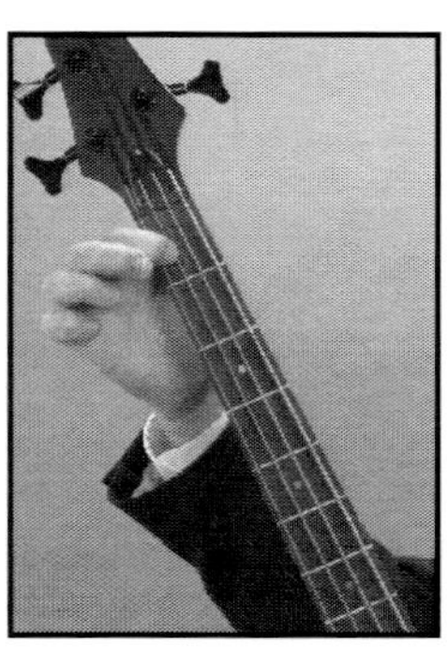

Root – E♭

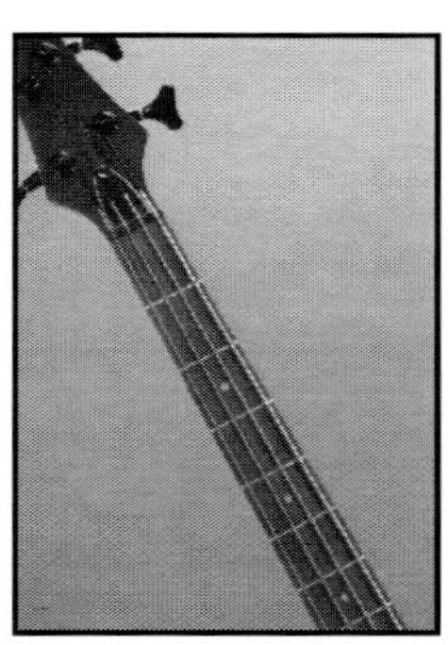

3rd – G

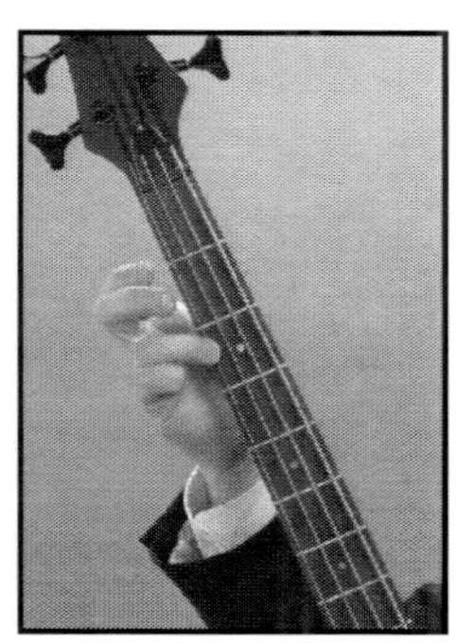

5th – B♭

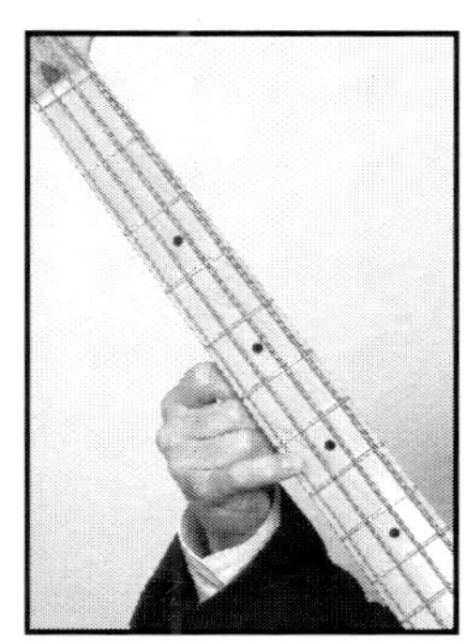

7th – D

Key of E♭ (cont.)

E♭dim

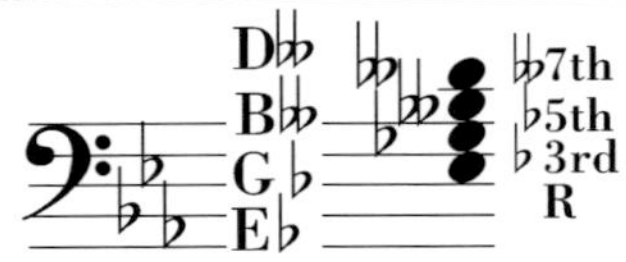

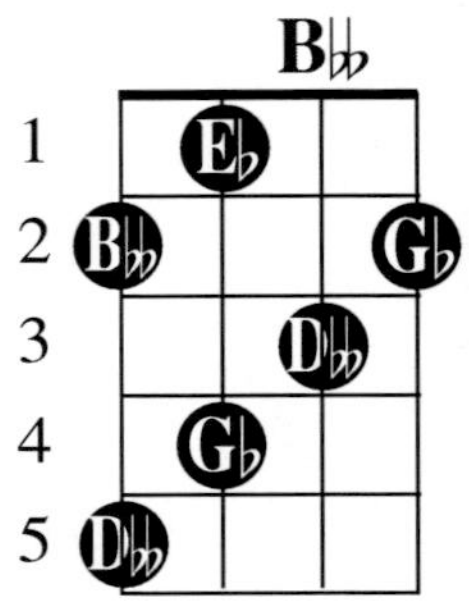

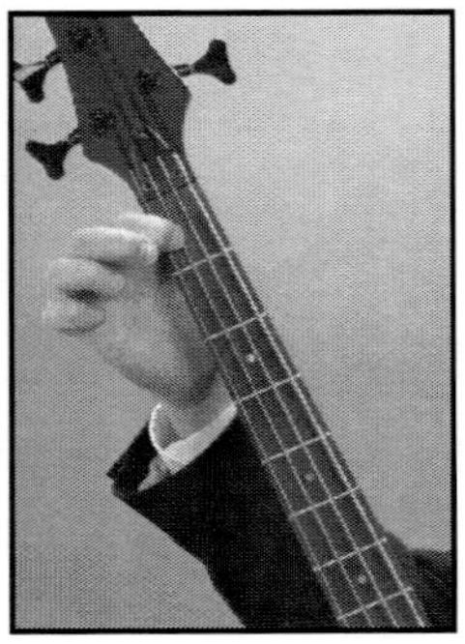

Root – E♭

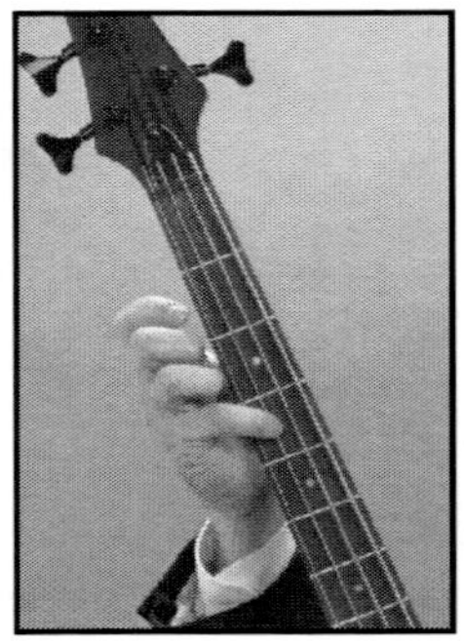

♭3rd – G♭

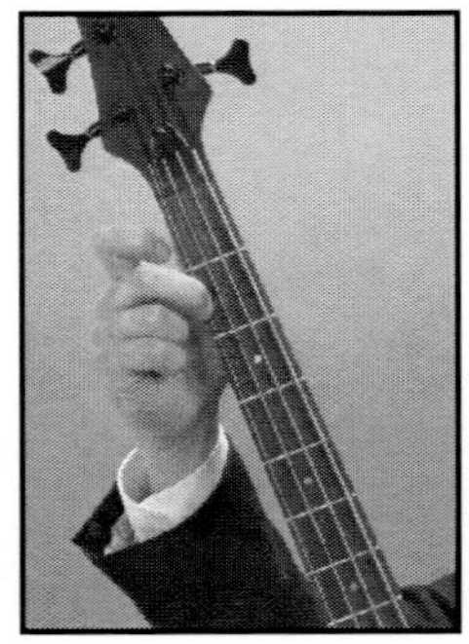

♭5th – B𝄫

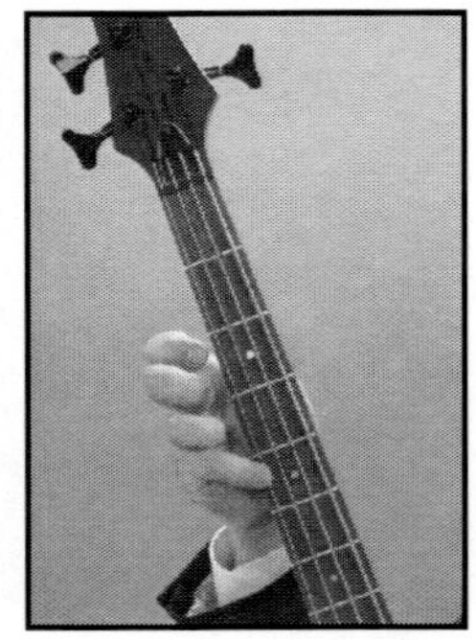

𝄫7th – D𝄫

E♭aug

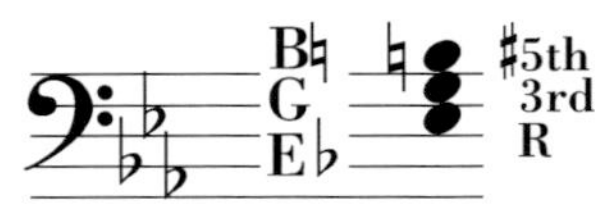

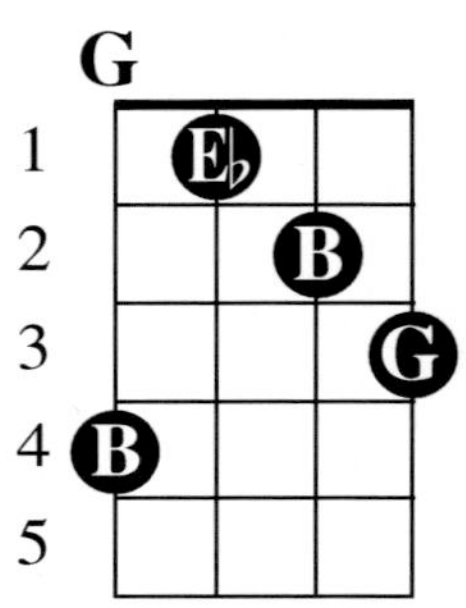

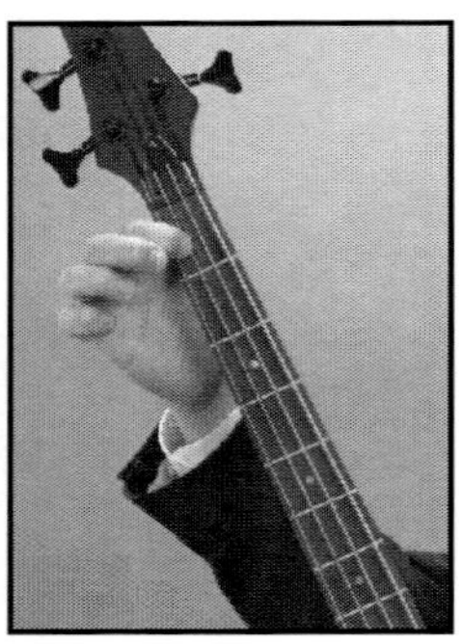

Root – E♭

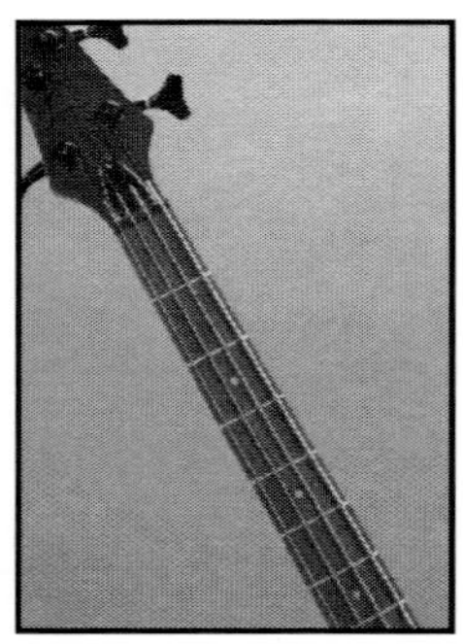

3rd – G

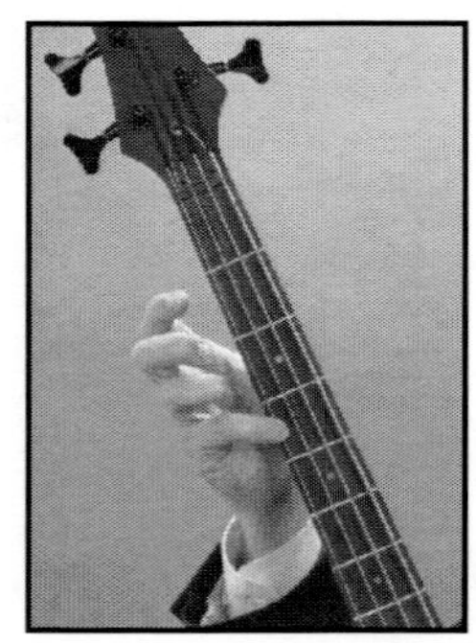

♯5th – B♮

E♭6

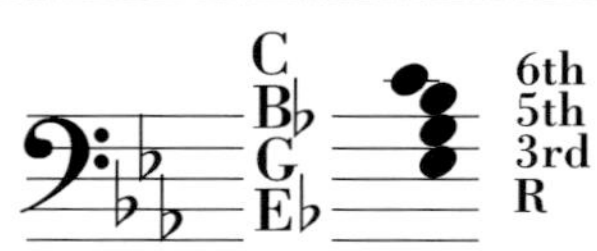

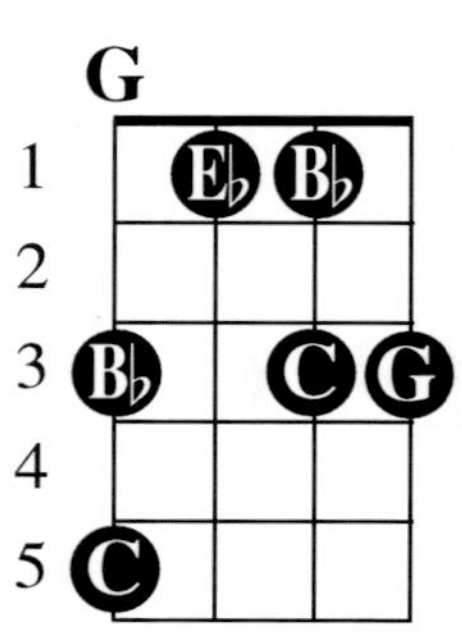

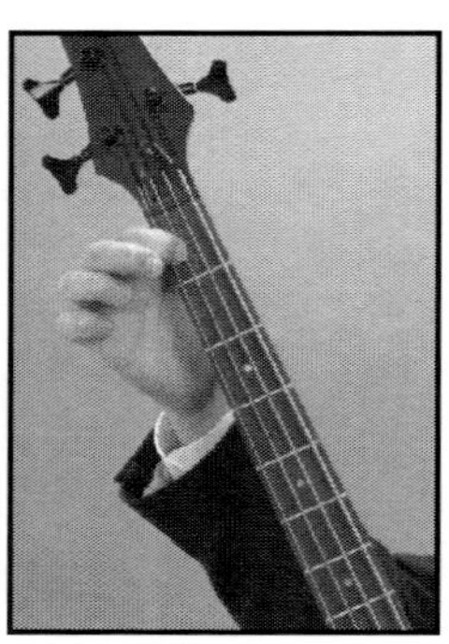

Root – E♭

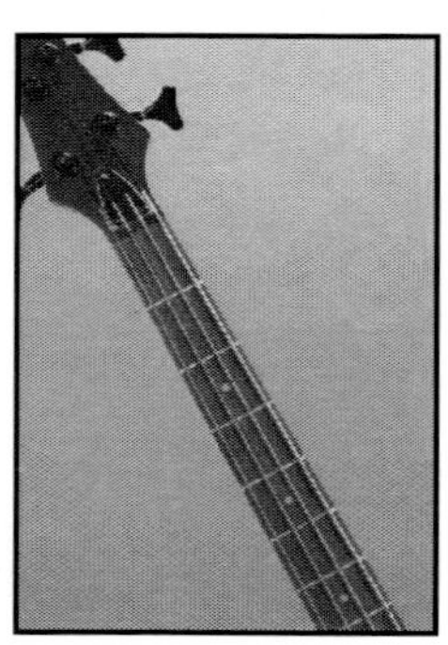

3rd – G

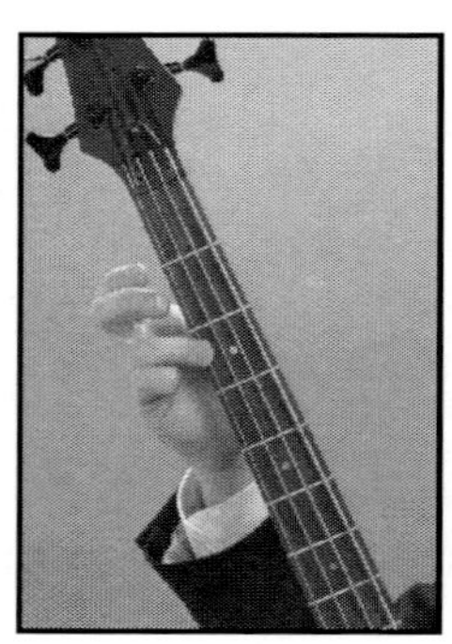

5th – B♭

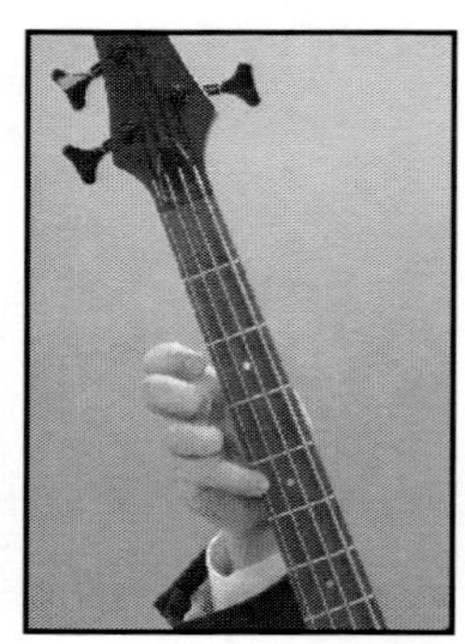

6th – C

Key of E♭ (cont.)

E♭m6

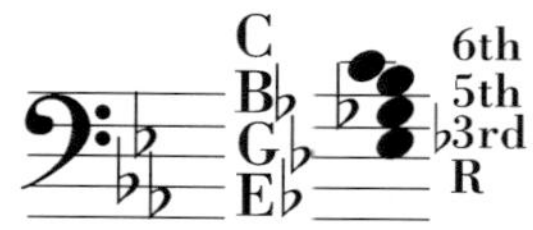

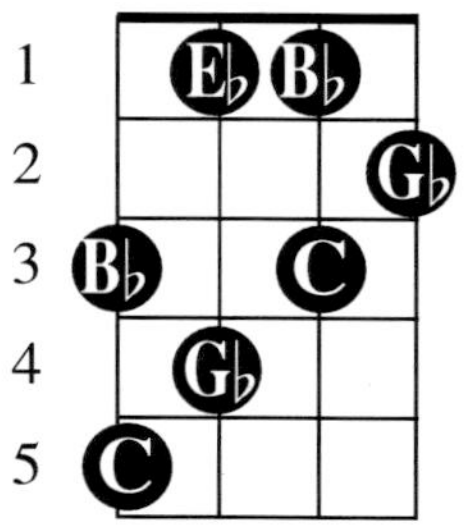

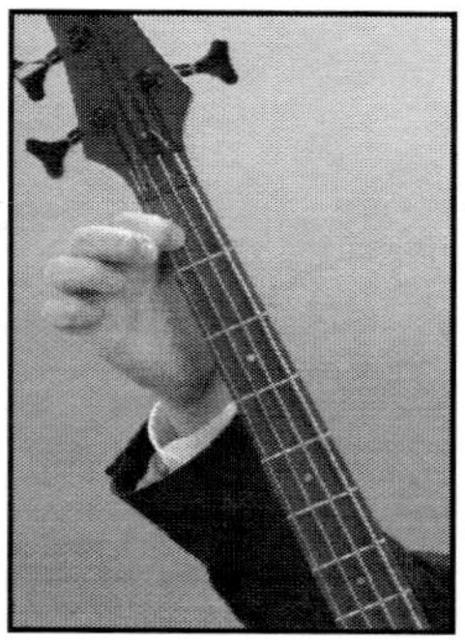
Root – E♭

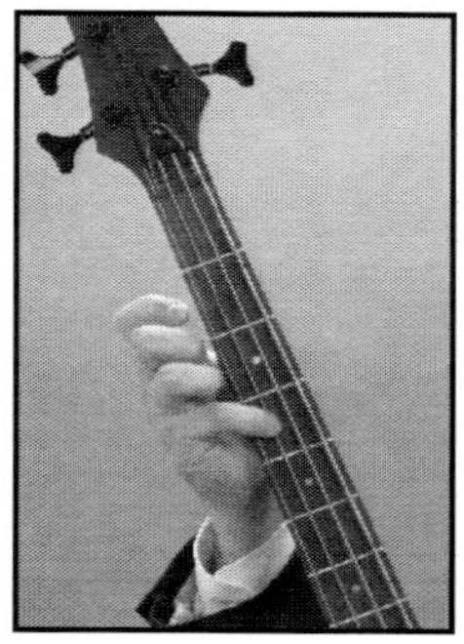
♭3rd – G♭

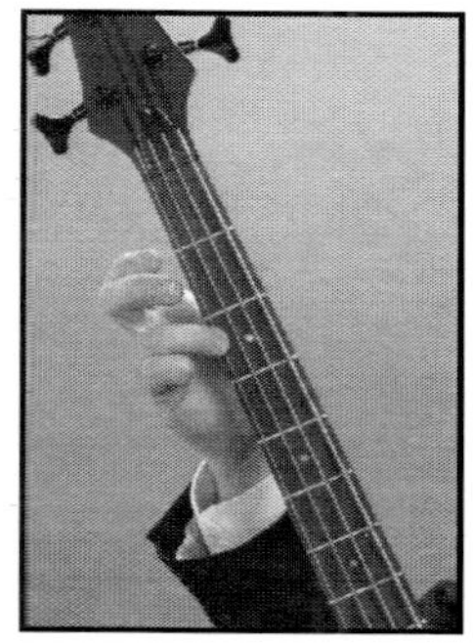
5th – B♭

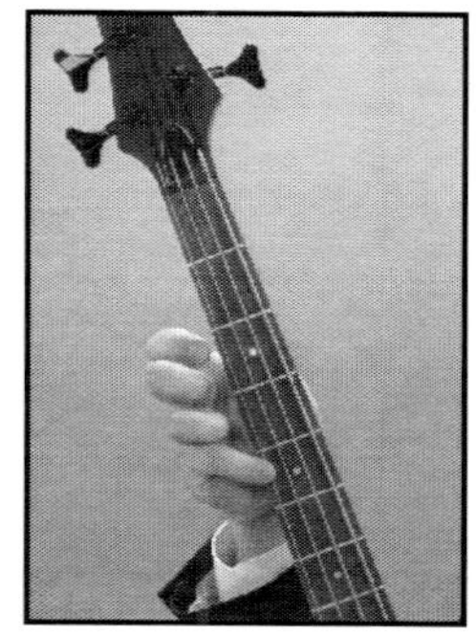
6th – C

E♭7♯5

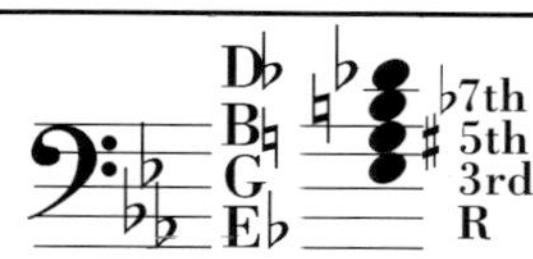

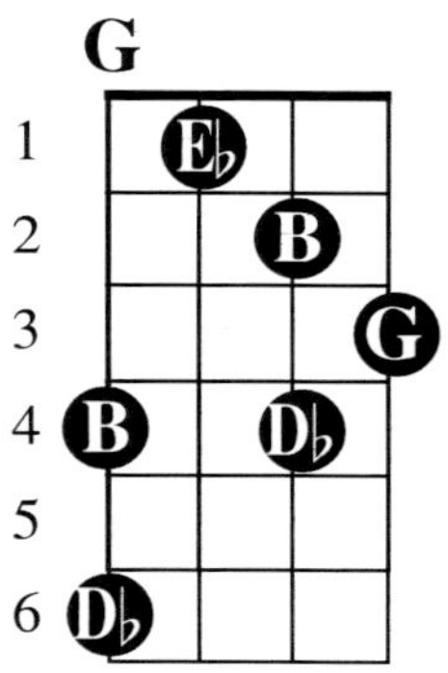

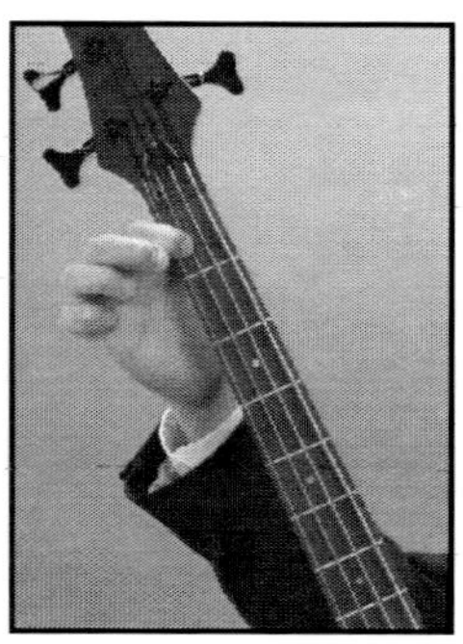
Root – E♭

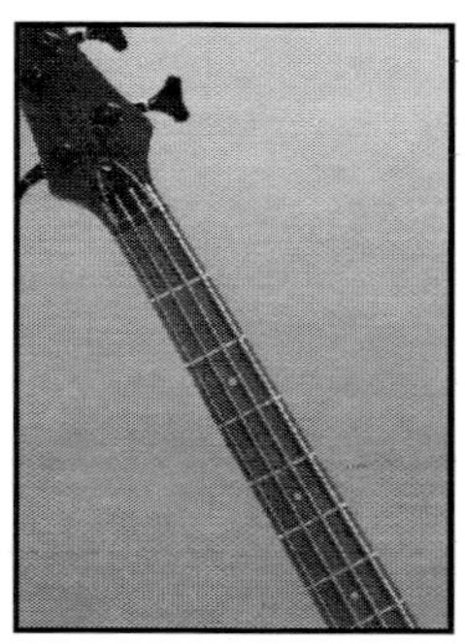
3rd – G

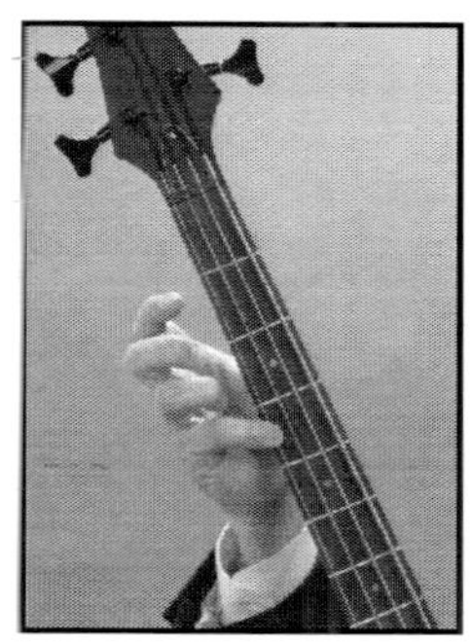
♯5th – B♮

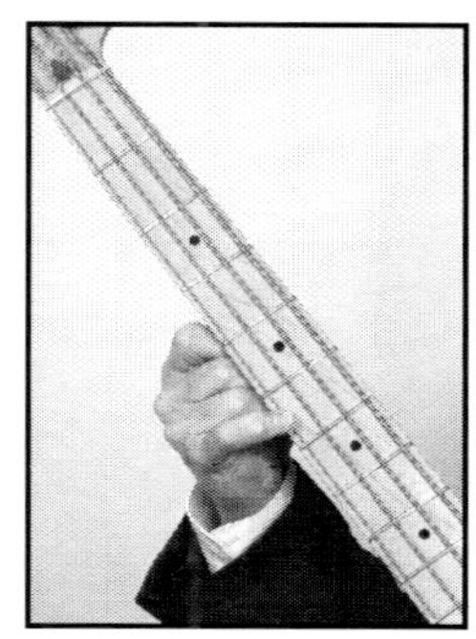
♭7th – D♭

E♭7♭5

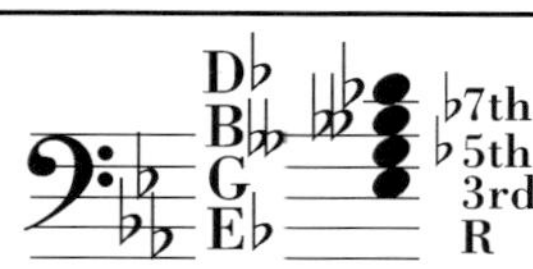

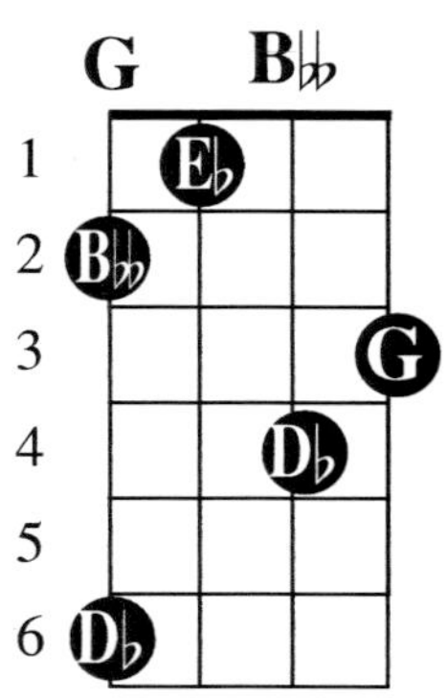

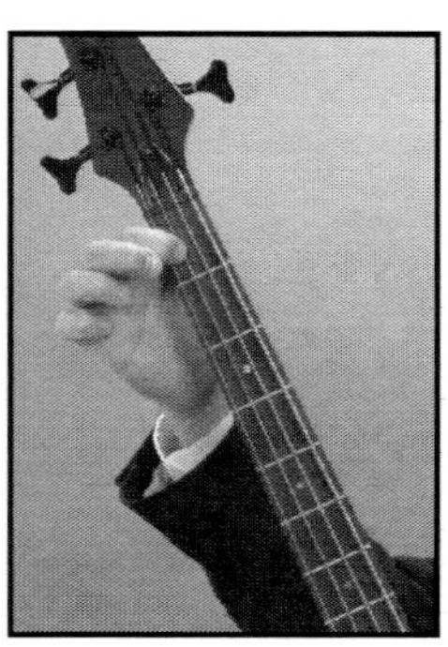
Root – E♭

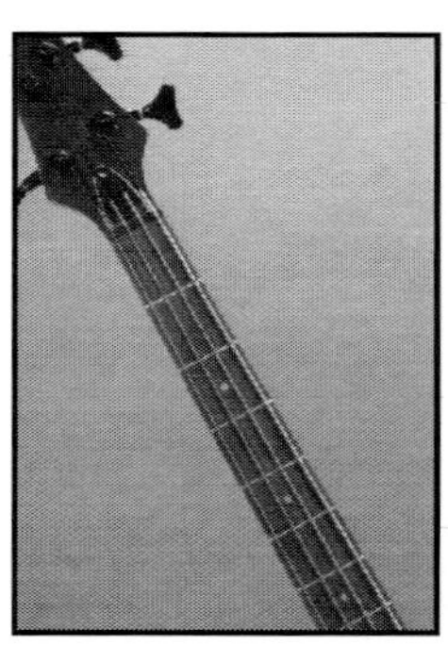
3rd – G

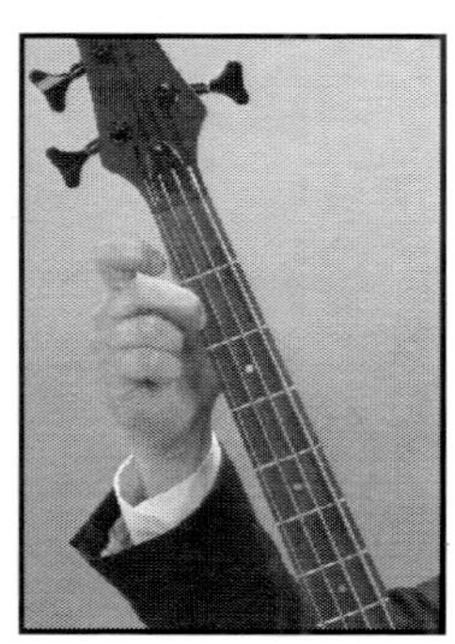
♭5th – B𝄫

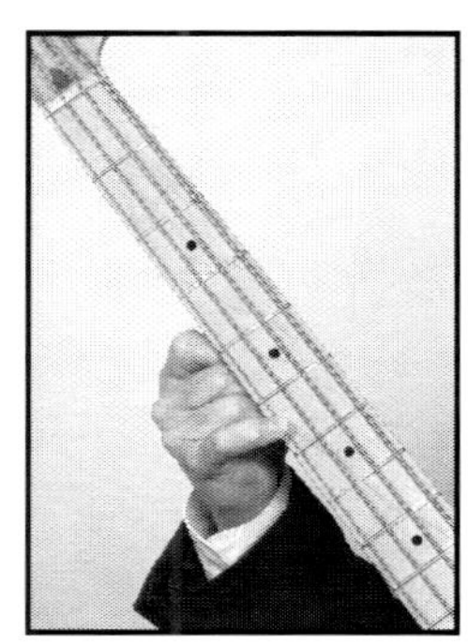
♭7th – D♭

Key of E

EMaj

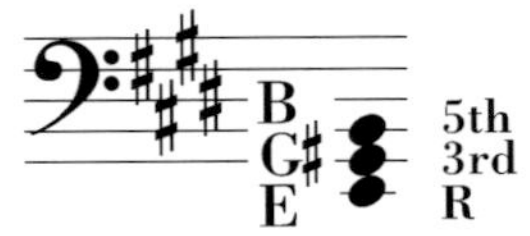

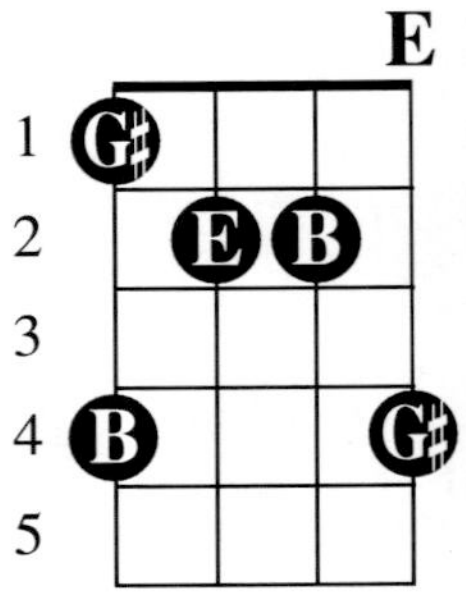

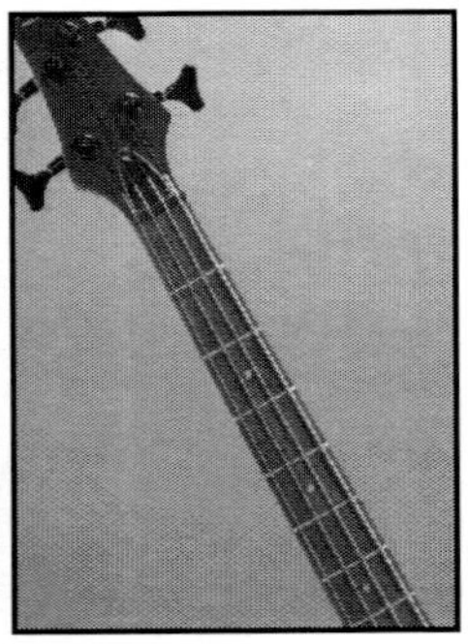

Root – E

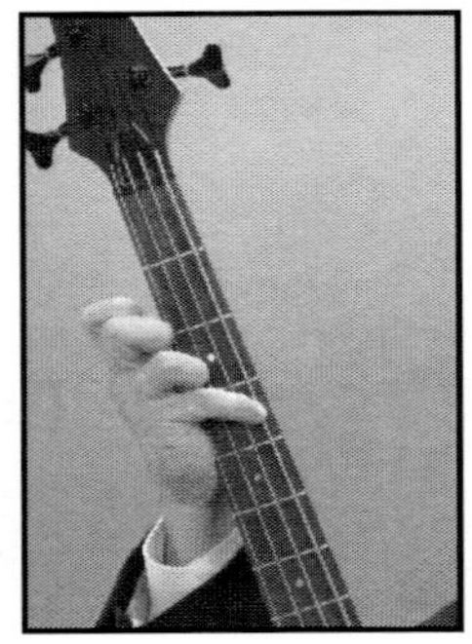

3rd – G♯

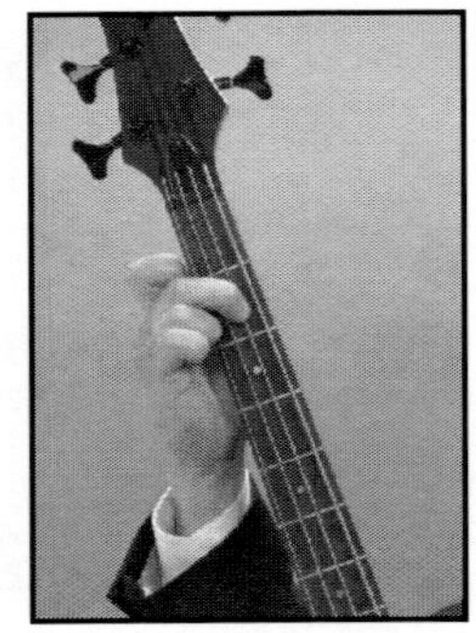

5th – B

Emin

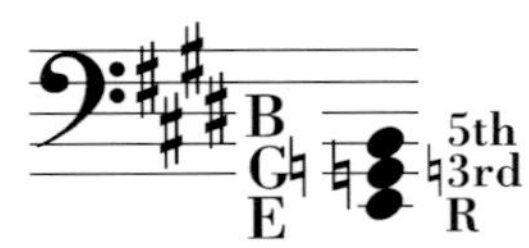

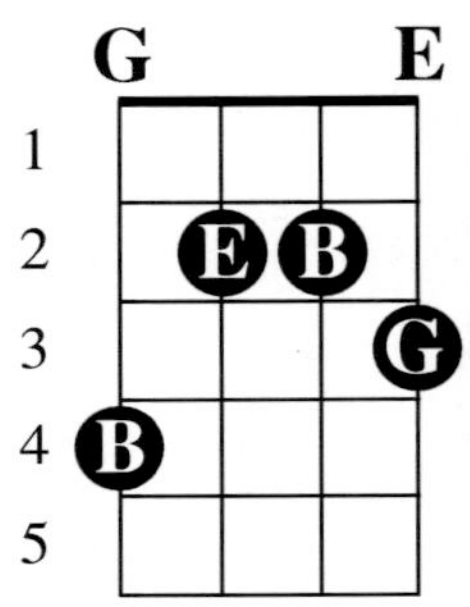

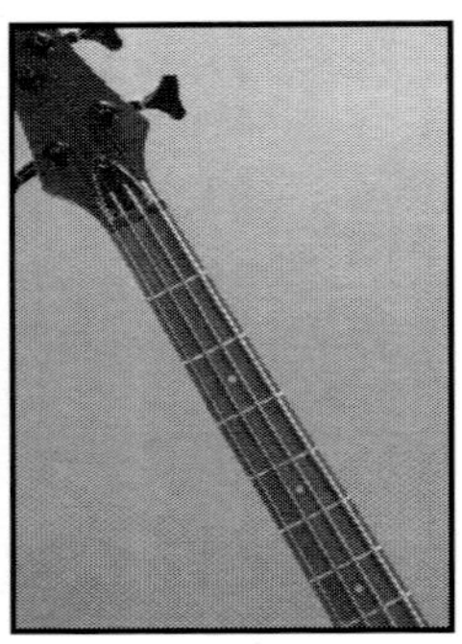

Root – E

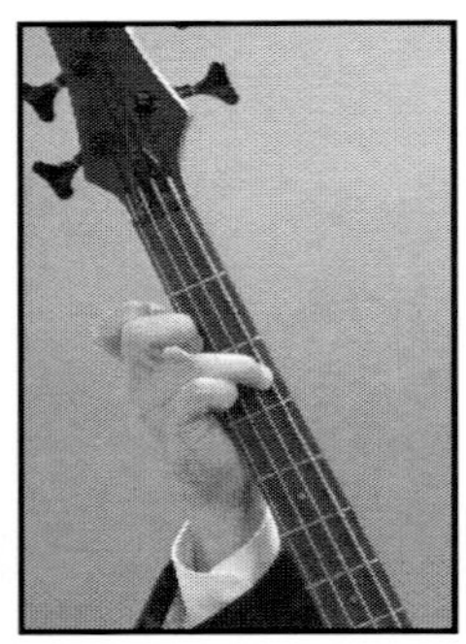

♭3rd – G♮

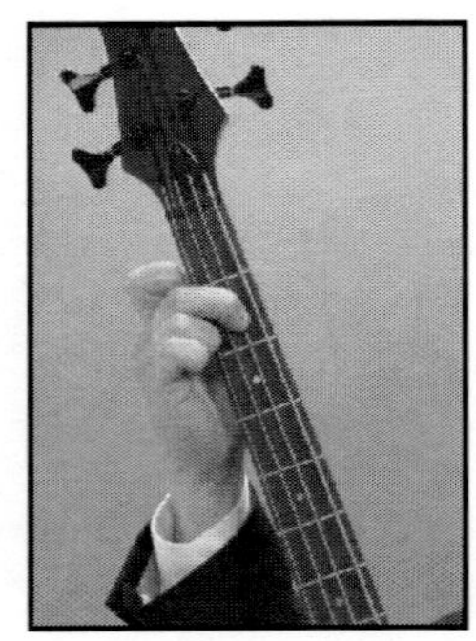

5th – B

E7

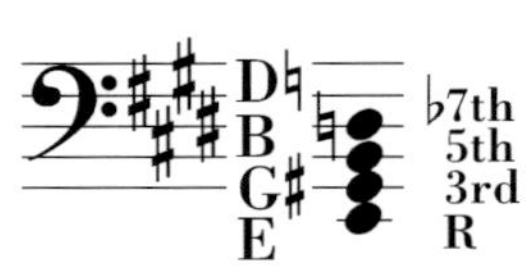

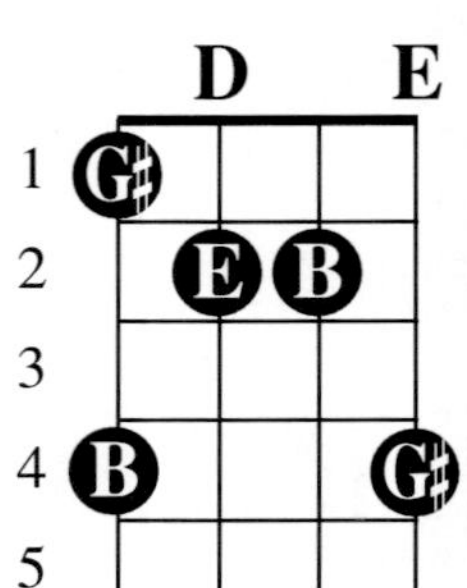

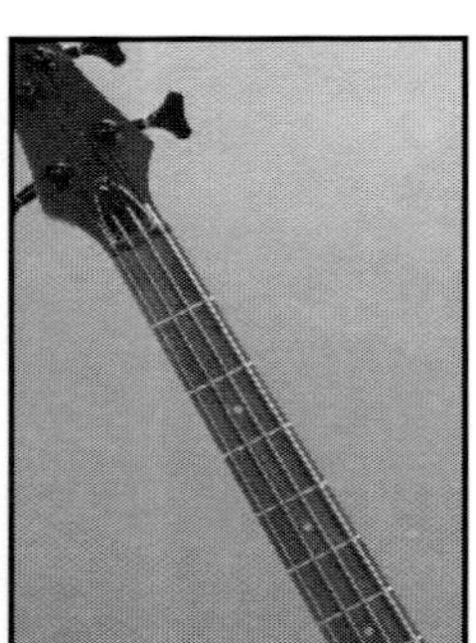

Root – E

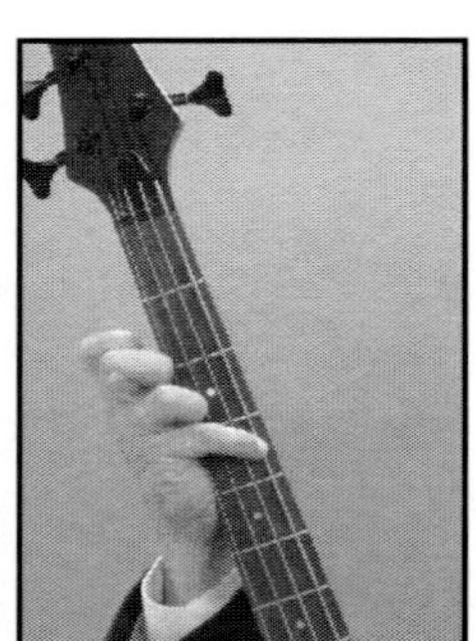

3rd – G♯

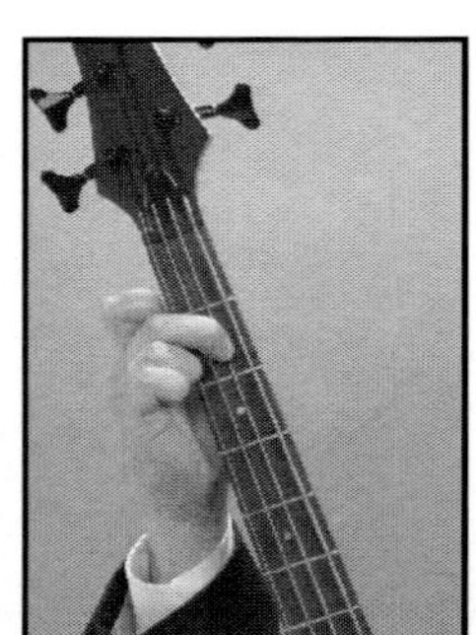

5th – B

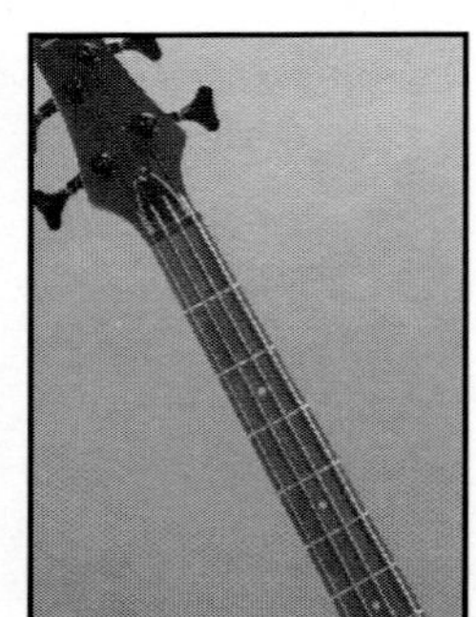

♭7th – D♮

Key of E (cont.)

E7sus

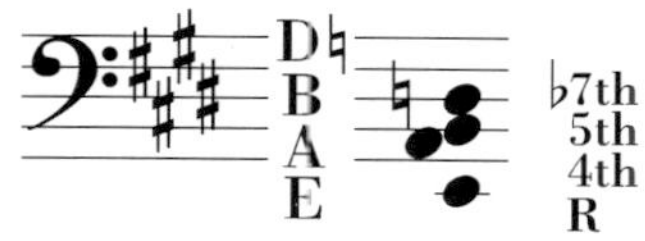

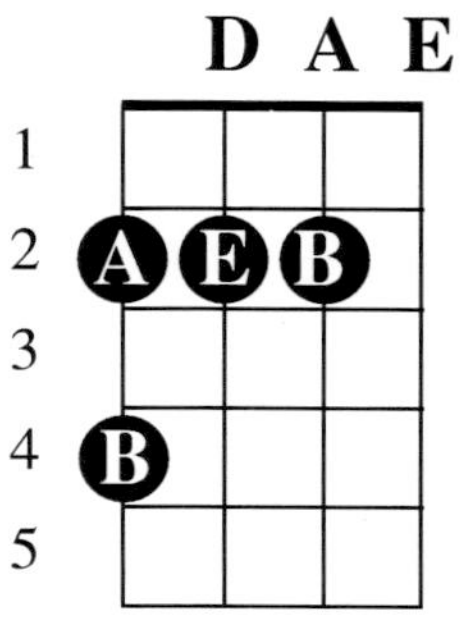

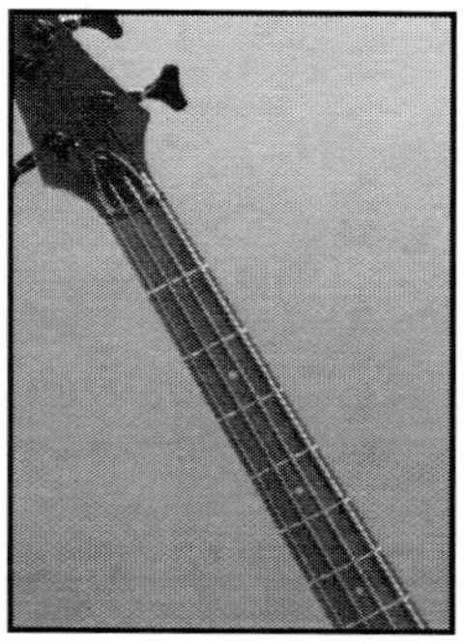

Root – E

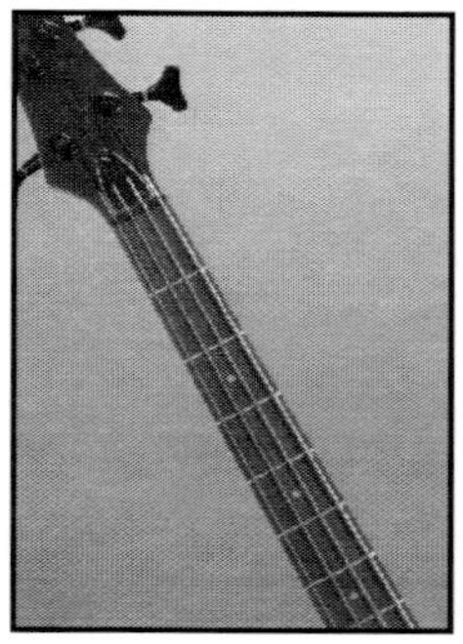

4th – A

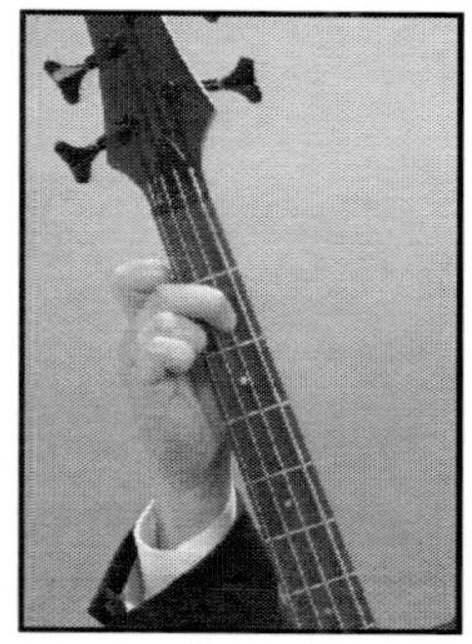

5th – B

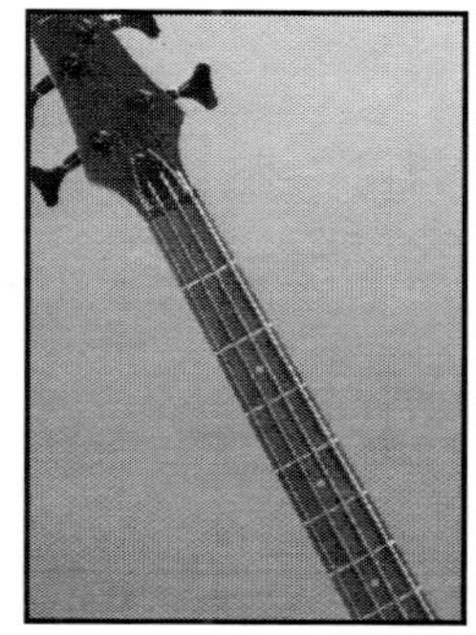

♭7th – D♮

Em7

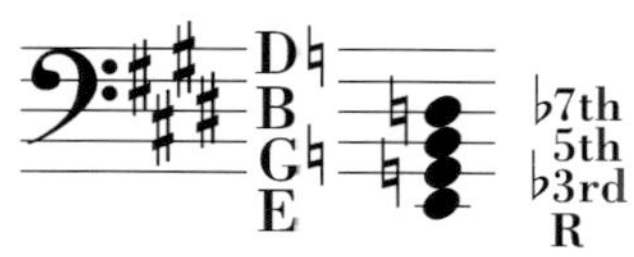

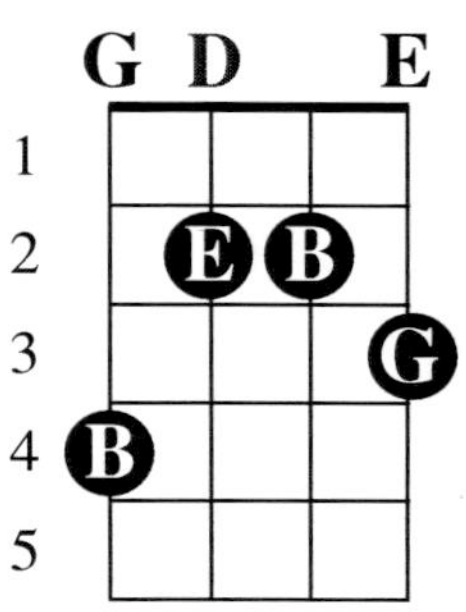

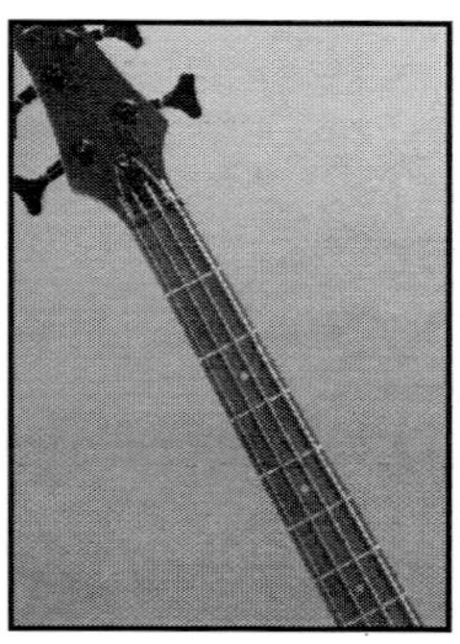

Root – E

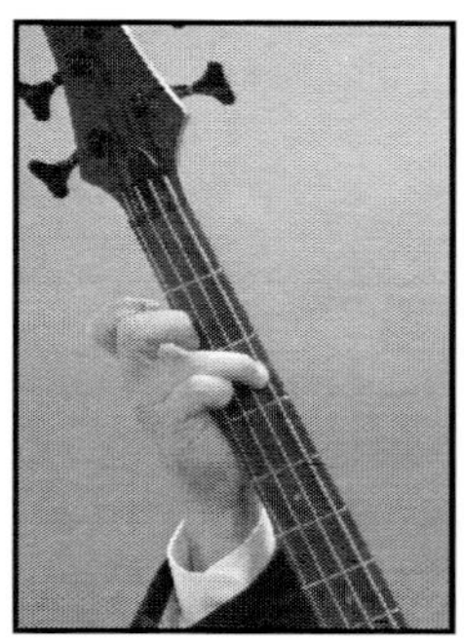

♭3rd – G♮

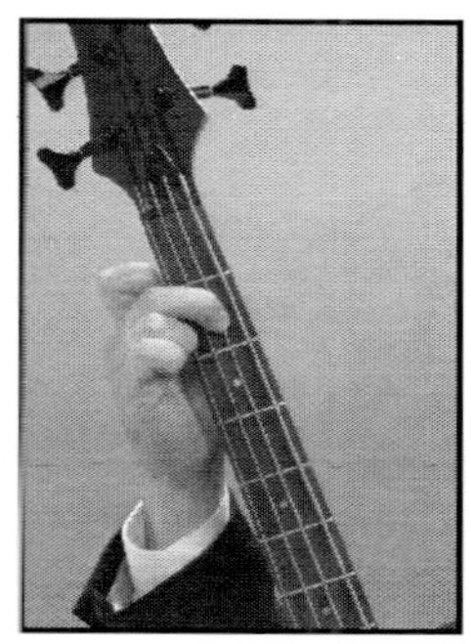

5th – B

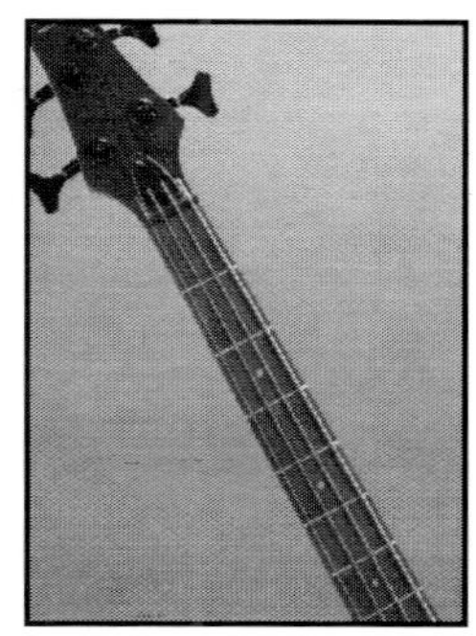

♭7th – D♮

EMa7

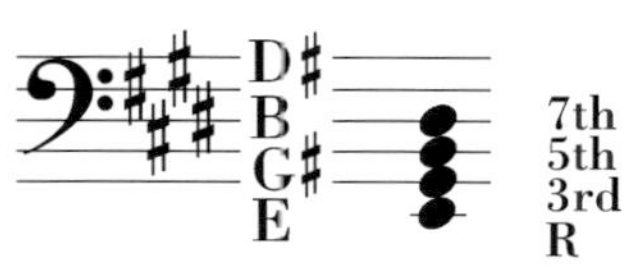

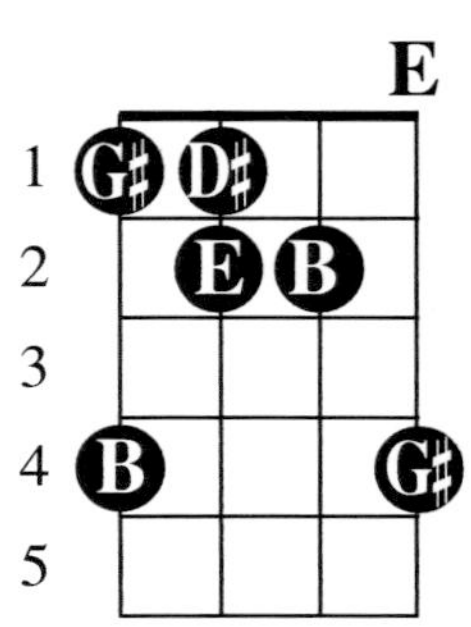

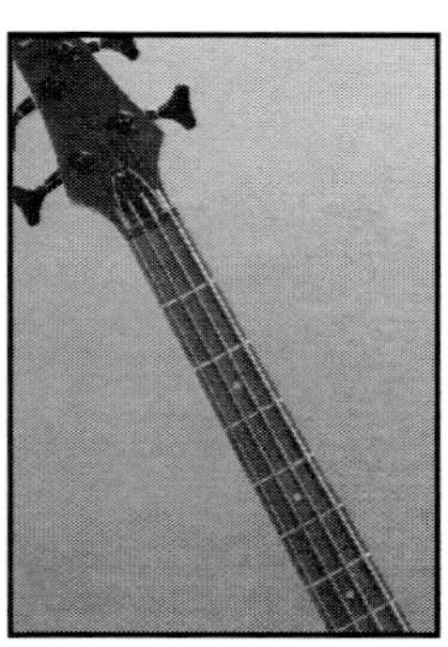

Root – E

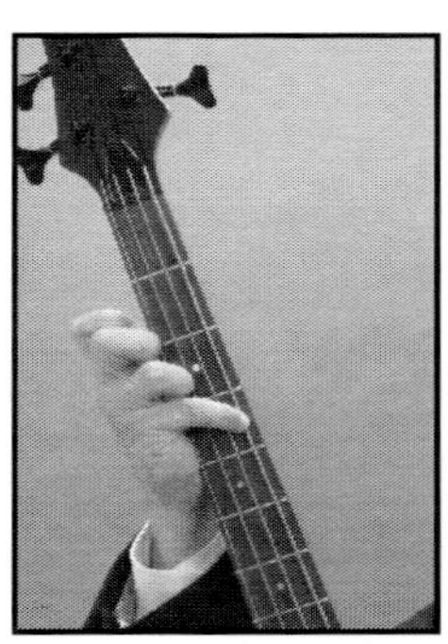

3rd – G♯

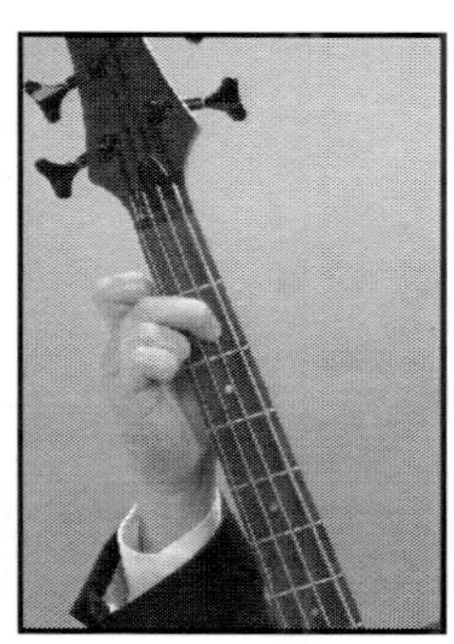

5th – B

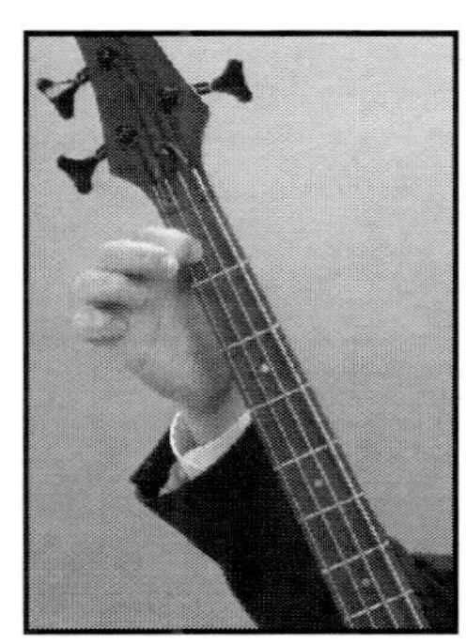

7th – D♯

Key of E (cont.)

Edim

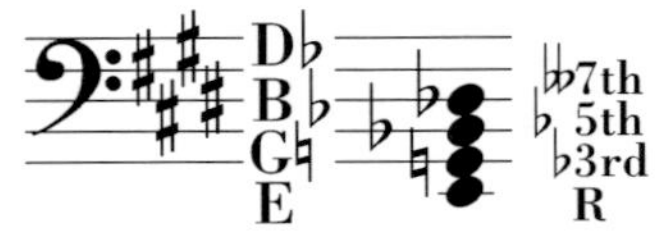

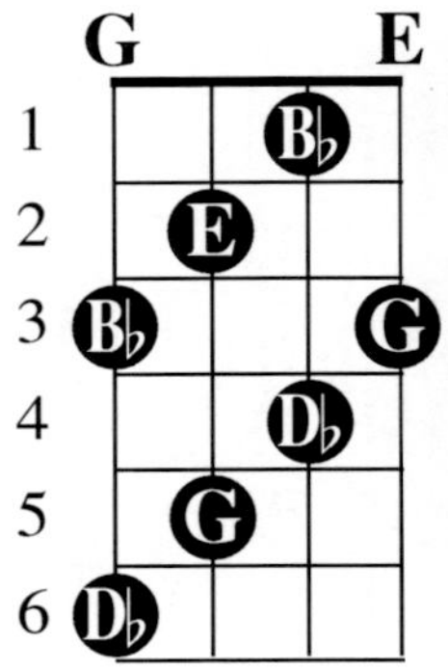

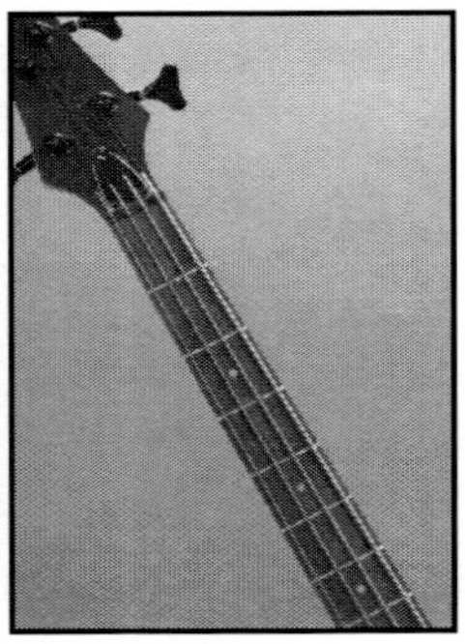

Root – E

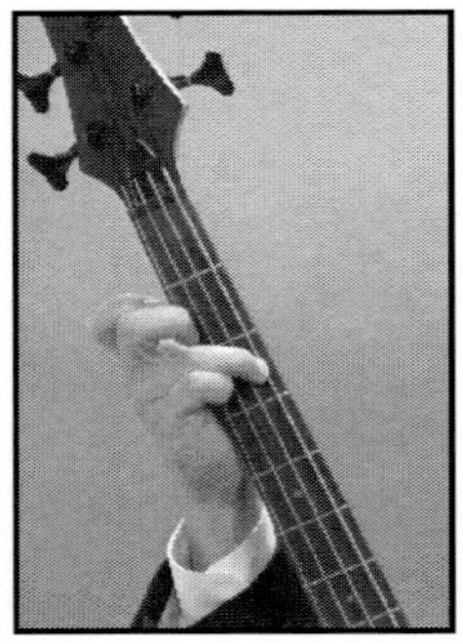

♭3rd – G♮

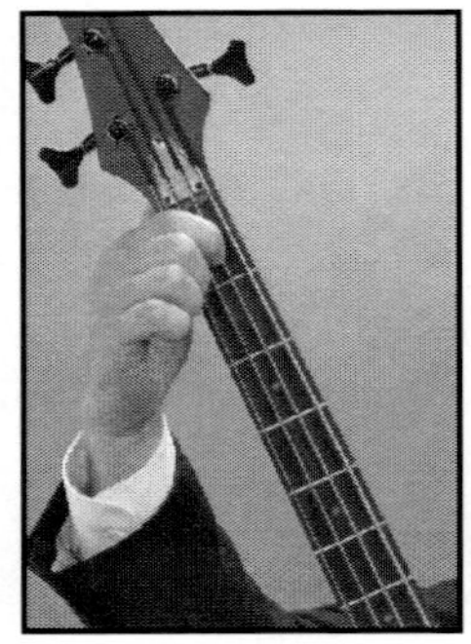

♭5th – B♭

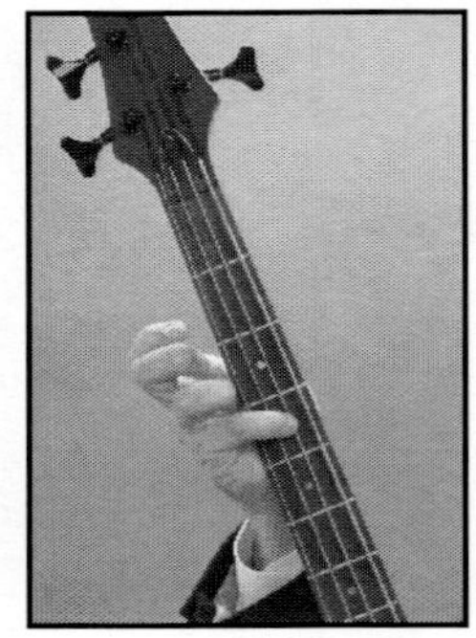

♭♭7th – D♭

Eaug

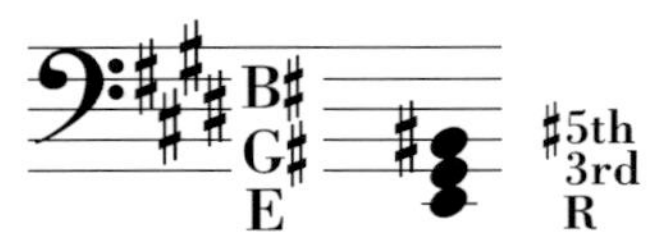

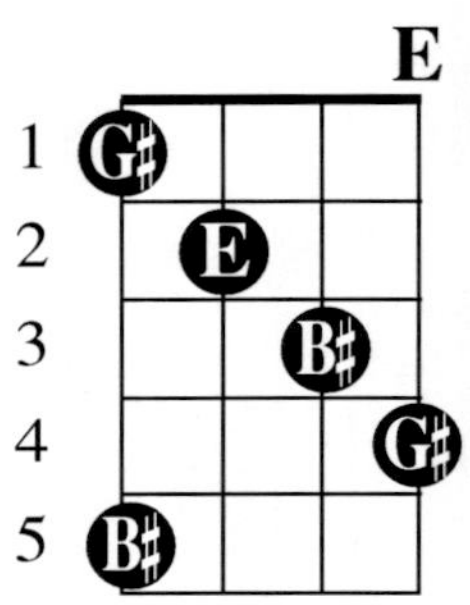

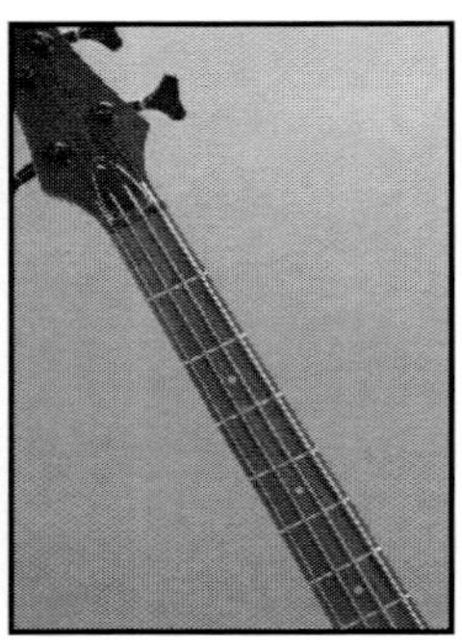

Root – E

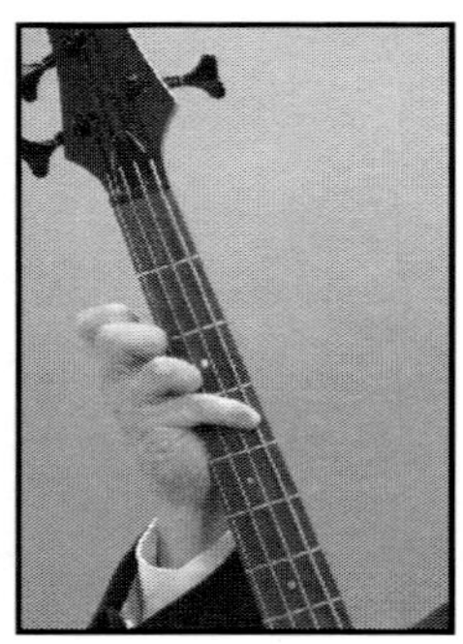

3rd – G♯

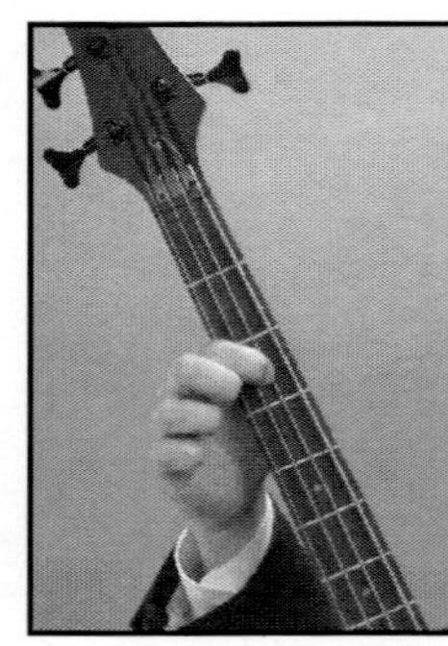

♯5th – B♯

E6

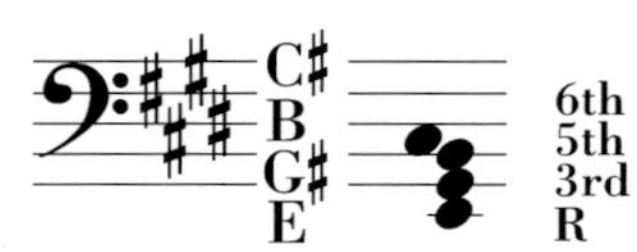

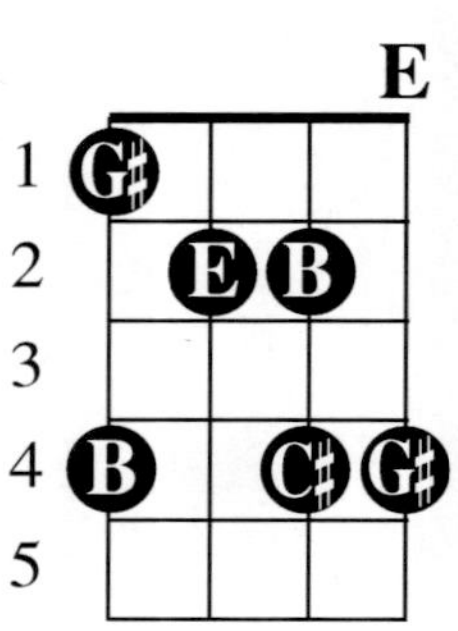

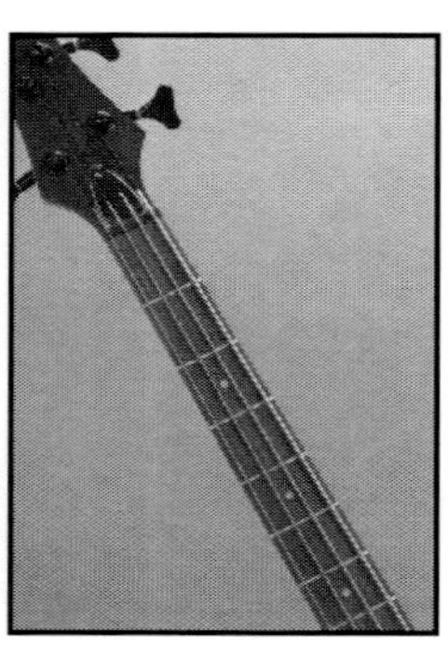

Root – E

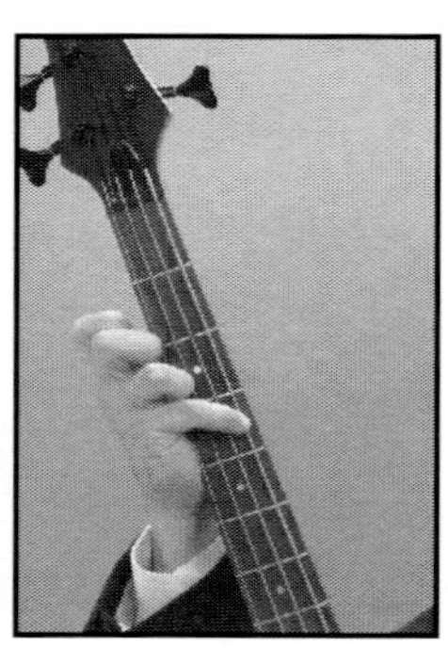

3rd – G♯

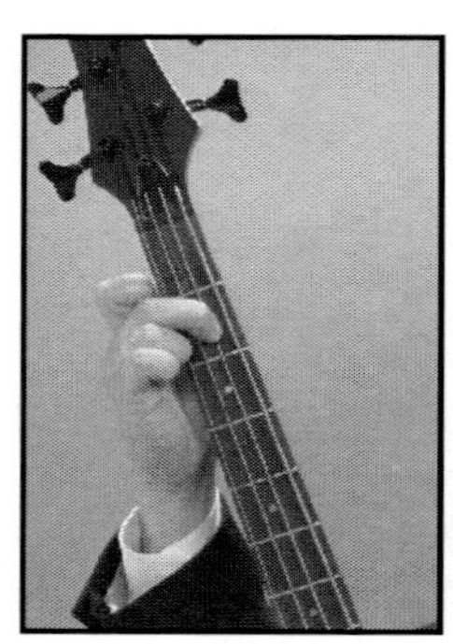

5th – B

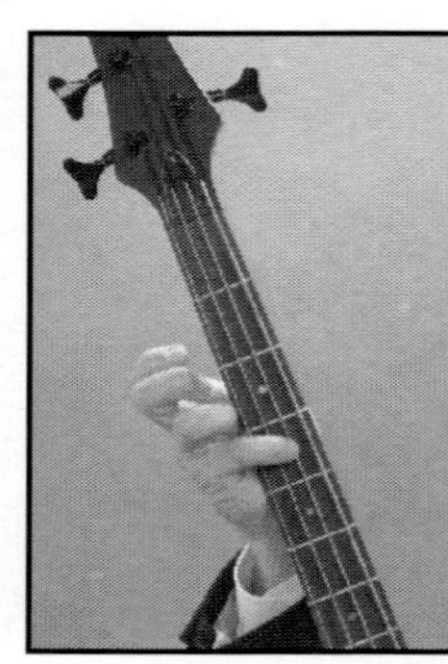

6th – C♯

Key of E (cont.)

Em6

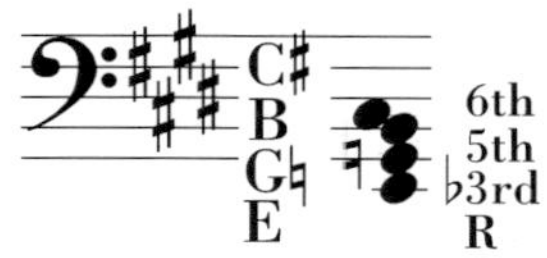

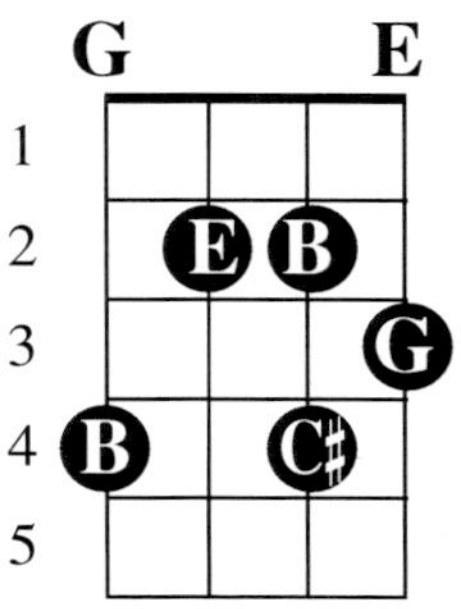

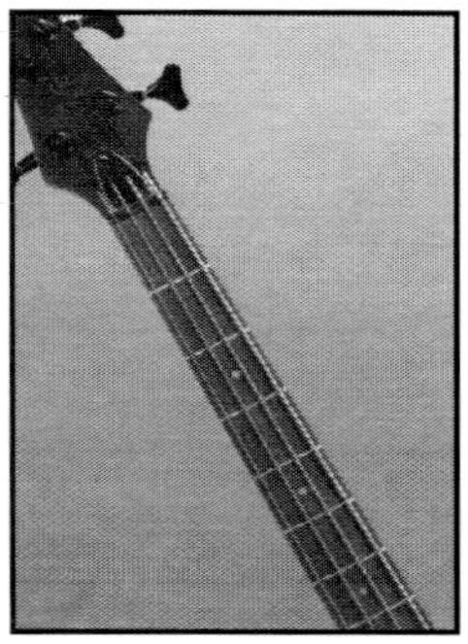

Root – E

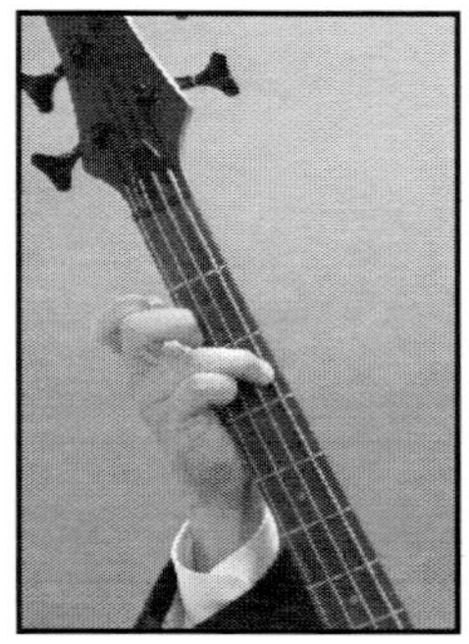

♭3rd – G♮

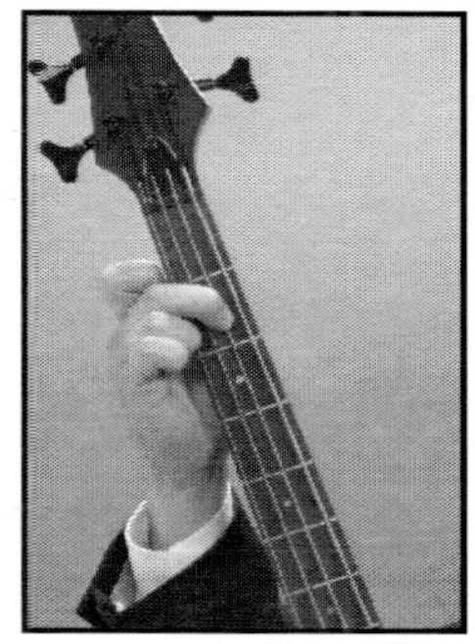

5th – B

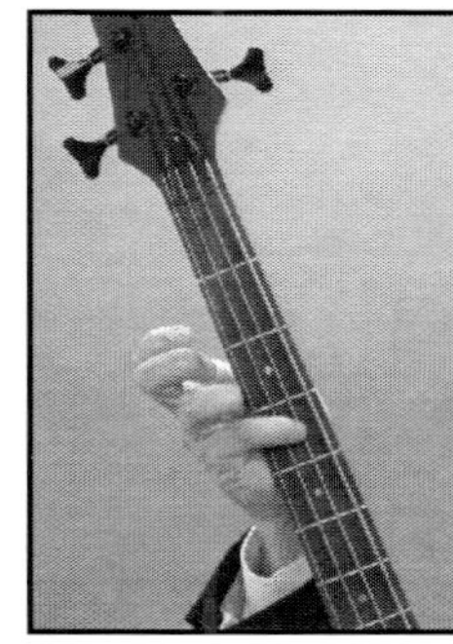

6th – C♯

E7♯5

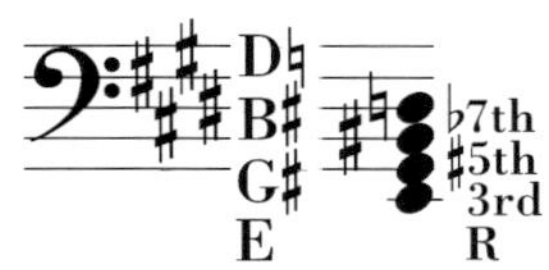

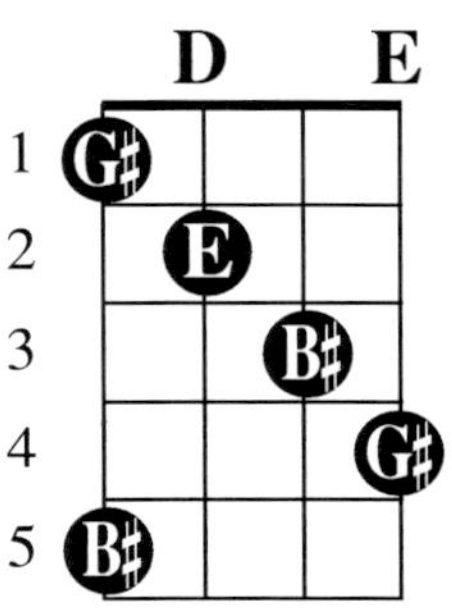

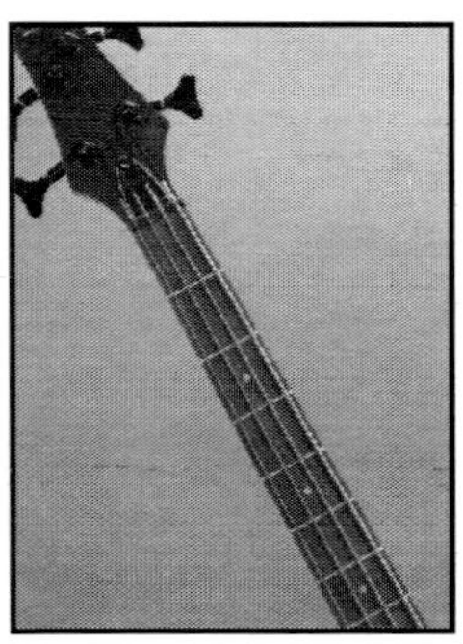

Root – E

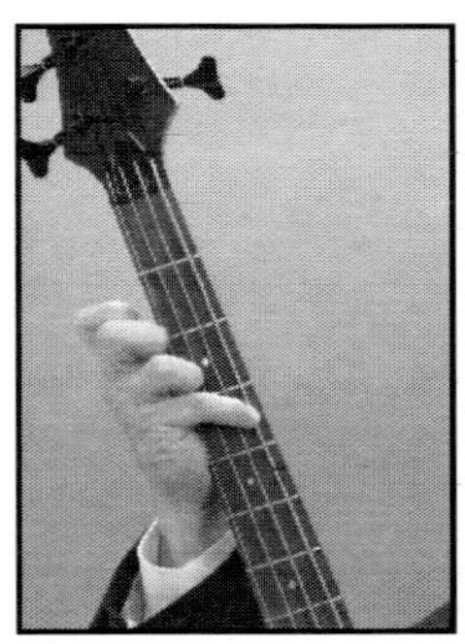

3rd – G♯

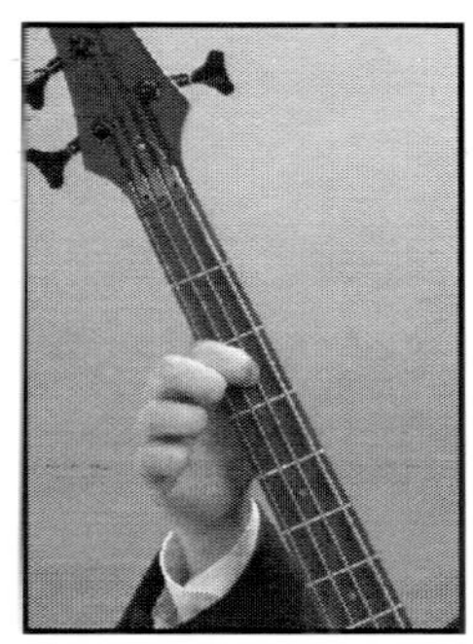

♯5th – B♯ or C

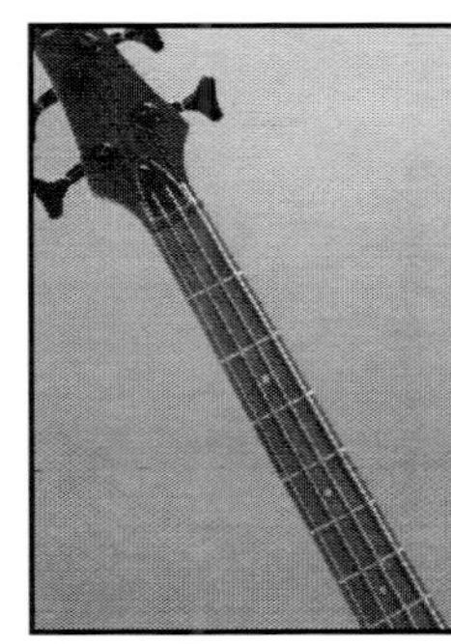

♭7th – D♮

E7♭5

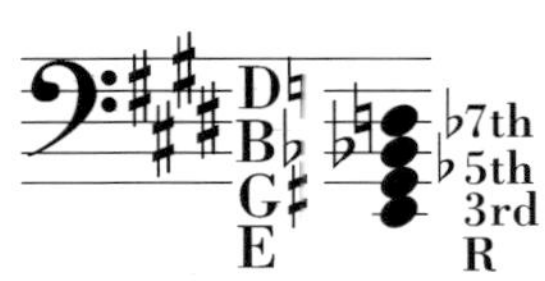

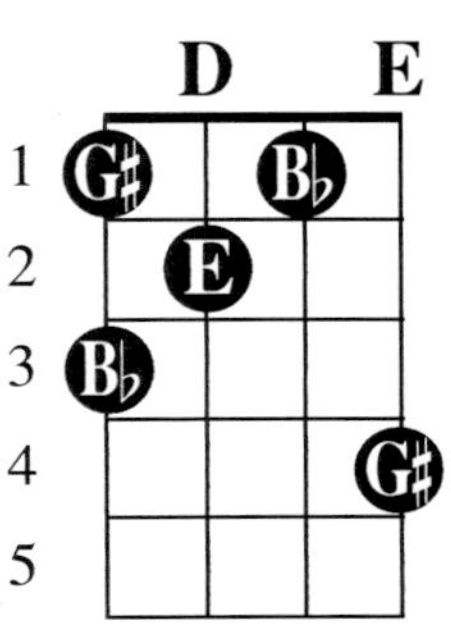

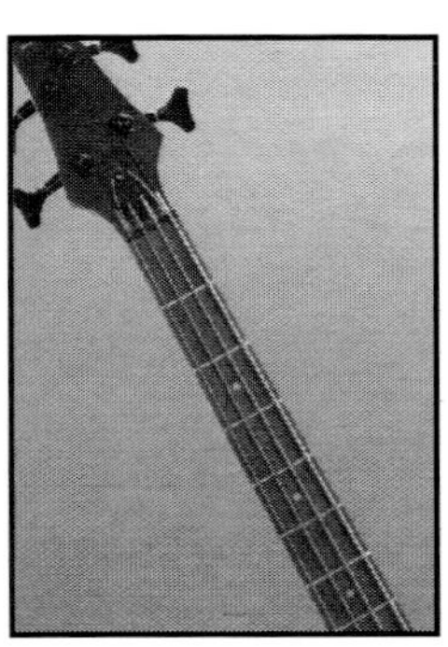

Root – E

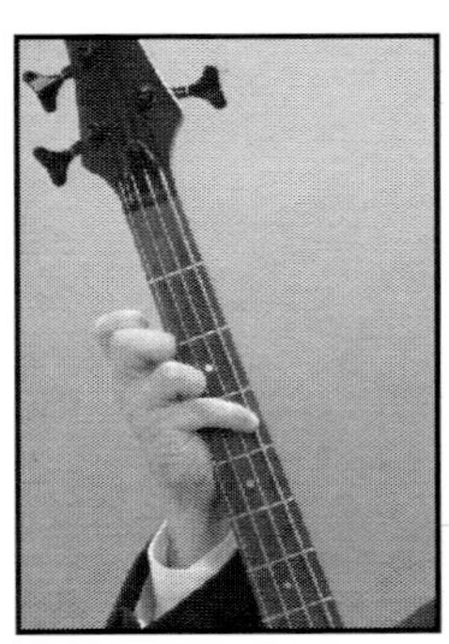

3rd – G♯

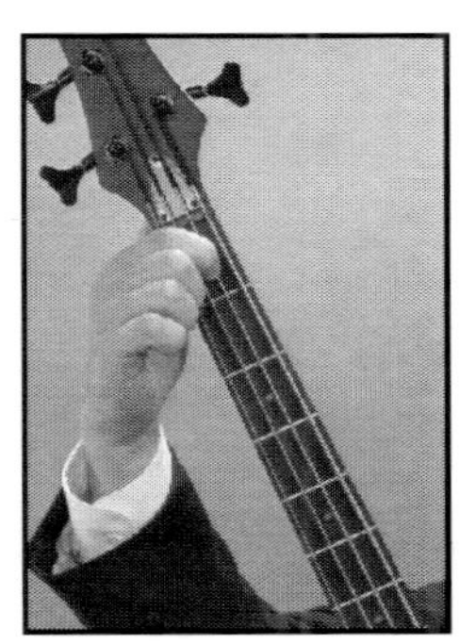

♭5th – B♭

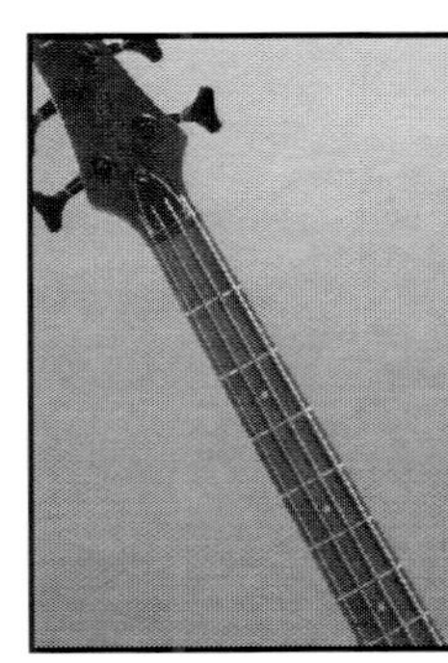

♭7th – D♮

Key of F

FMaj

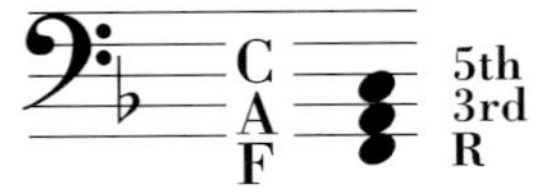

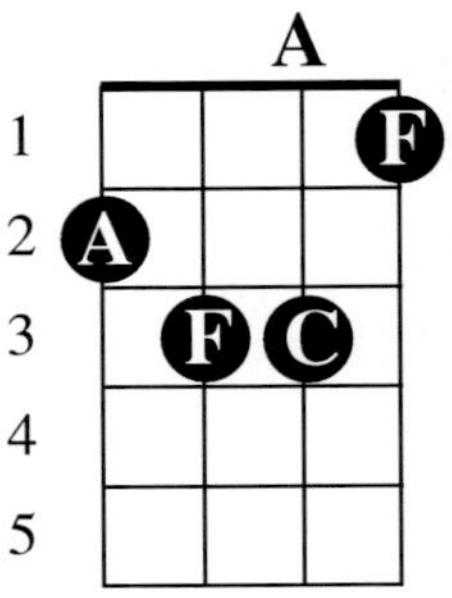

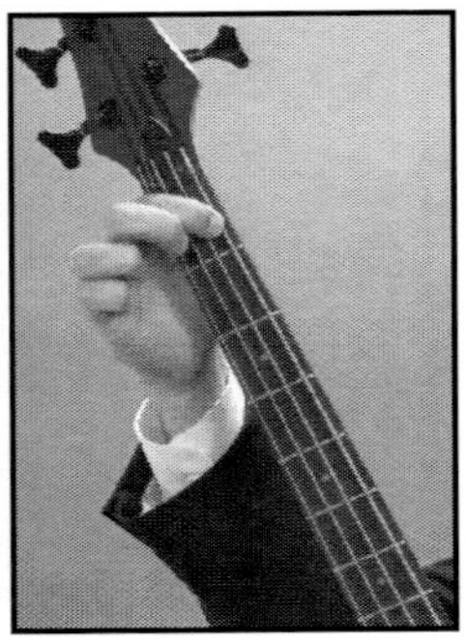

Root – F

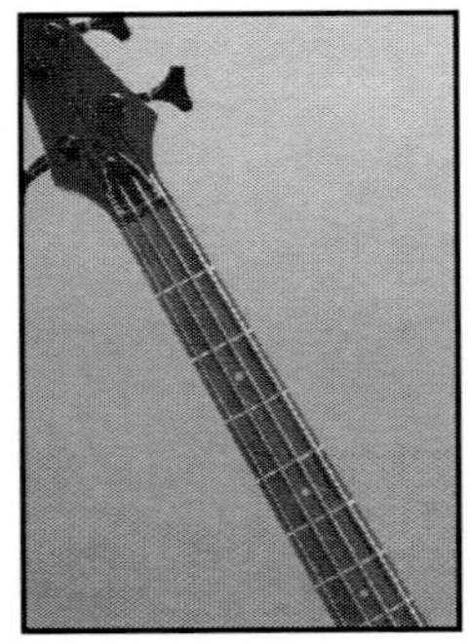

3rd – A

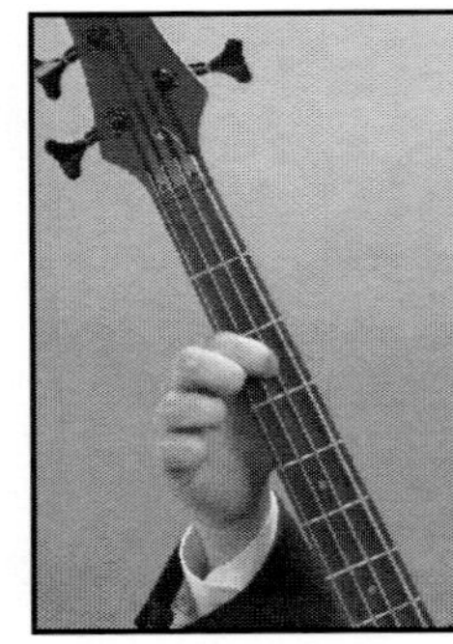

5th – C

Fmin

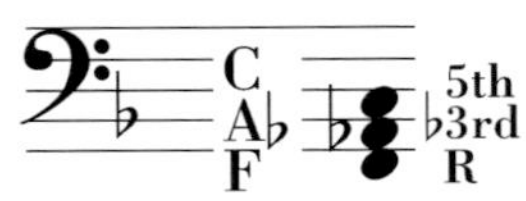

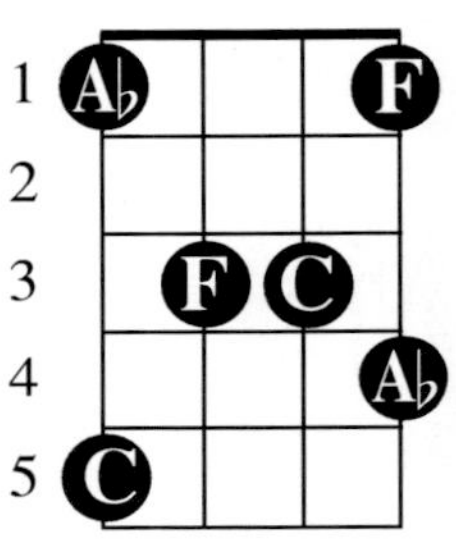

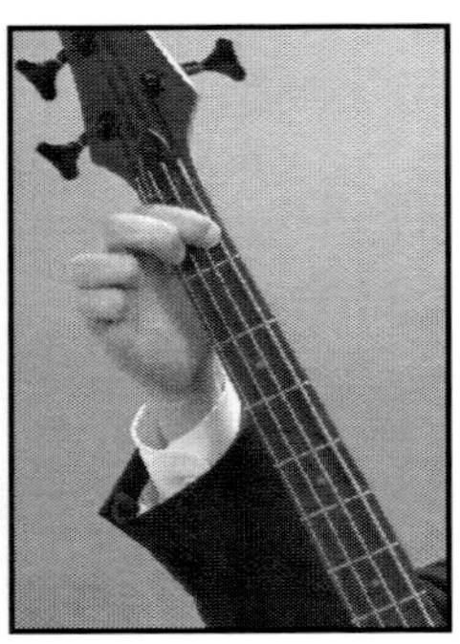

Root – F

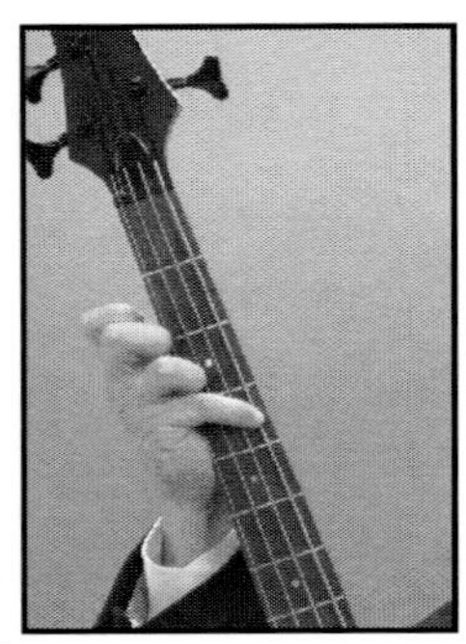

♭3rd – A♭

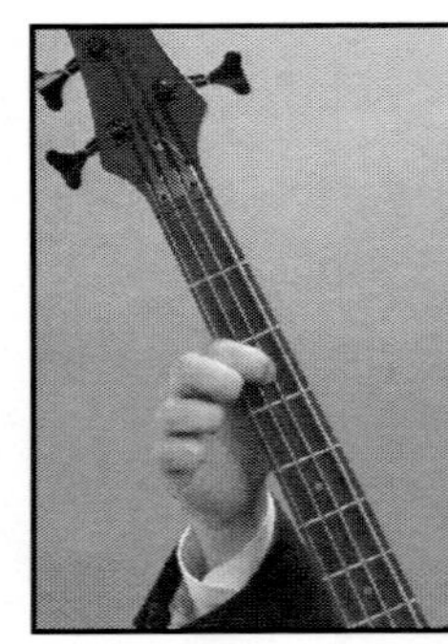

5th – C

F7

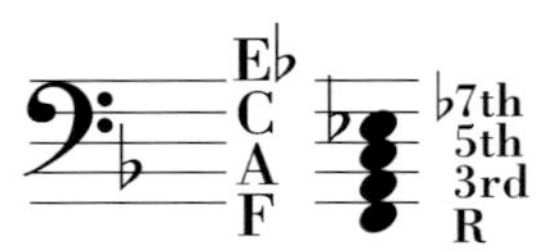

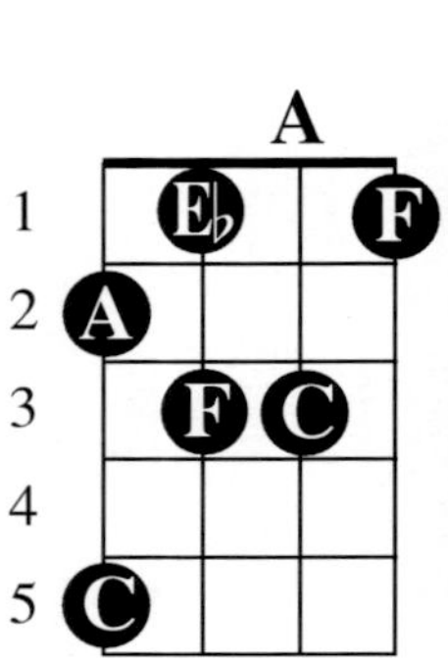

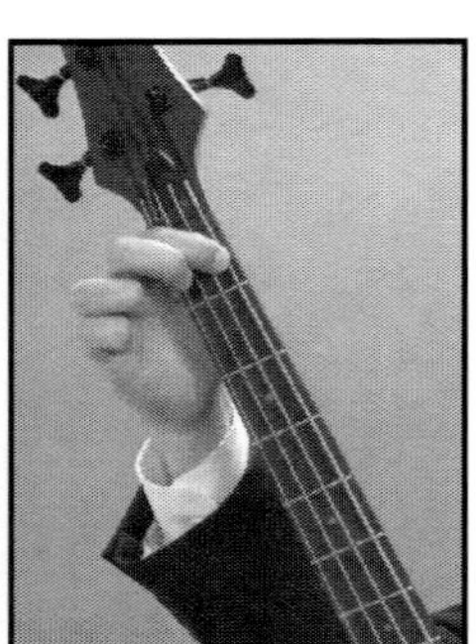

Root – F

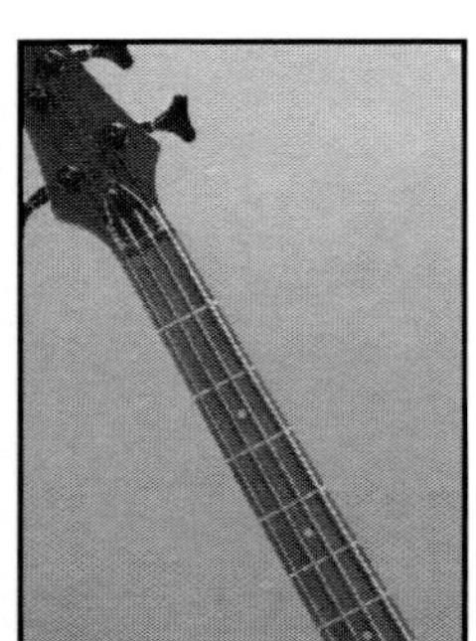

3rd – A

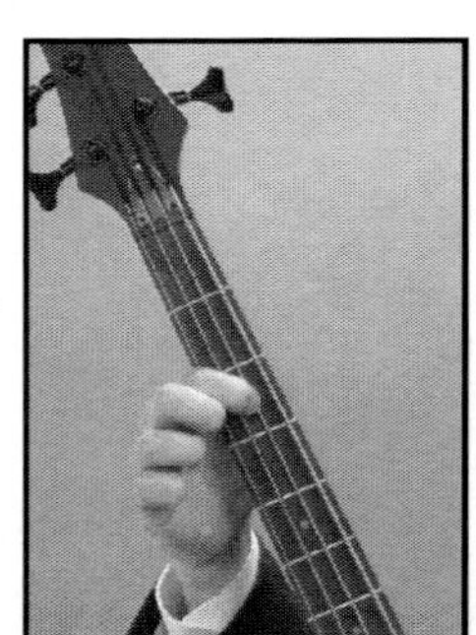

5th – C

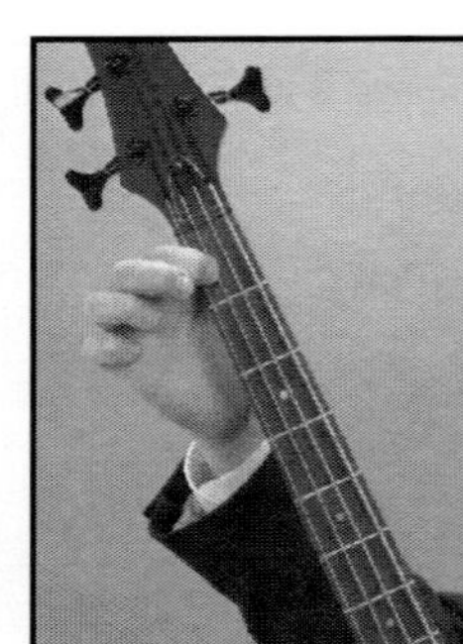

♭7th – E♭

F7sus

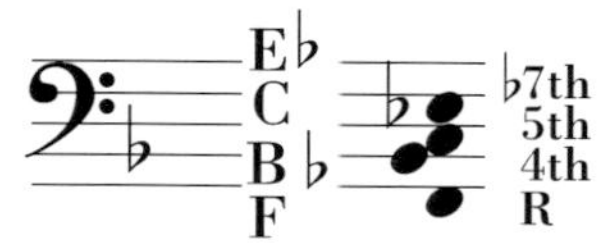

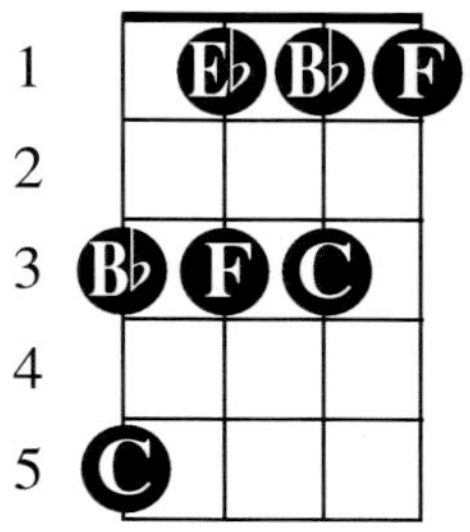

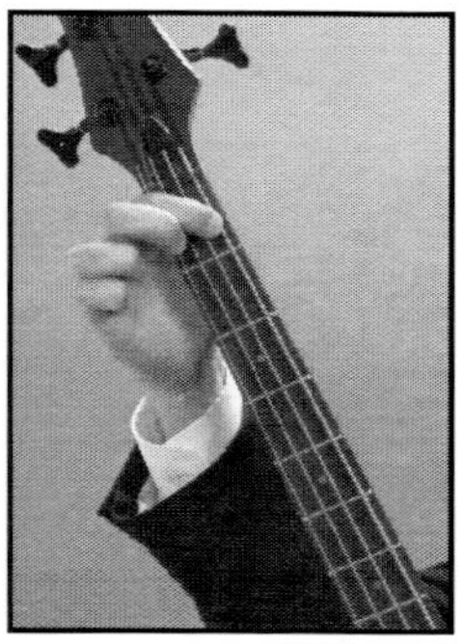

Root – F

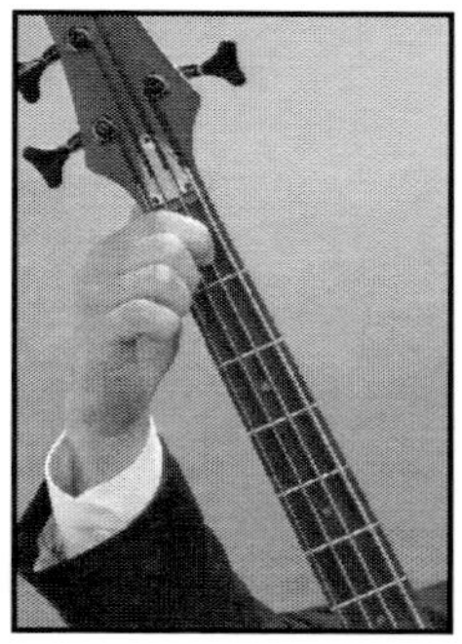

4th – B♭

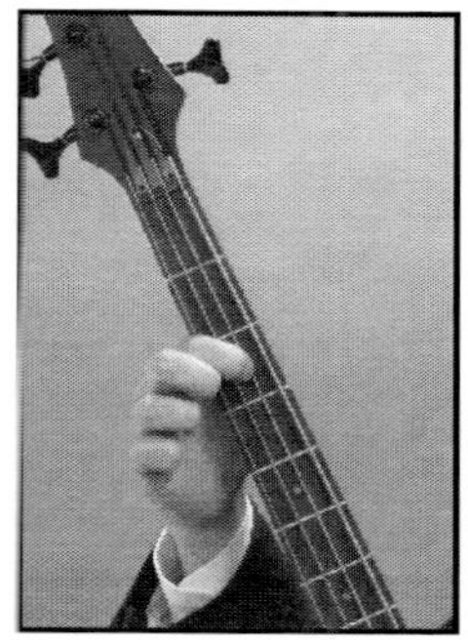

5th – C

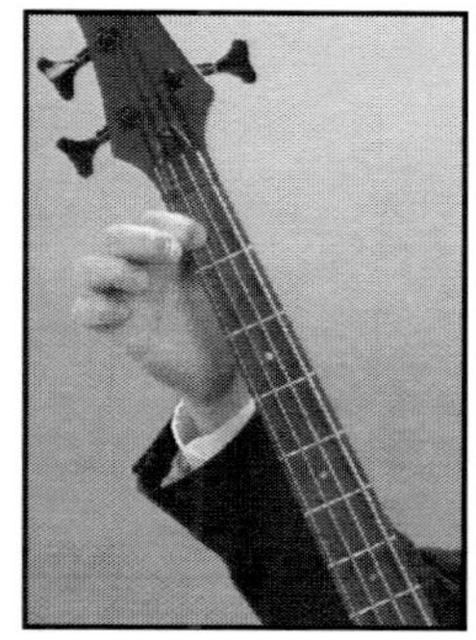

♭7th – E♭

Fm7

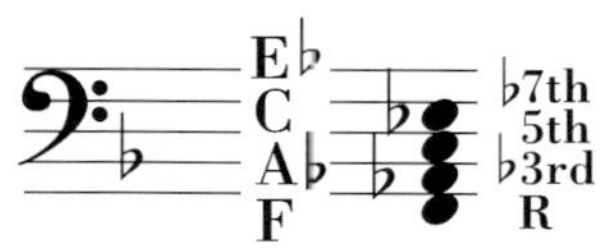

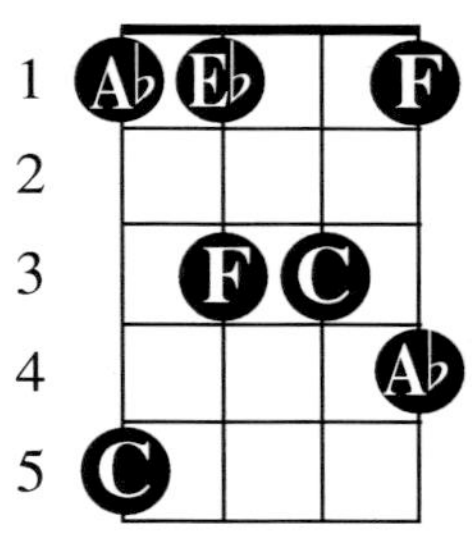

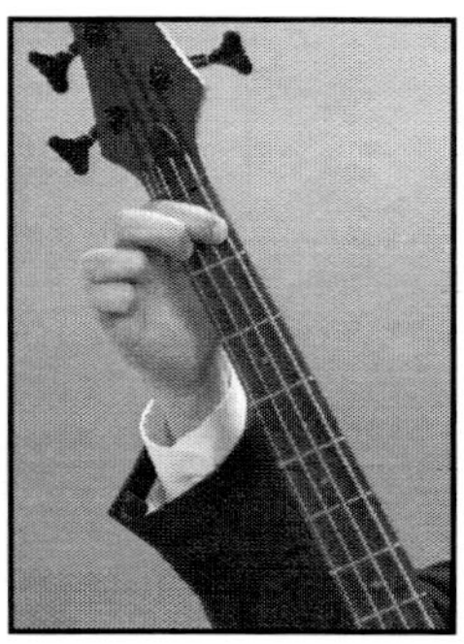

Root – F

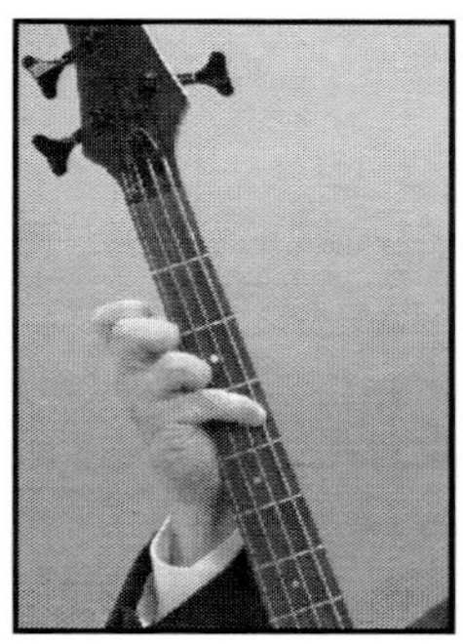

♭3rd – A♭

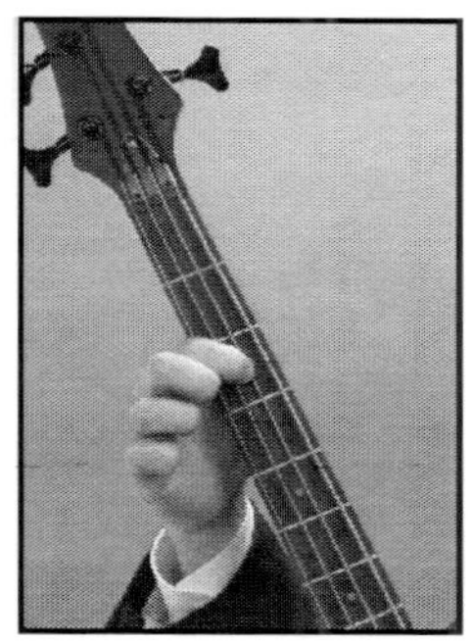

5th – C

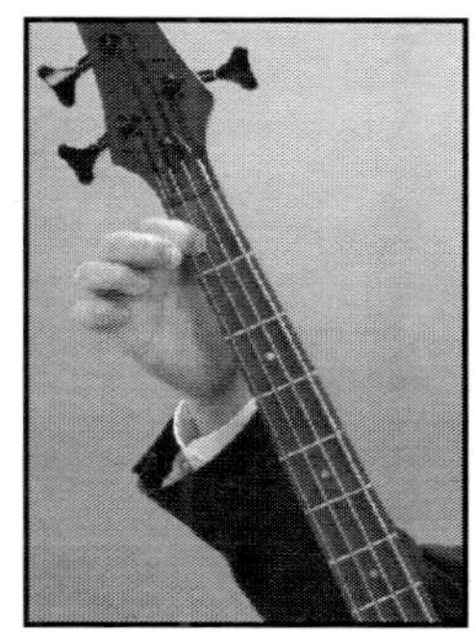

♭7th – E♭

FMa7

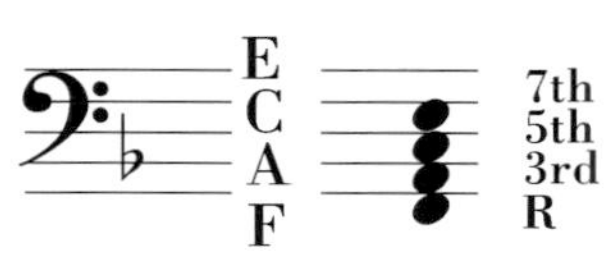

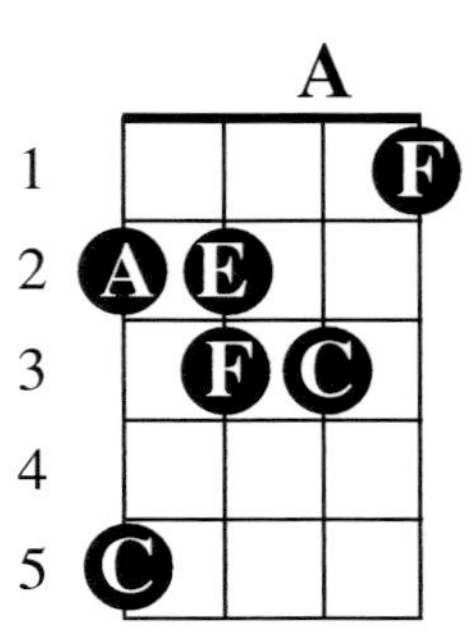

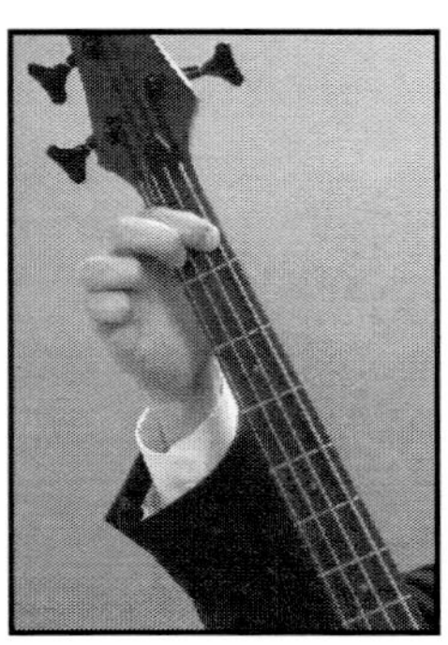

Root – F

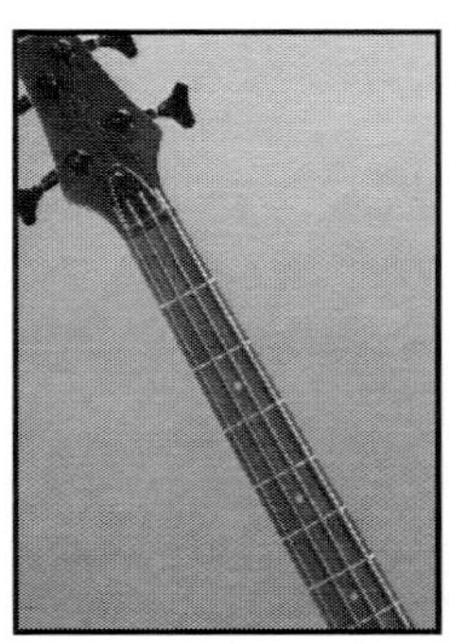

3rd – A

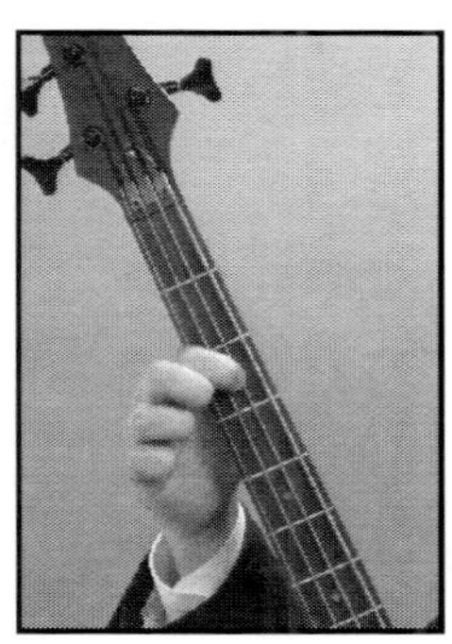

5th – C

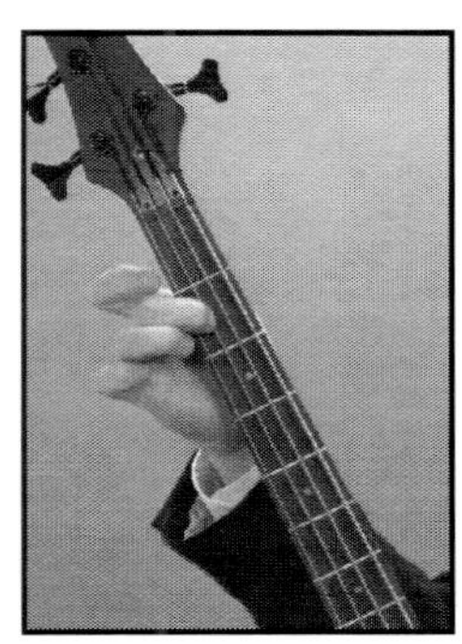

7th – E

Key of F (cont.)

Fdim

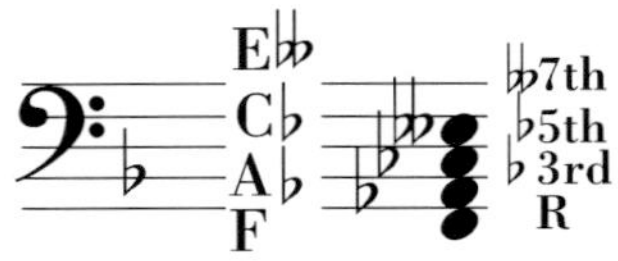

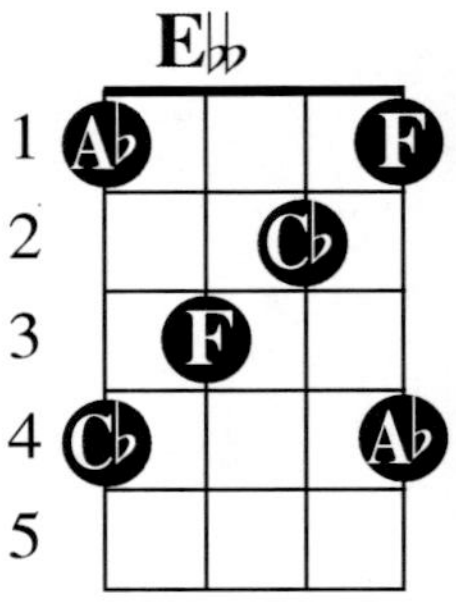

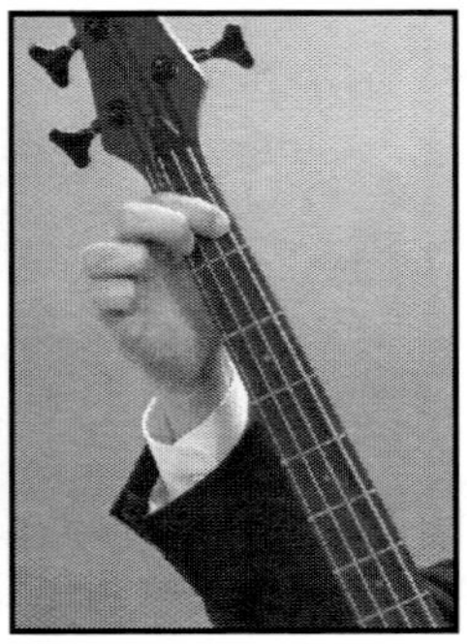
Root – F

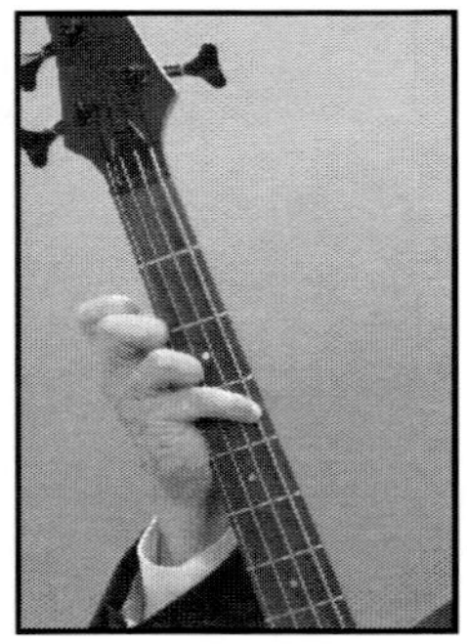
♭3rd – A♭

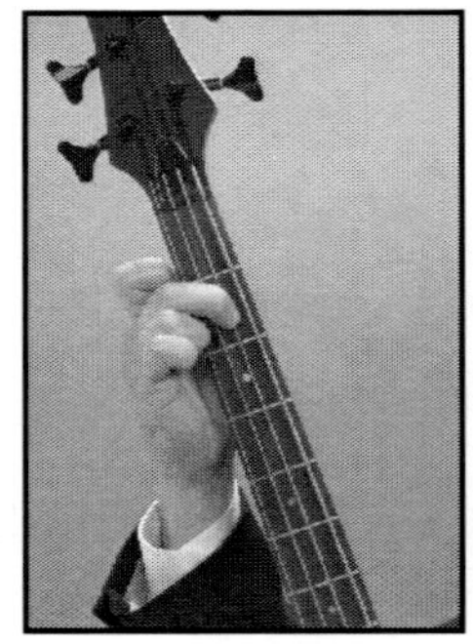
♭5th – C♭ or B♮

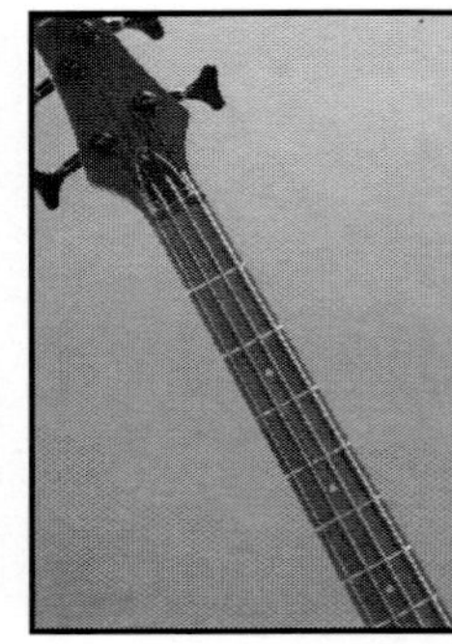
♭♭7th – E♭♭ or D

Faug

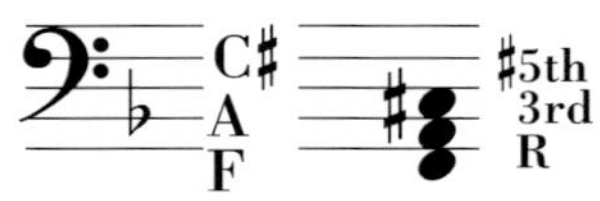

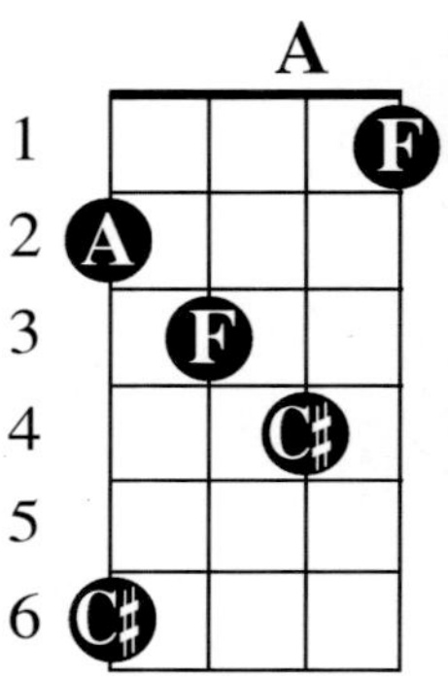

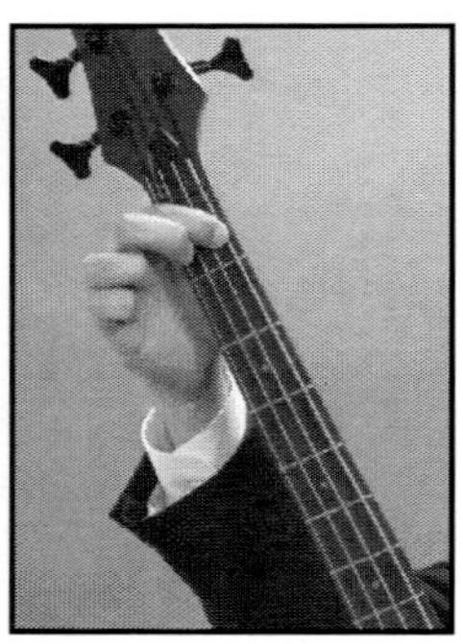
Root – F

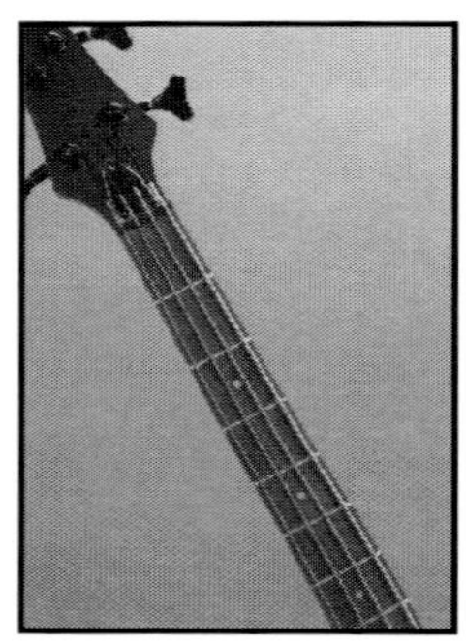
3rd – A

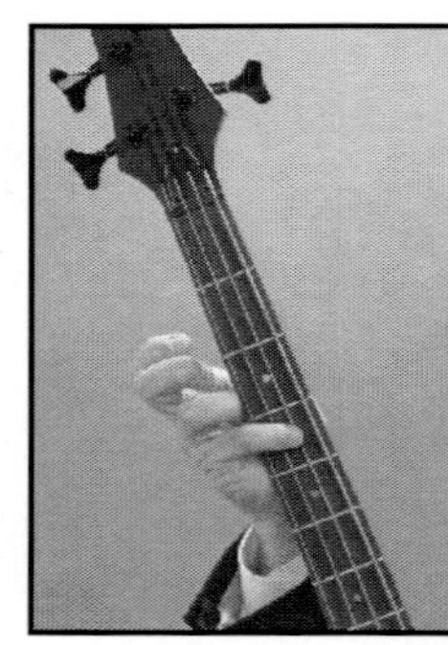
♯5th – C♯

F6

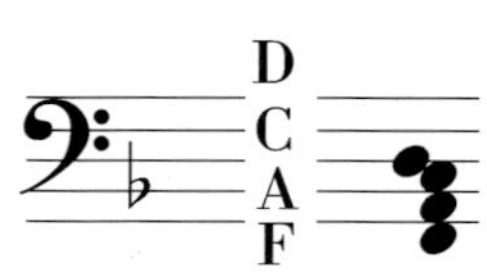

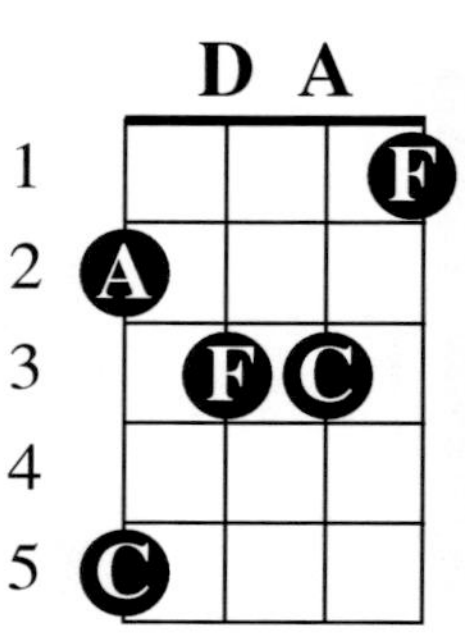

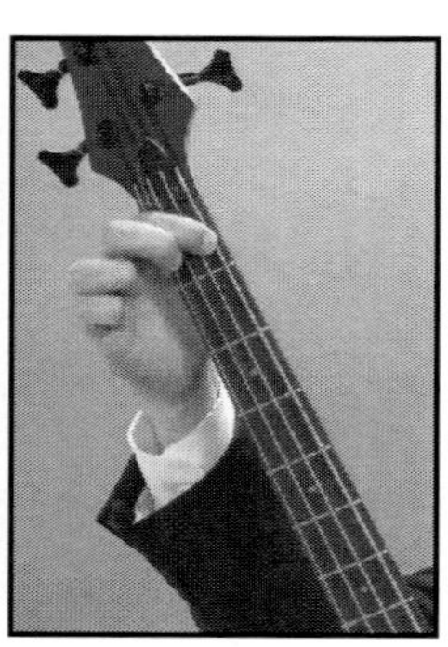
Root – F

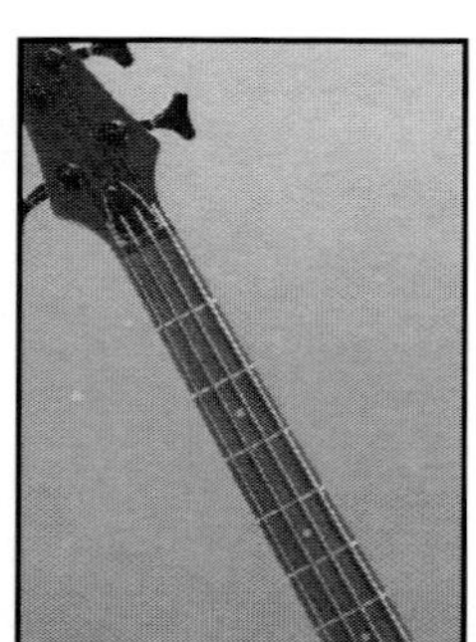
3rd – A

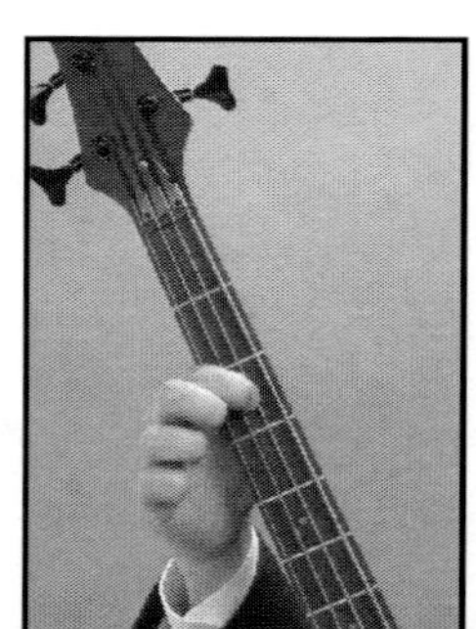
5th – C

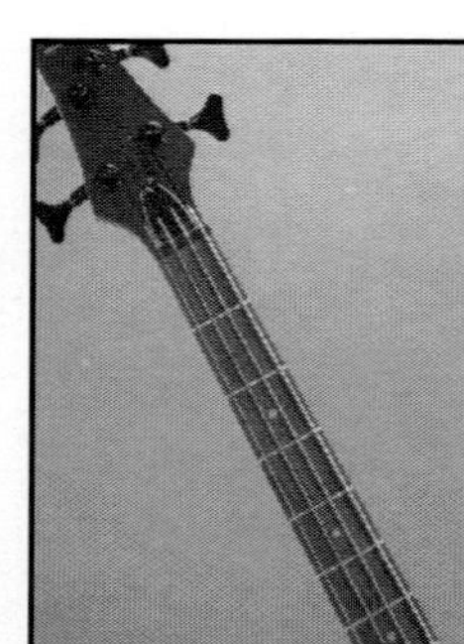
6th – D

Key of F (cont.)

Fm6

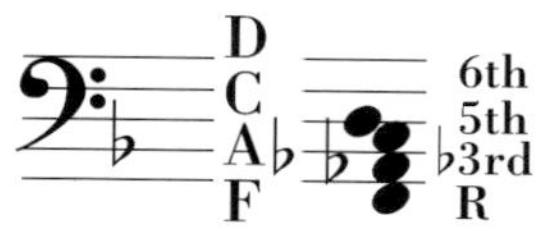

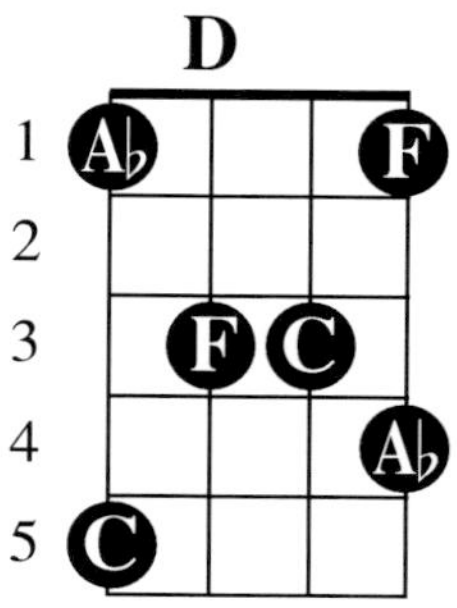

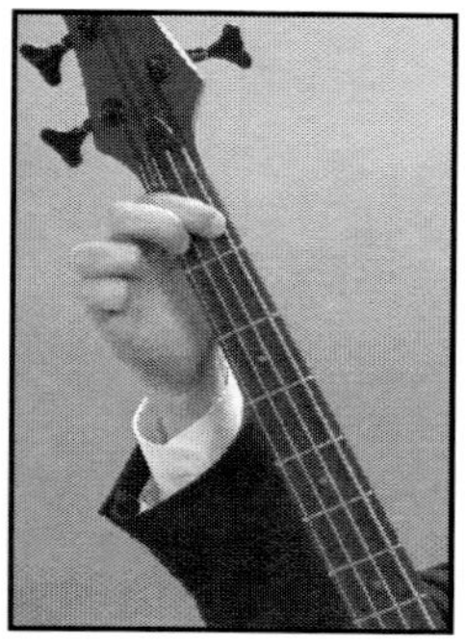
Root – F

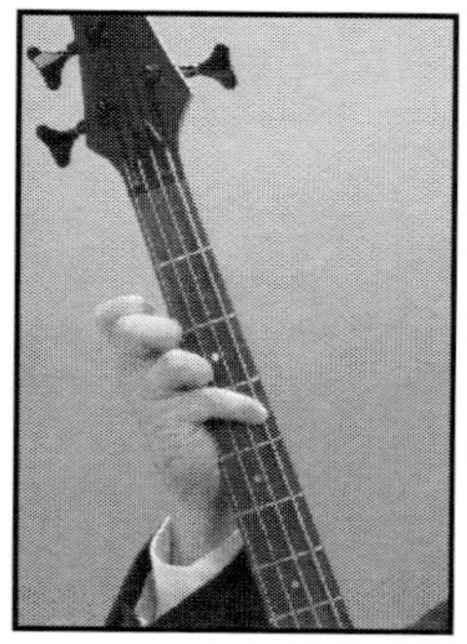
♭3rd – A♭

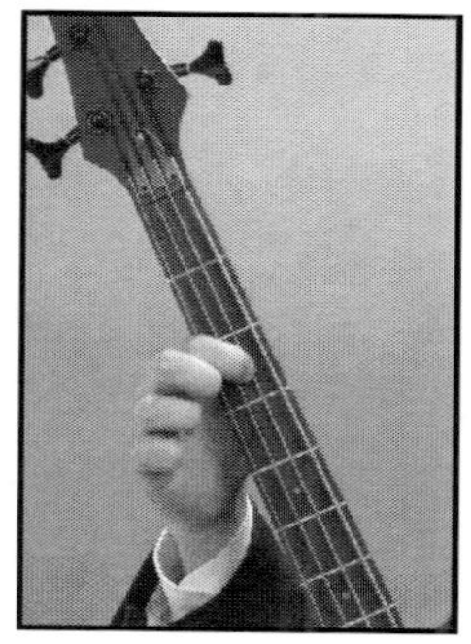
5th – C

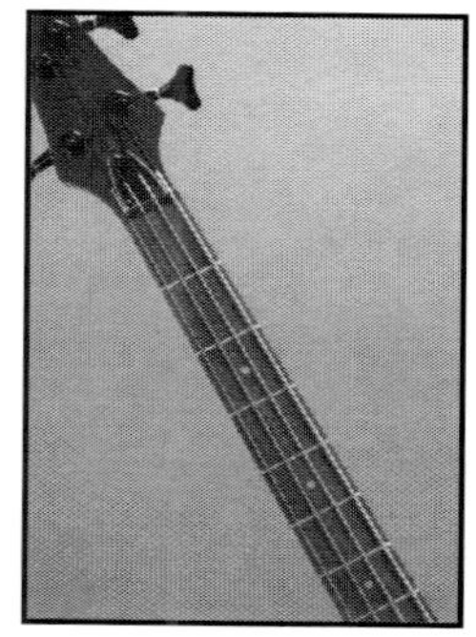
6th – D

F7♯5

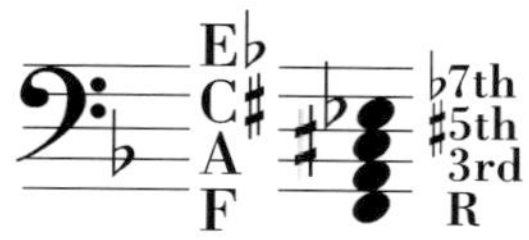

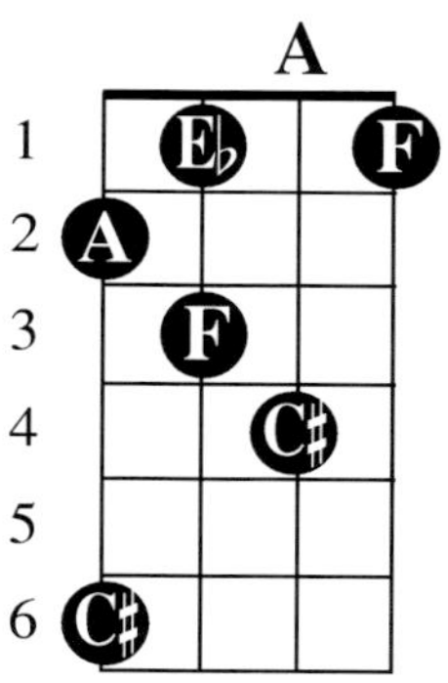

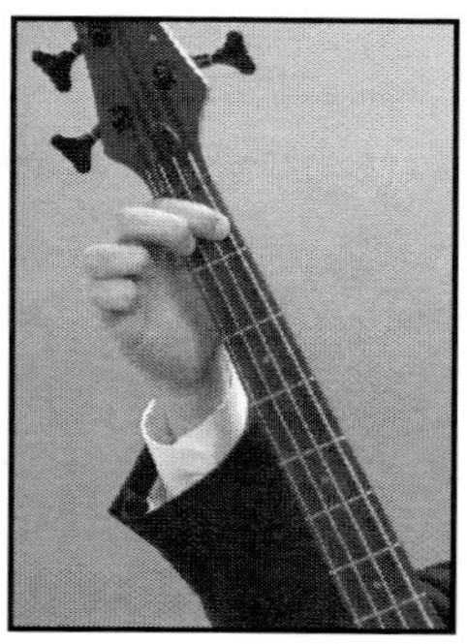
Root – F

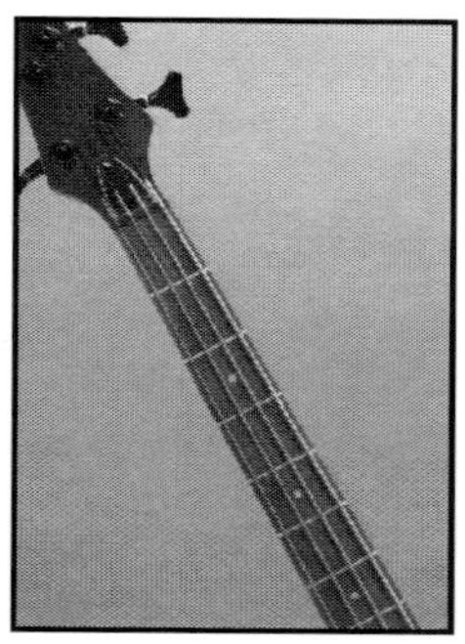
3rd – A

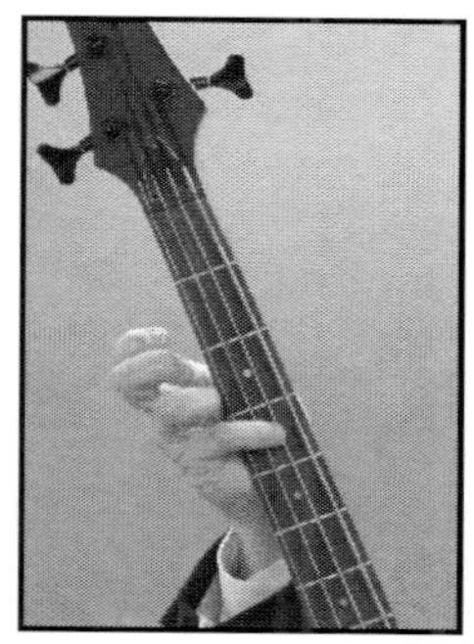
♯5th – C♯

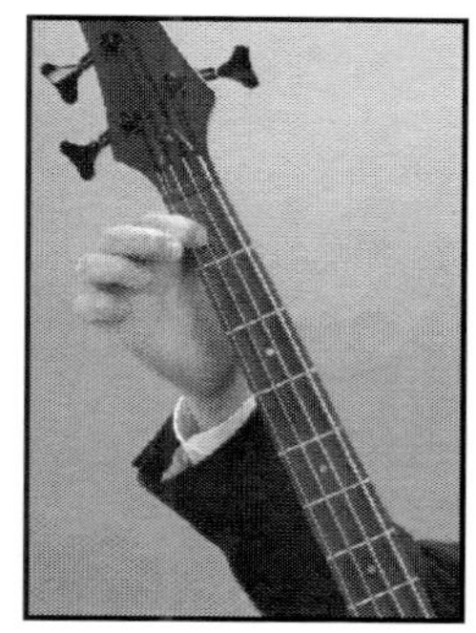
♭7th – E♭

F7♭5

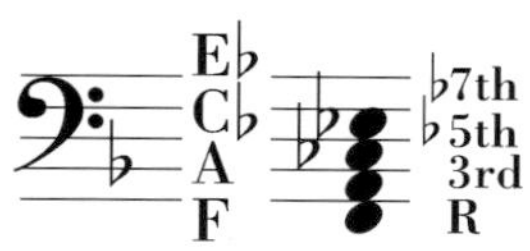

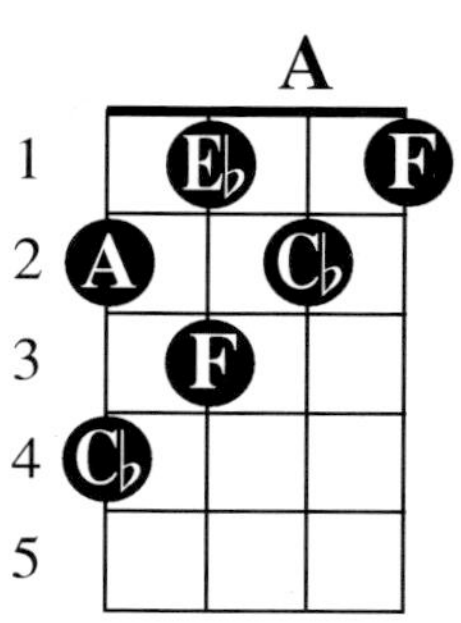

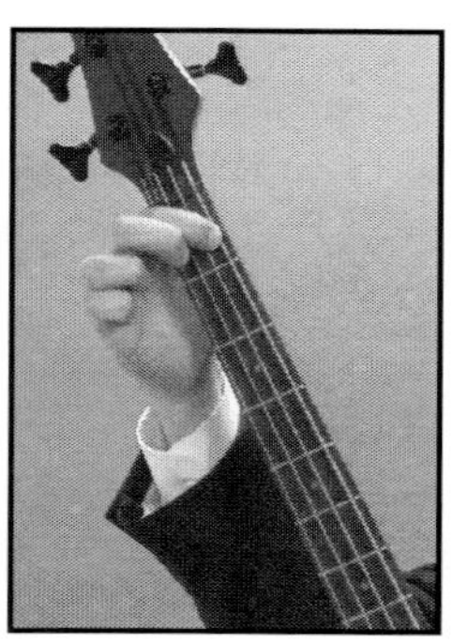
Root – F

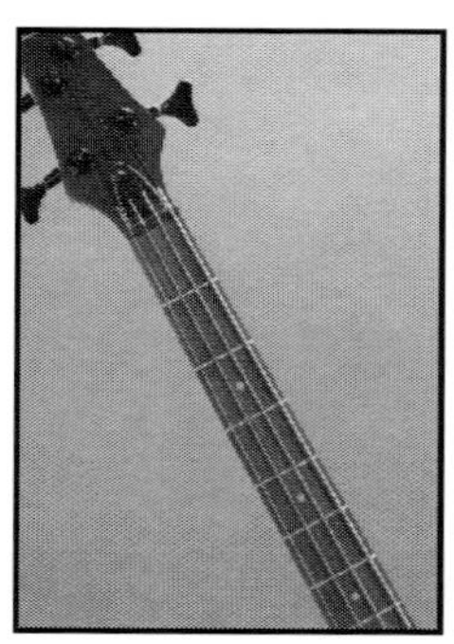
3rd – A

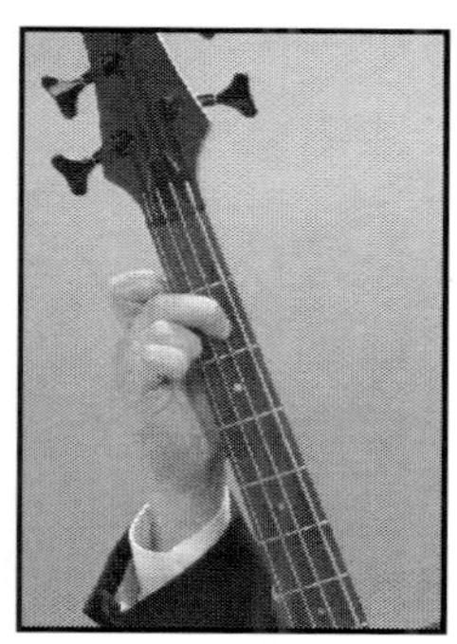
♭5th – C♭ or B♮

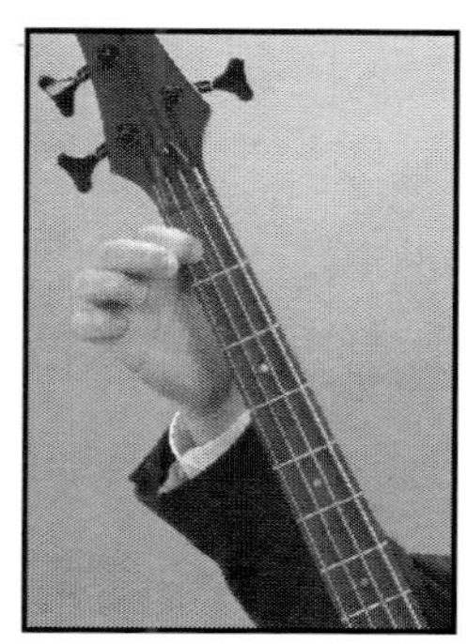
♭7th – E♭

Key of F♯/G♭

G♭Major

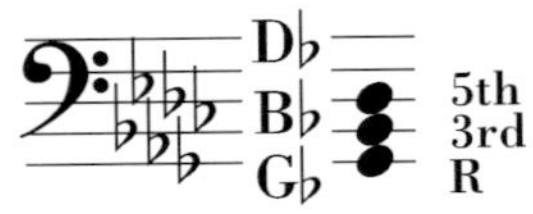

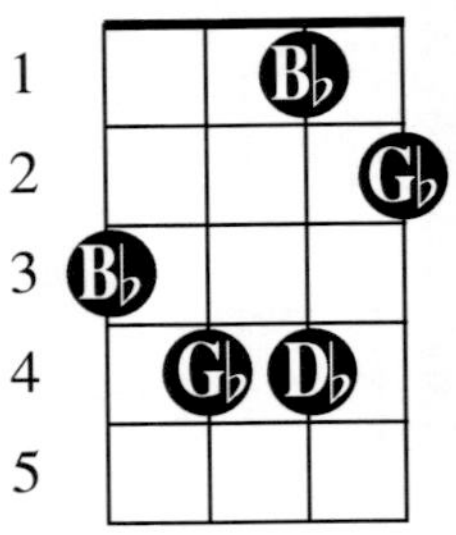

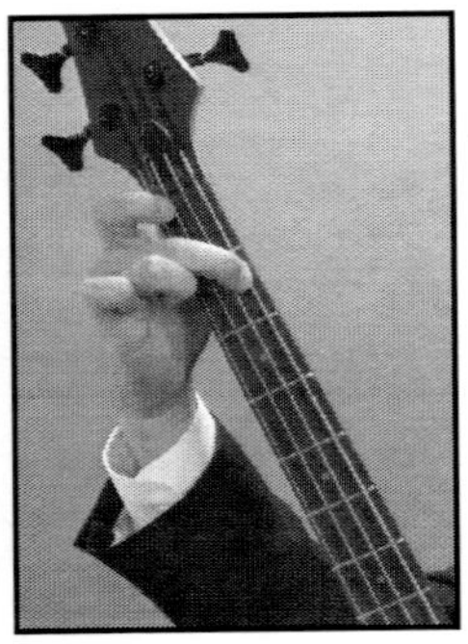

Root – G♭

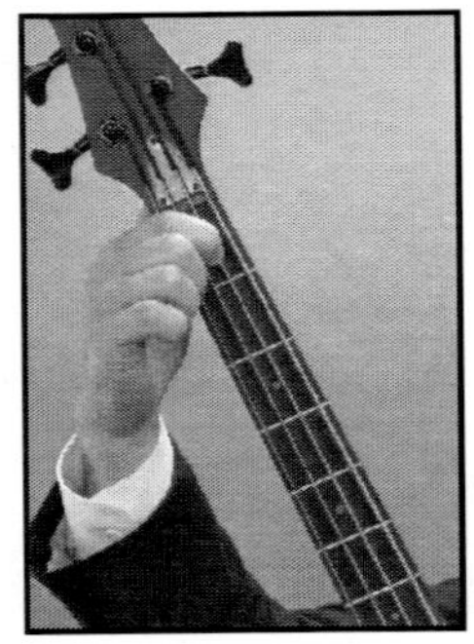

3rd – B♭

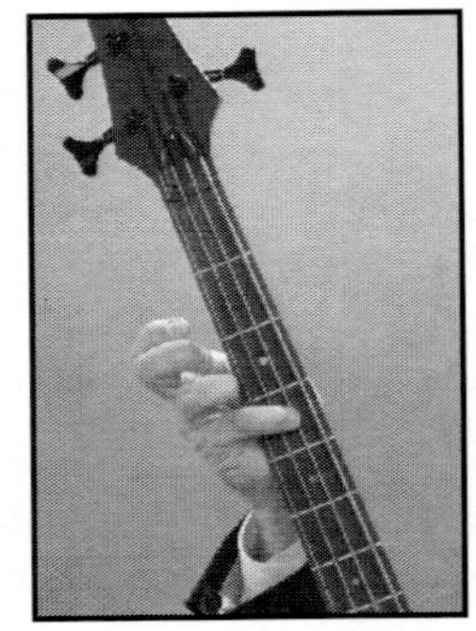

5th – D♭

G♭minor

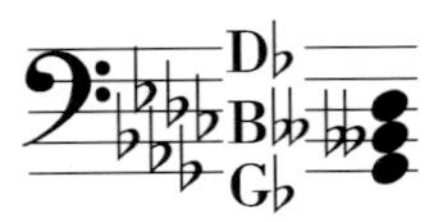

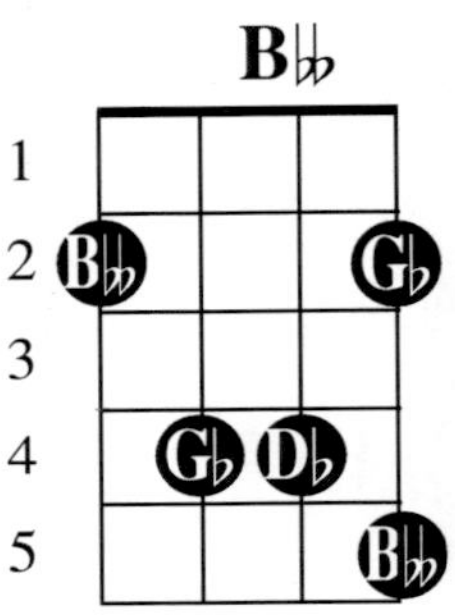

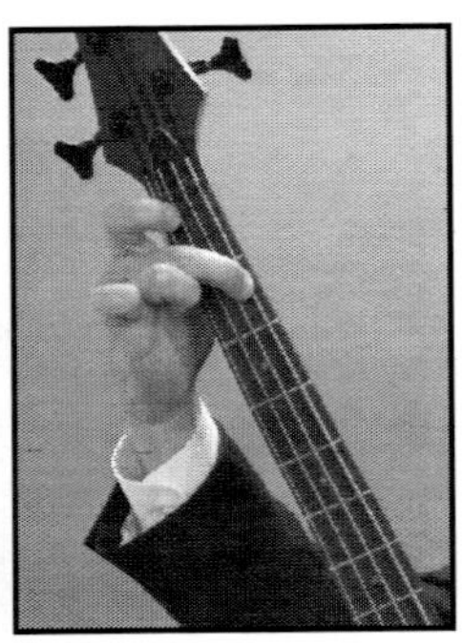

Root – G♭

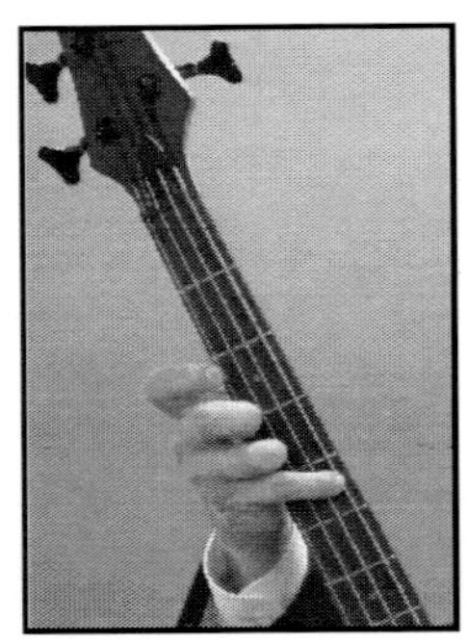

♭3rd – B♭♭ or A

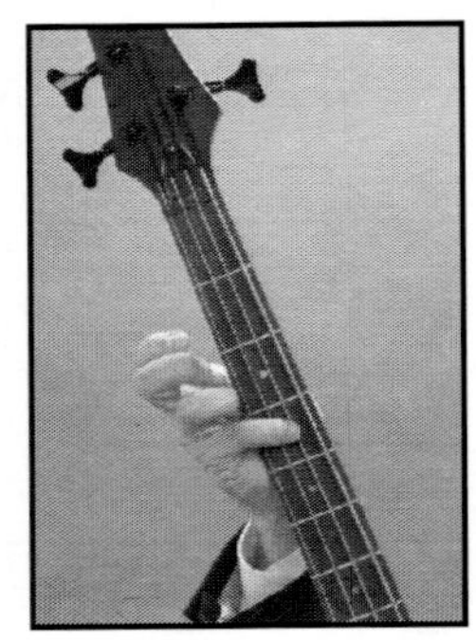

5th – D♭

G♭7

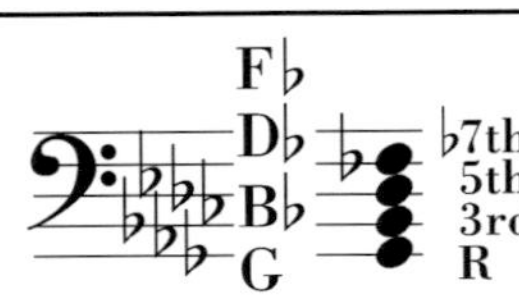

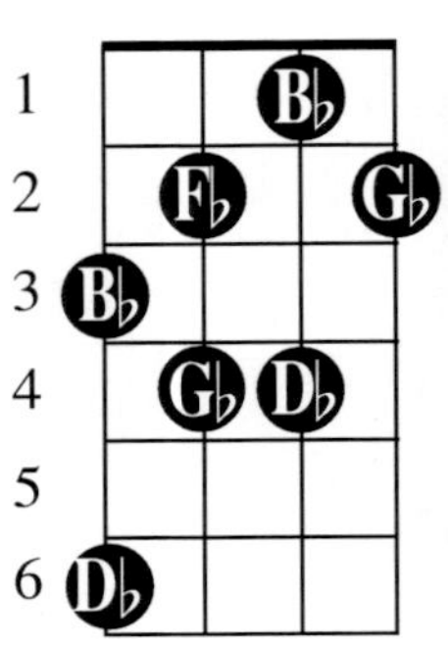

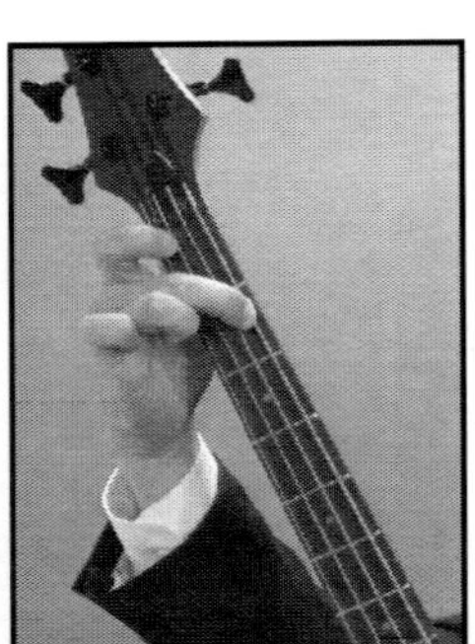

Root – G♭

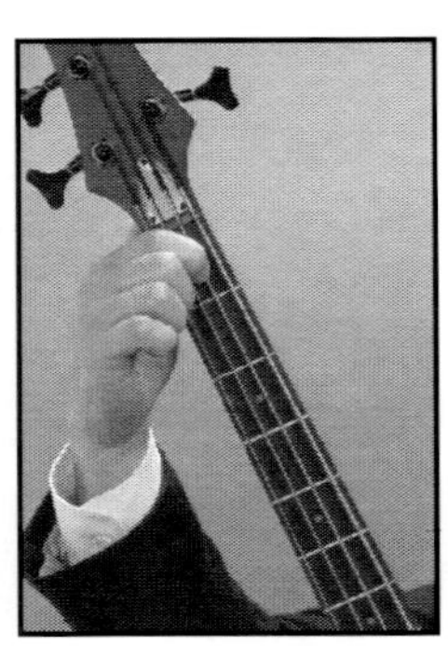

3rd – B♭

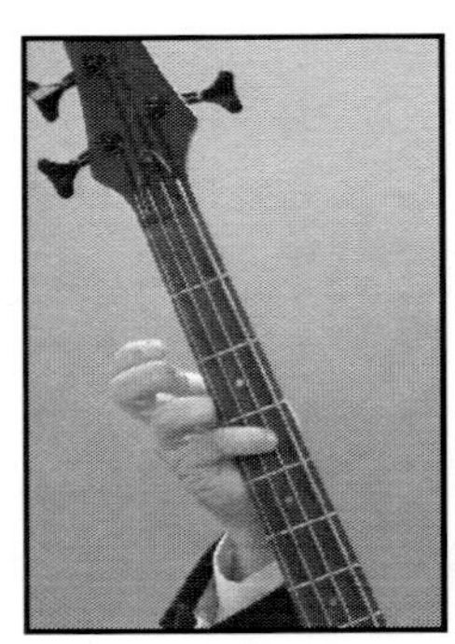

5th – D♭

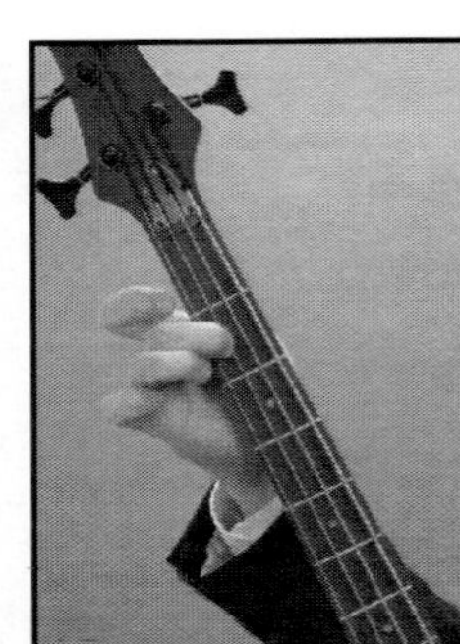

♭7th – F♭ or E

Key of F♯/G♭ (cont.)

G♭7sus

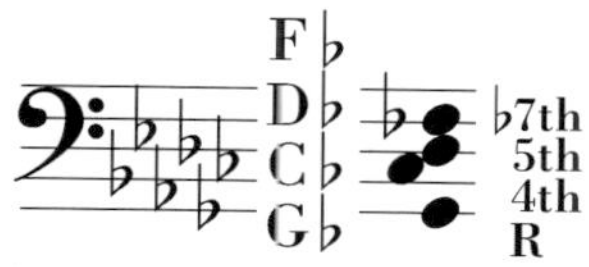

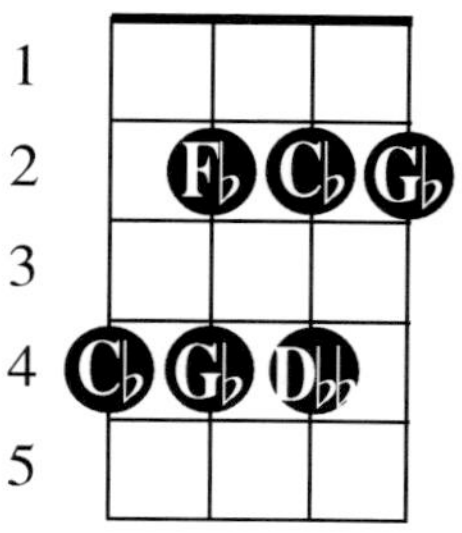

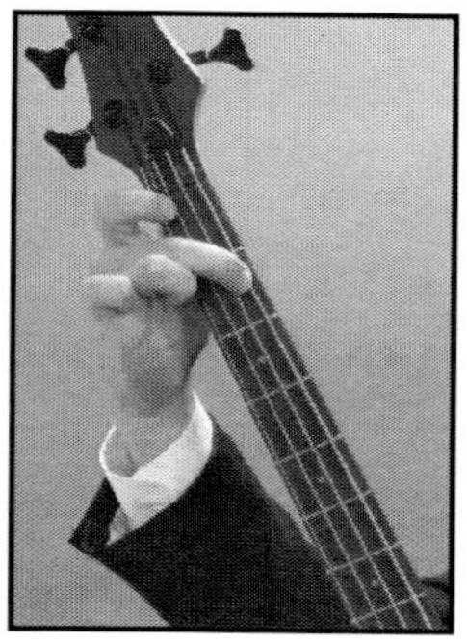
Root – G♭

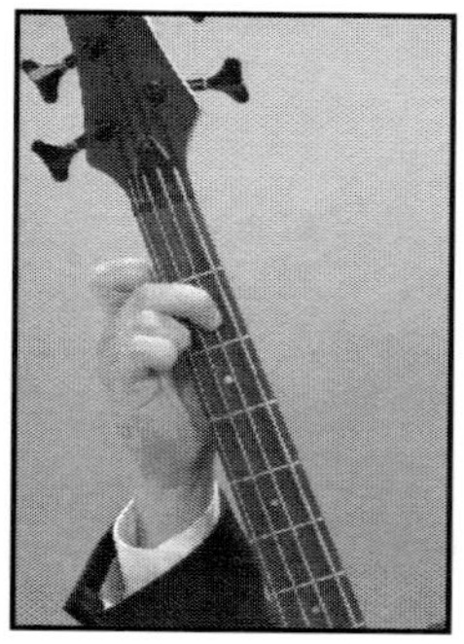
4th – C♭ or B

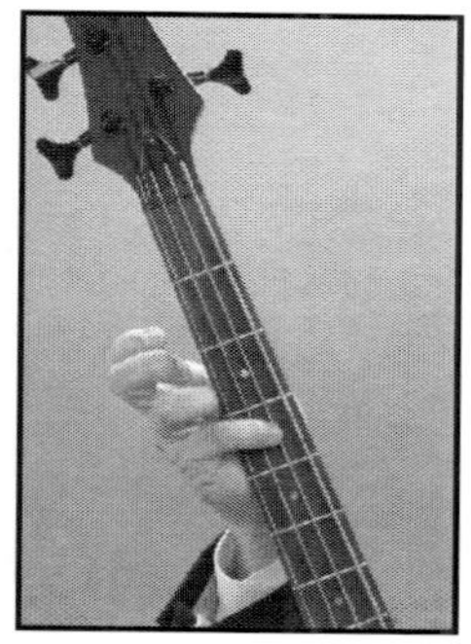
5th – D♭

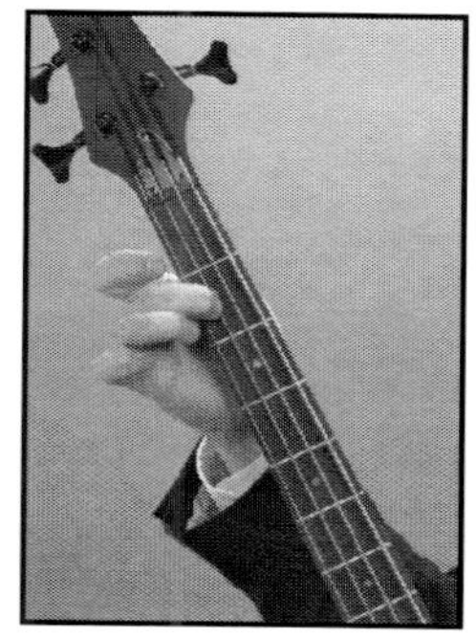
♭7th – F♭ or E

G♭m7

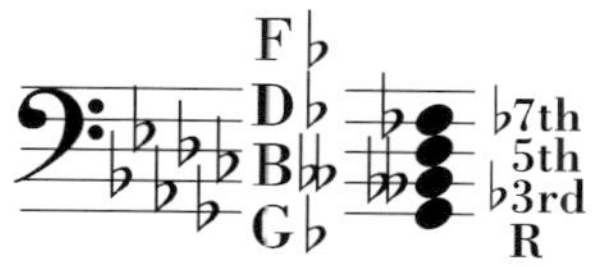

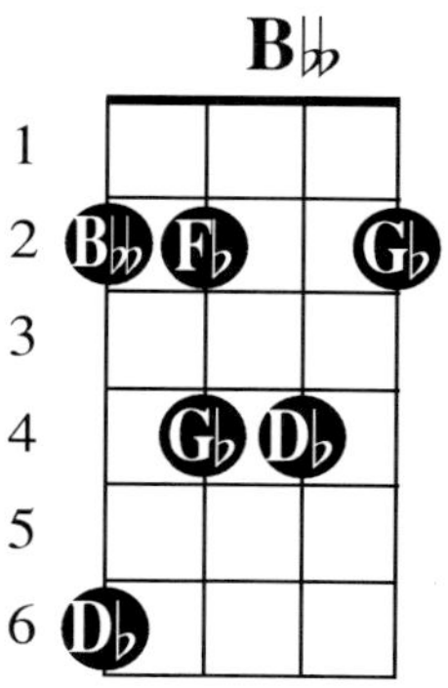

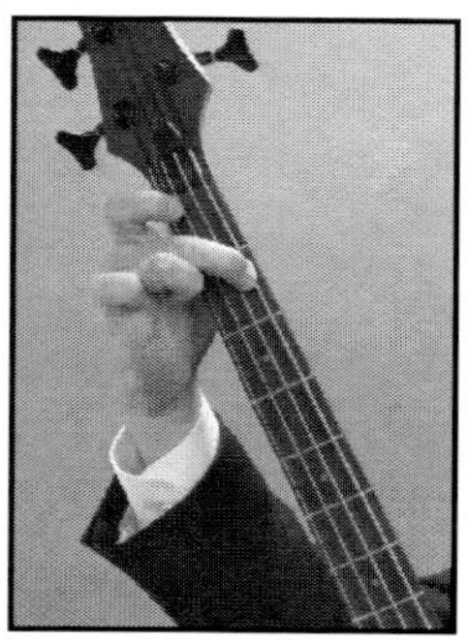
Root – G♭

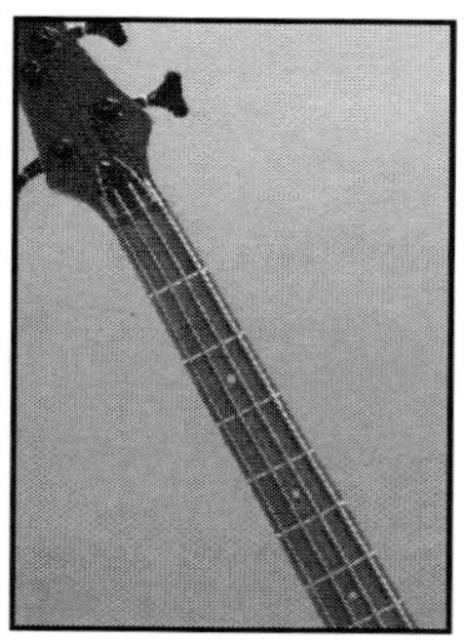
♭3rd – B♭♭ or A

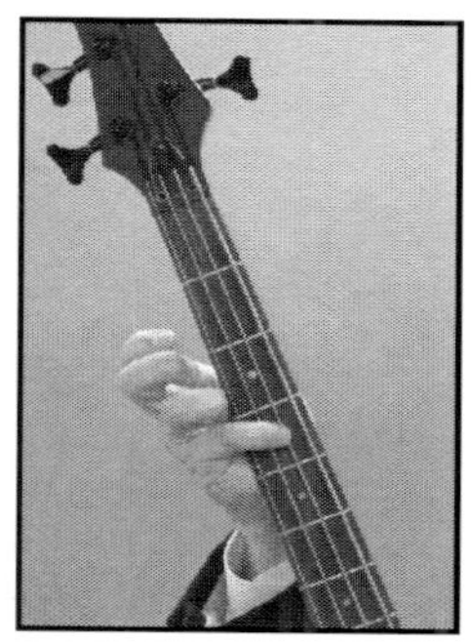
5th – D♭

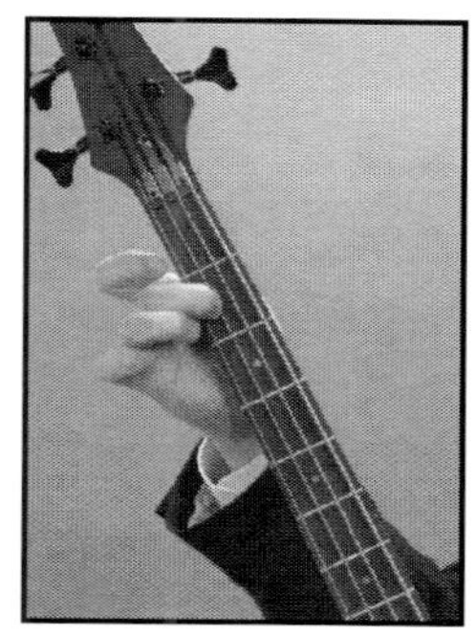
♭7th – F♭ or E

G♭Ma7

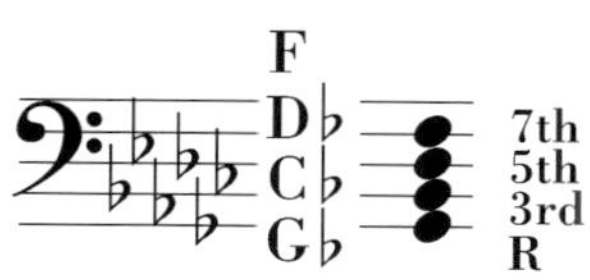

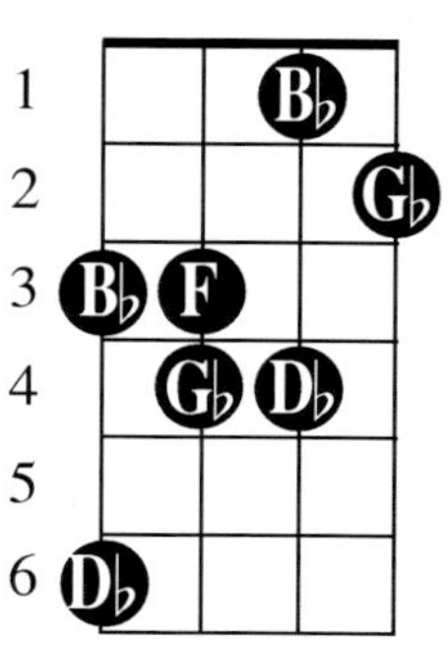

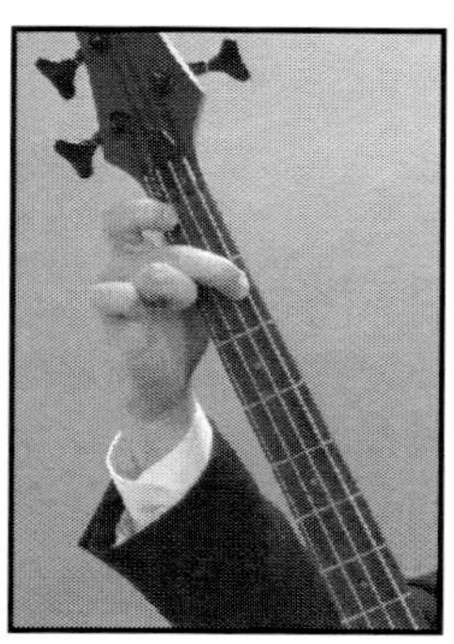
Root – G♭

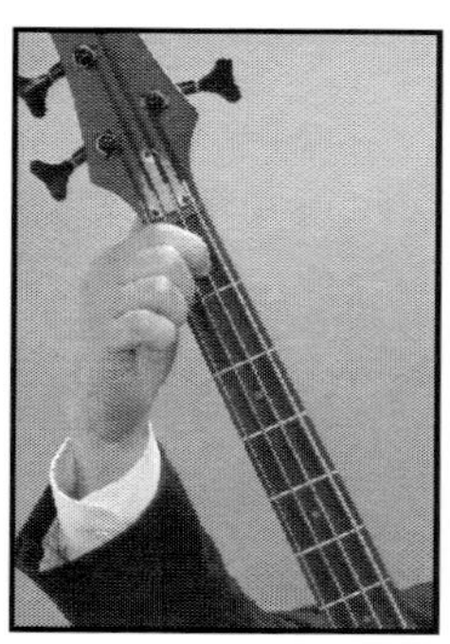
3rd – B♭

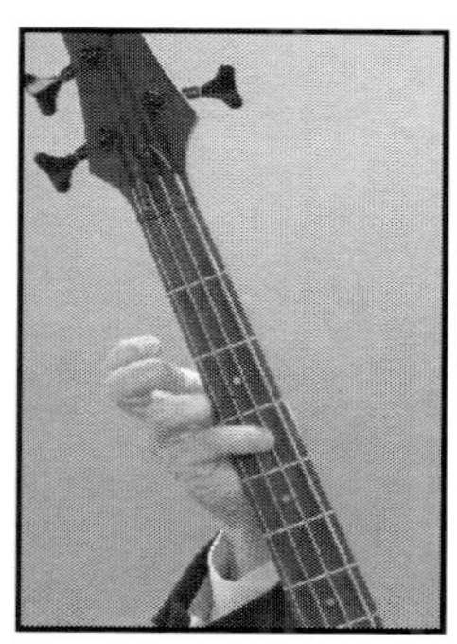
5th – D♭

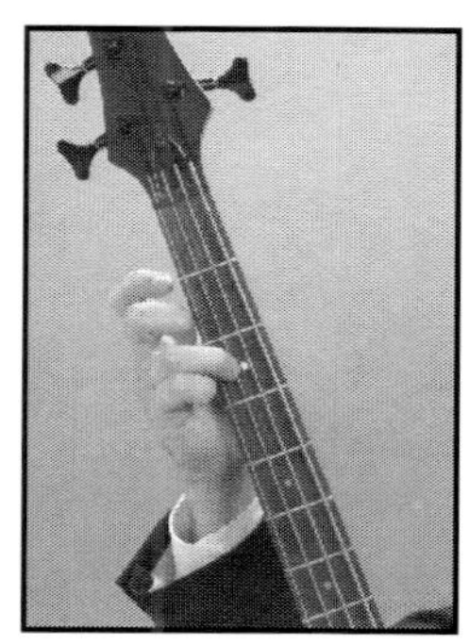
7th – F

Key of F♯/G♭ (cont.)

G♭dim

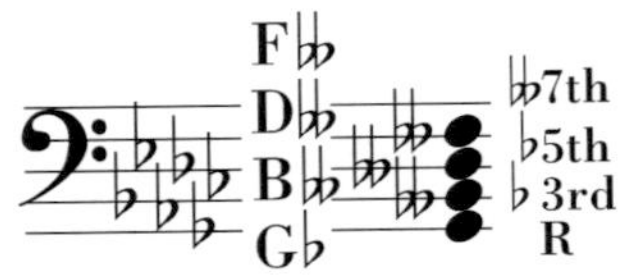

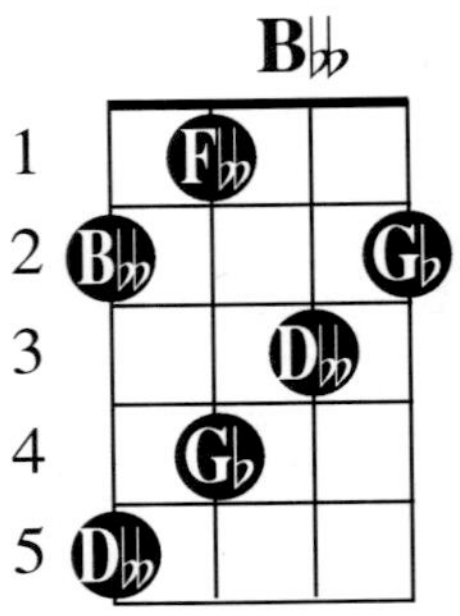

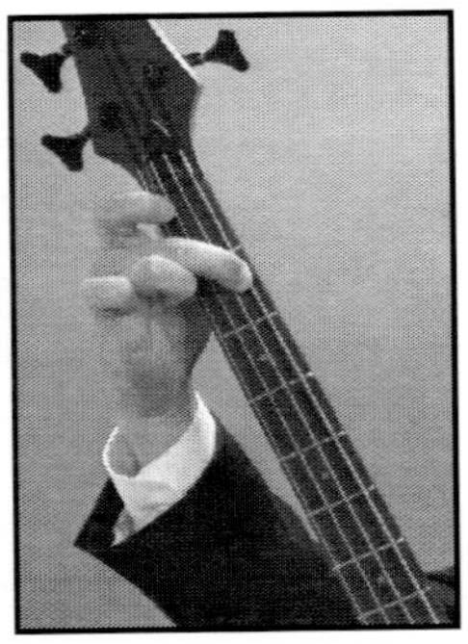

Root – G♭

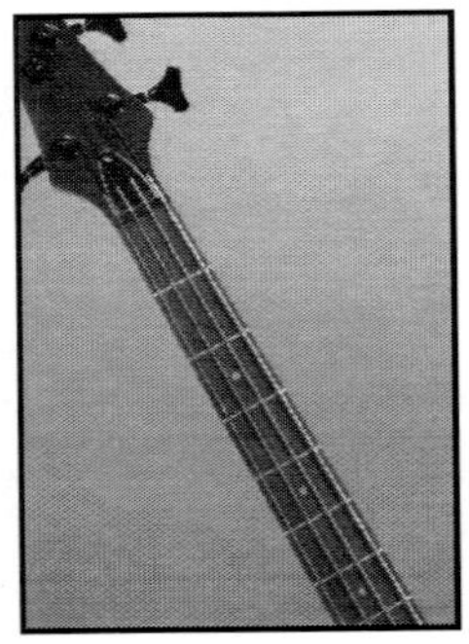

♭3rd – B𝄫 or A

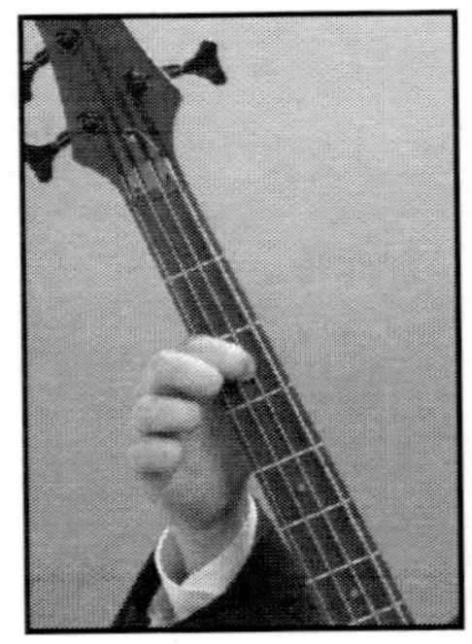

♭5th – D𝄫 or C

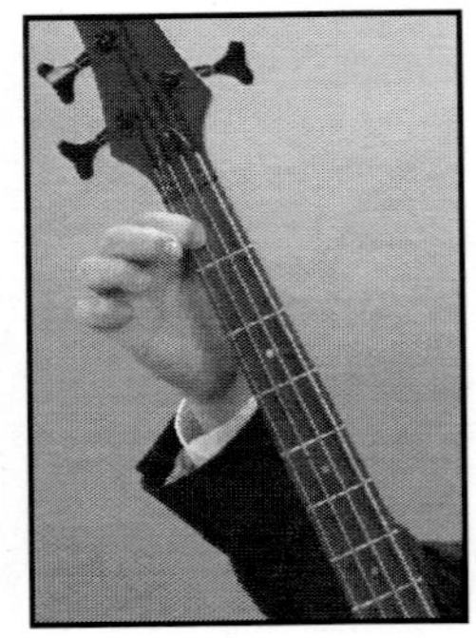

𝄫7th – F𝄫 or E♭

G♭aug

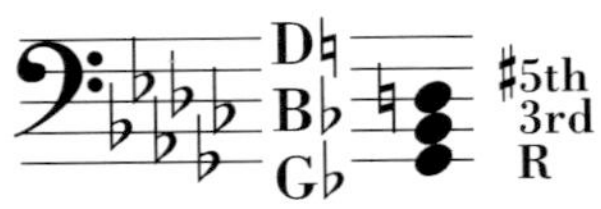

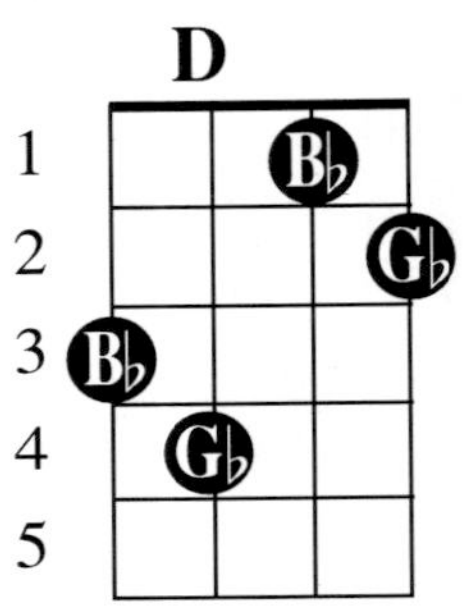

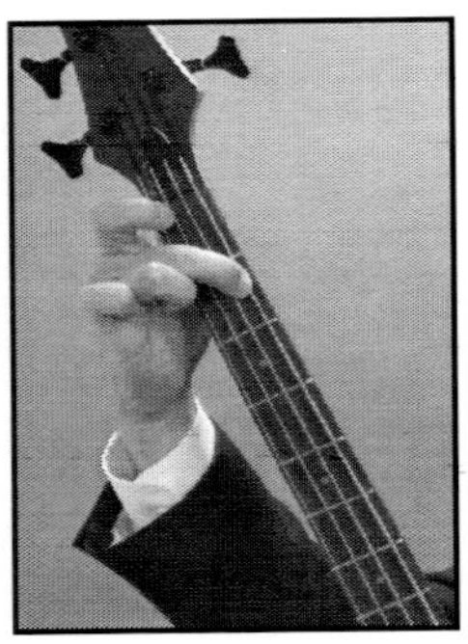

Root – G♭

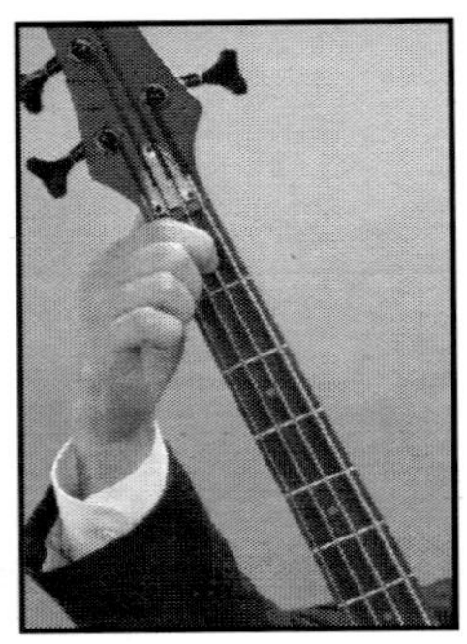

3rd – B♭

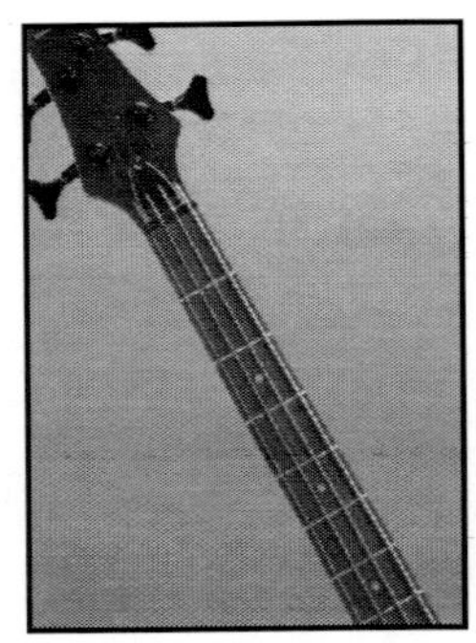

♯5th – D♮

G♭6

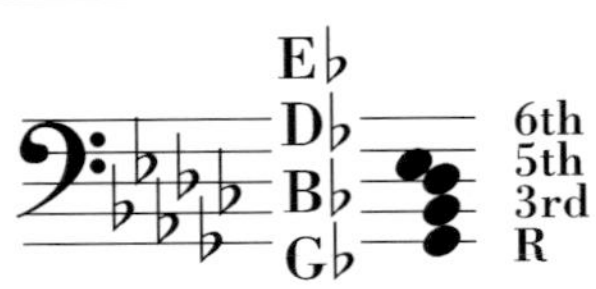

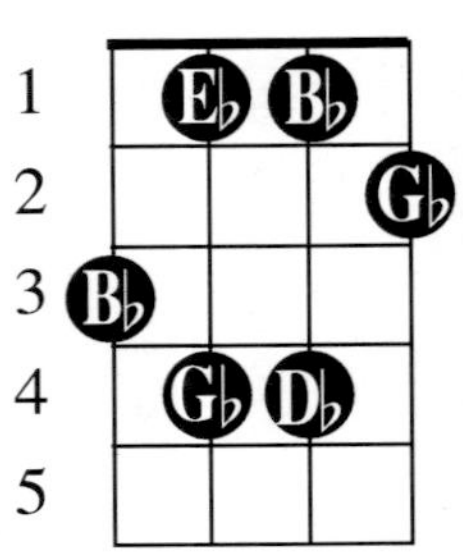

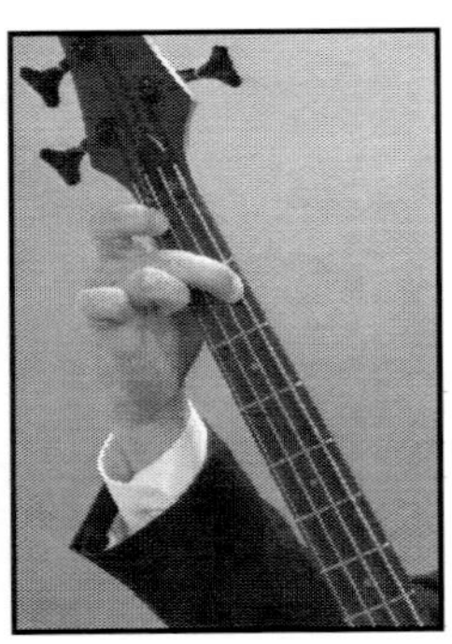

Root – G♭

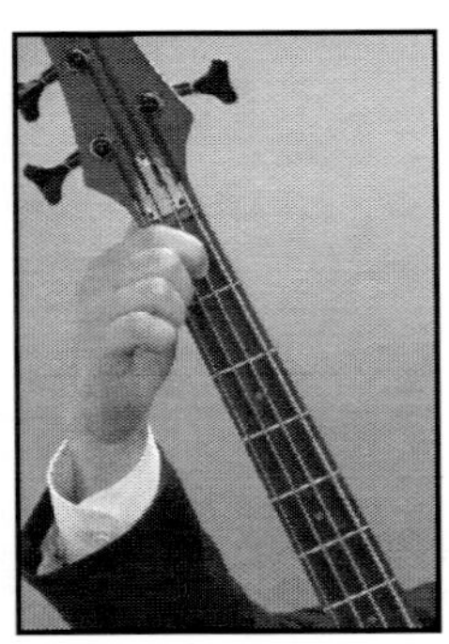

3rd – B♭

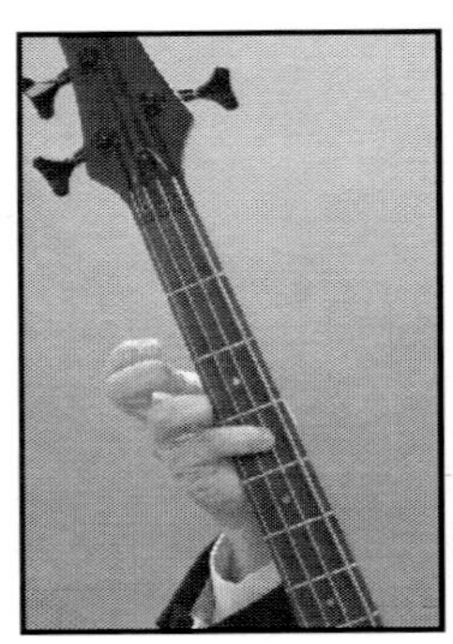

5th – D♭

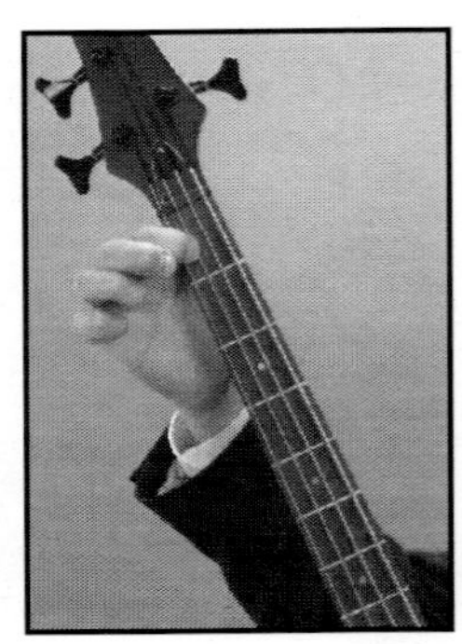

6th – E♭

Key of F♯/G♭ (cont.)

G♭m6

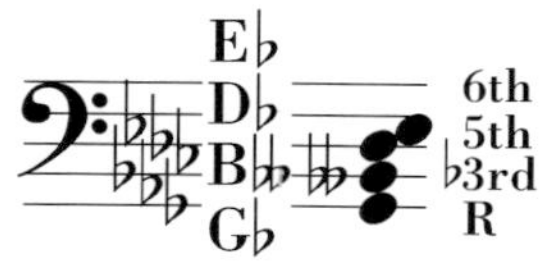

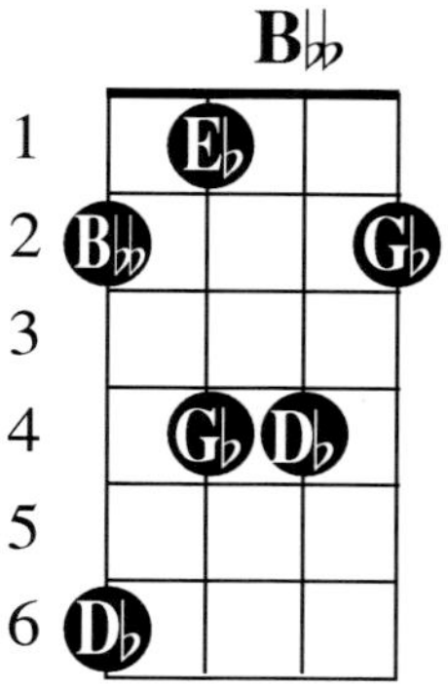

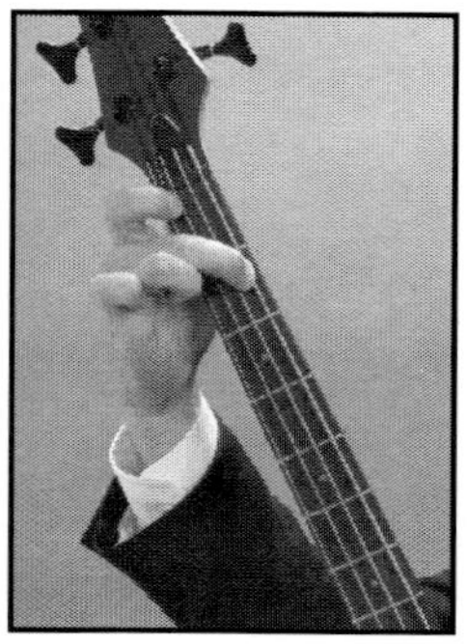
Root – G♭

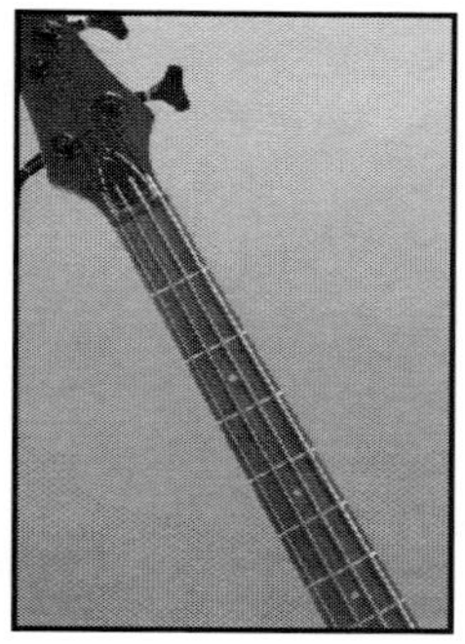
♭3rd – B♭♭ or A

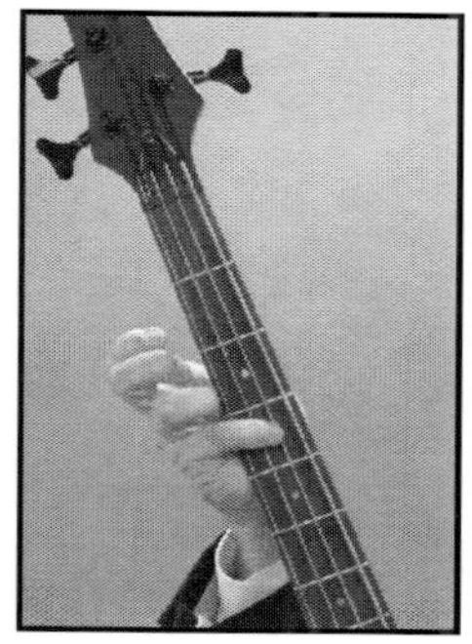
5th – D♭

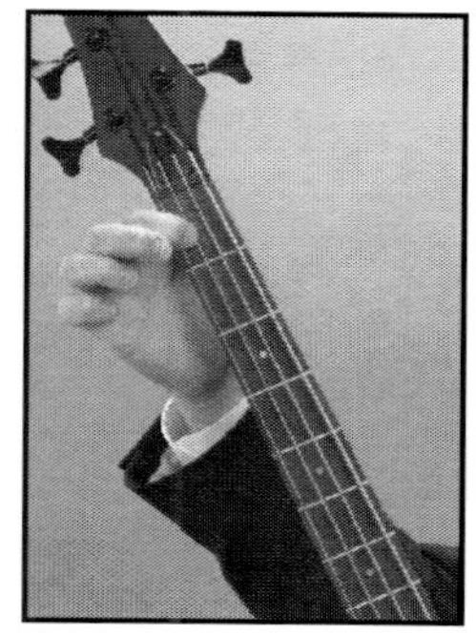
6th – E♭

G♭7♯5

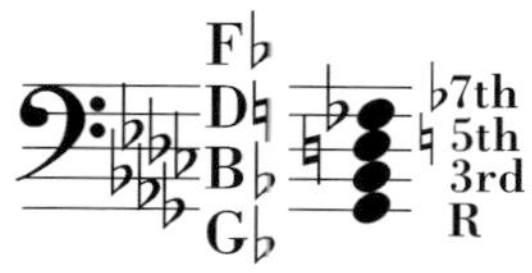

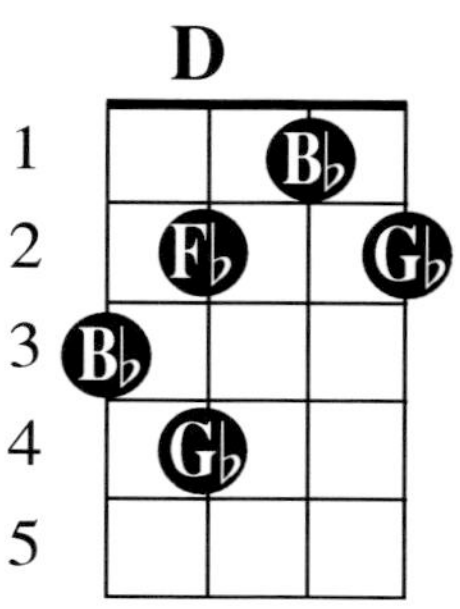

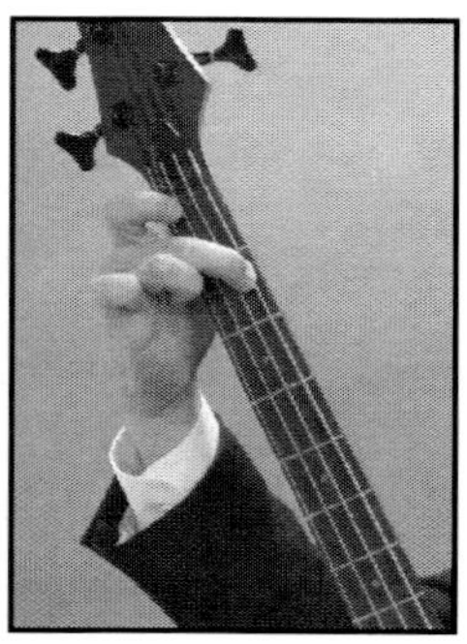
Root – G♭

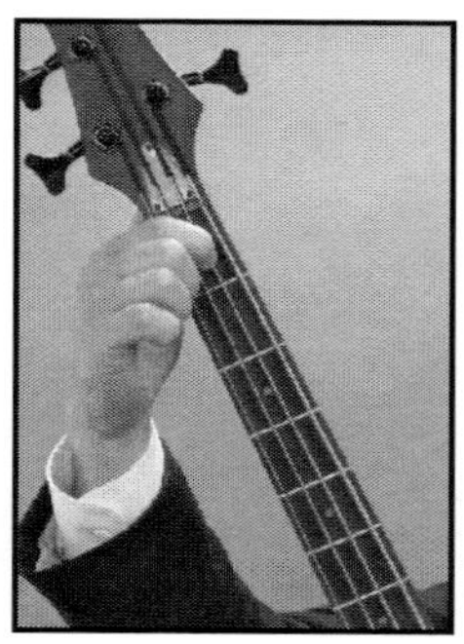
3rd – B♭

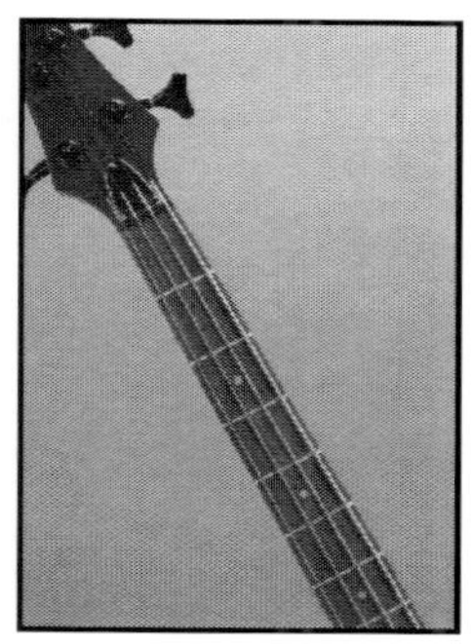
♯5th – D♮

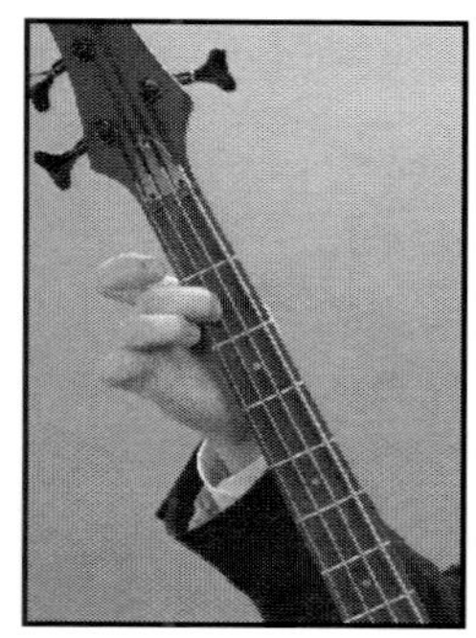
♭7th – F♭ or E♮

G♭7♭5

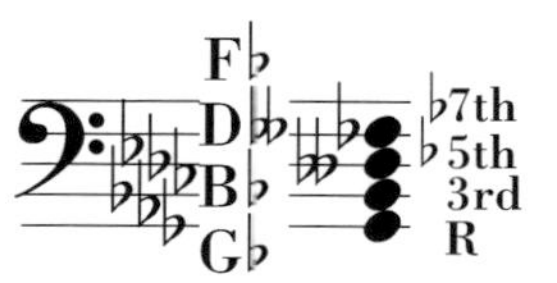

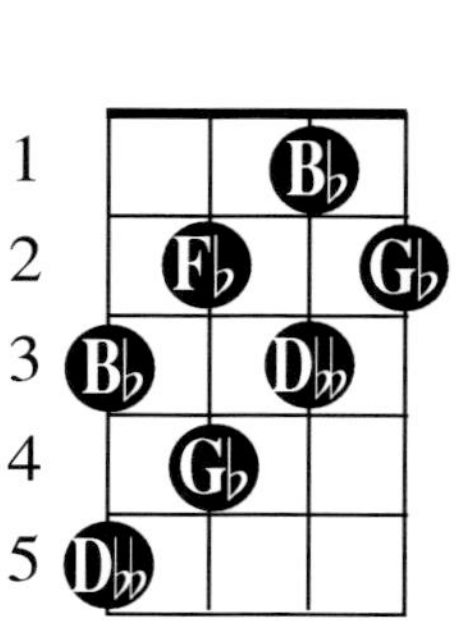

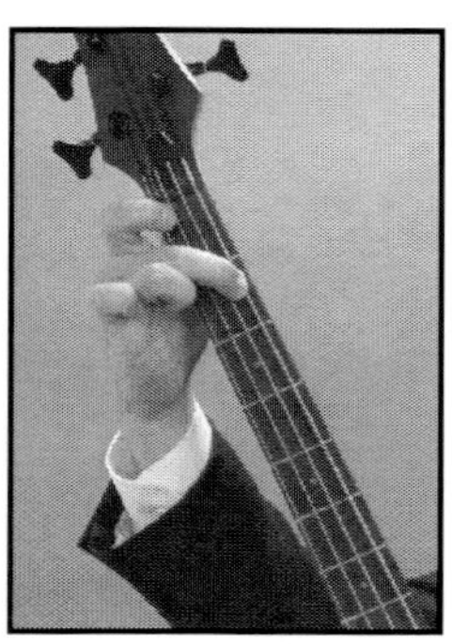
Root – G♭

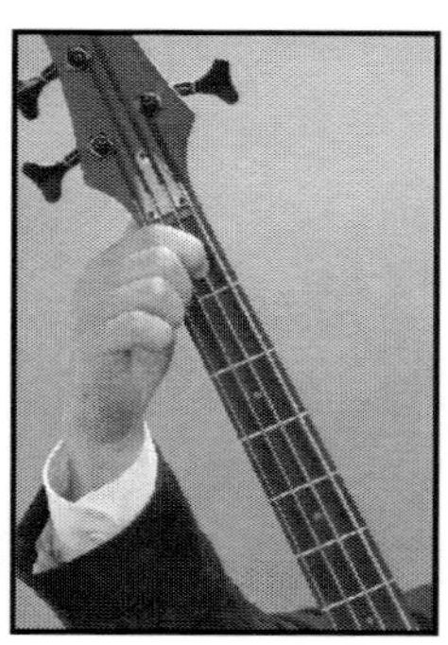
3rd – B♭

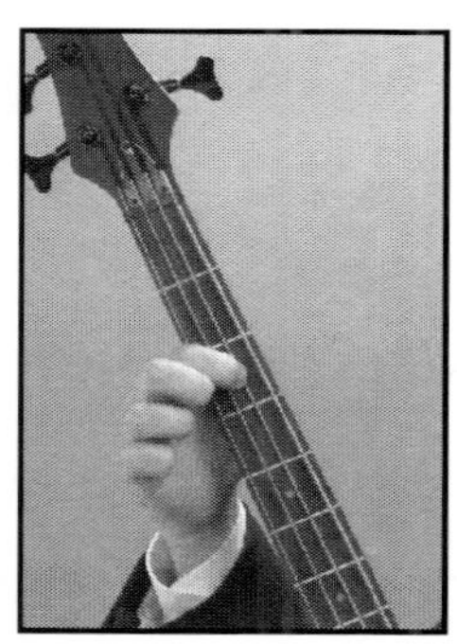
♭5th – D♭♭ or C

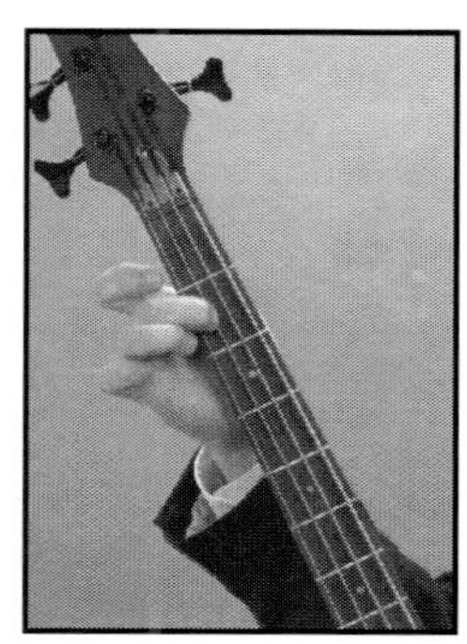
♭7th – F♭ or E

Key of G

GMaj

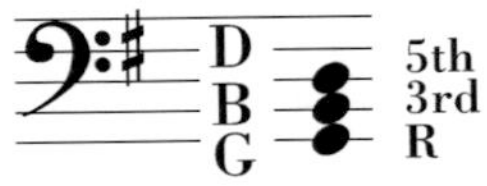

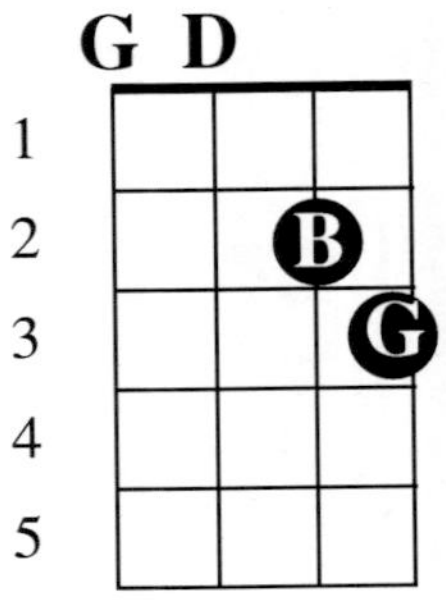

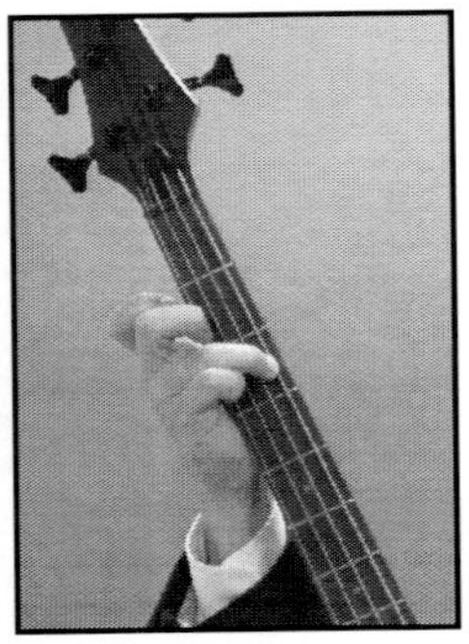

Root – G

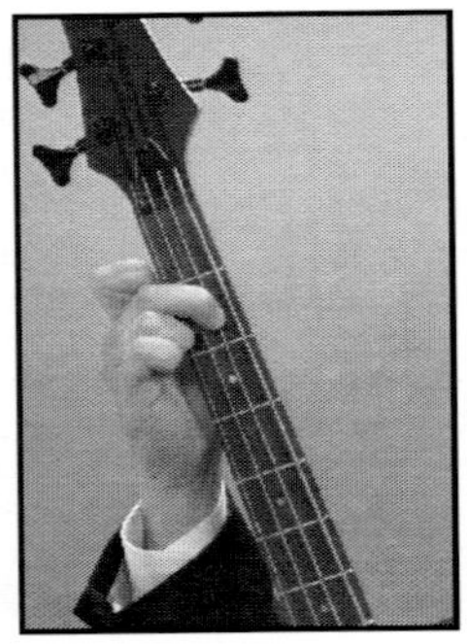

3rd – B

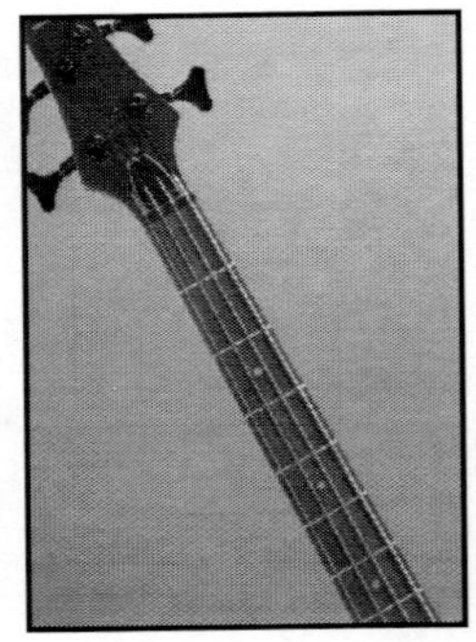

5th – D

Gmin

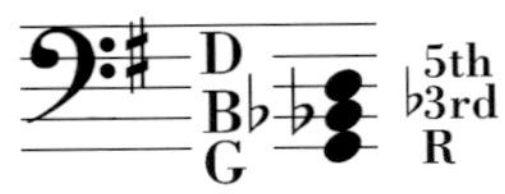

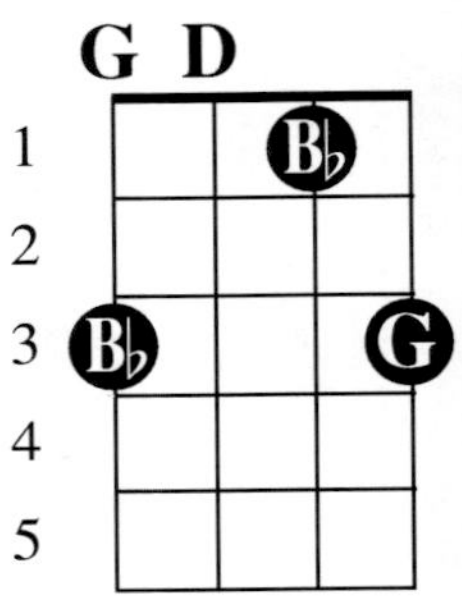

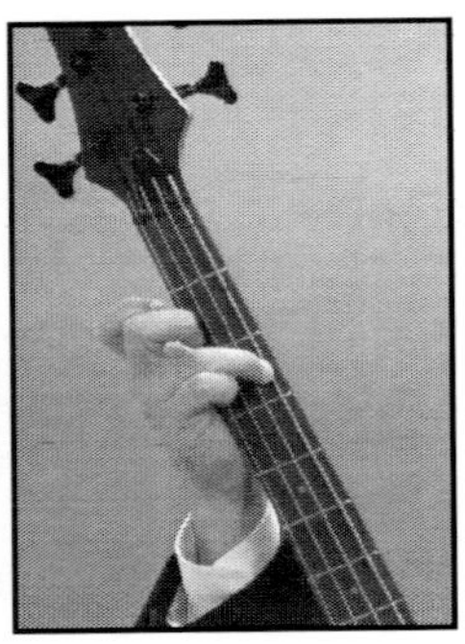

Root – G

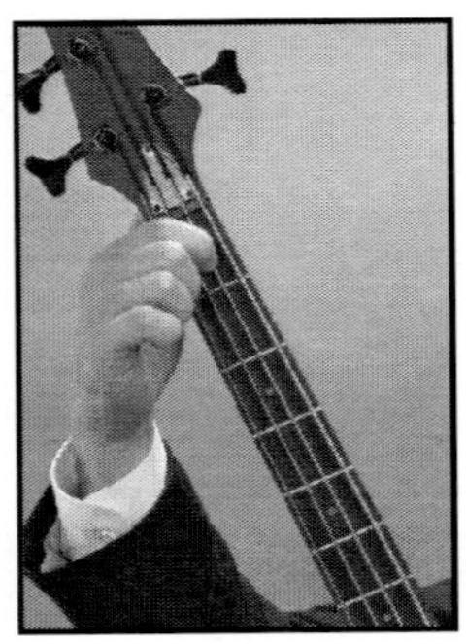

♭3rd – B♭

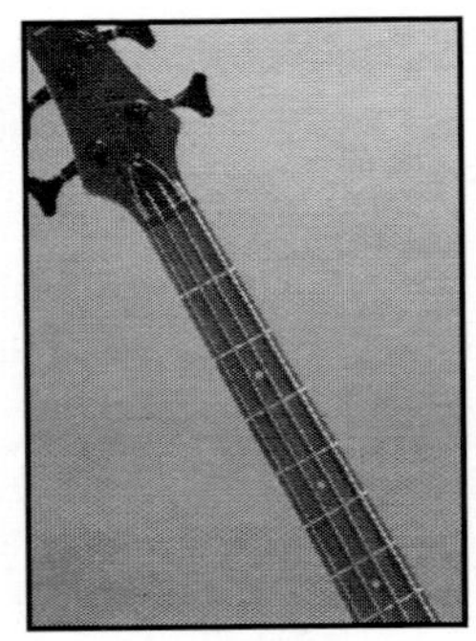

5th – D

G7

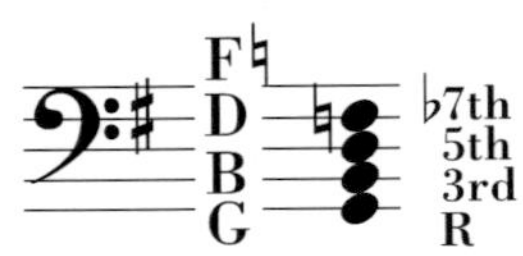

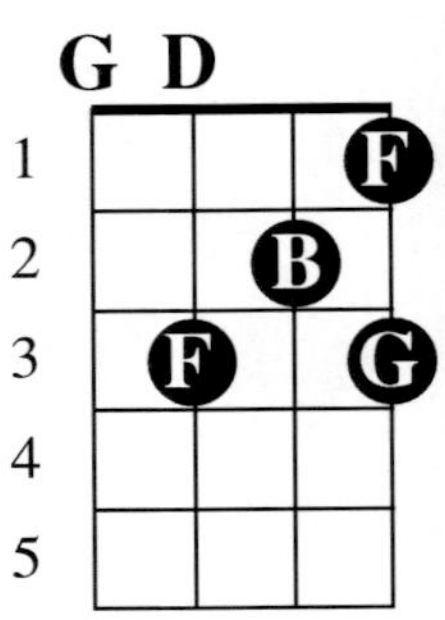

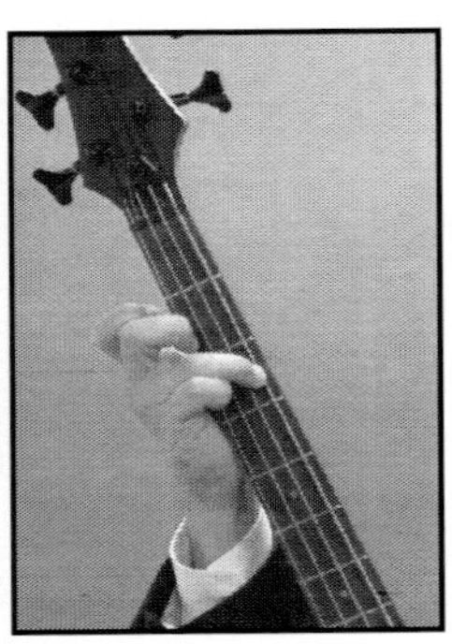

Root – G

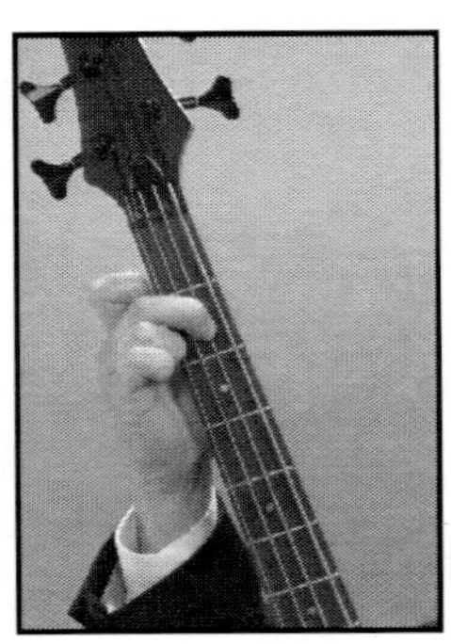

3rd – B

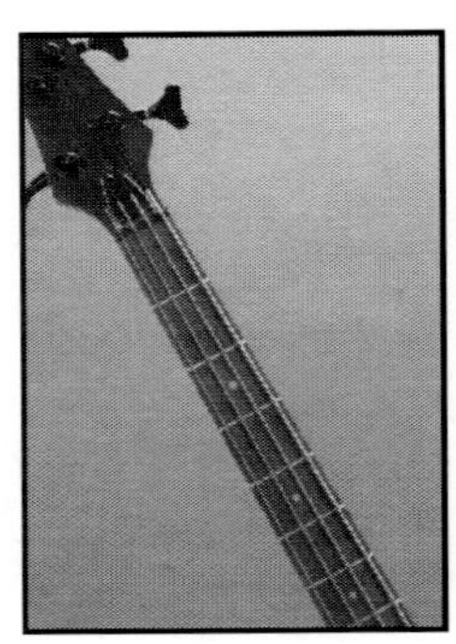

5th – D

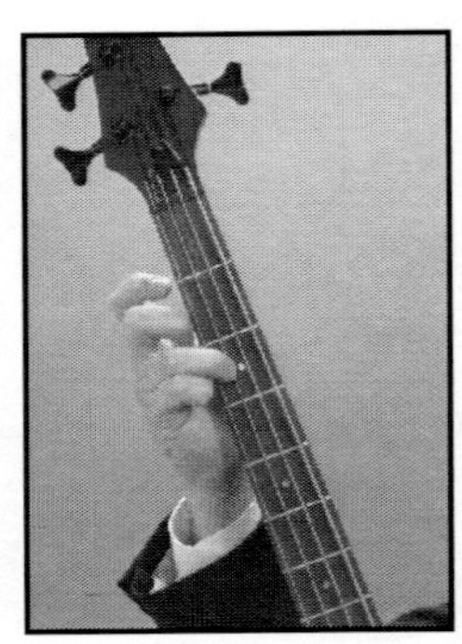

♭7th – F♮

Key of G (cont.)

G7sus

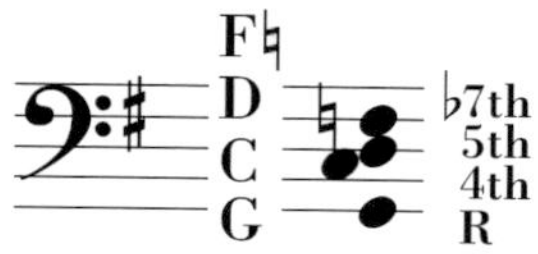

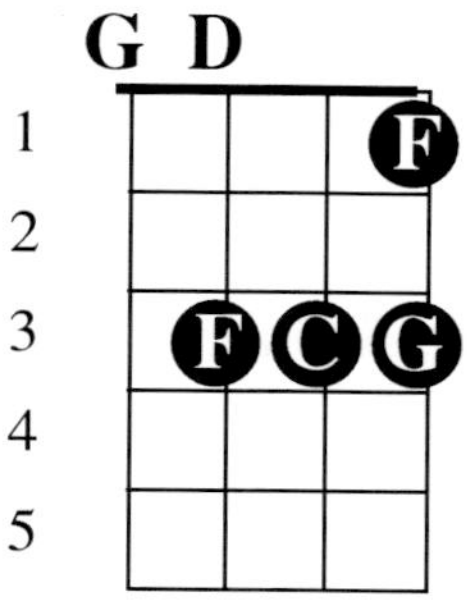

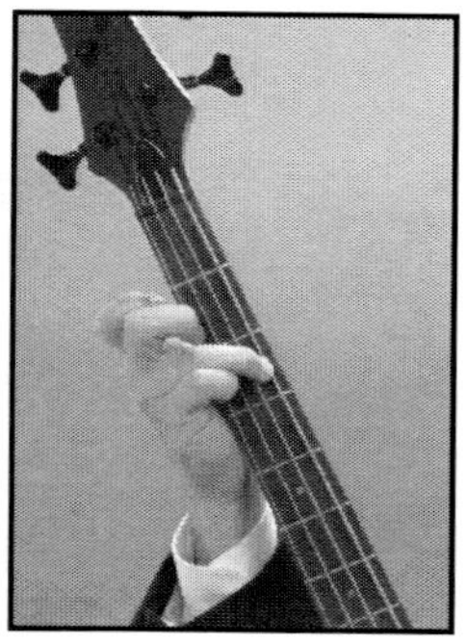

Root – G

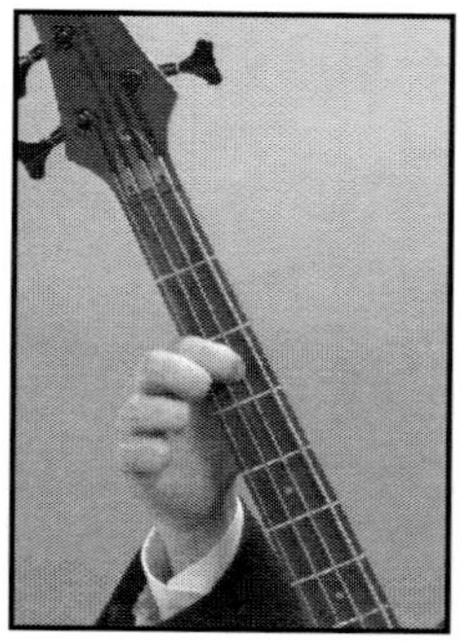

4th – C

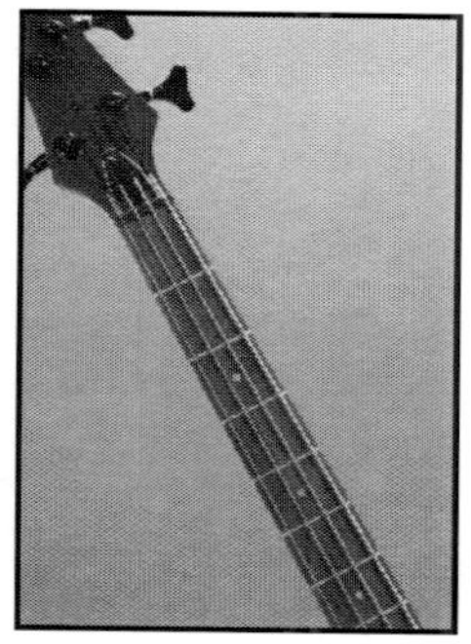

5th – D

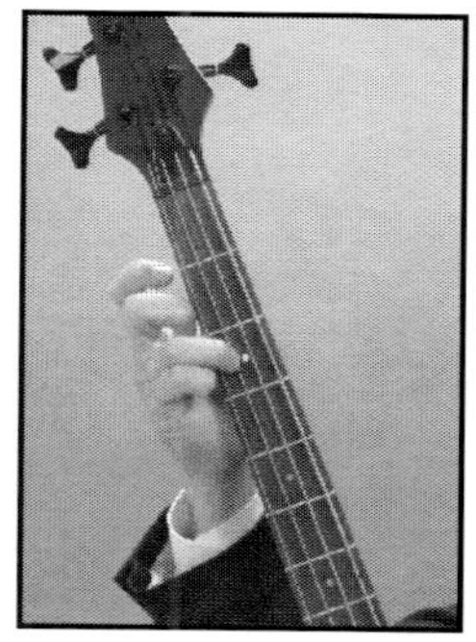

♭7th – F♮

Gm7

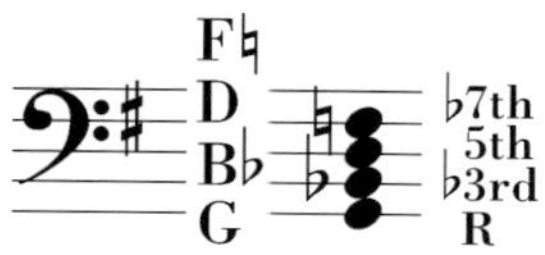

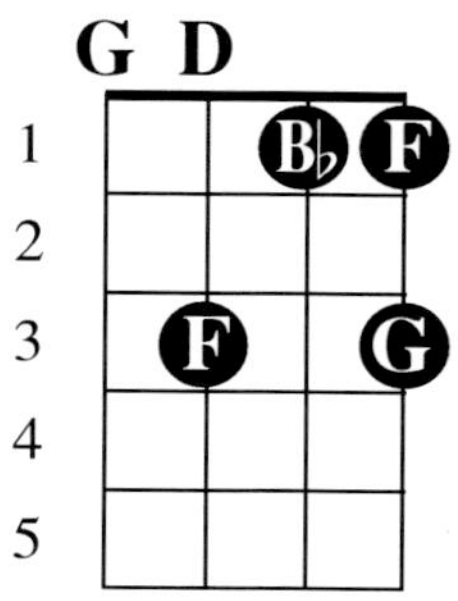

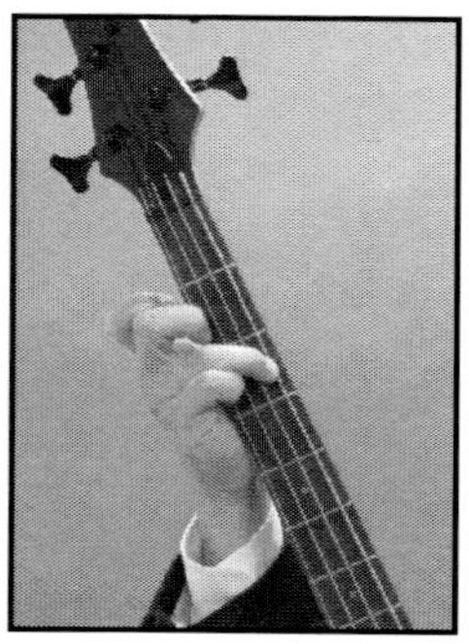

Root – G

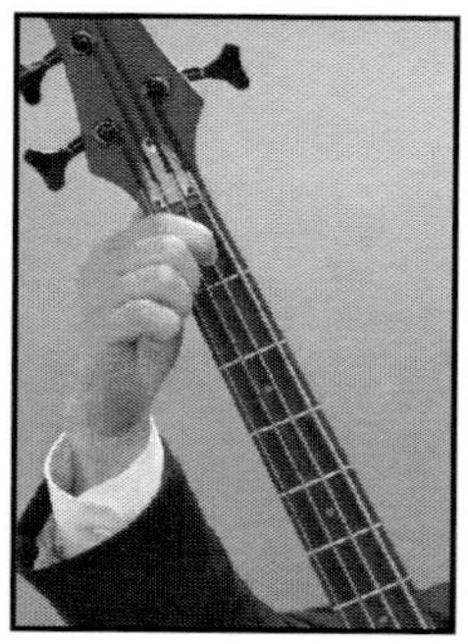

♭3rd – B♭

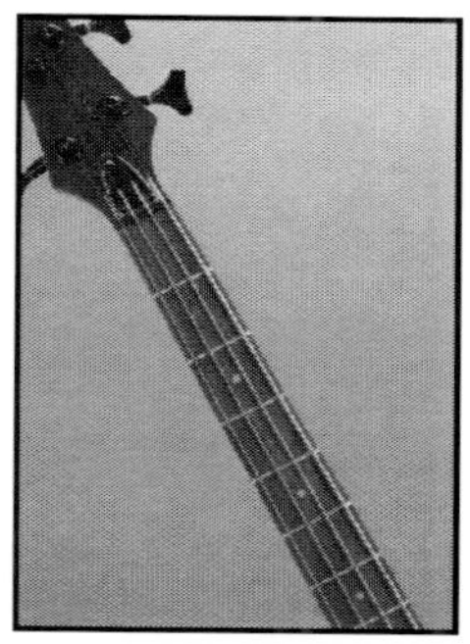

5th – D

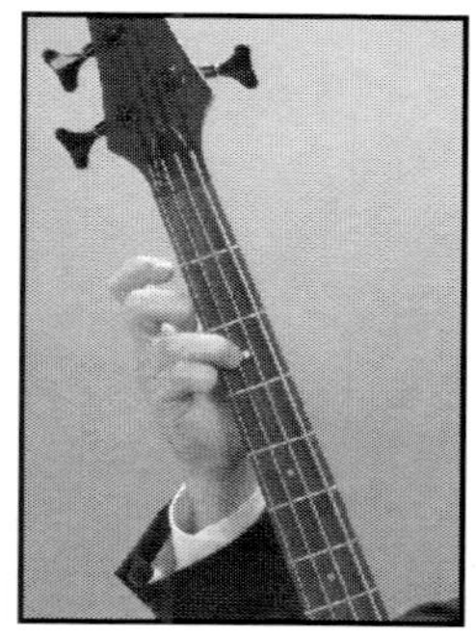

♭7th – F♮

GMa7

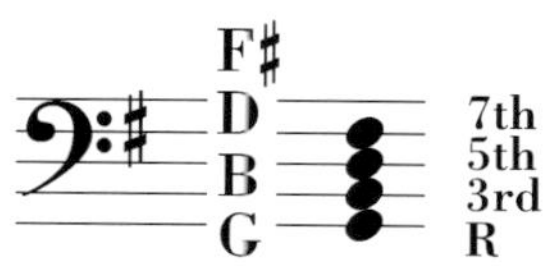

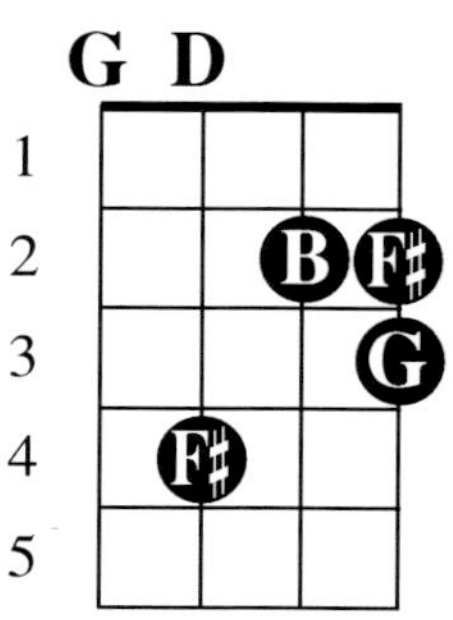

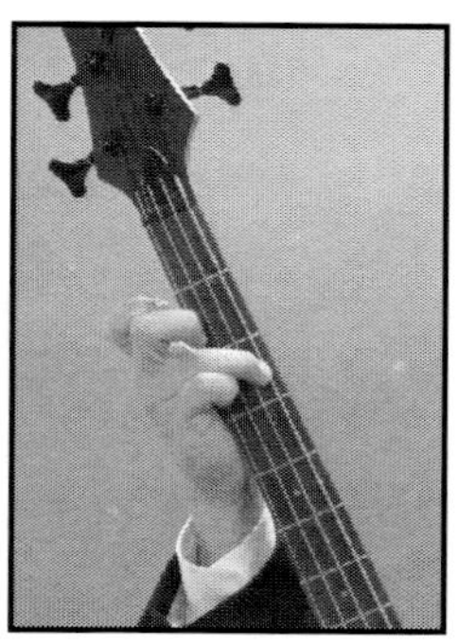

Root – G

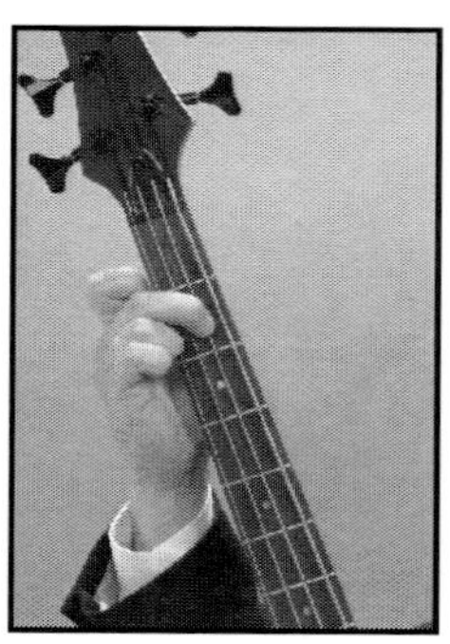

3rd – B

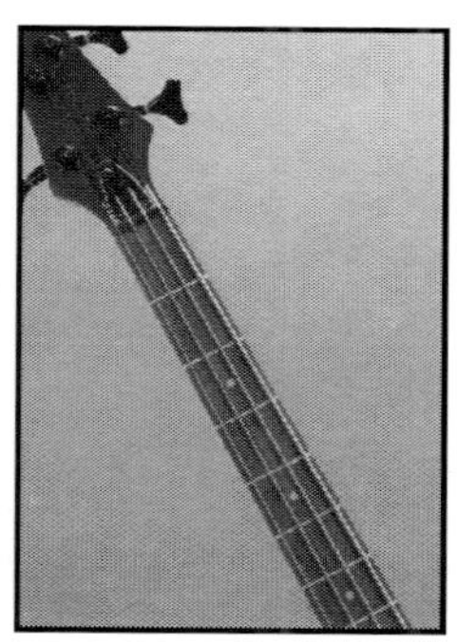

5th – D

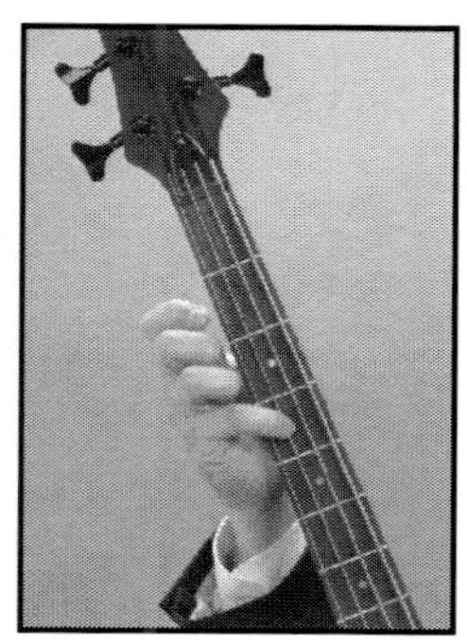

7th – F♯

Key of G (cont.)

Gdim

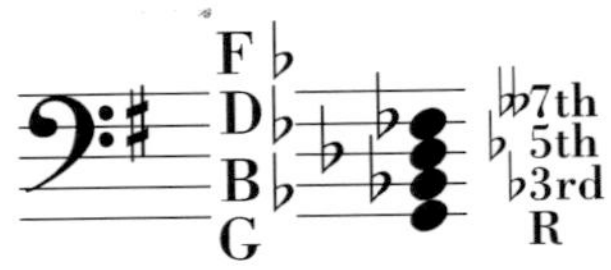

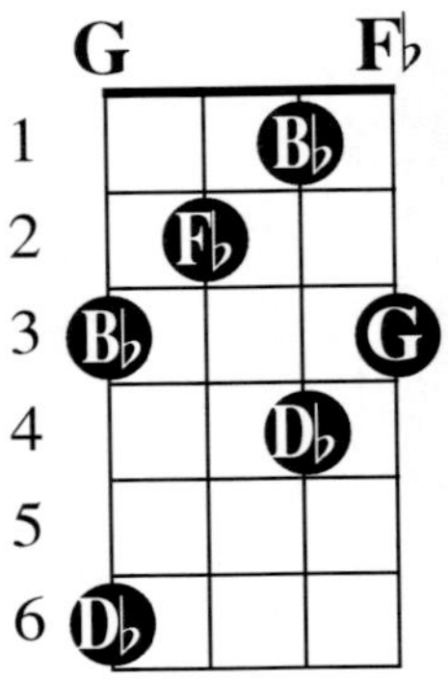

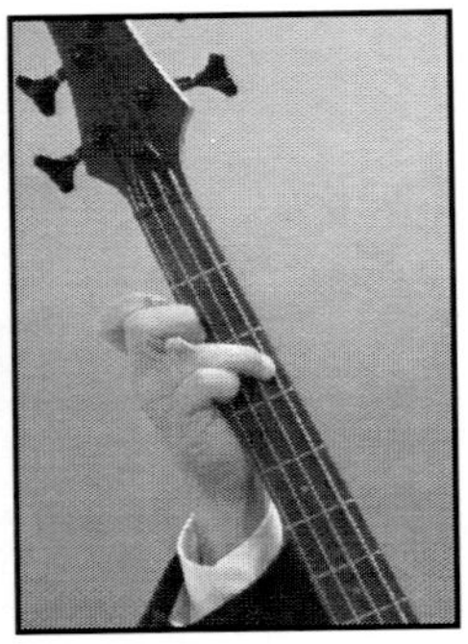
Root – G

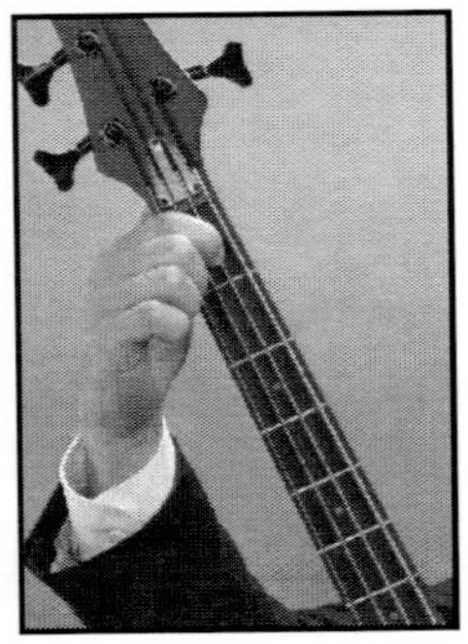
♭3rd – B♭

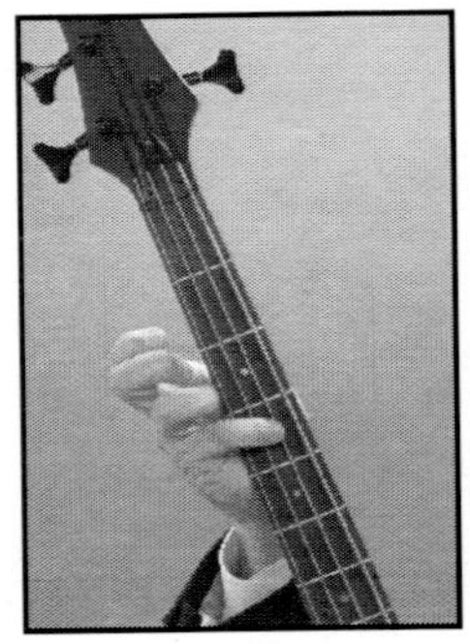
♭5th – D♭

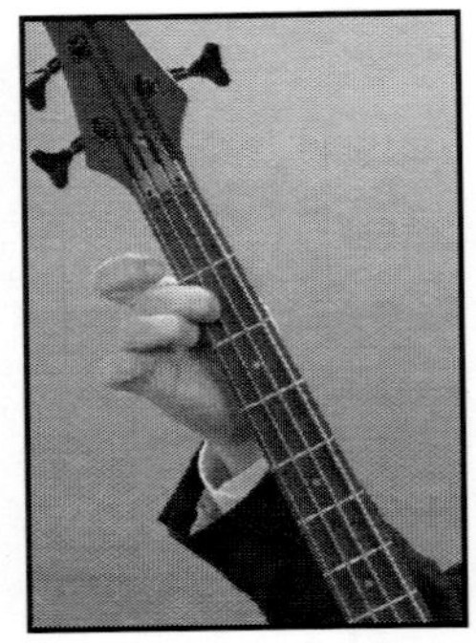
♭♭7th – F♭ or E

Gaug

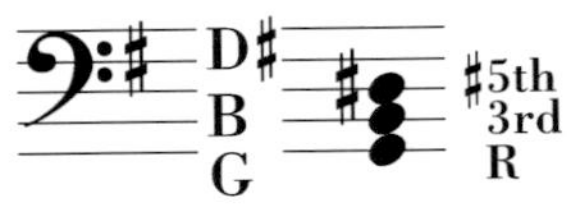

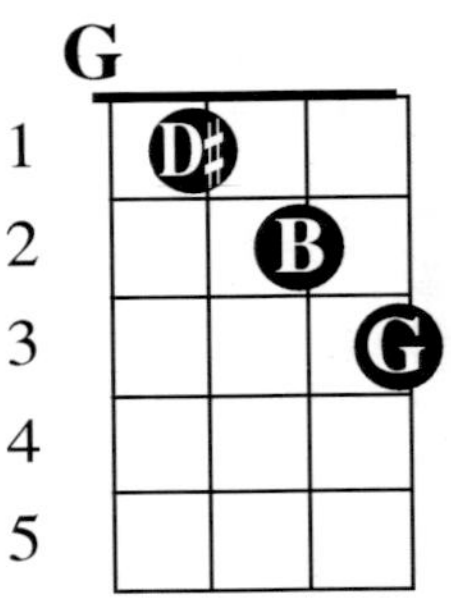

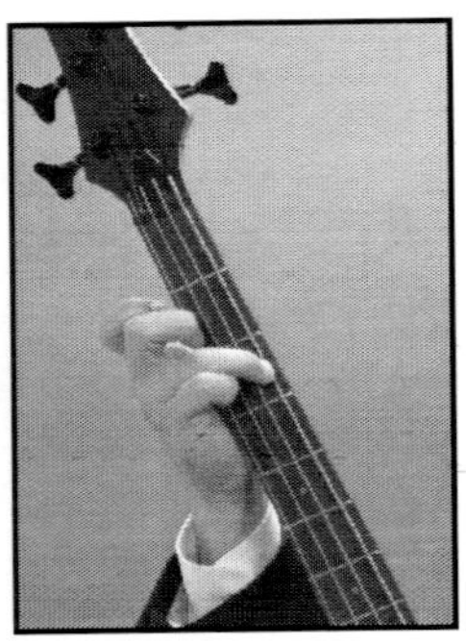
Root – G

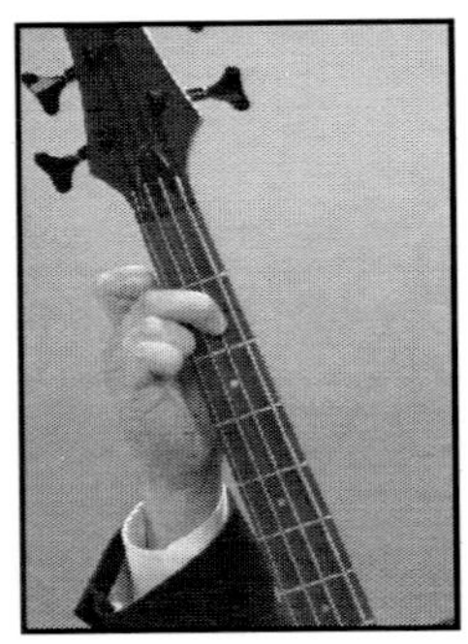
3rd – B

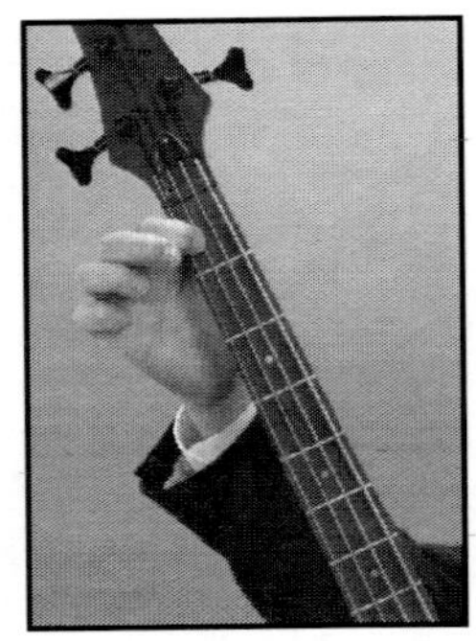
♯5th – D♯

G6

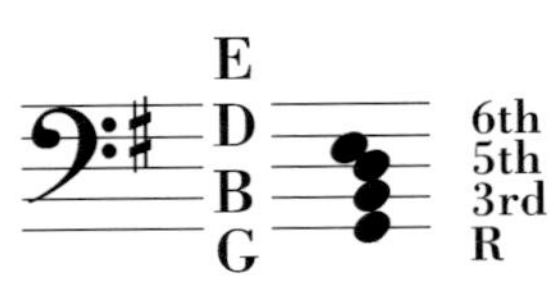

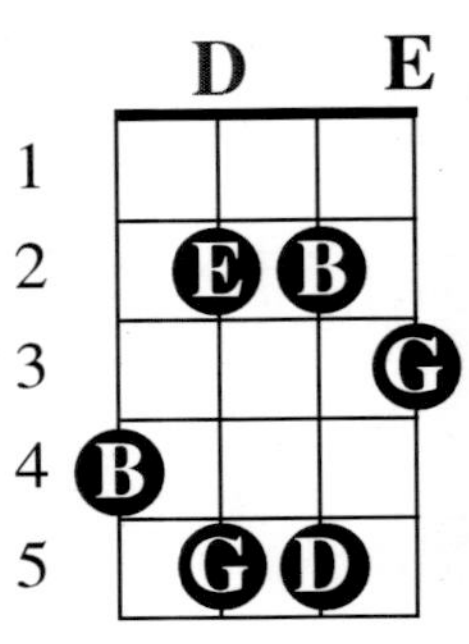

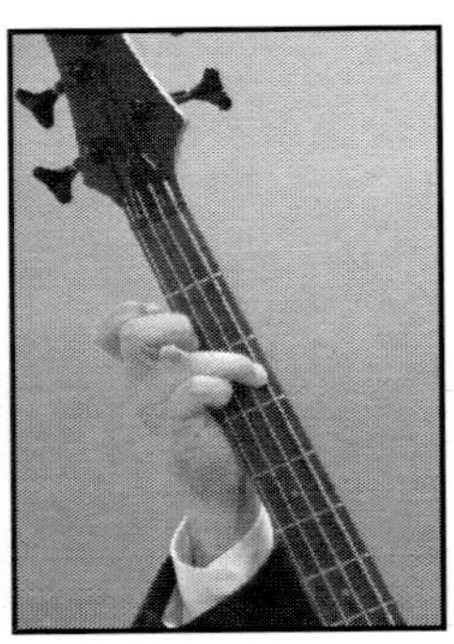
Root – G

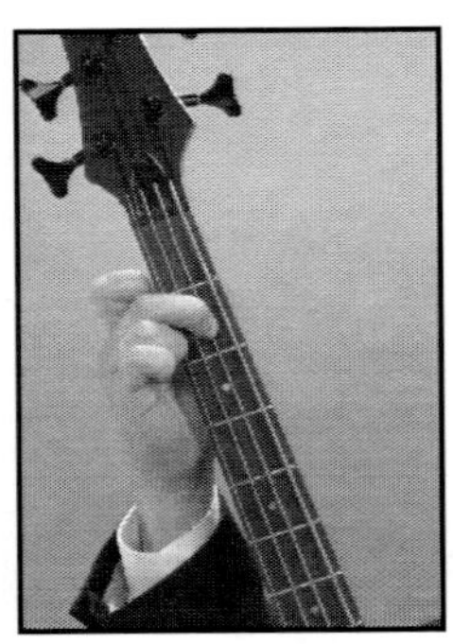
3rd – B

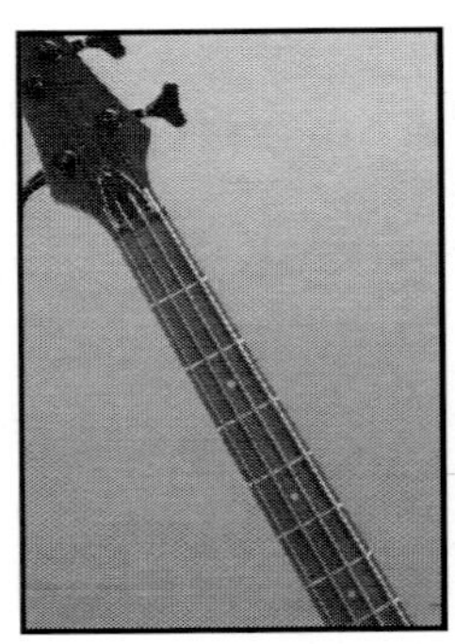
5th – D

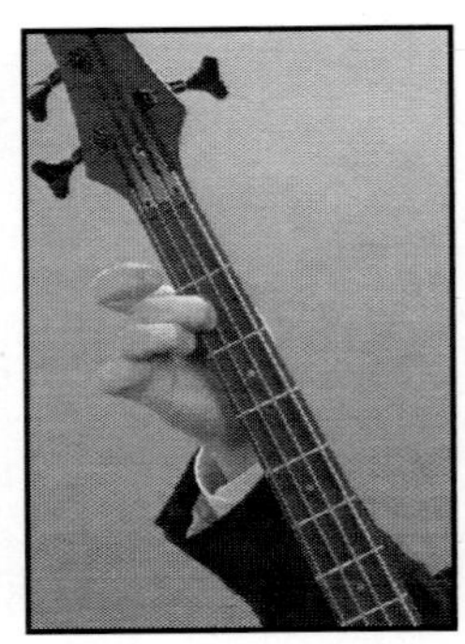
6th – E

Key of G (cont.)

Gm6

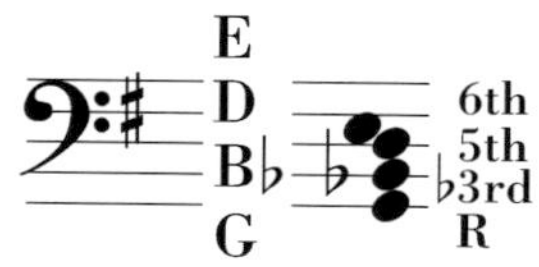

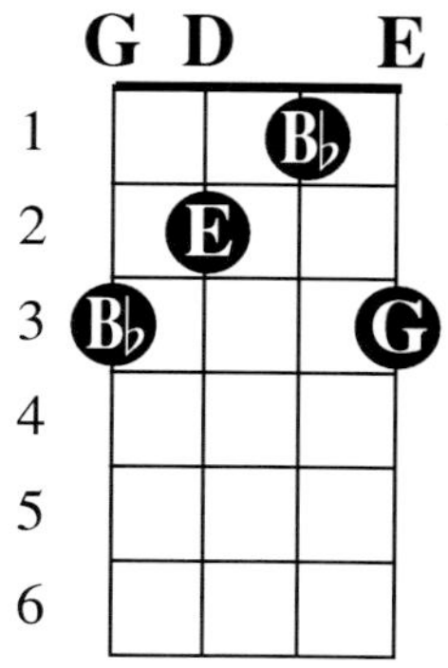

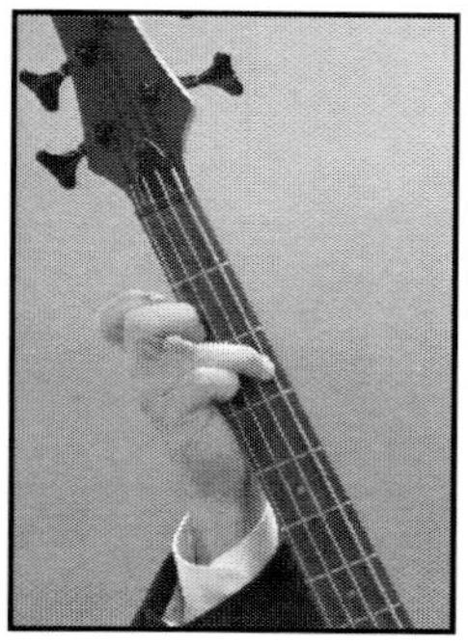

Root – G

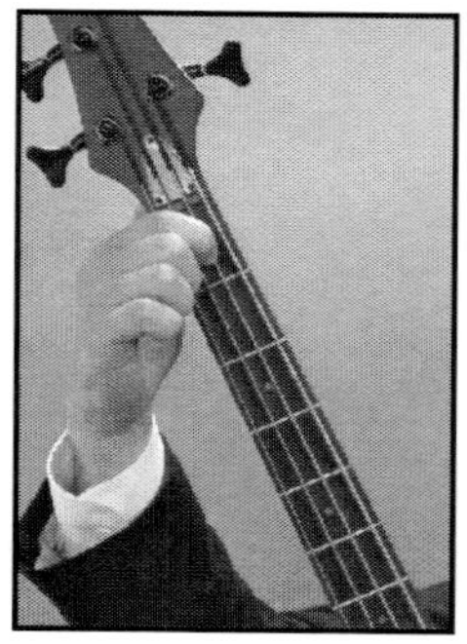

♭3rd – B♭

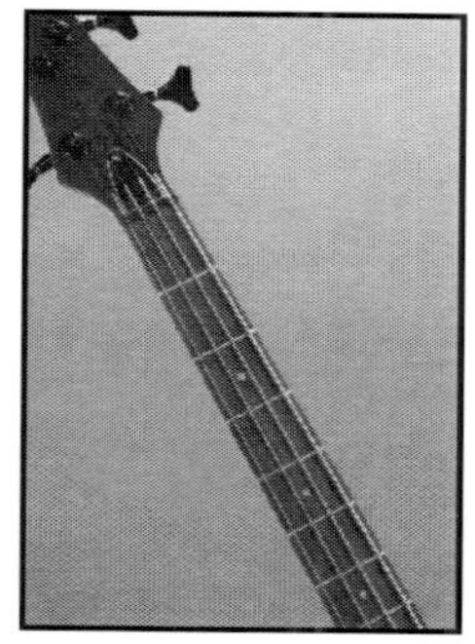

5th – D

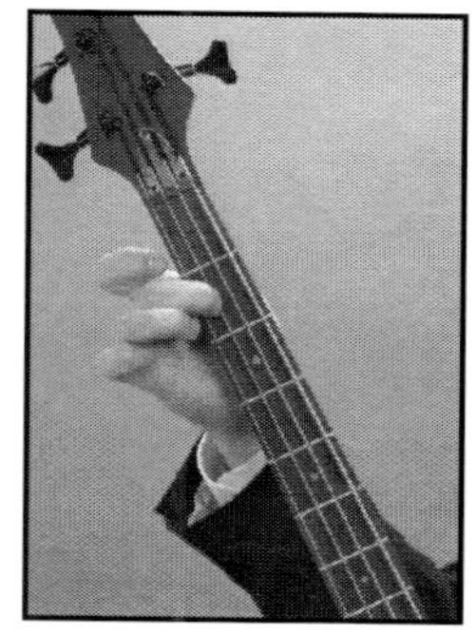

6th – E

G7♯5

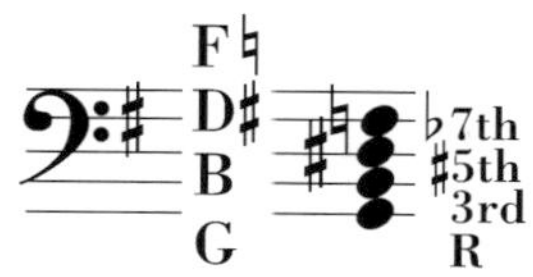

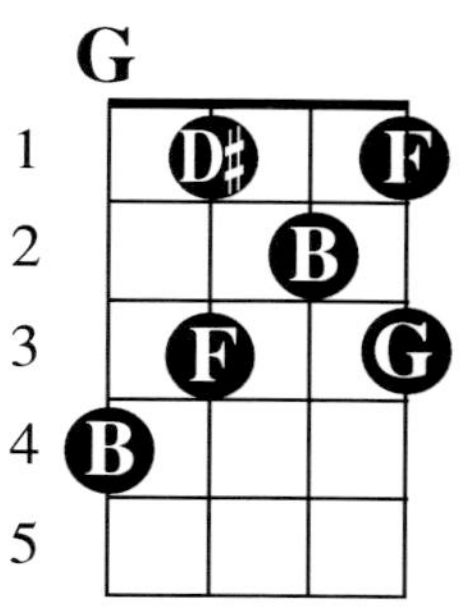

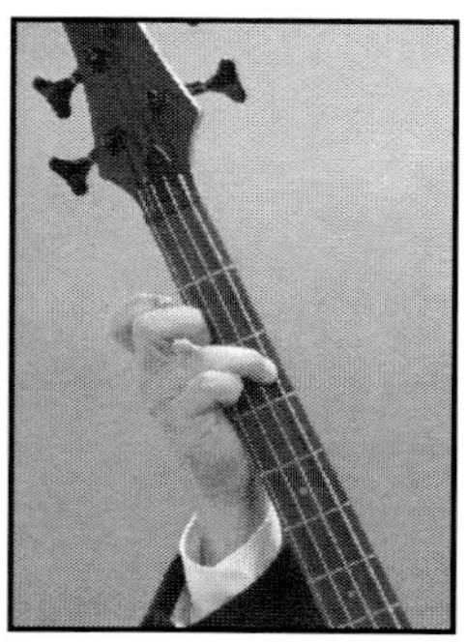

Root – G

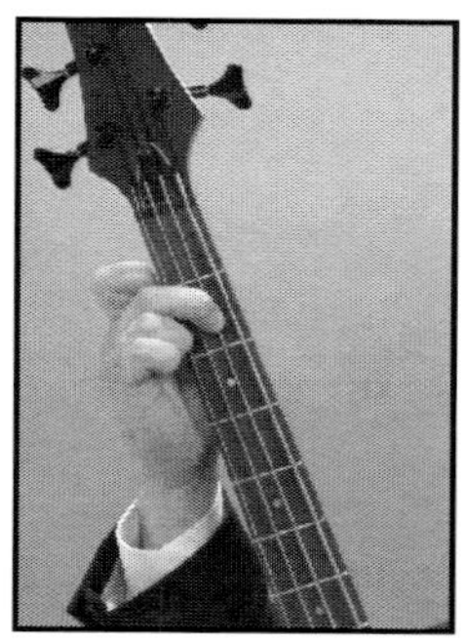

3rd – B

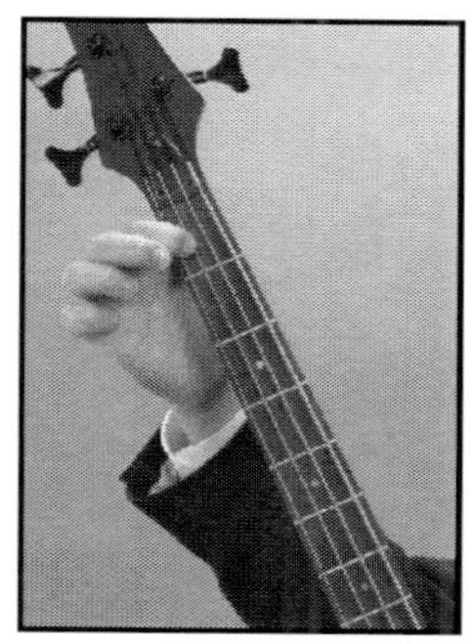

♯5th – D♯

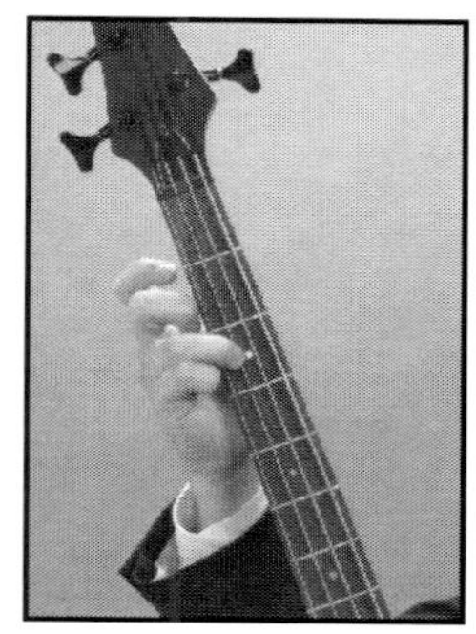

♭7th – F♮

G7♭5

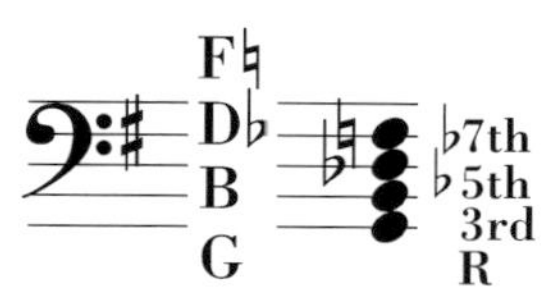

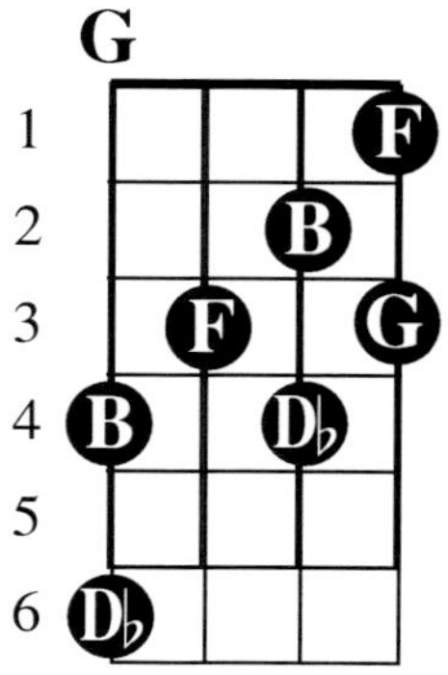

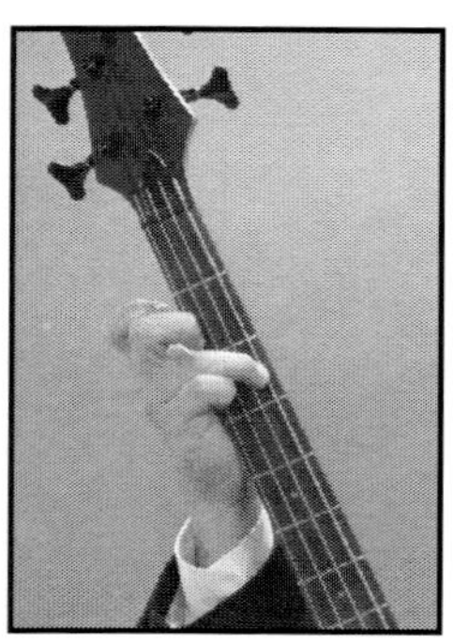

Root – G

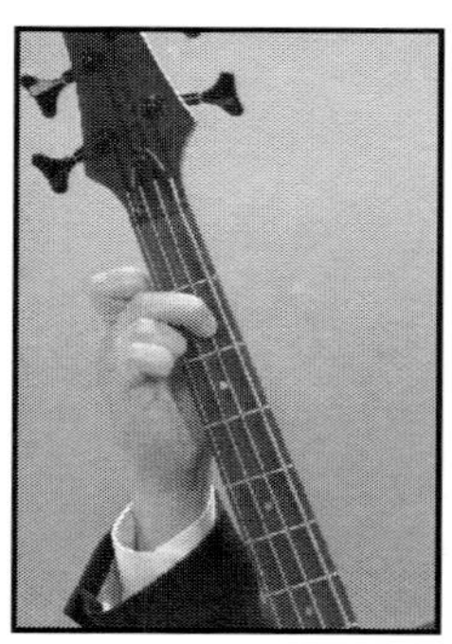

3rd – B

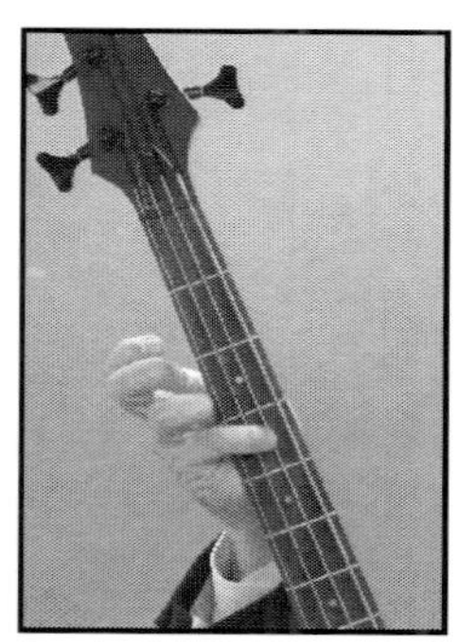

♭5th – D♭

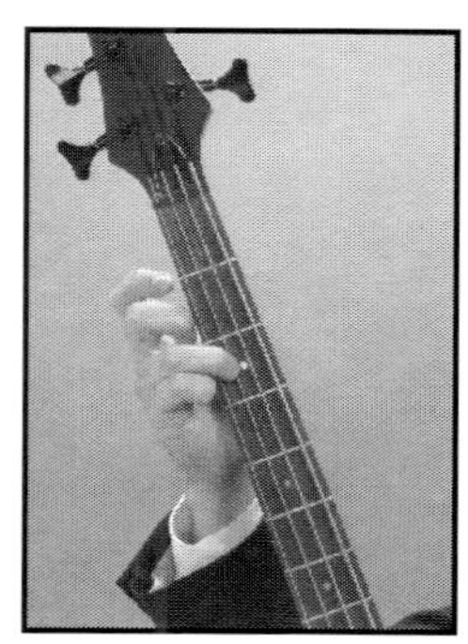

♭7th – F♮

Key of A♭

A♭Major

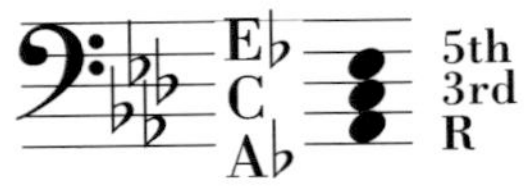

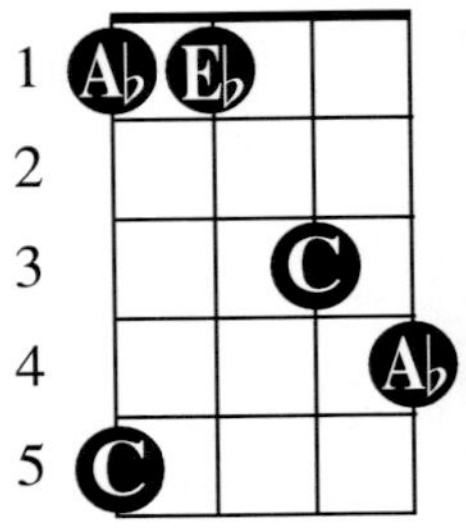

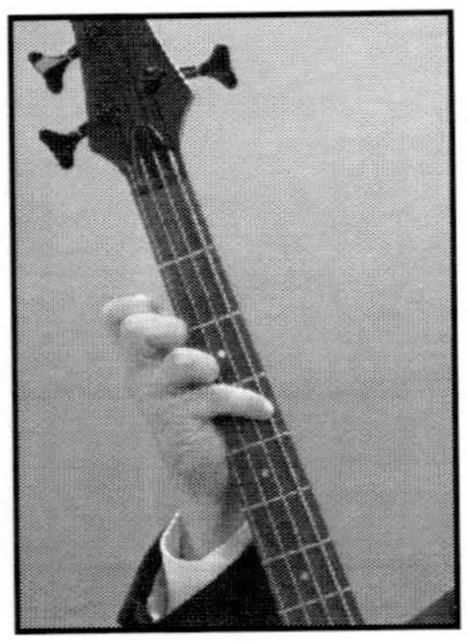

Root – A♭

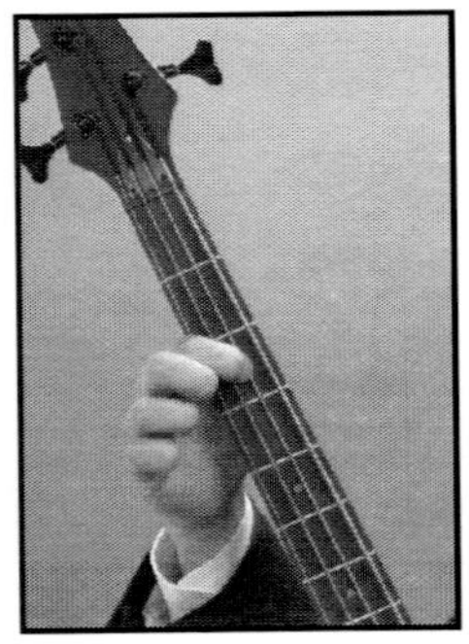

3rd – C

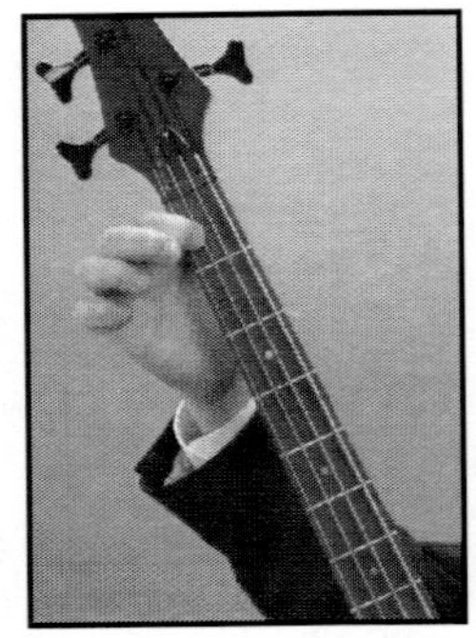

5th – E♭

A♭minor

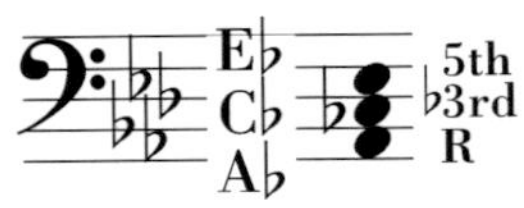

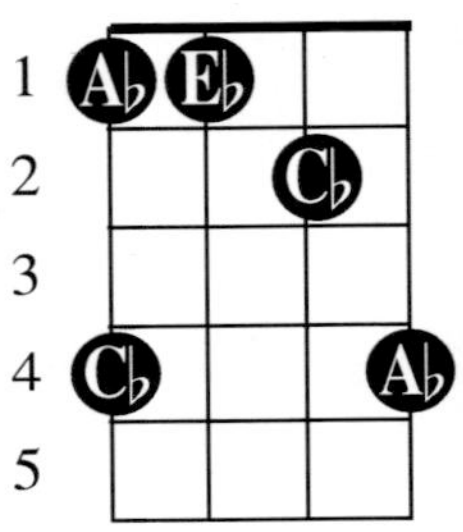

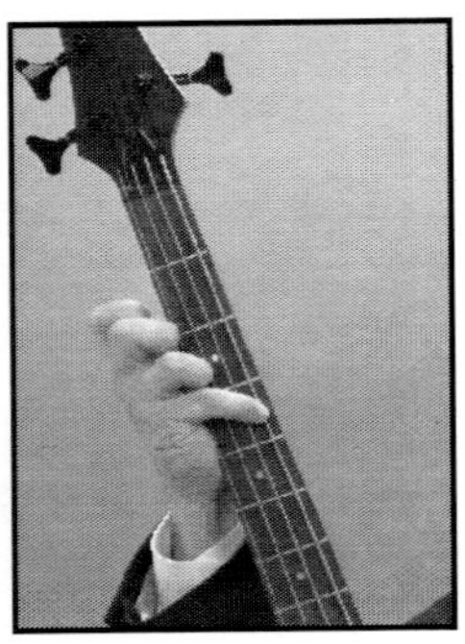

Root – A♭

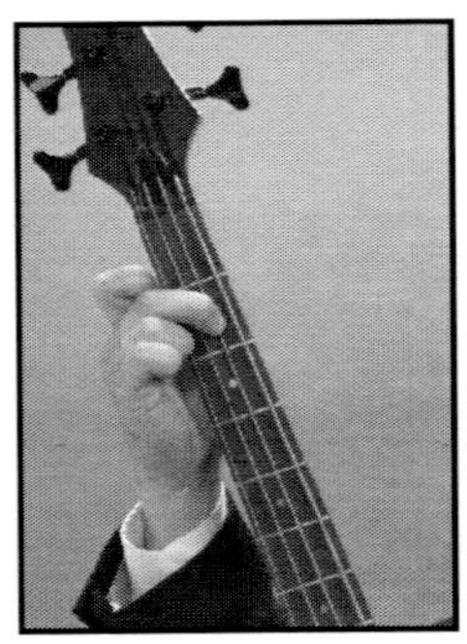

♭3rd – C♭ or B

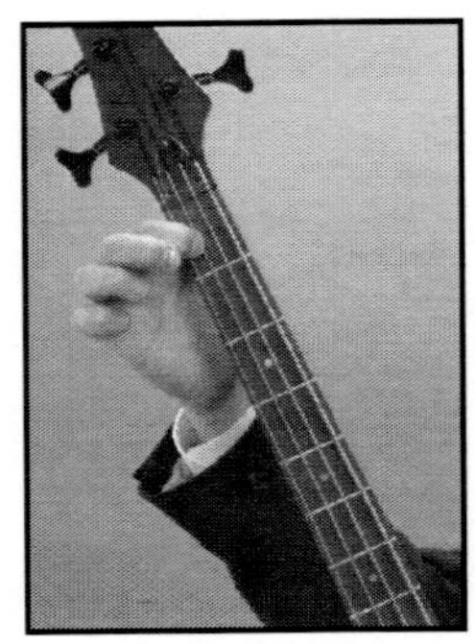

5th – E♭

A♭7

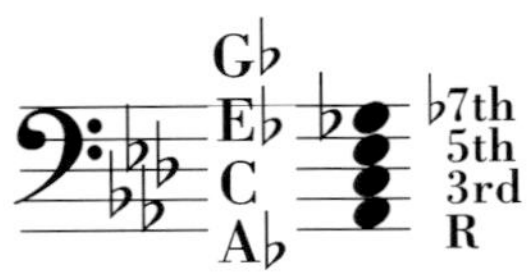

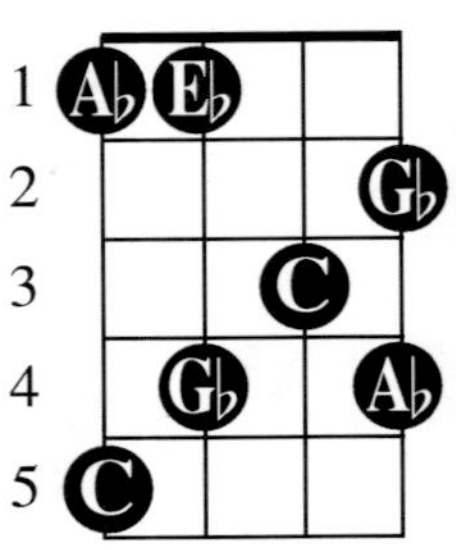

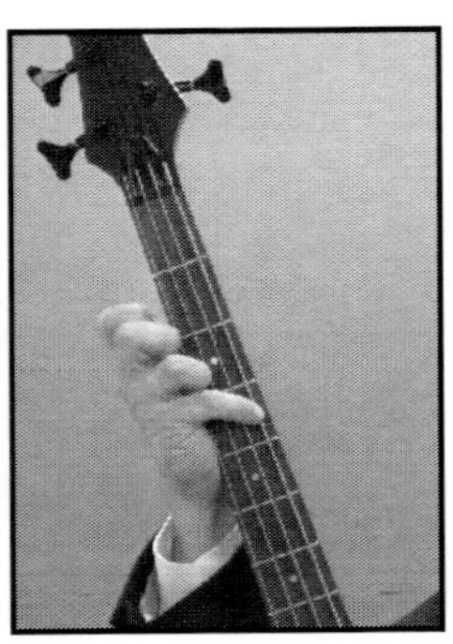

Root – A♭

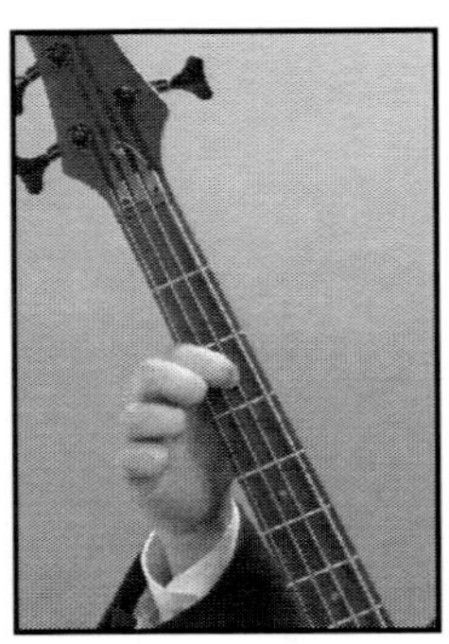

3rd – C

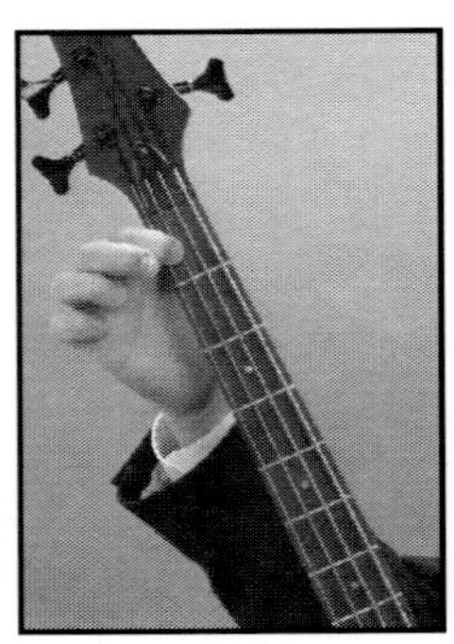

5th – E♭

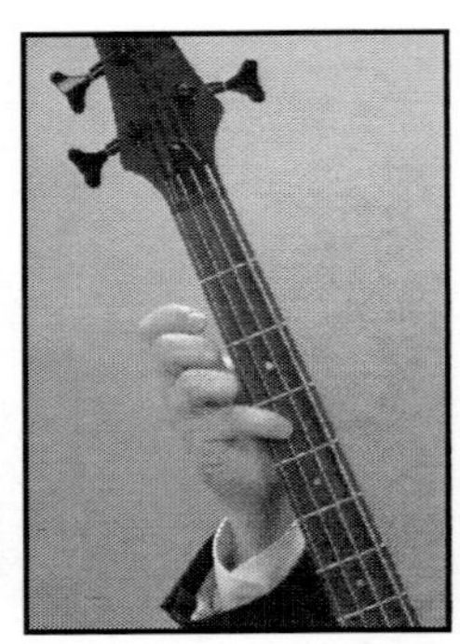

♭7th – G♭

Key of A♭ (cont.)

A♭7sus

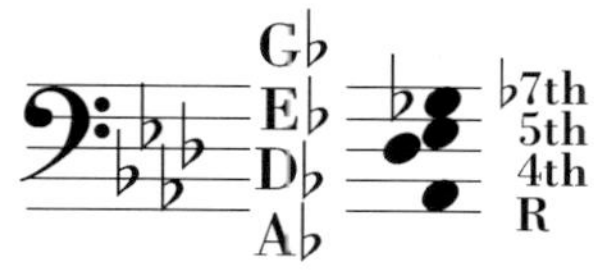

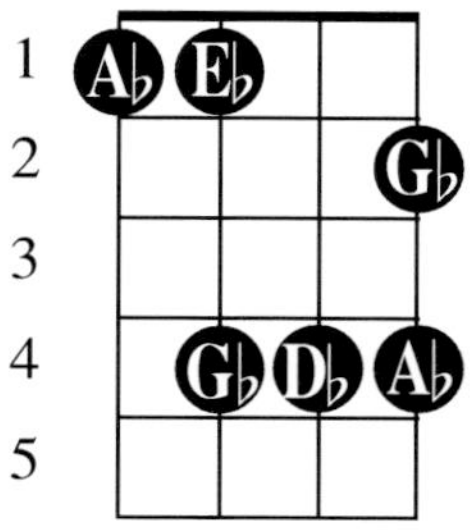

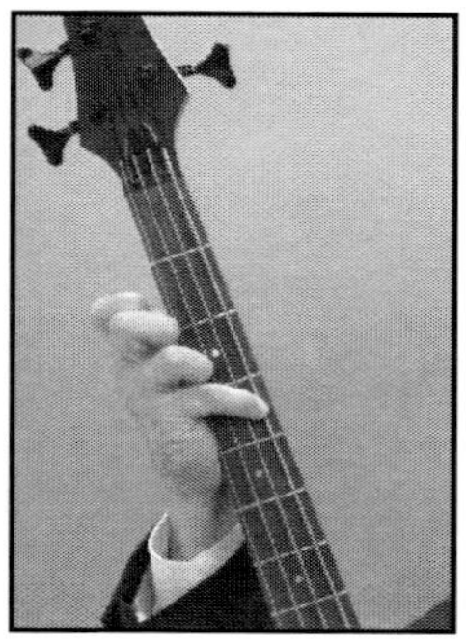

Root – A♭

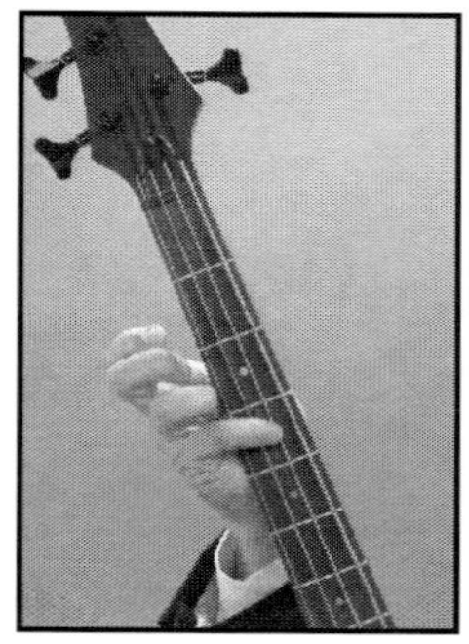

4th – D♭

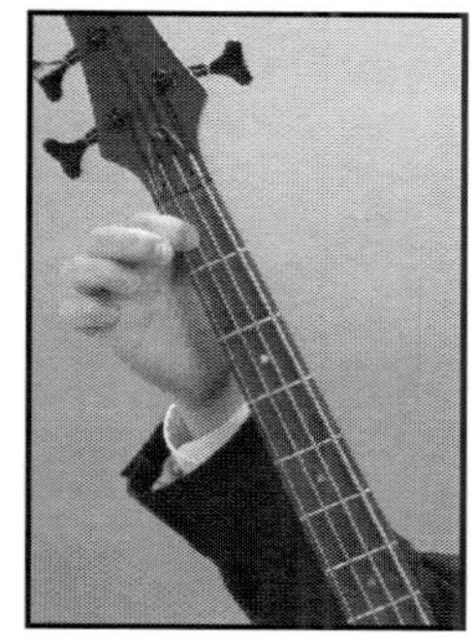

5th – E♭

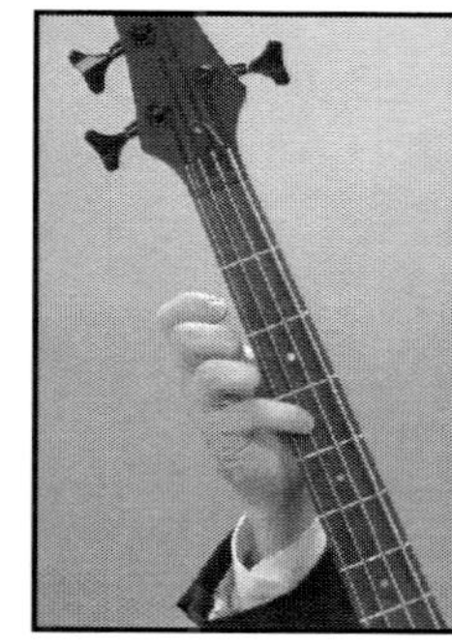

♭7th – G♭

A♭m7

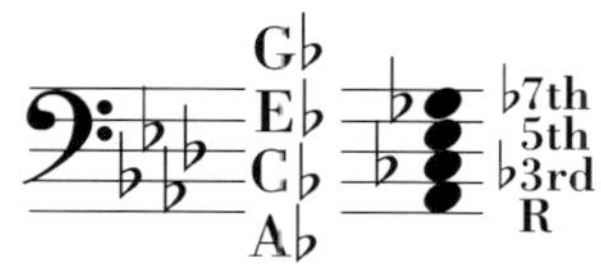

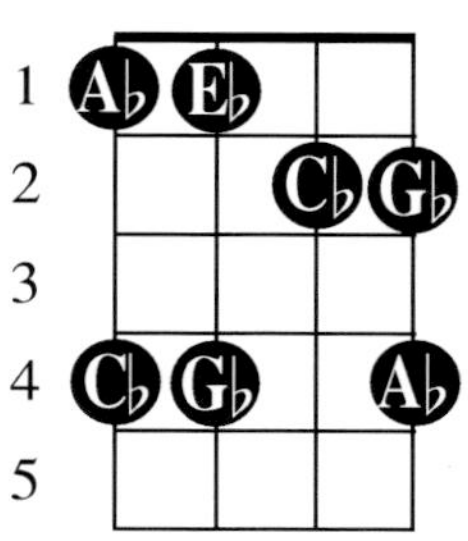

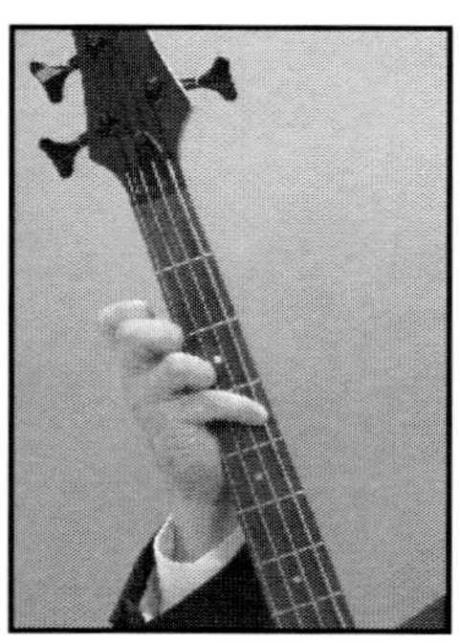

Root – A♭

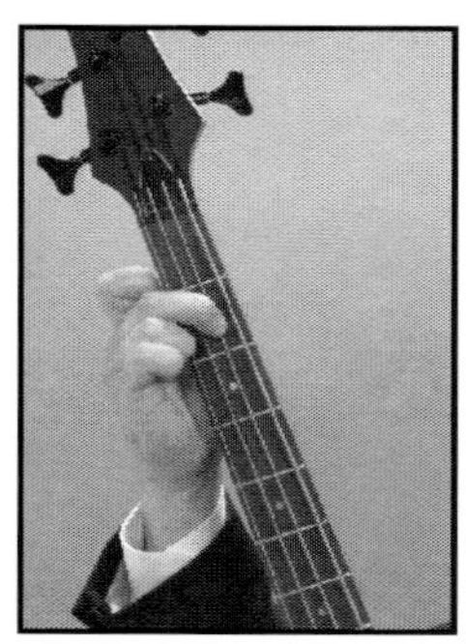

♭3rd – C♭ or B

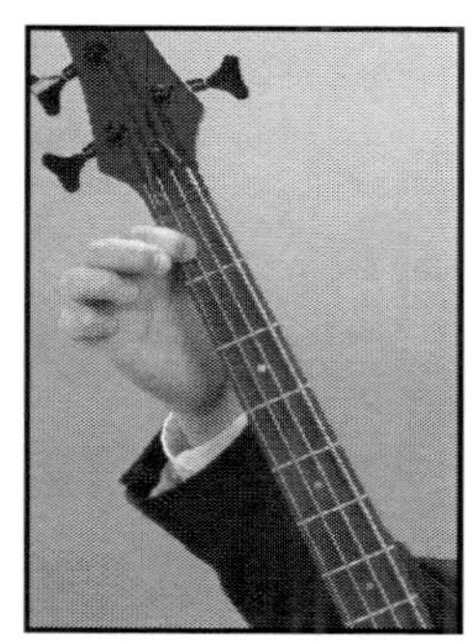

5th – E♭

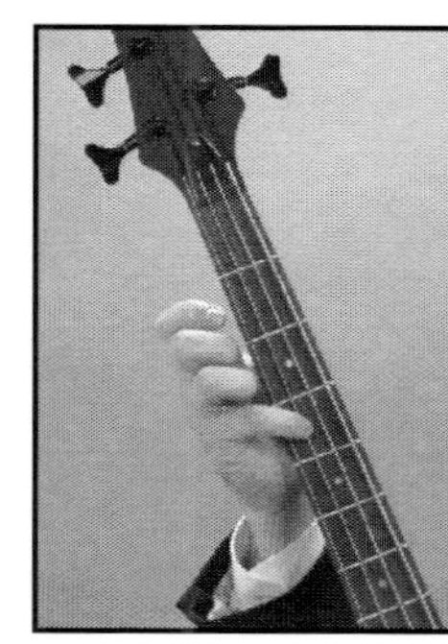

♭7th – G♭

A♭Ma7

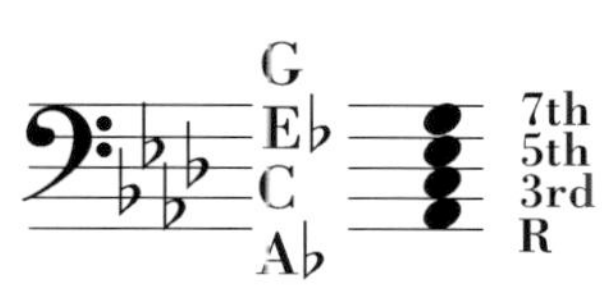

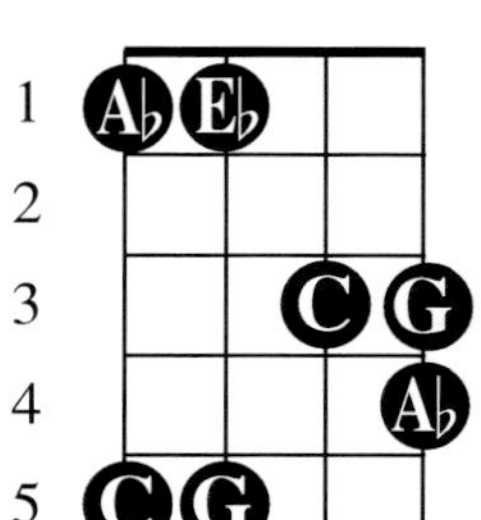

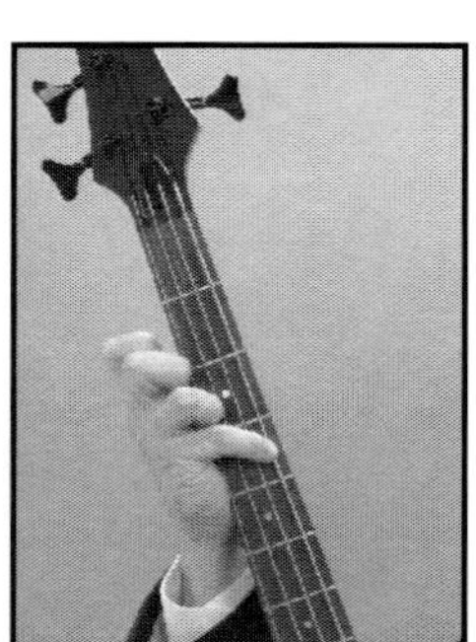

Root – A♭

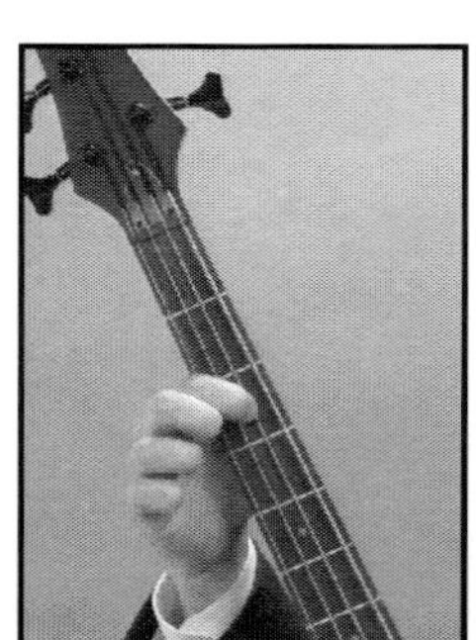

3rd – C

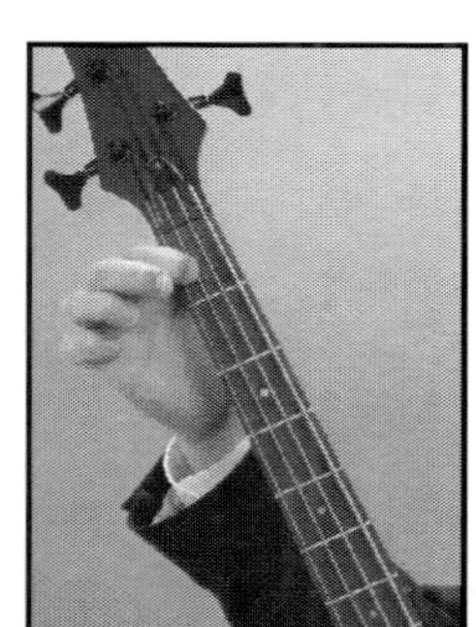

5th – E♭

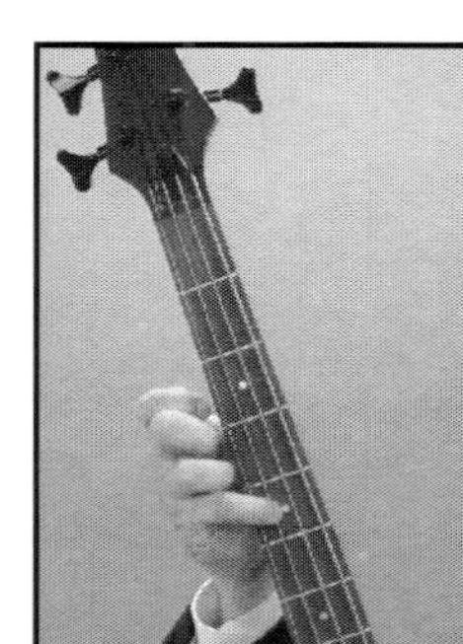

7th – G

Key of A♭ (cont.)

A♭dim

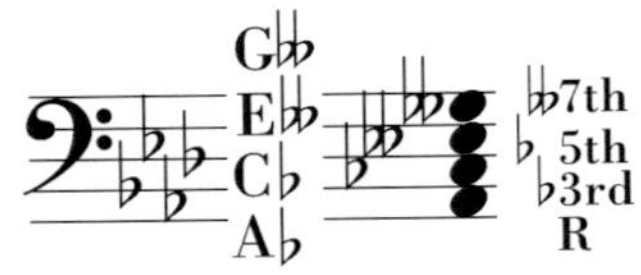

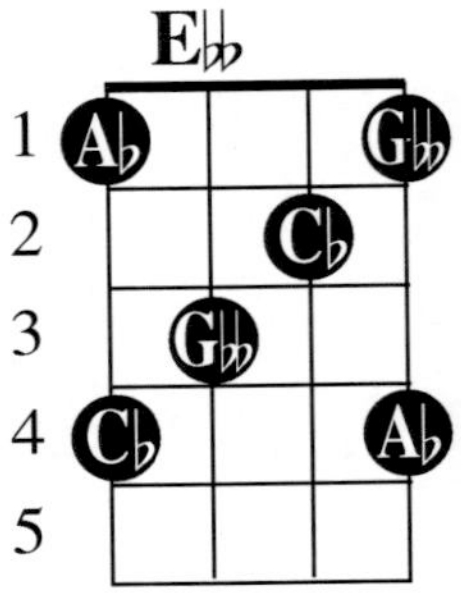

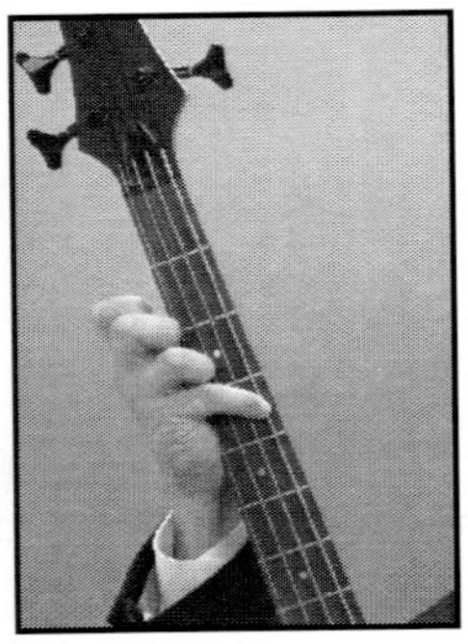

Root – A♭

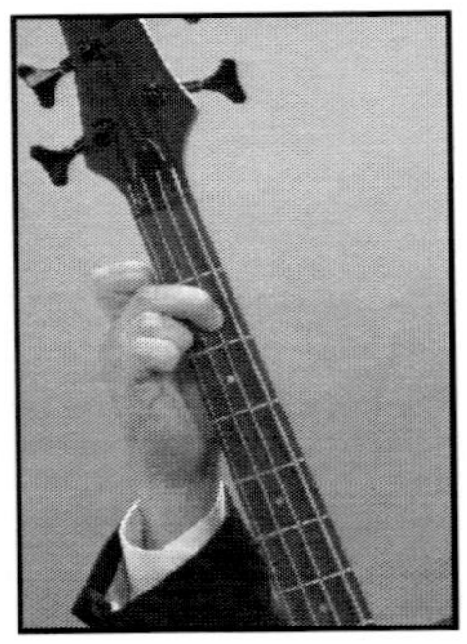

♭3rd – C♭ or B

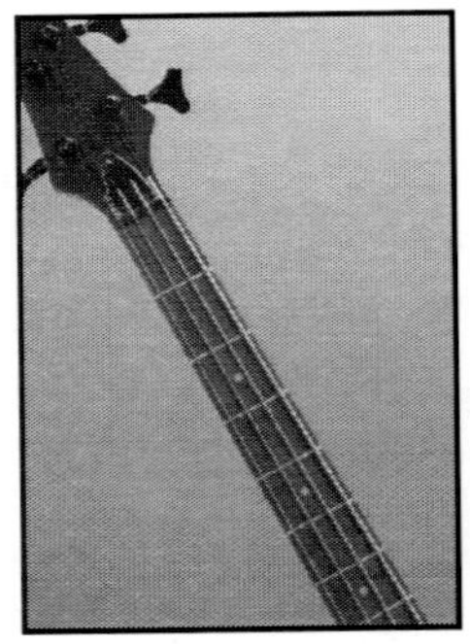

♭5th – E♭♭ or D

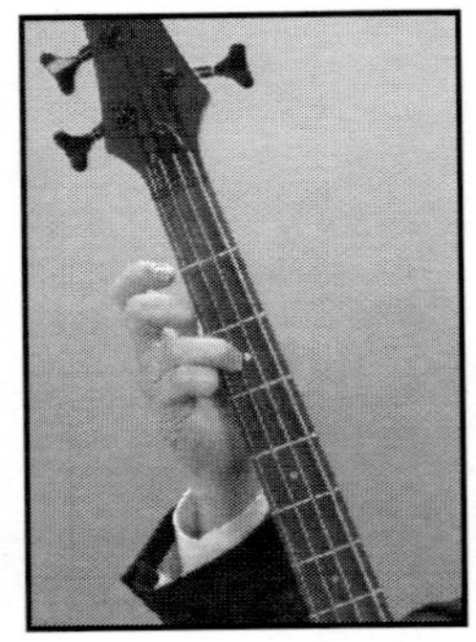

♭♭7th – G♭♭ or F

A♭aug

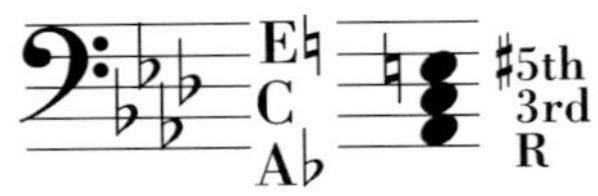

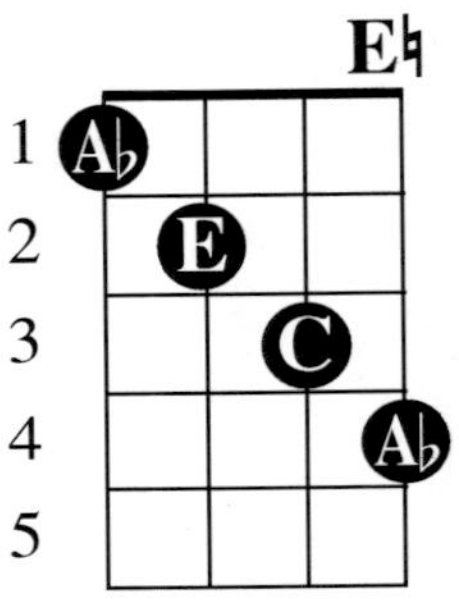

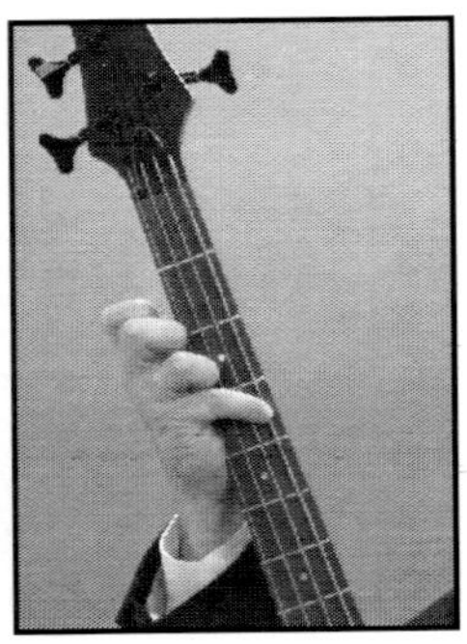

Root – A♭

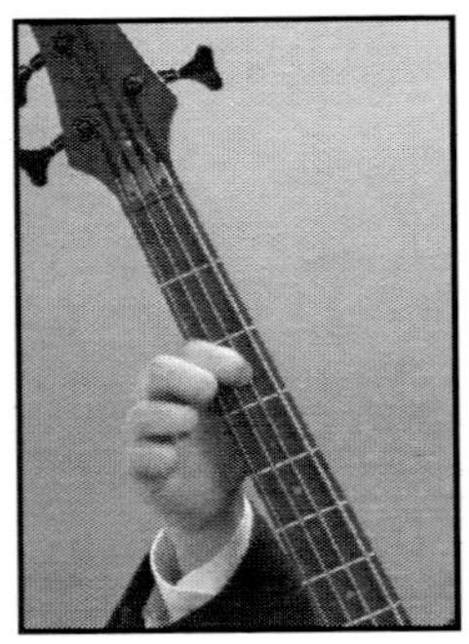

3rd – C

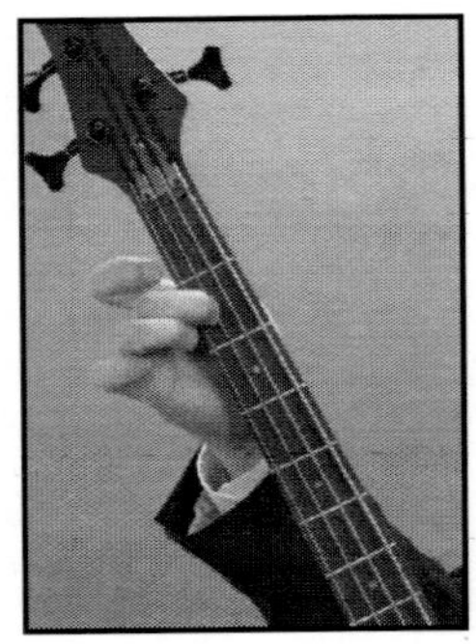

♯5th – E♮

A♭6

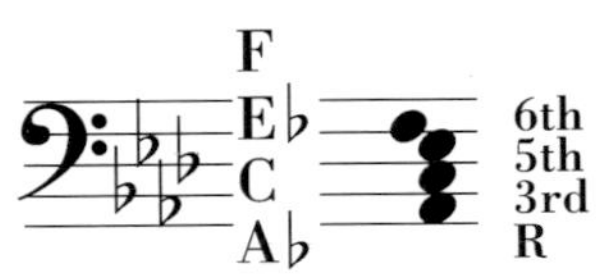

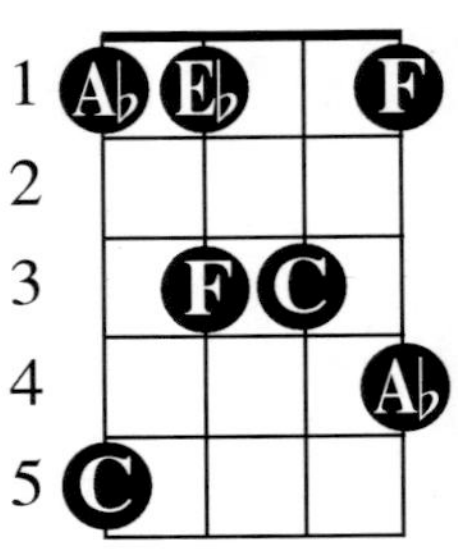

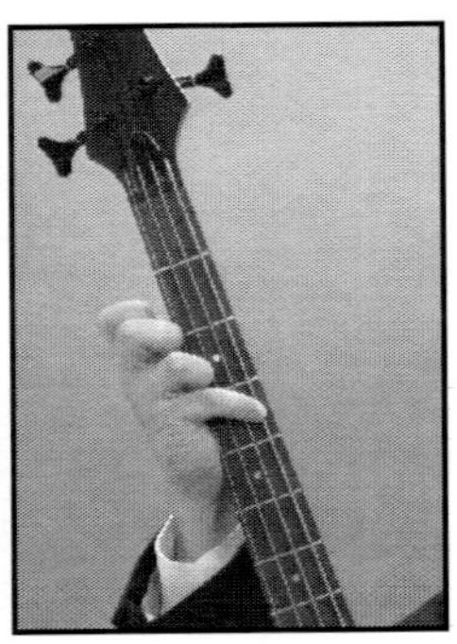

Root – A♭

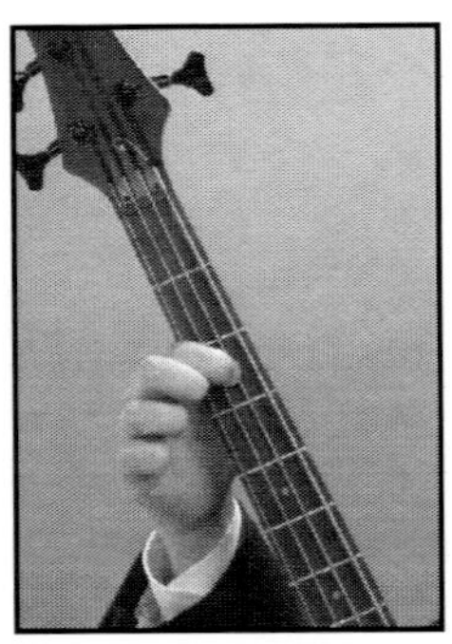

3rd – C

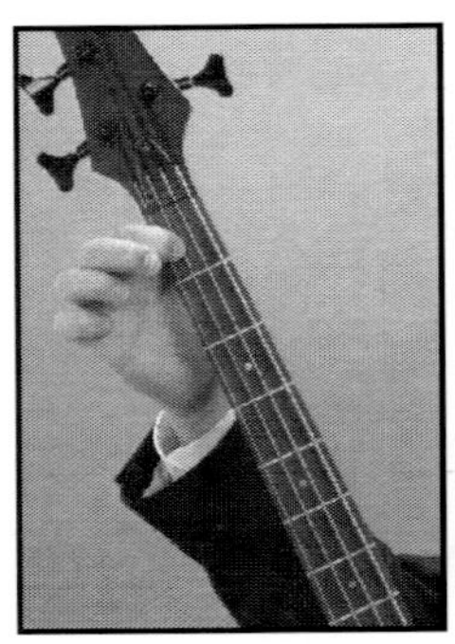

5th – E♭

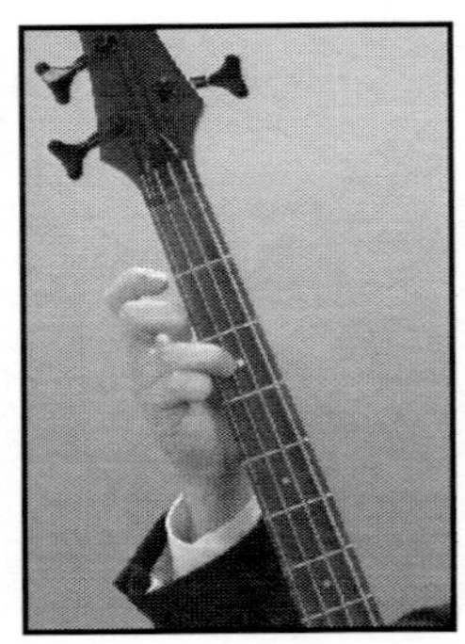

6th – F

Key of A♭ (cont.)

A♭m6

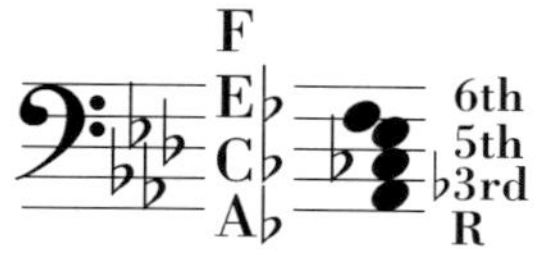

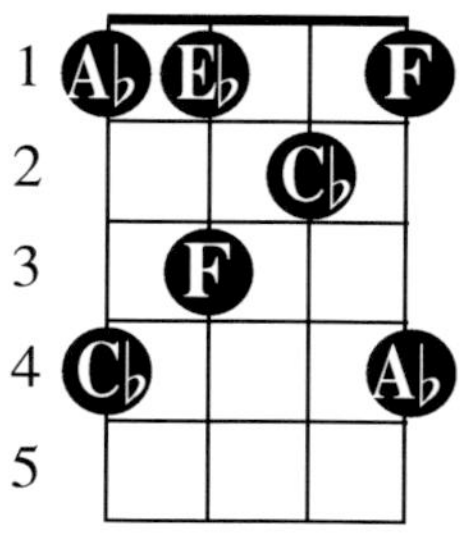

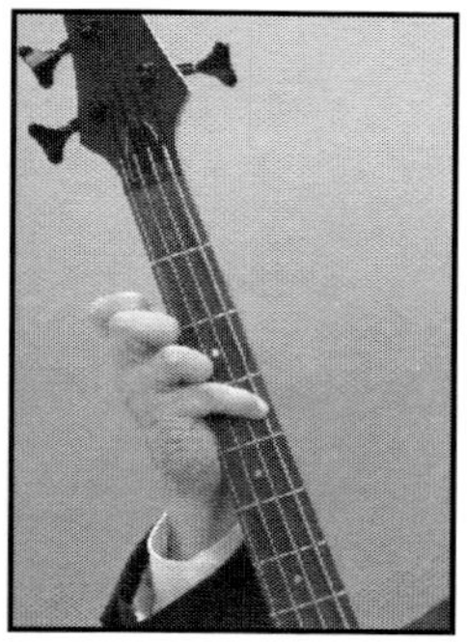
Root – A♭

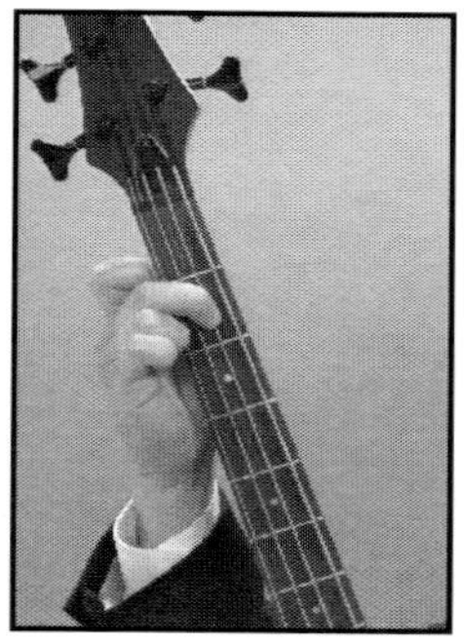
♭3rd – C♭ or B

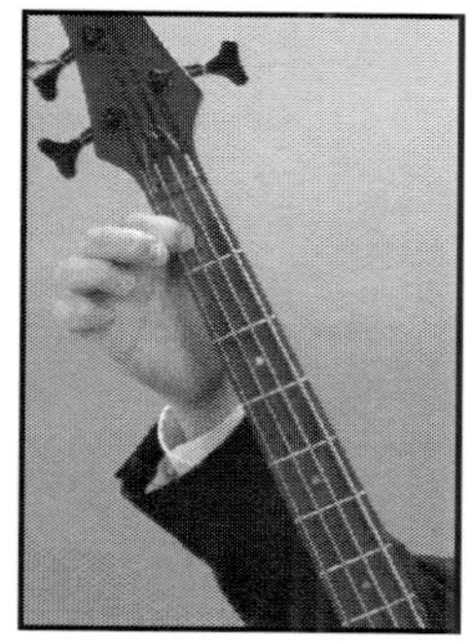
5th – E♭

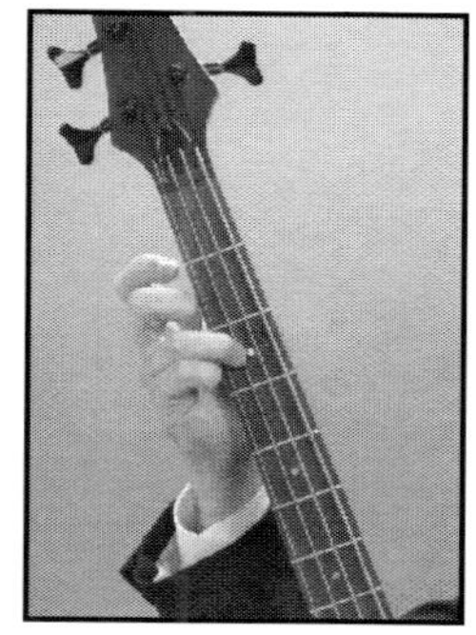
6th – F

A♭7♯5

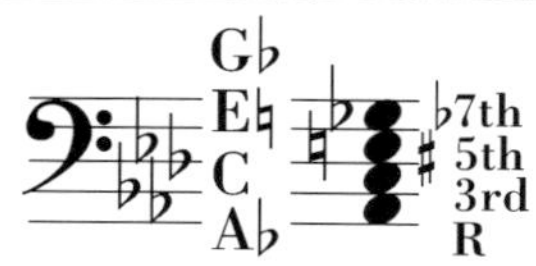

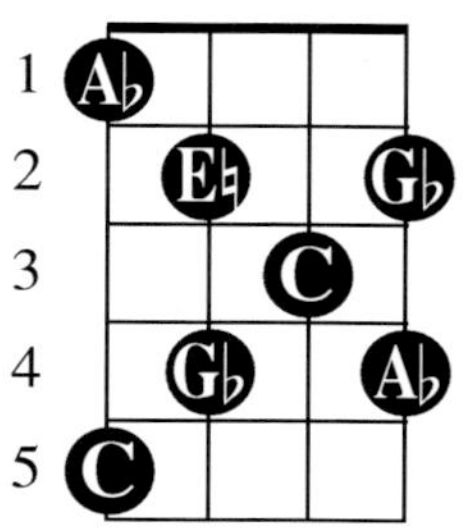

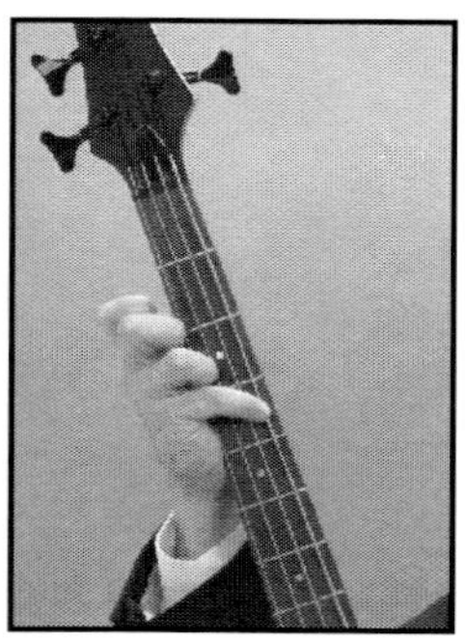
Root – A♭

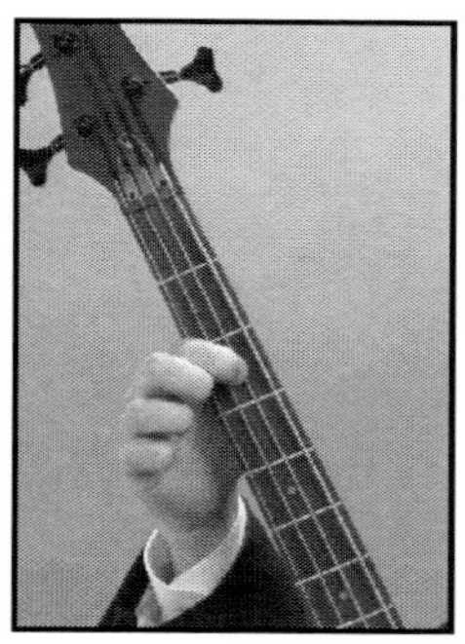
3rd – C

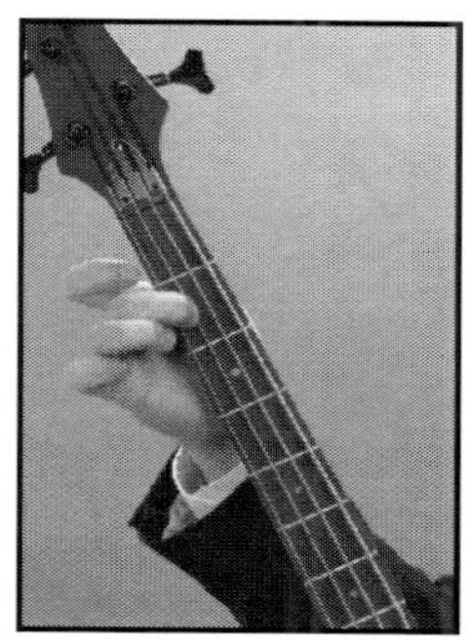
♯5th – E♮

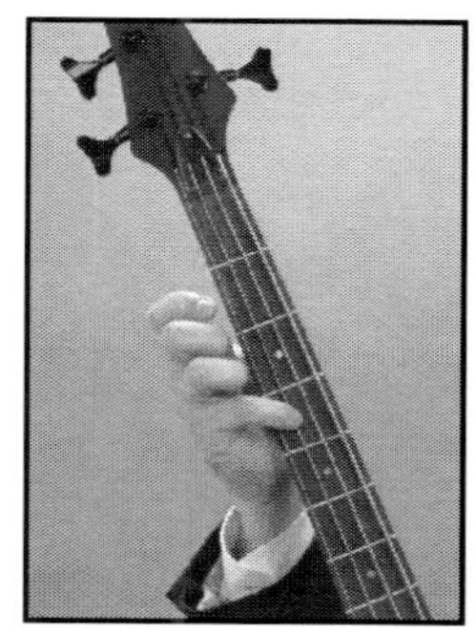
♭7th – G♭

A♭7♭5

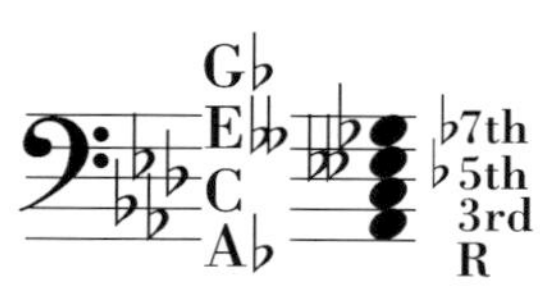

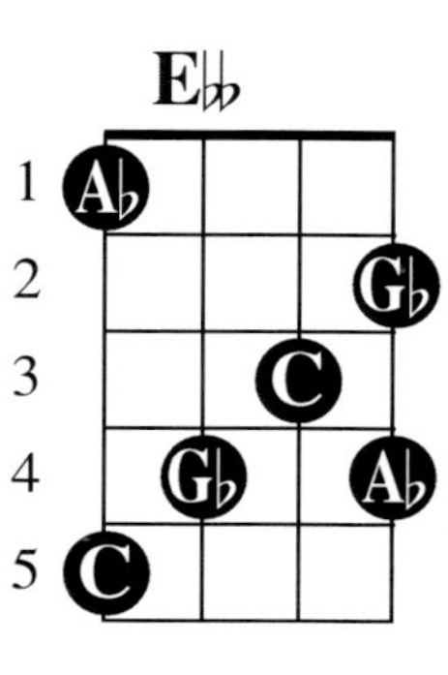

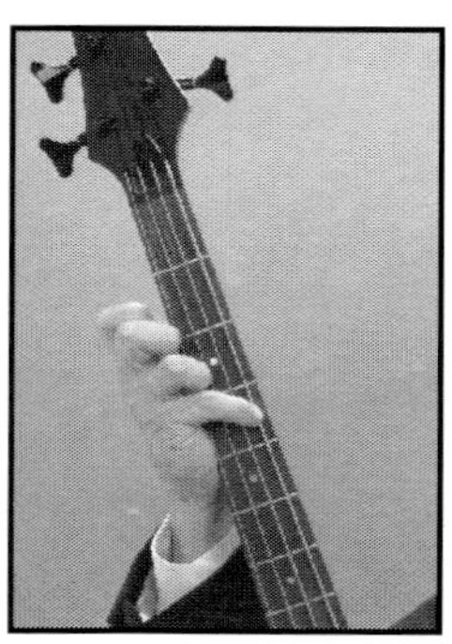
Root – A♭

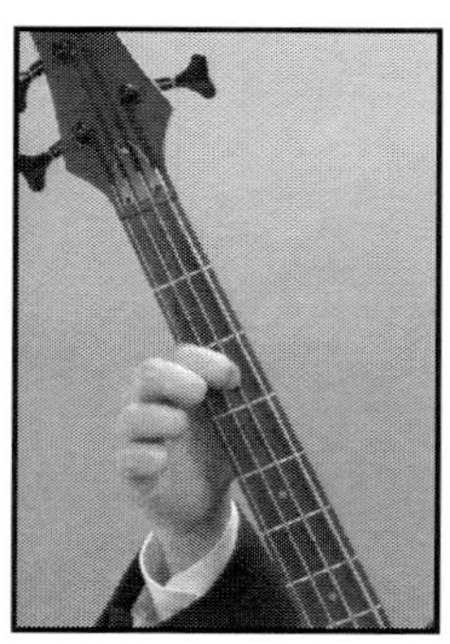
3rd – C

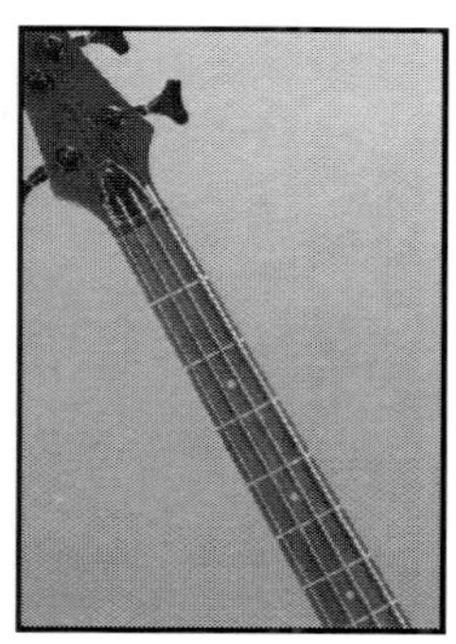
♭5th – E𝄫 or D

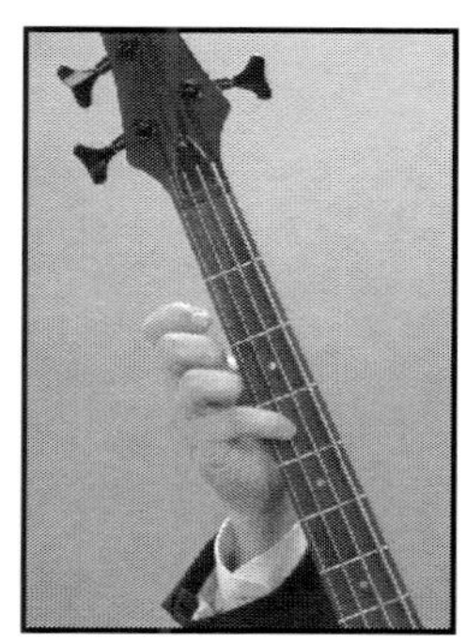
♭7th – G♭

Key of A

AMaj

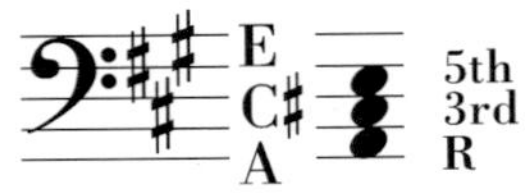

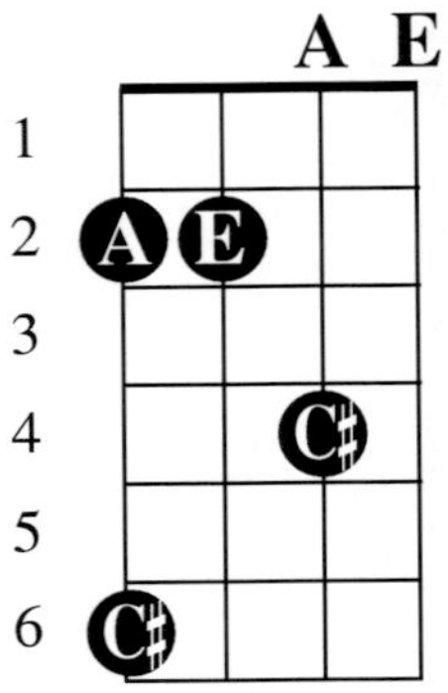

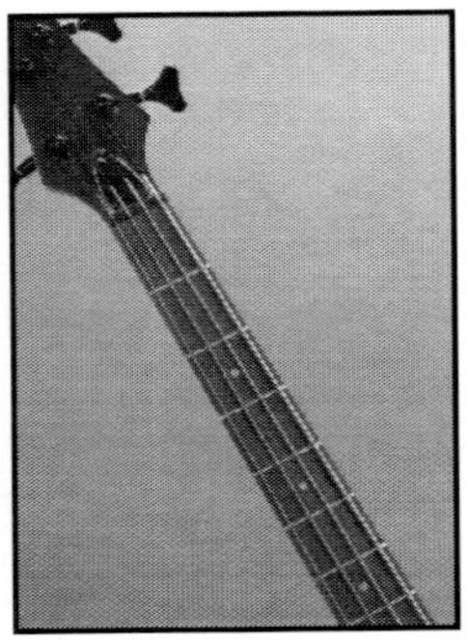

Root – A

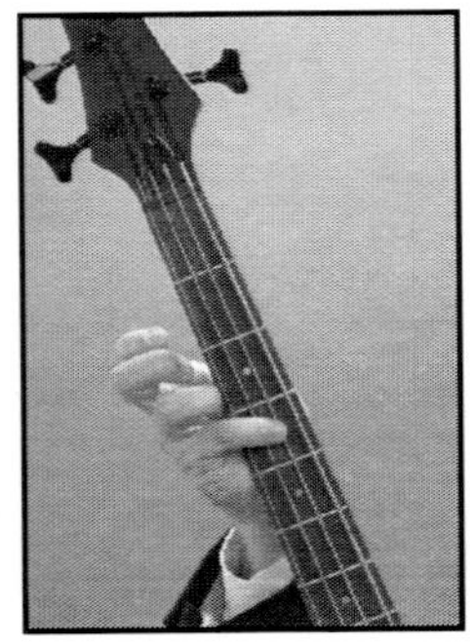

3rd – C♯

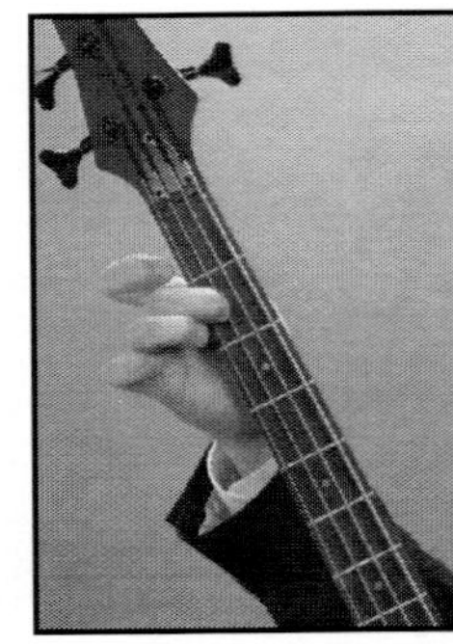

5th – E

Amin

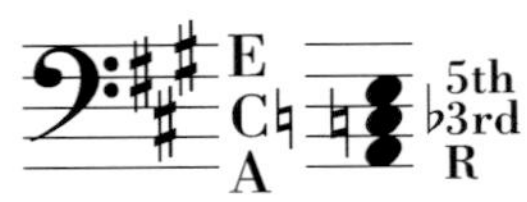

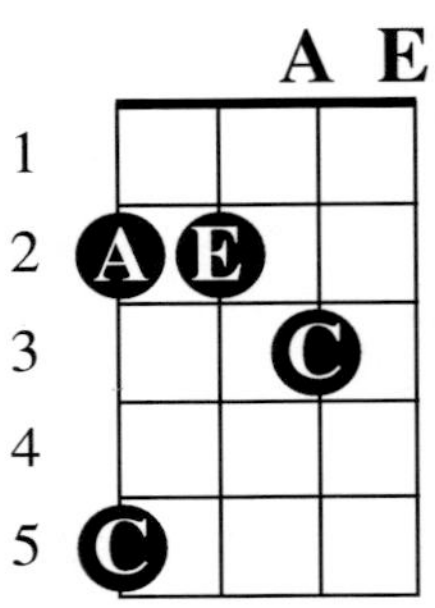

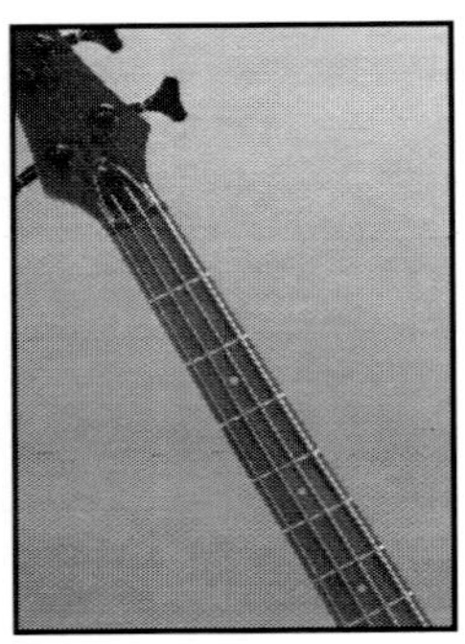

Root – A

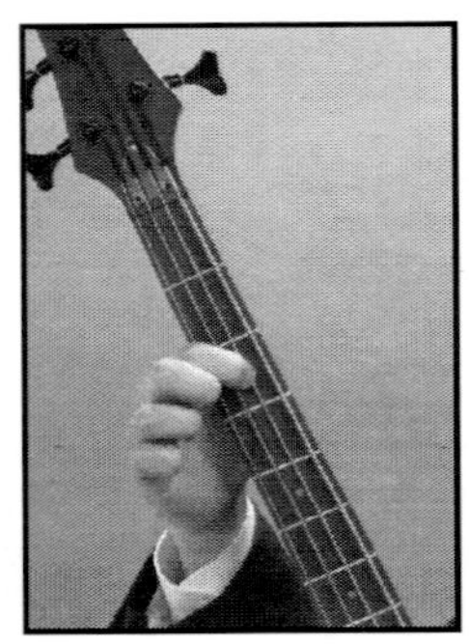

♭3rd – C♮

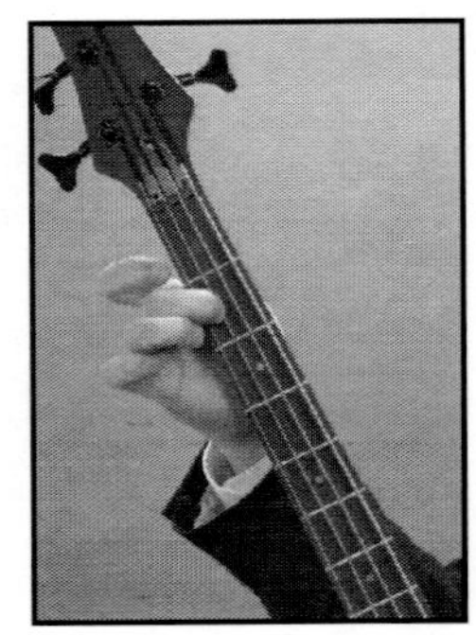

5th – E

A7

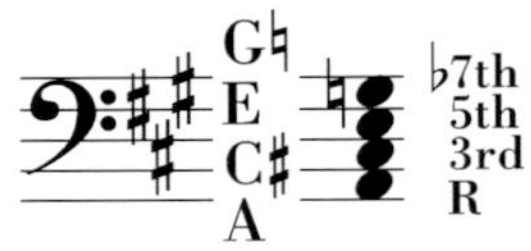

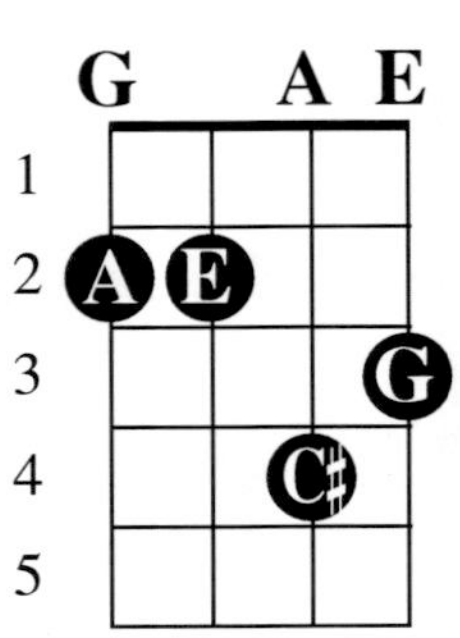

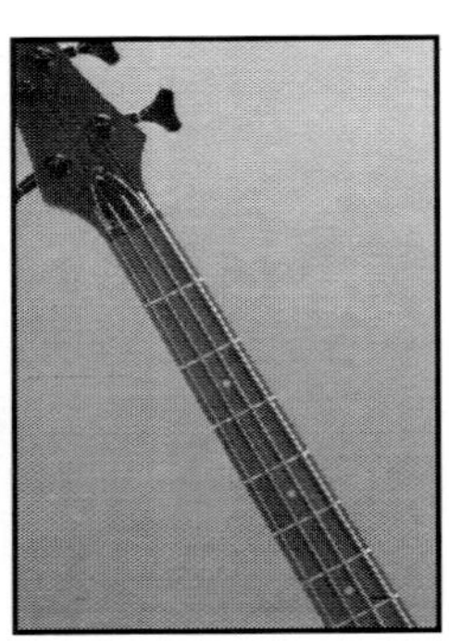

Root – A

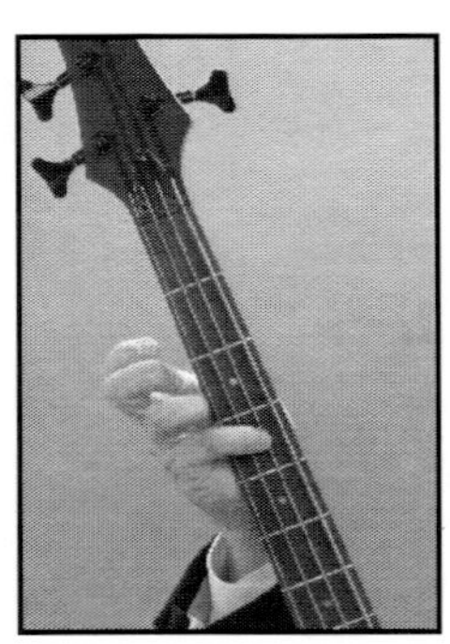

3rd – C♯

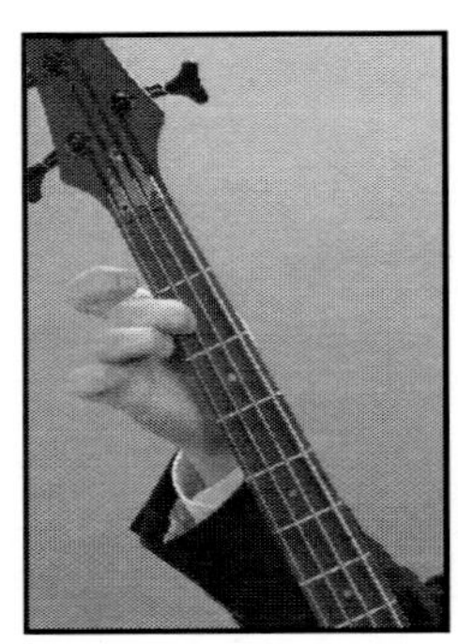

5th – E

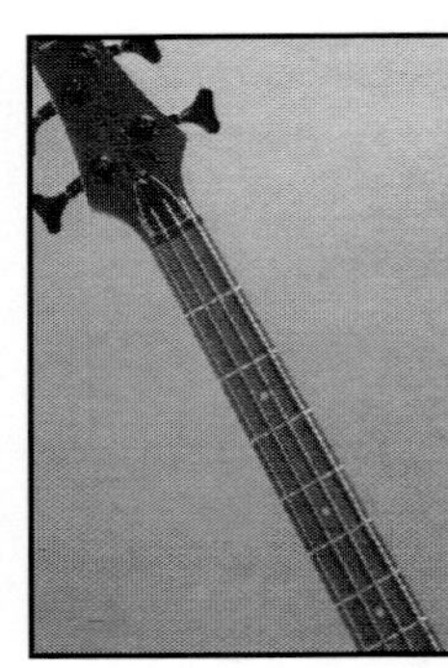

♭7th – G♮

Key of A (cont.)

A7sus

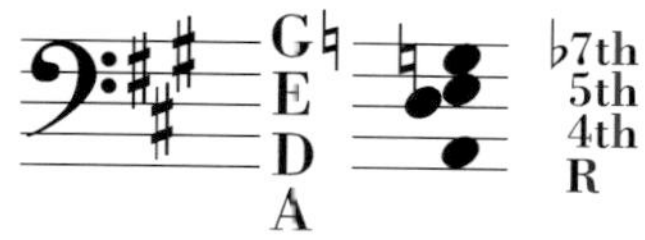

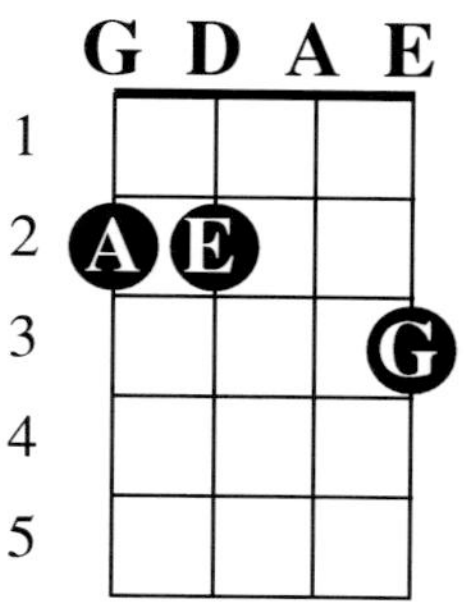

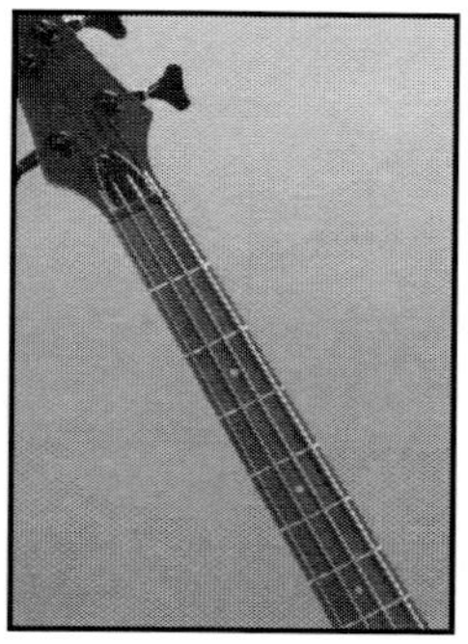

Root – A

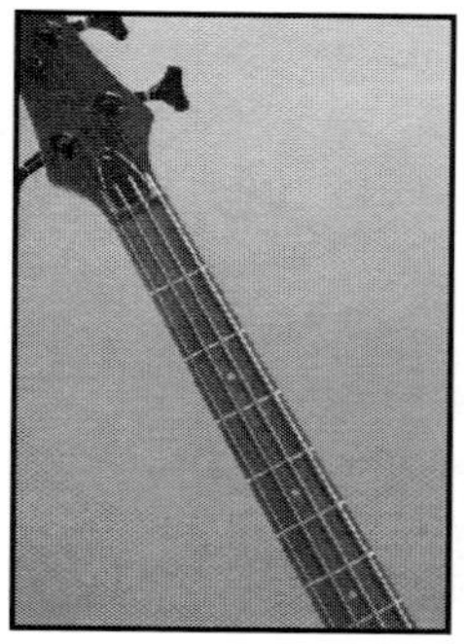

4th – D

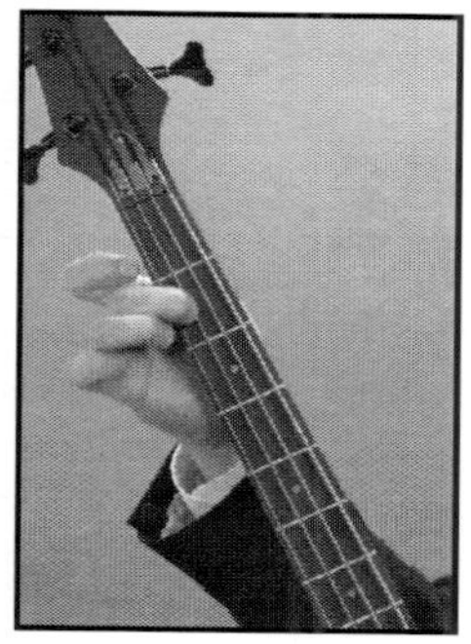

5th – E

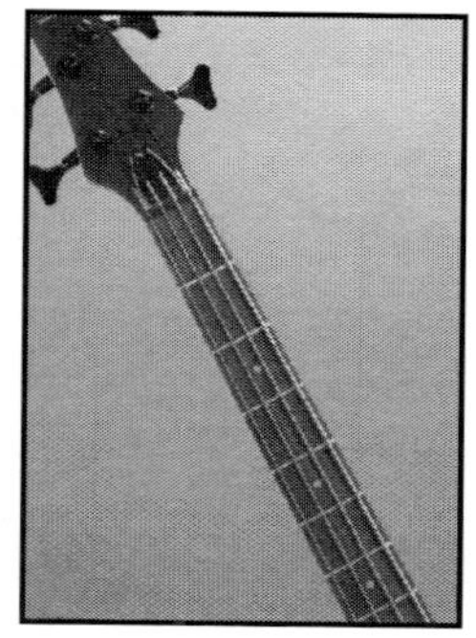

♭7th – G♮

Am7

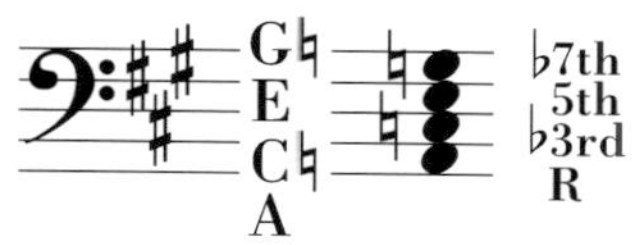

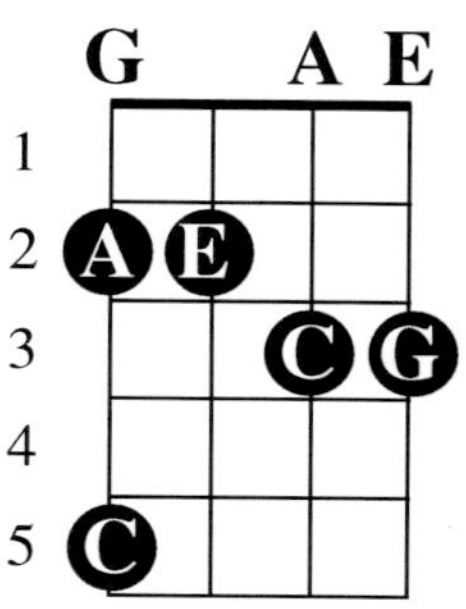

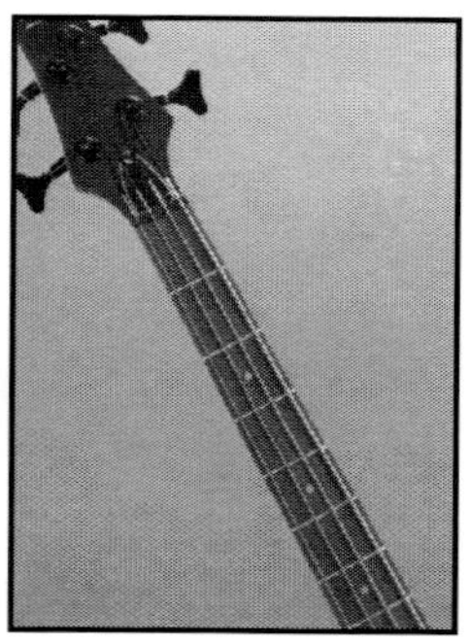

Root – A

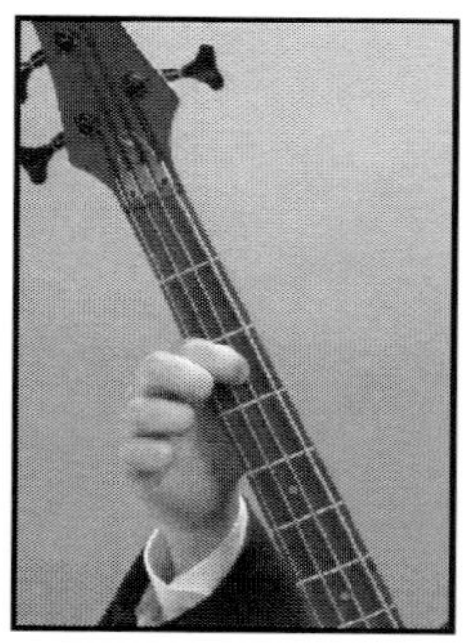

♭3rd – C♮

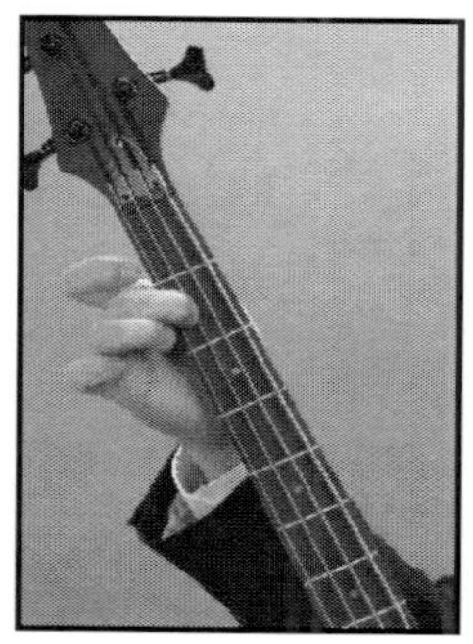

5th – E

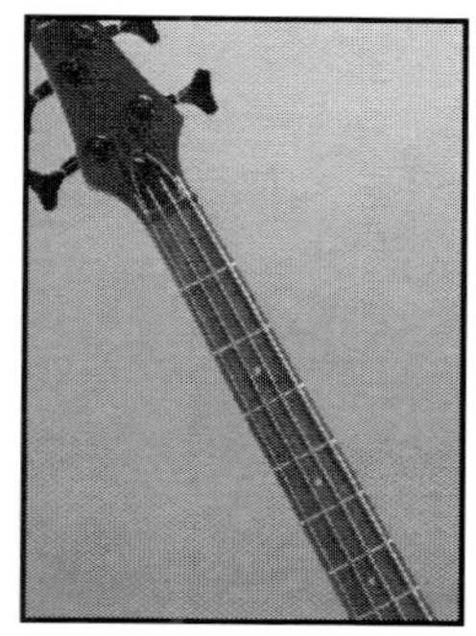

♭7th – G♮

AMa7

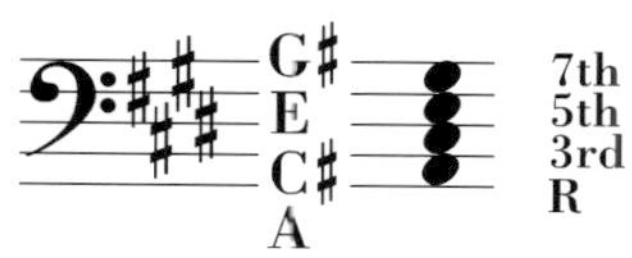

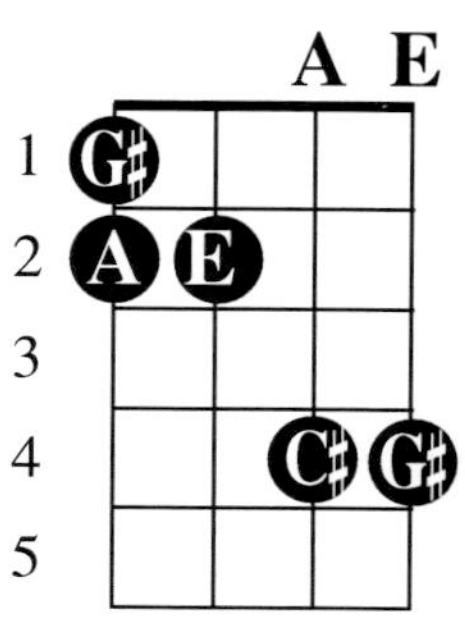

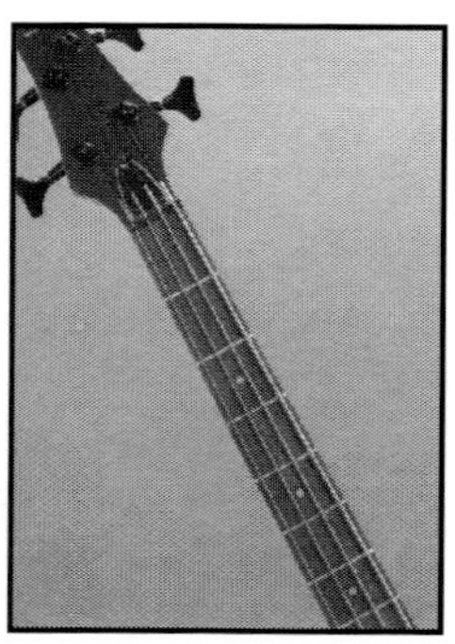

Root – A

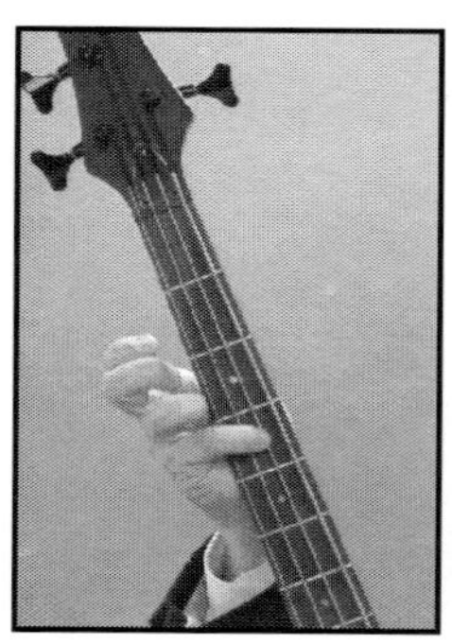

3rd – C♯

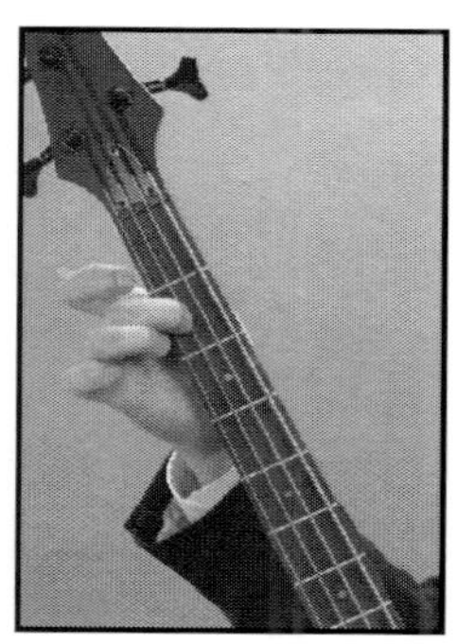

5th – E

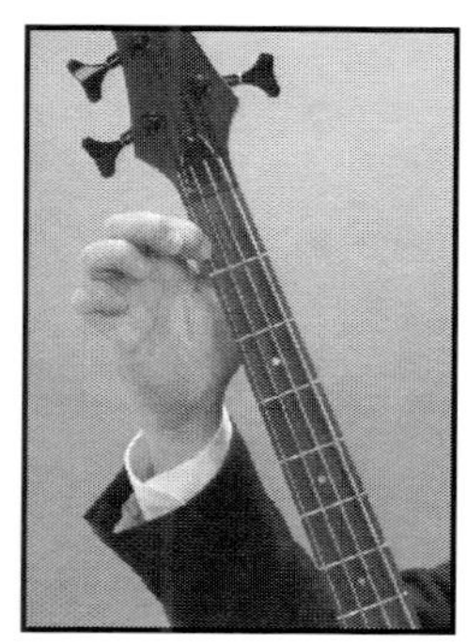

7th – G♯

Key of A (cont.)

Adim

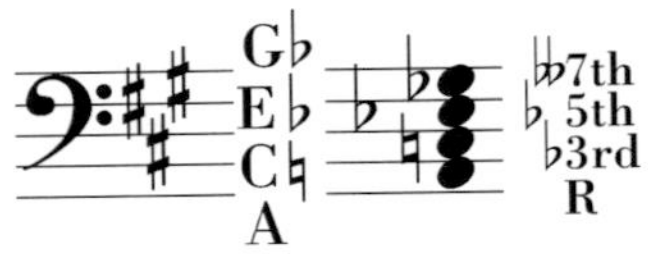

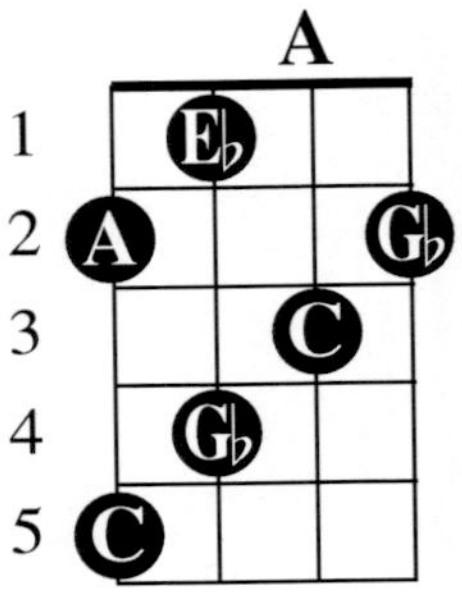

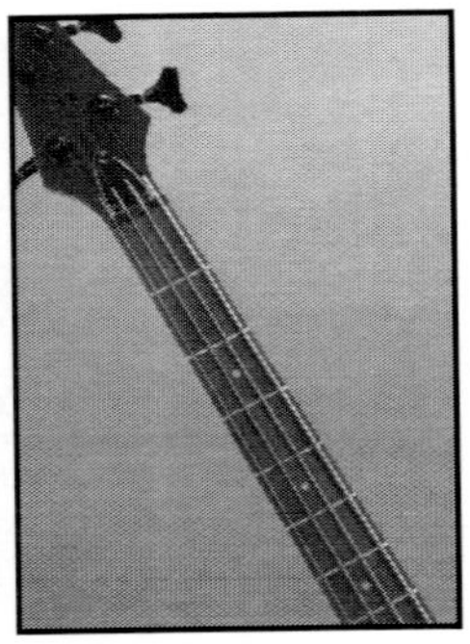

Root – A

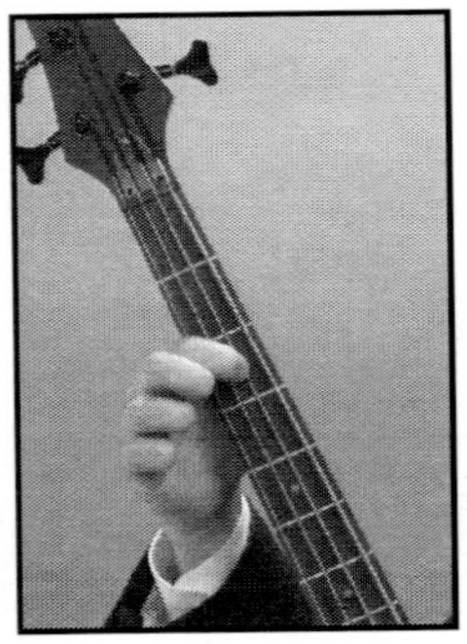

♭3rd – C♮

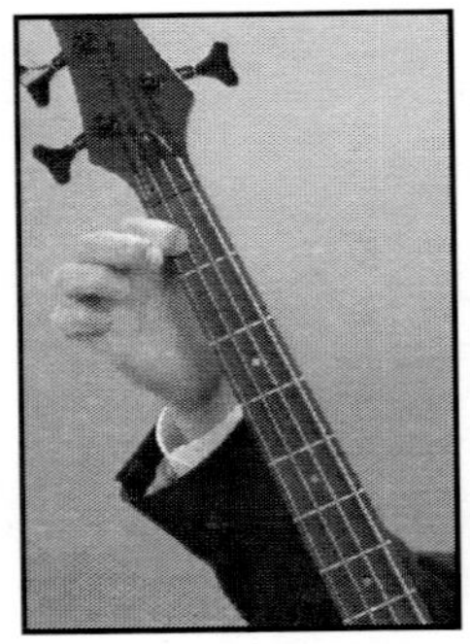

♭5th – E♭

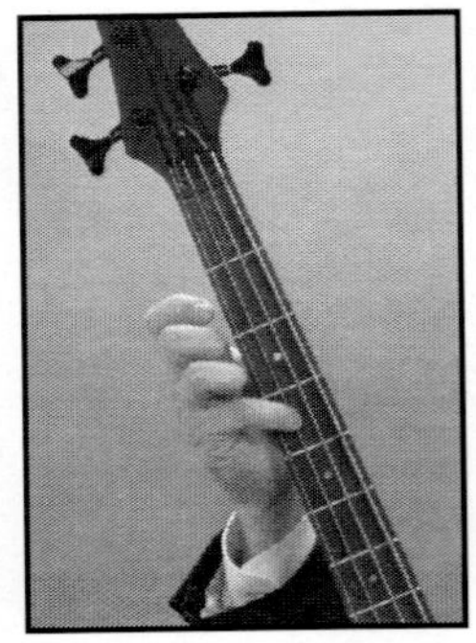

♭♭7th – G♭

Aaug

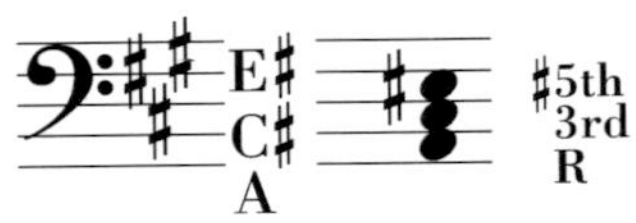

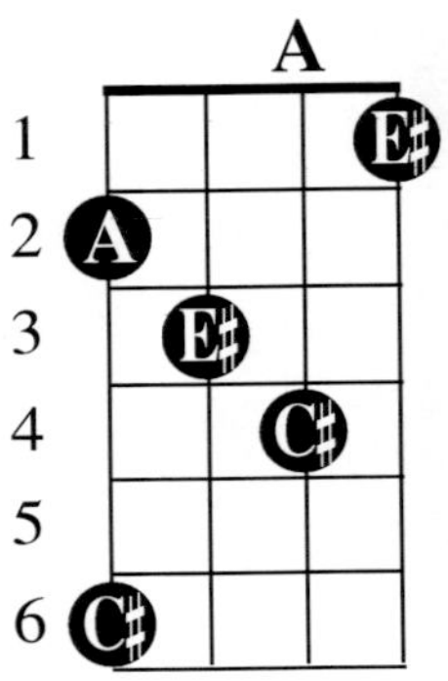

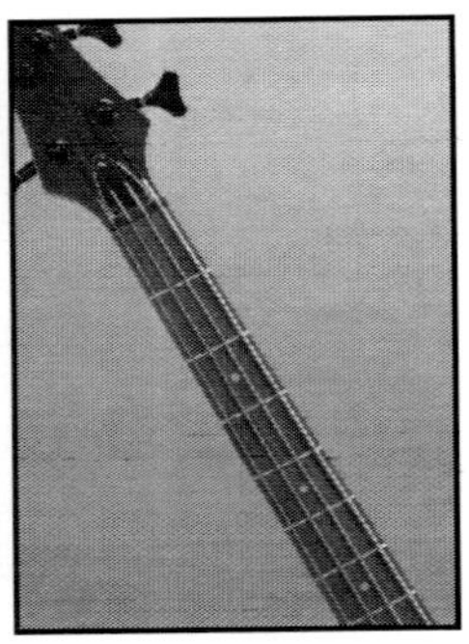

Root – A

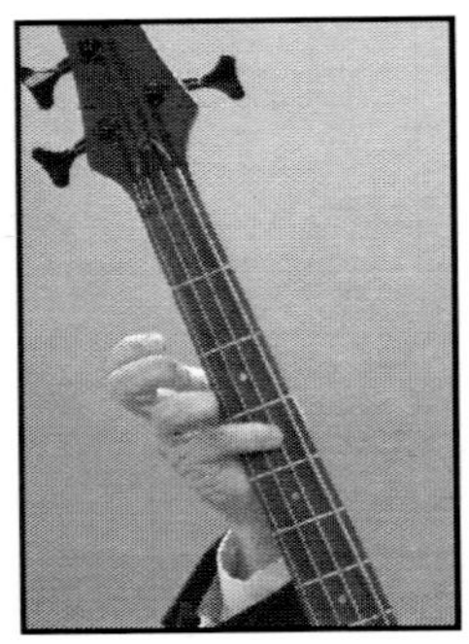

3rd – C♯

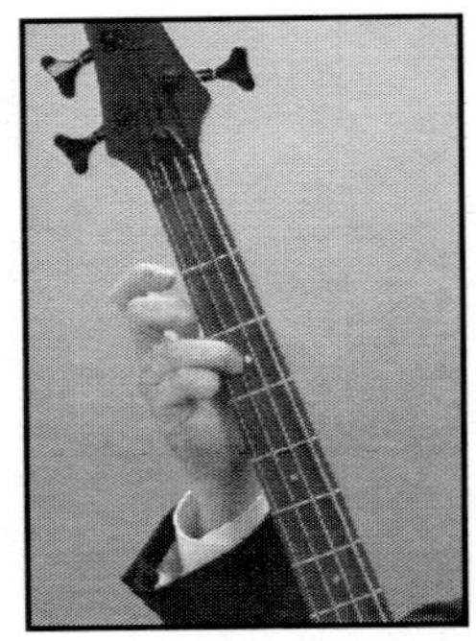

♯5th – E♯

A6

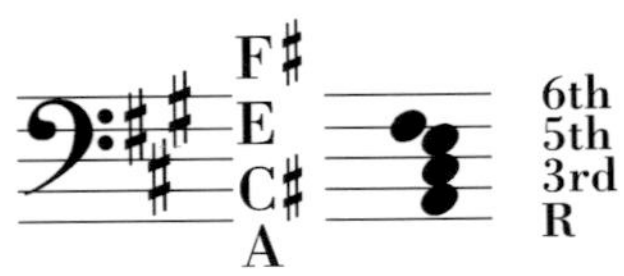

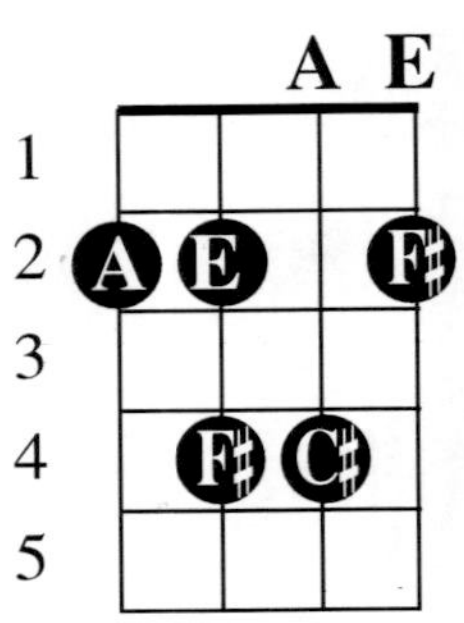

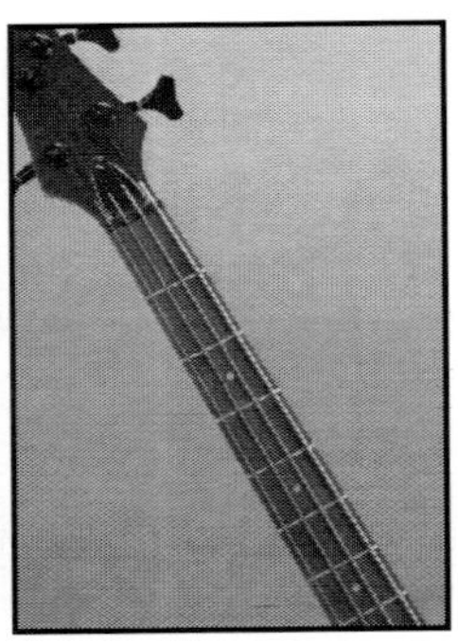

Root – A

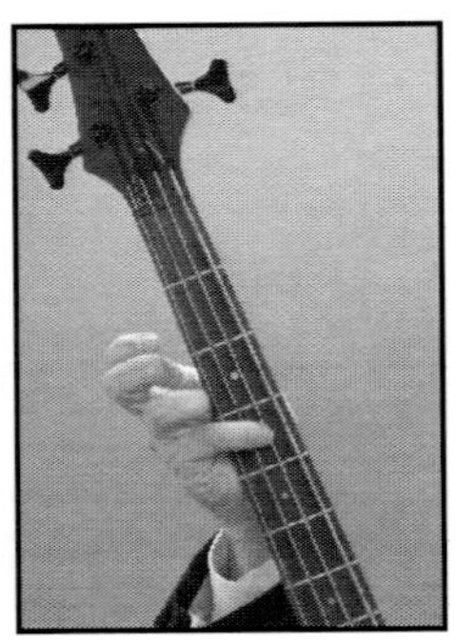

3rd – C♯

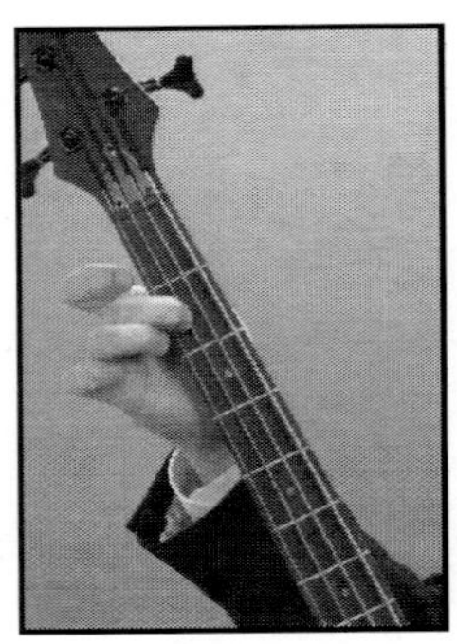

5th – E

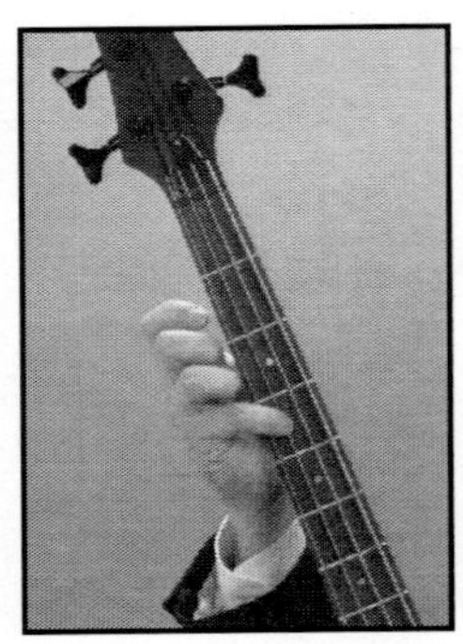

6th – F♯

Key of A (cont.)

Am6

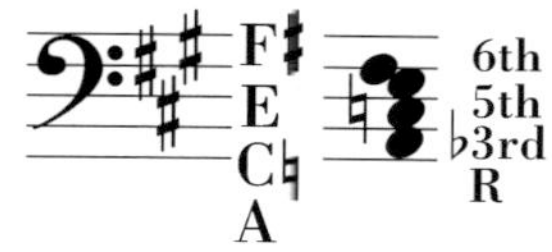

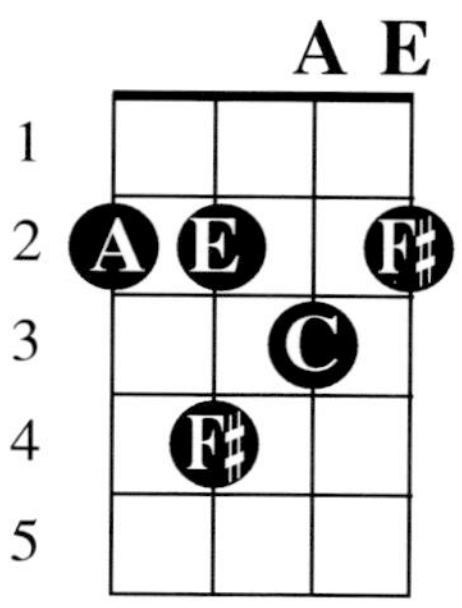

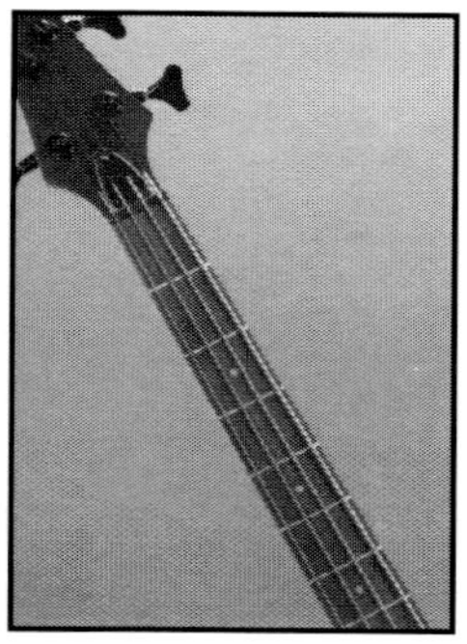

Root – A

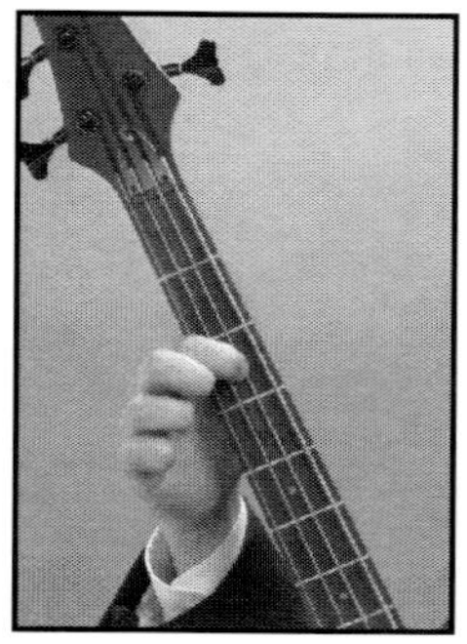

♭3rd – C♮

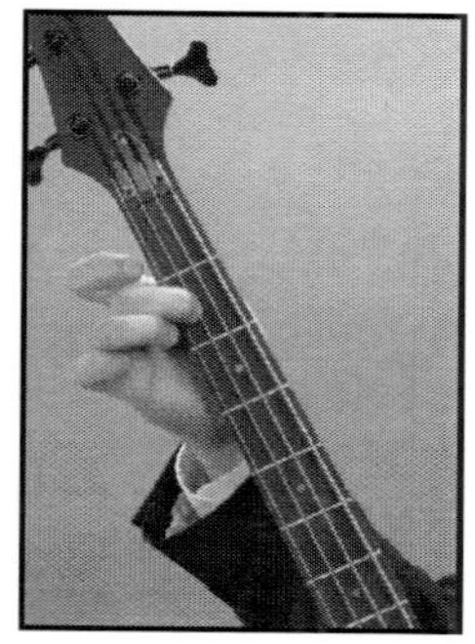

5th – E

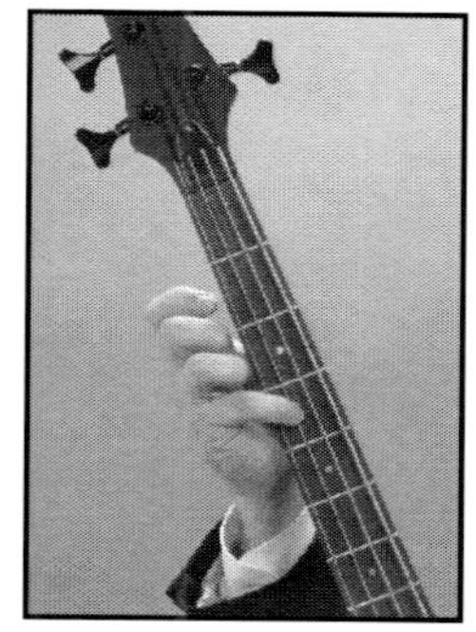

6th – F♯

A7♯5

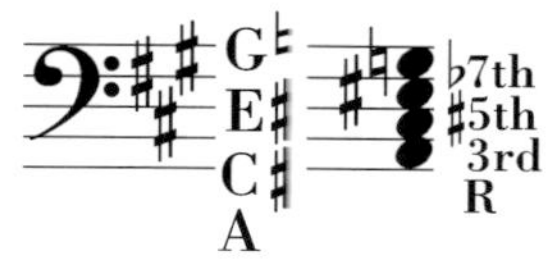

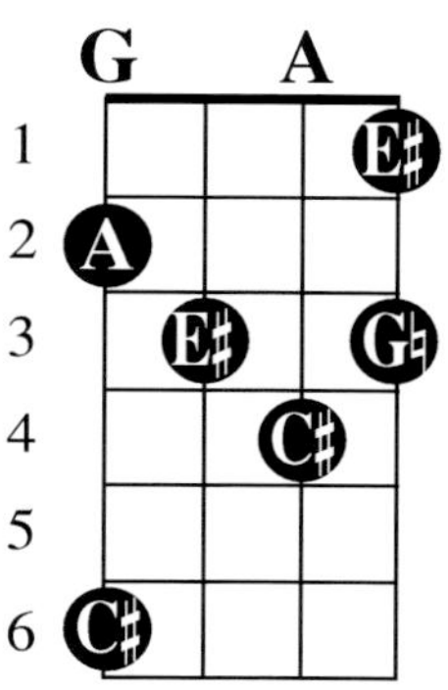

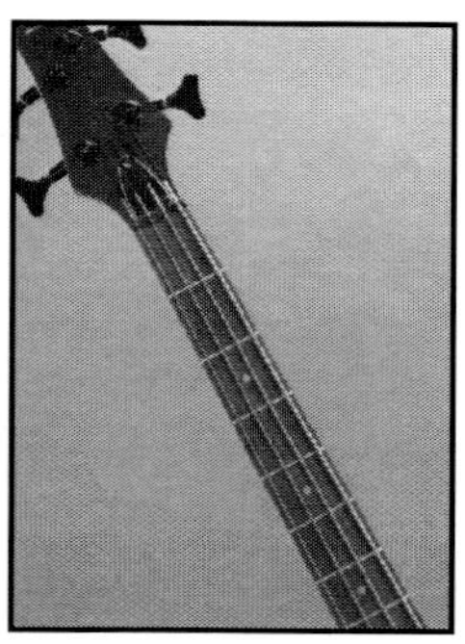

Root – A

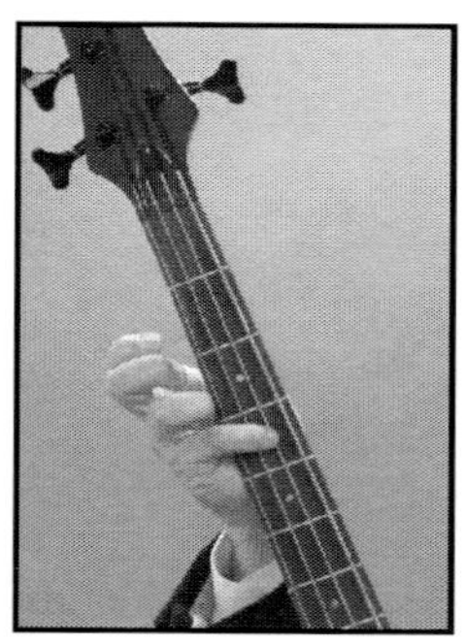

3rd – C♯

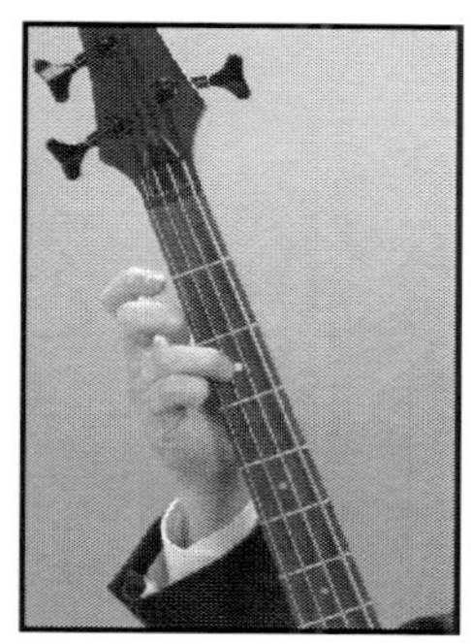

♯5th – E♯ or F

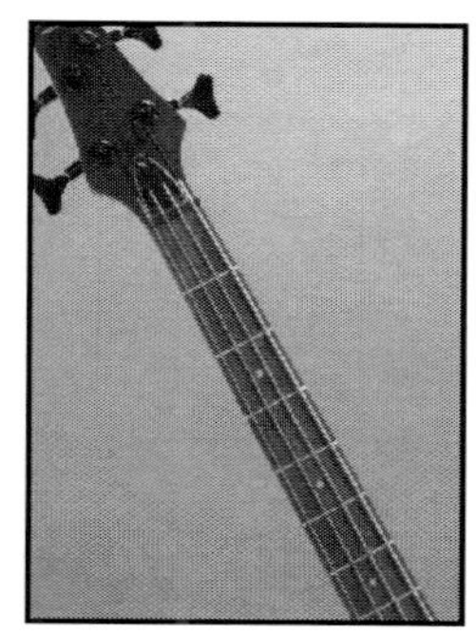

♭7th – G♮

A7♭5

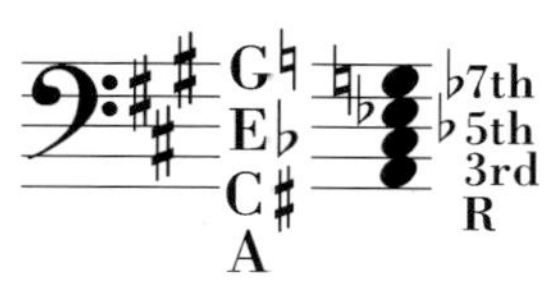

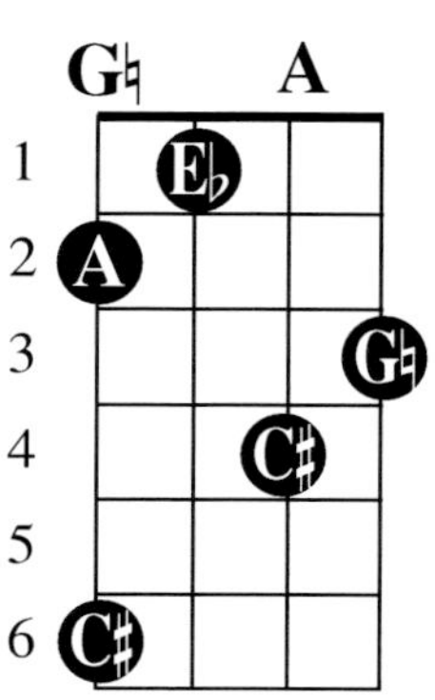

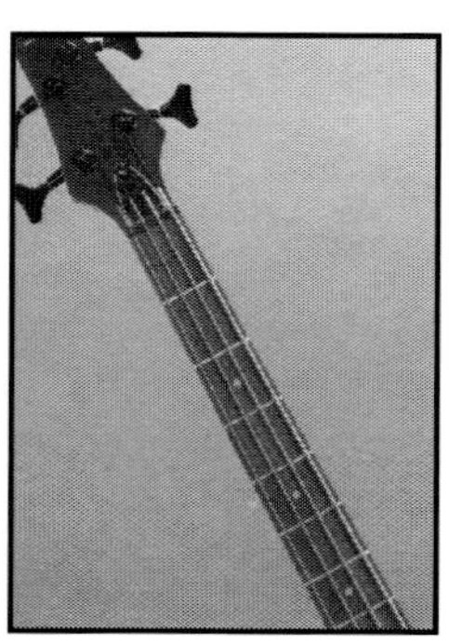

Root – A

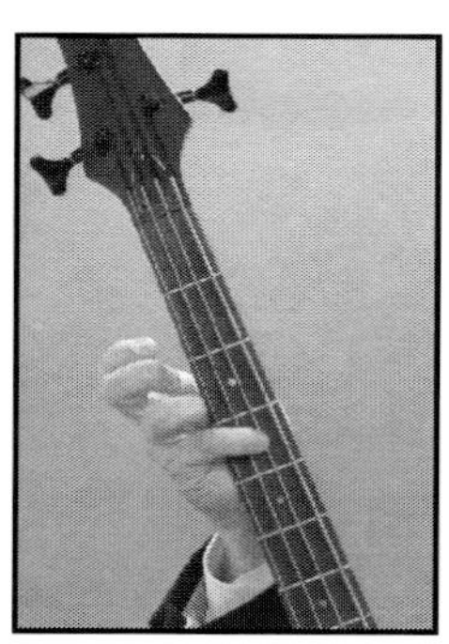

3rd – C♯

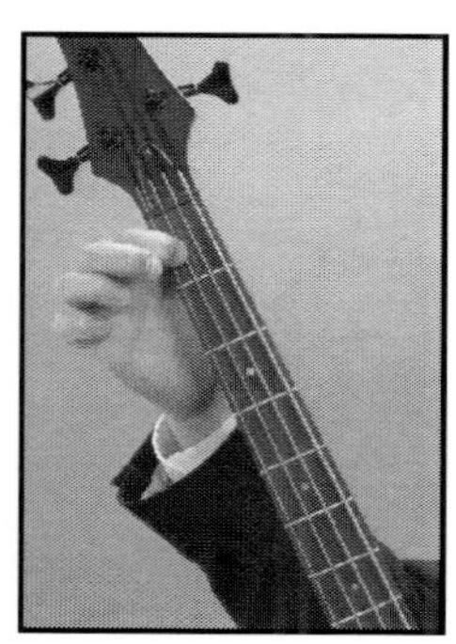

♭5th – E♭

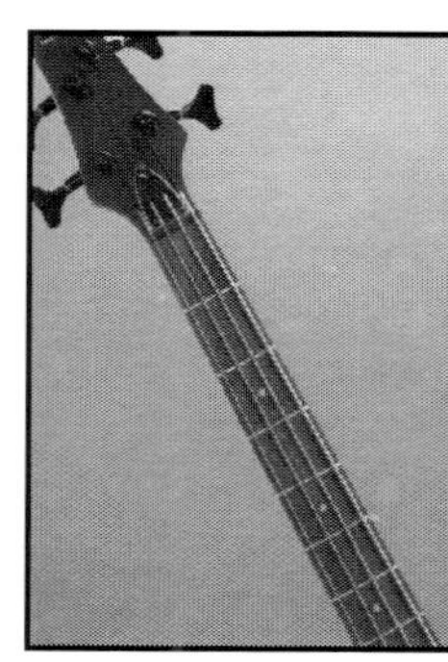

♭7th – G♮

Key of B♭

B♭Major

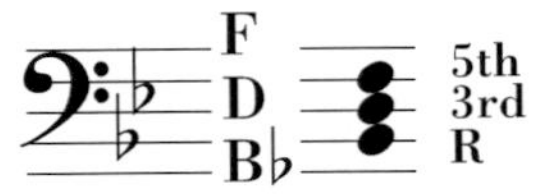

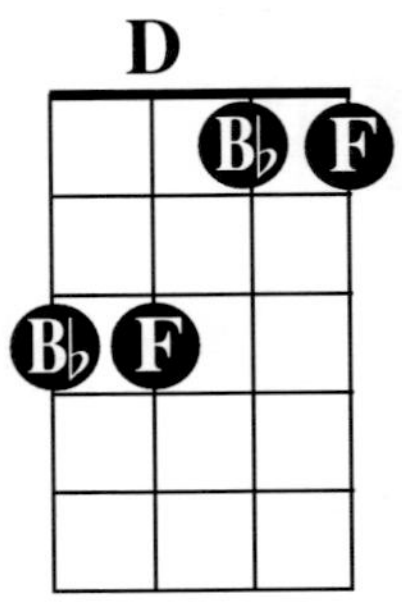

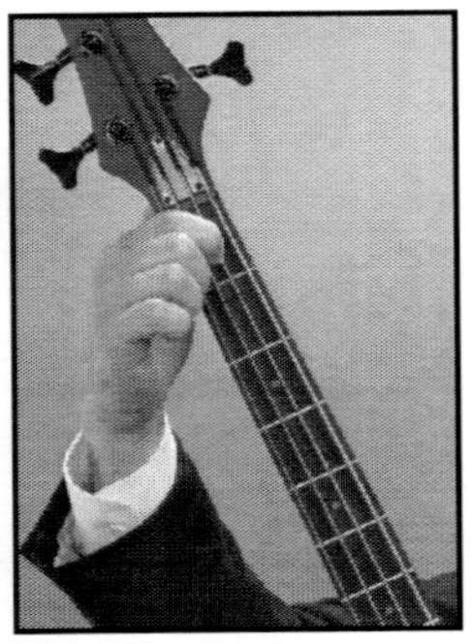

Root – B♭

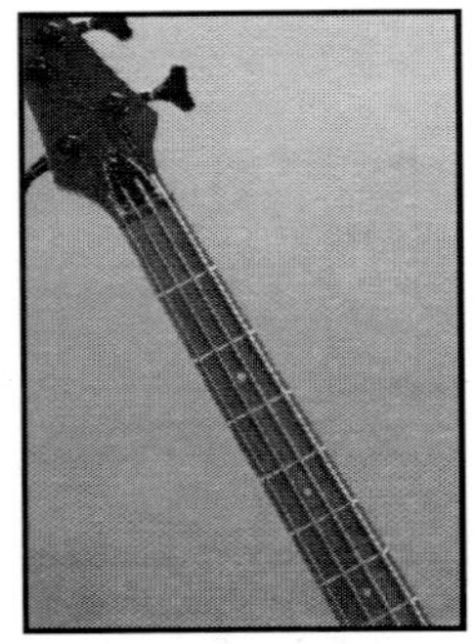

3rd – D

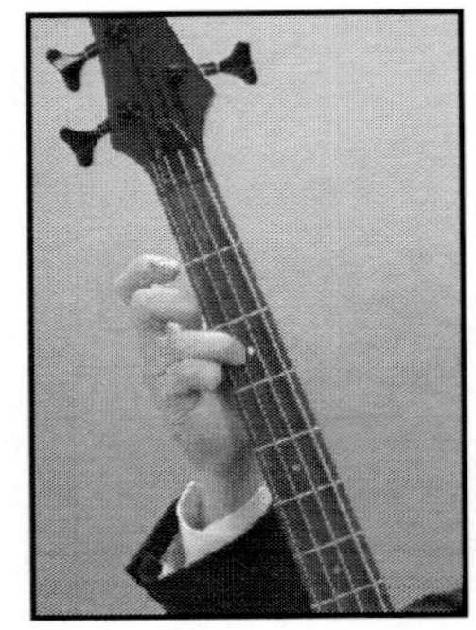

5th – F

B♭minor

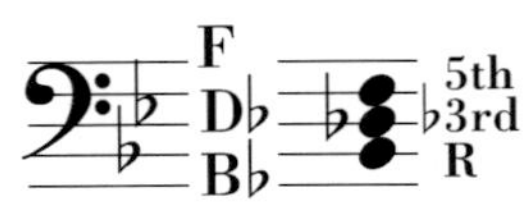

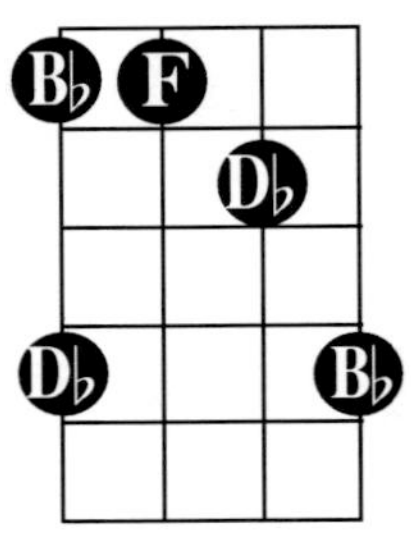

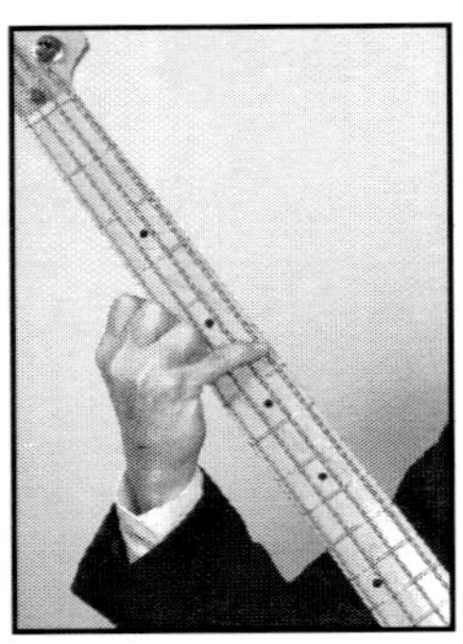

Root – B♭

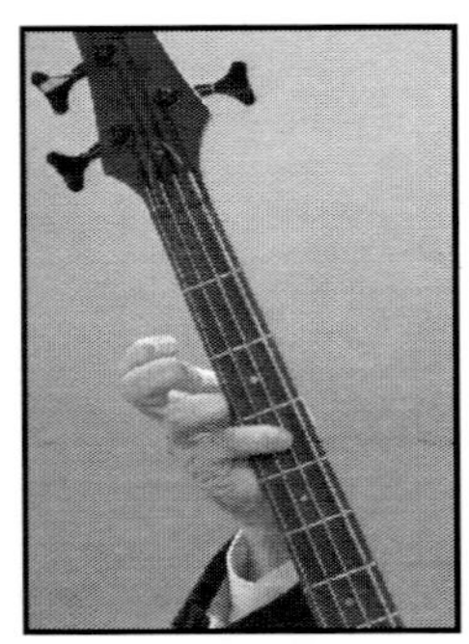

♭3rd – D♭

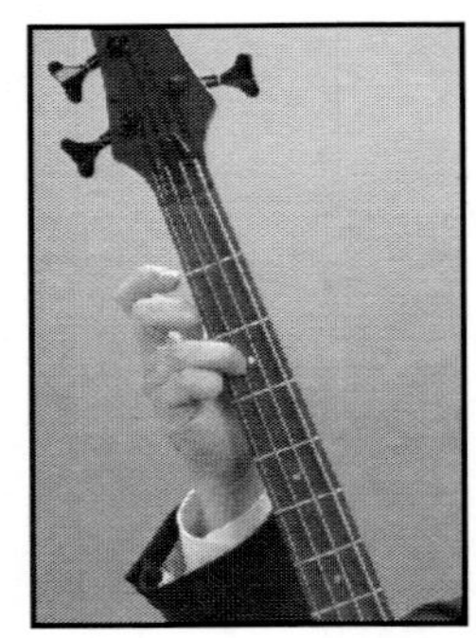

5th – F

B♭7

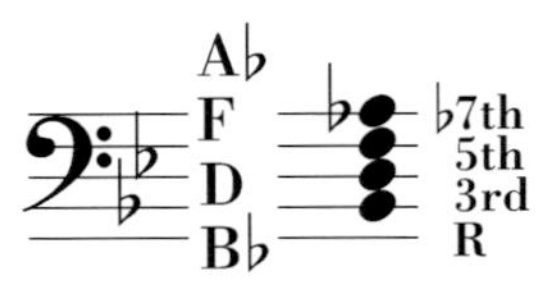

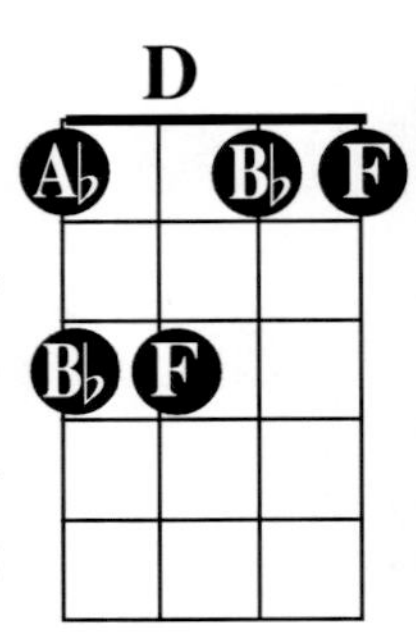

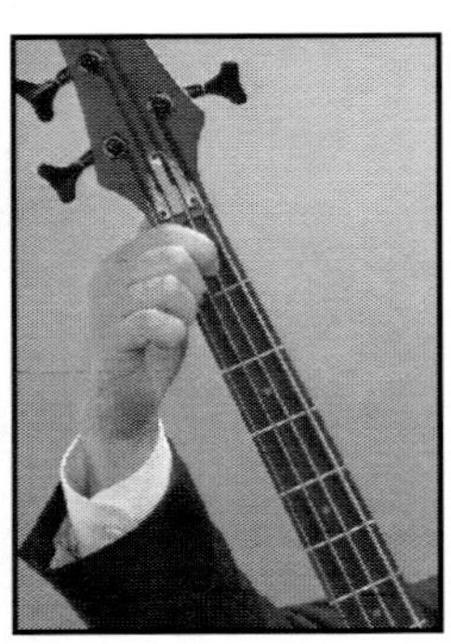

Root – B♭

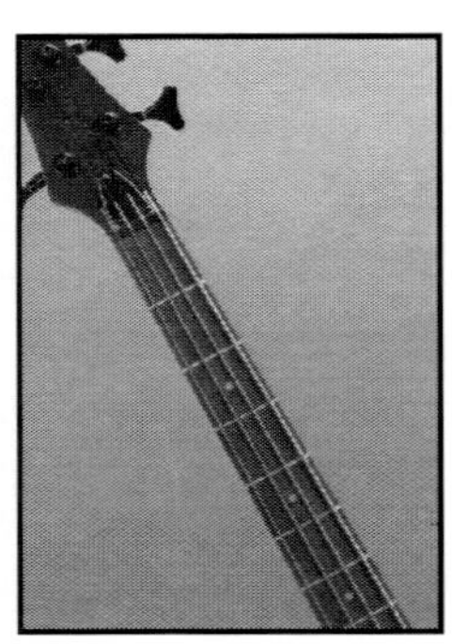

3rd – D

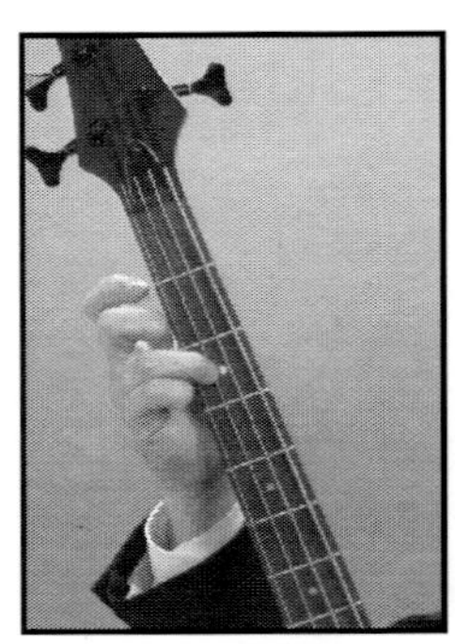

5th – F

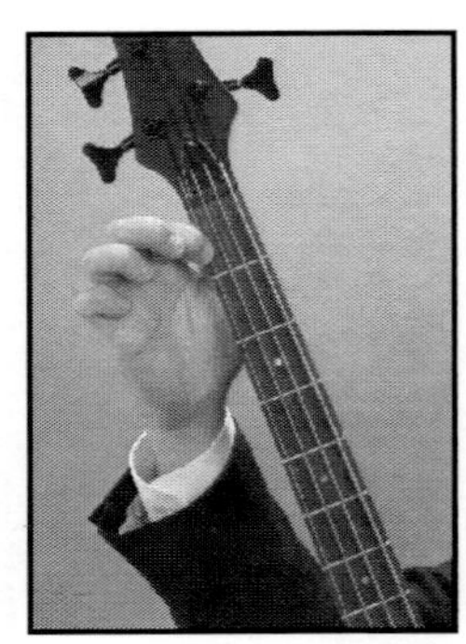

♭7th – A♭

Key of B♭ (cont.)

B♭7sus

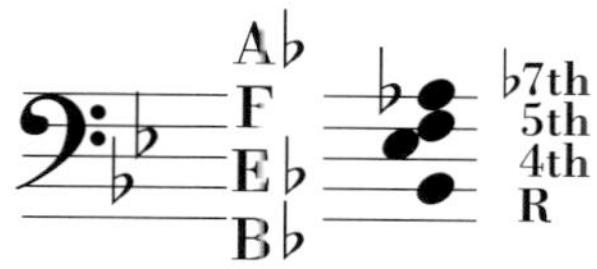

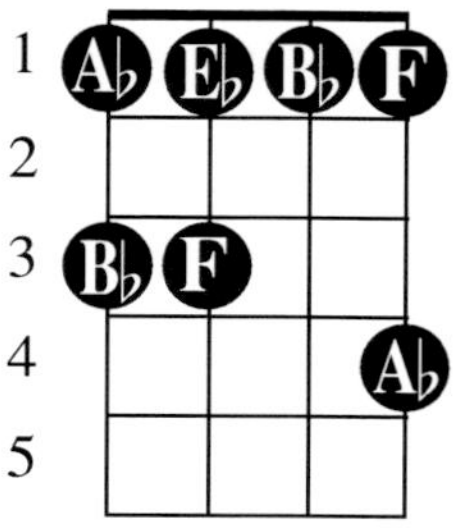

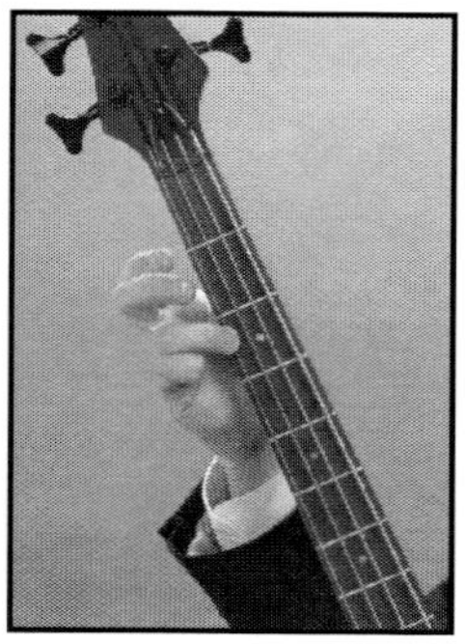

Root – B♭

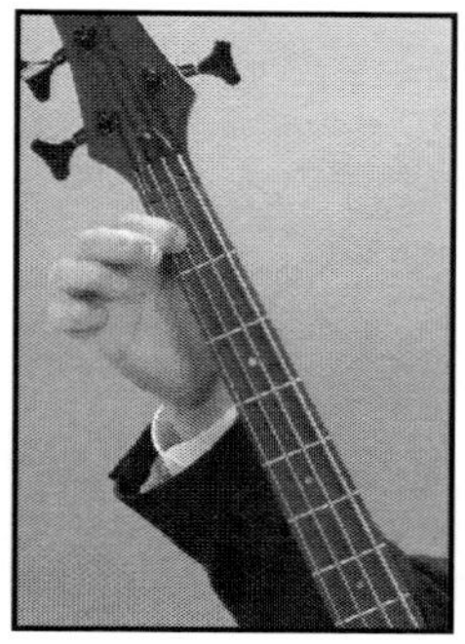

4th – E♭

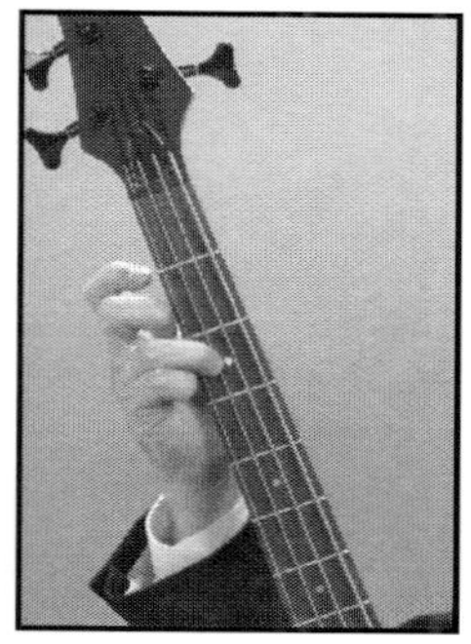

5th – F

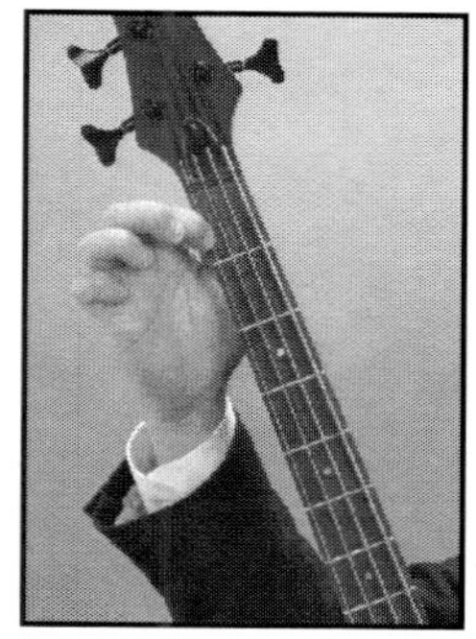

♭7th – A♭

B♭m7

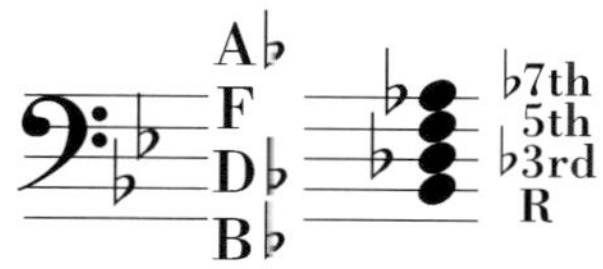

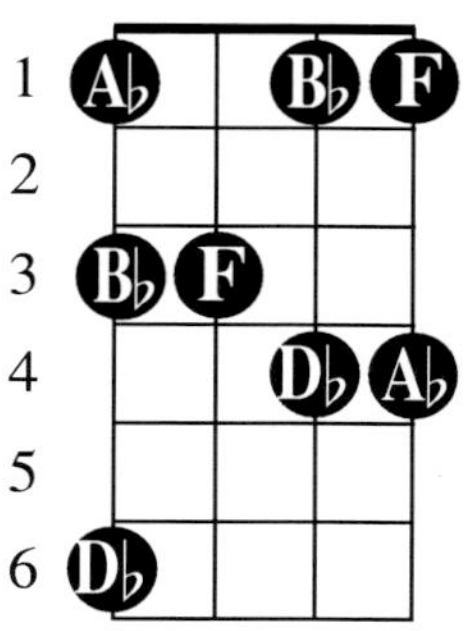

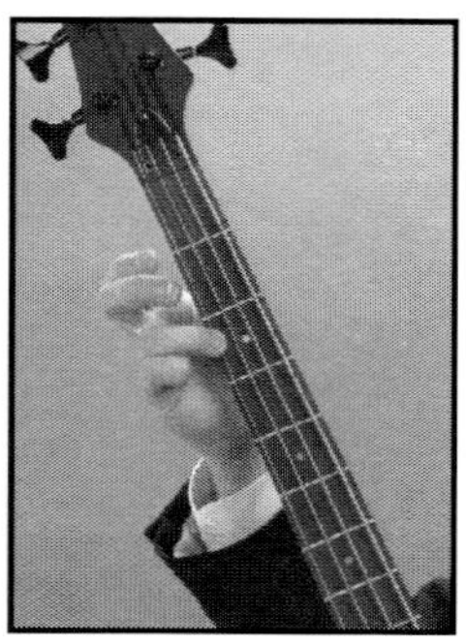

Root – B♭

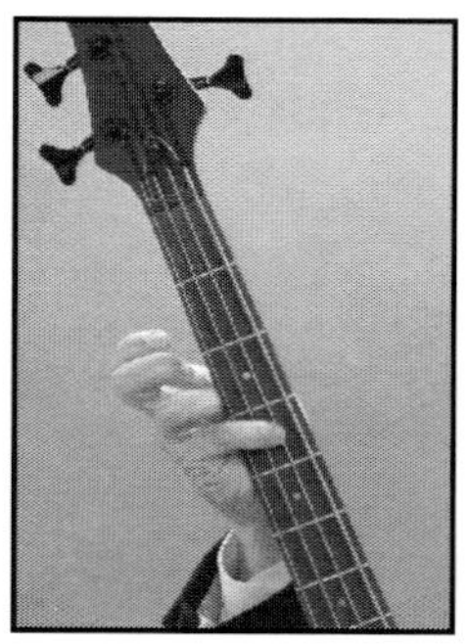

♭3rd – D♭

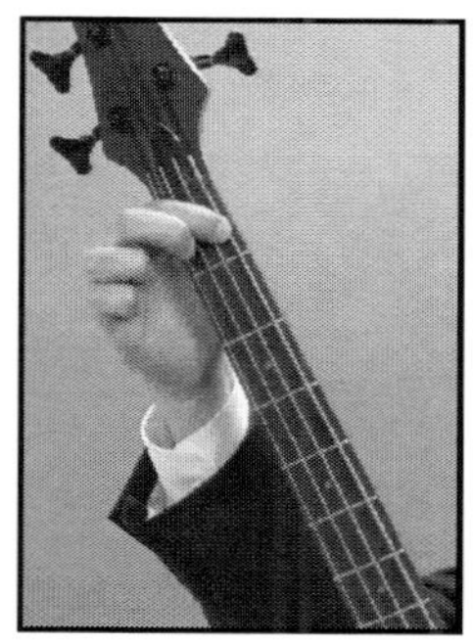

5th – F

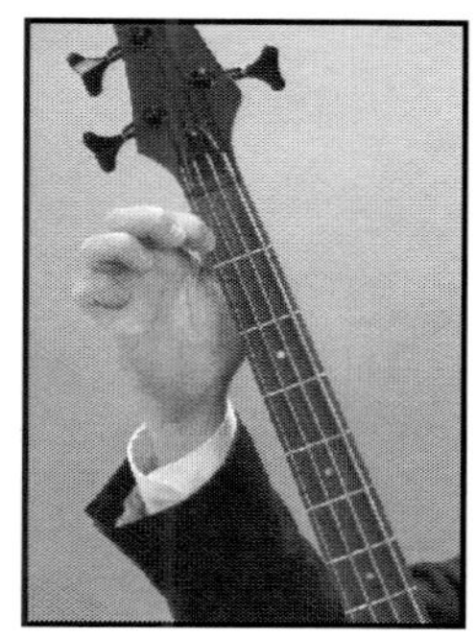

♭7th – A♭

B♭Ma7

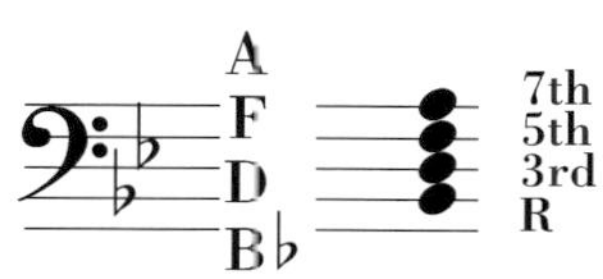

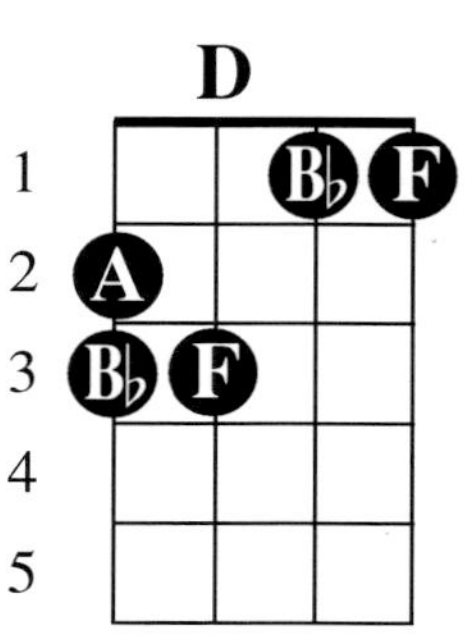

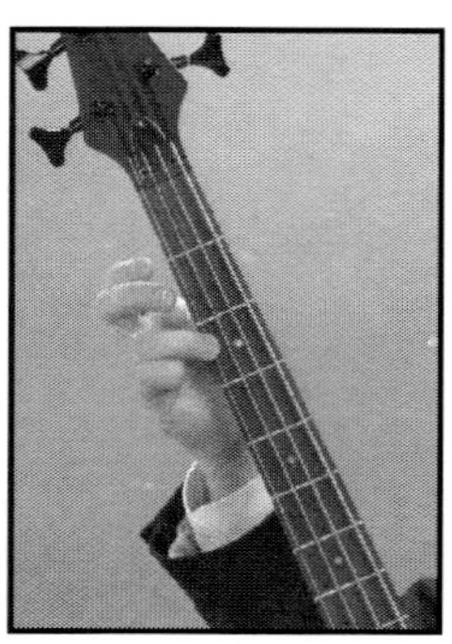

Root – B♭

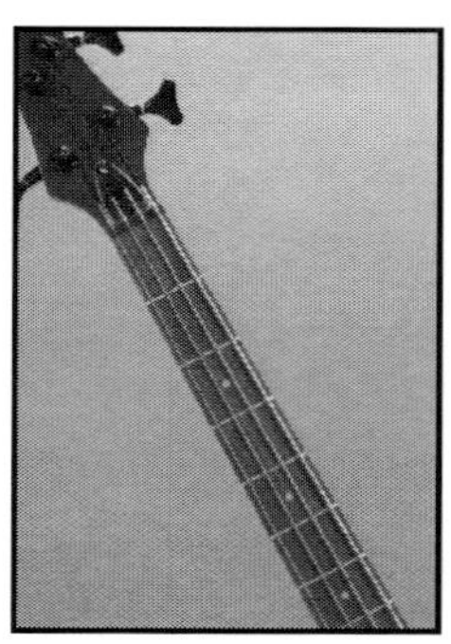

3rd – D

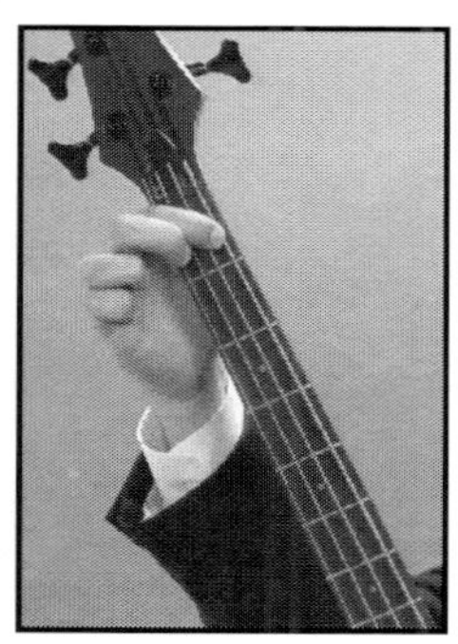

5th – F

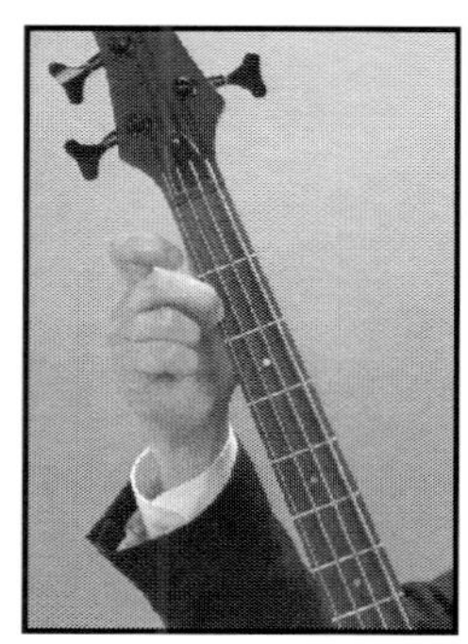

7th – A

Key of B♭ (cont.)

B♭dim

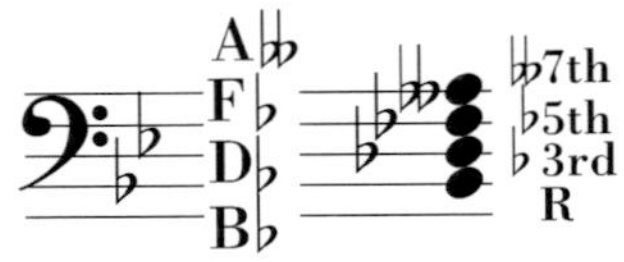

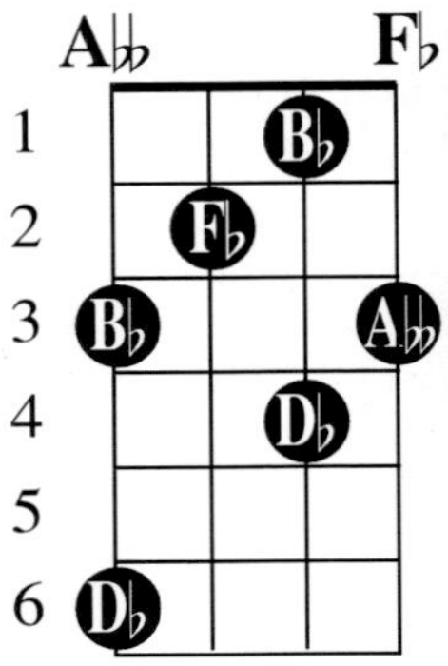

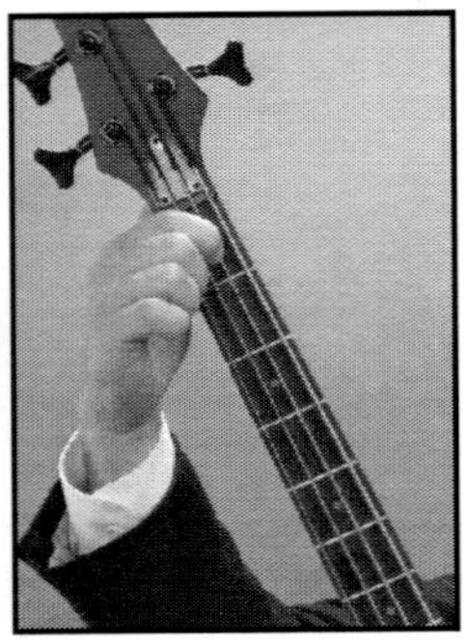

Root – B♭

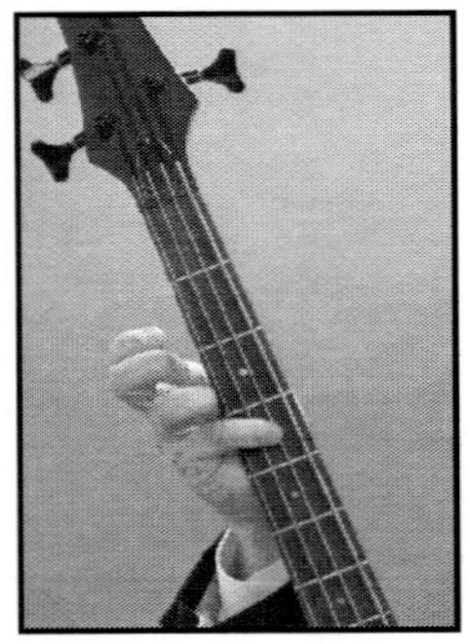

♭3rd – D♭

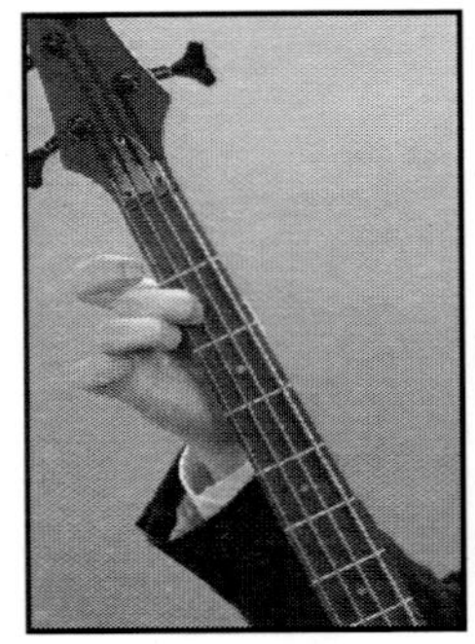

♭5th – F♭ or E

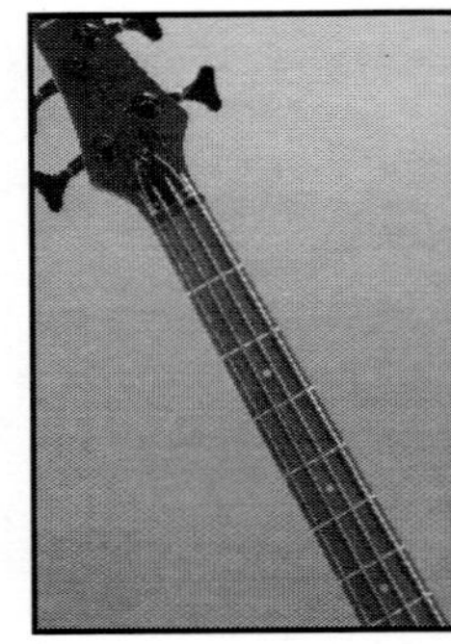

♭♭7th – A♭♭ or G

B♭aug

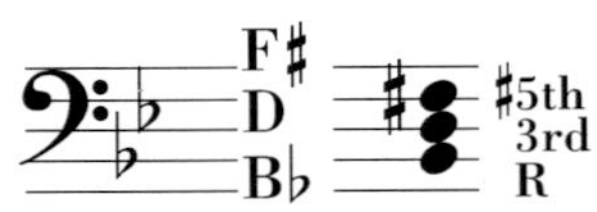

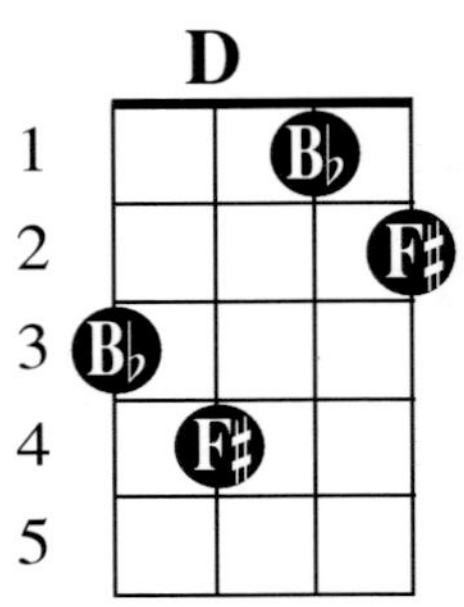

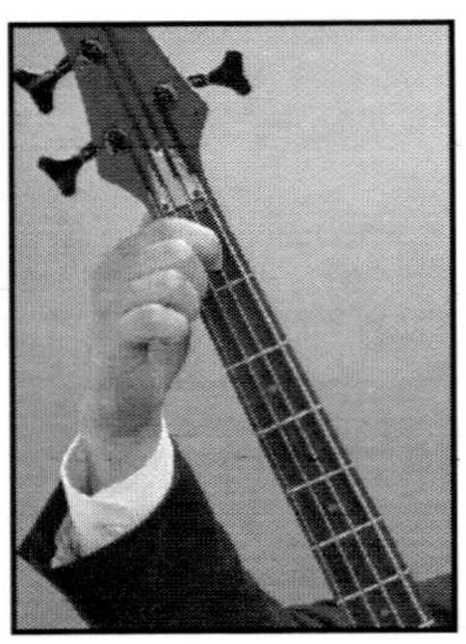

Root – B♭

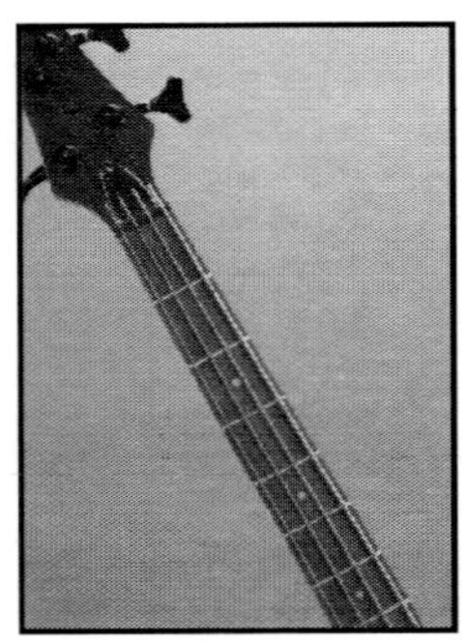

3rd – D

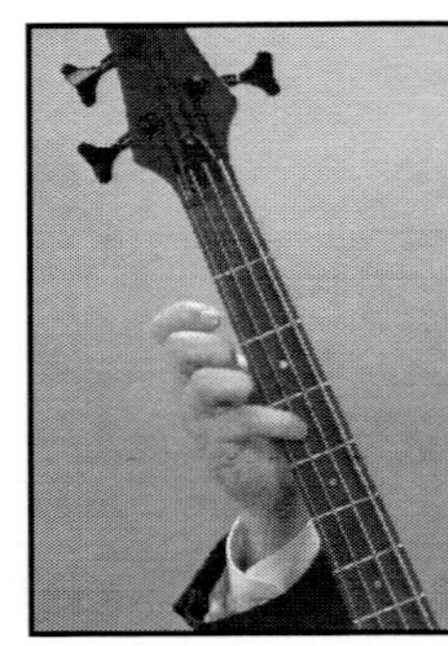

♯5th – F♯

B♭6

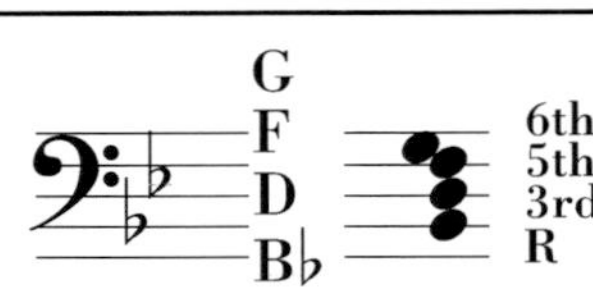

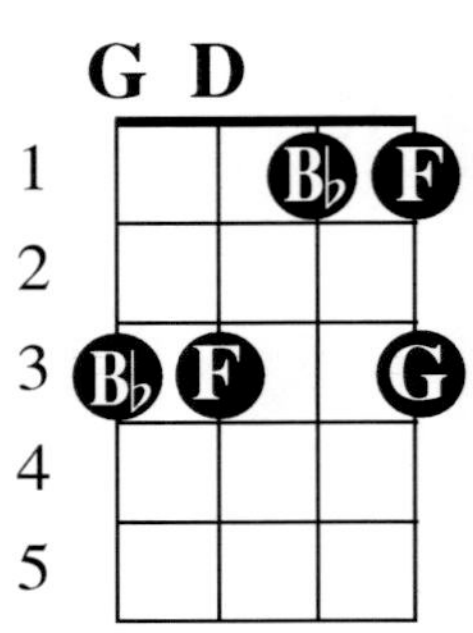

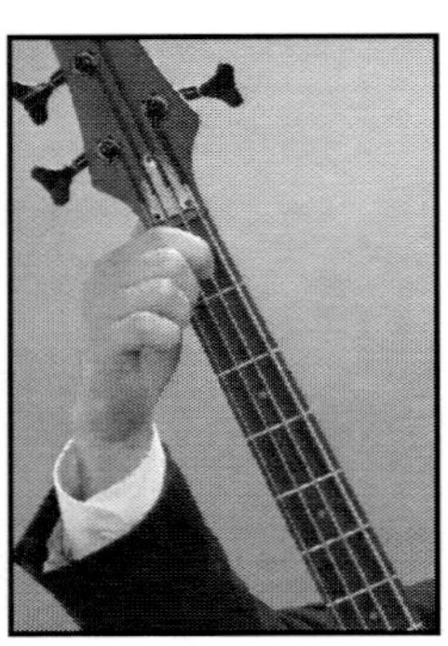

Root – B♭

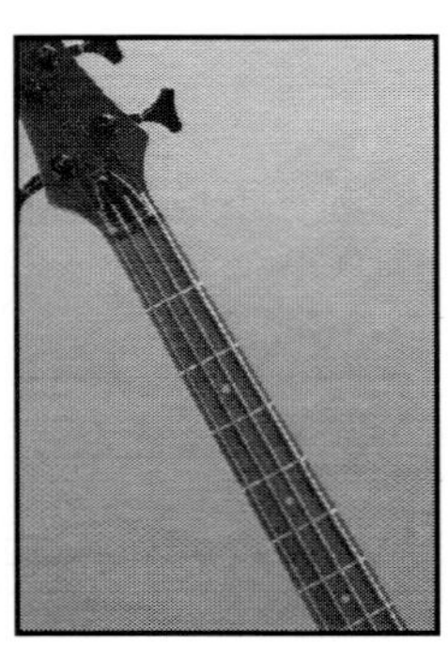

3rd – D

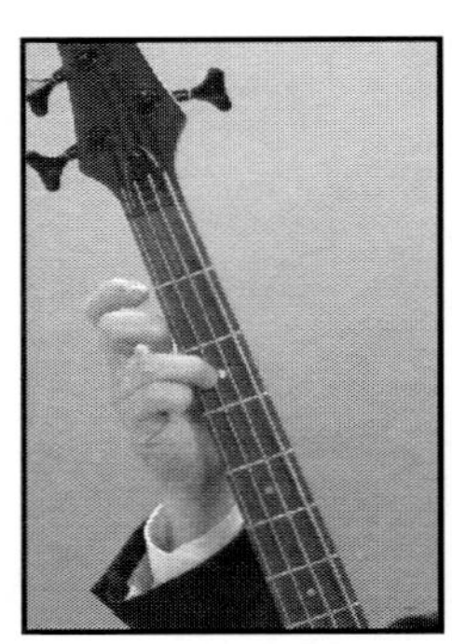

5th – F

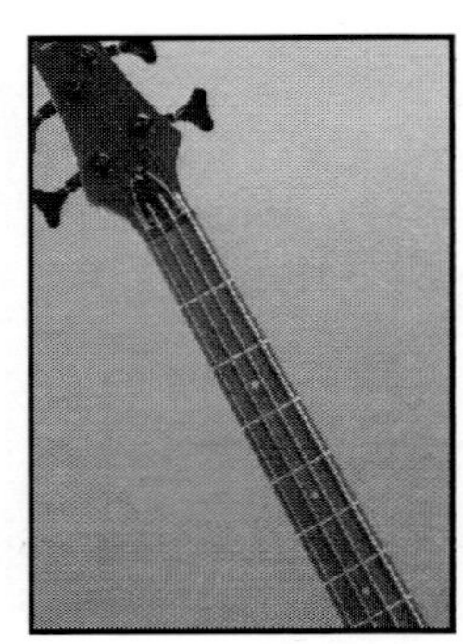

6th – G

Key of B♭ (cont.)

B♭m6

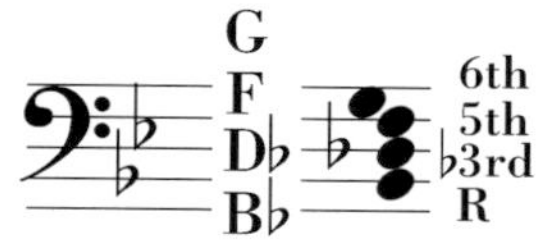

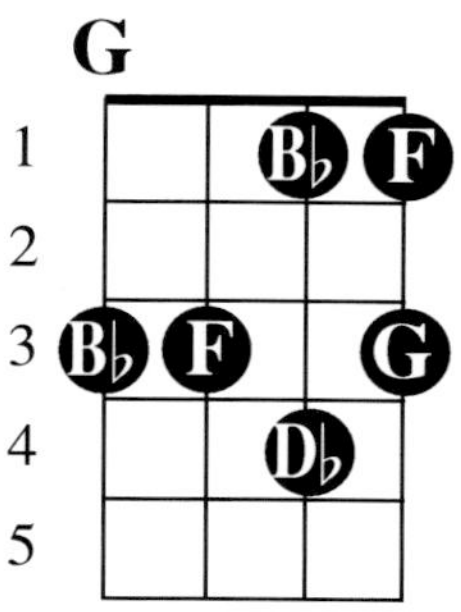

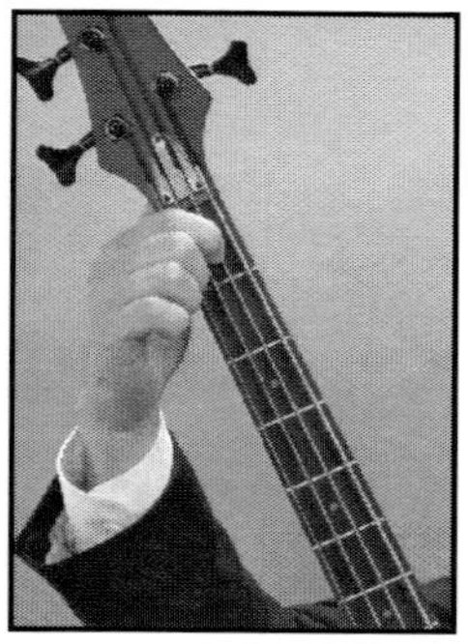
Root – B♭

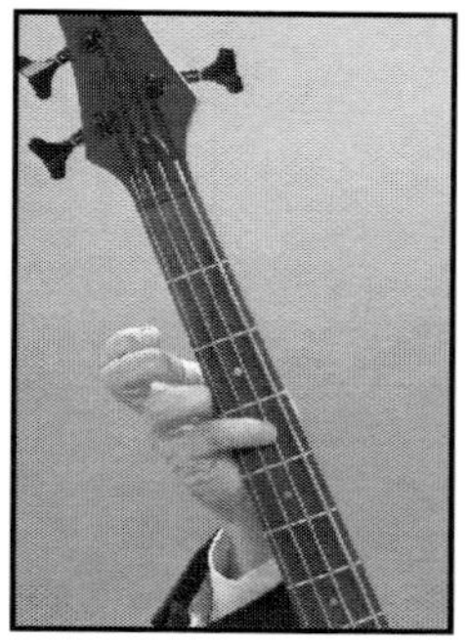
♭3rd – D♭

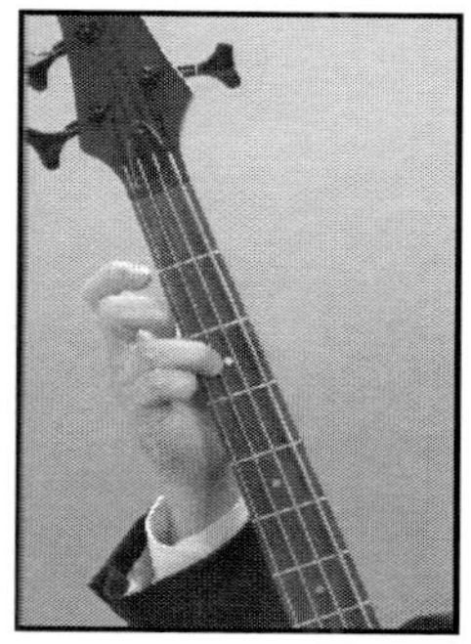
5th – F

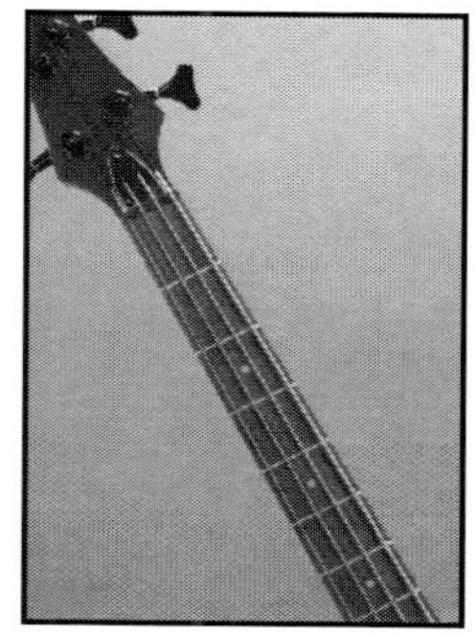
6th – G

B♭7♯5

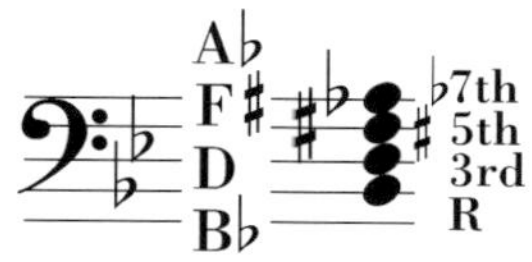

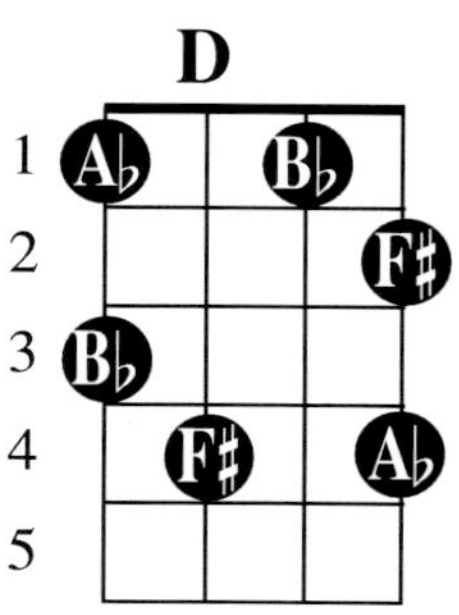

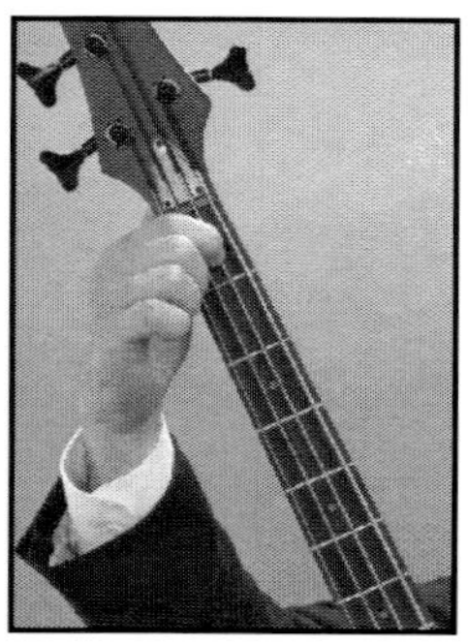
Root – B♭

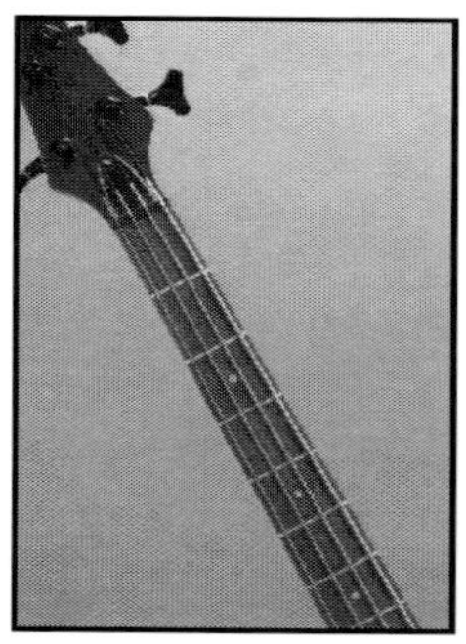
3rd – D

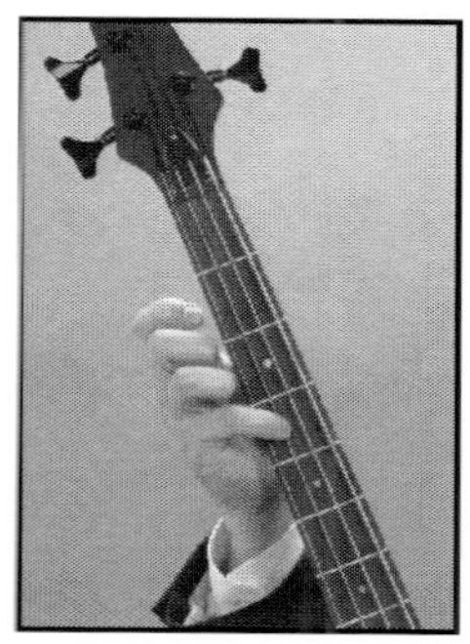
♯5th – F♯

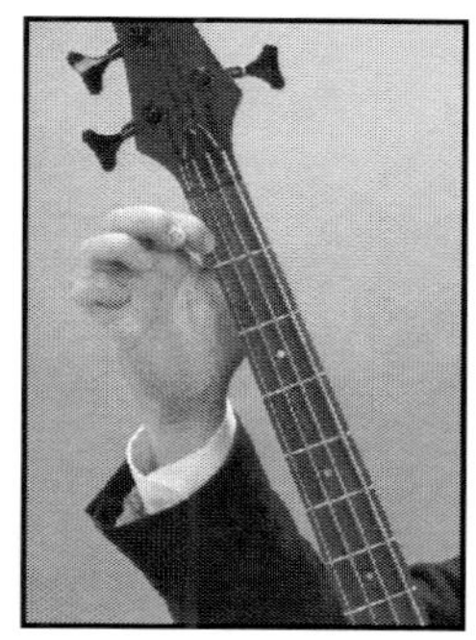
♭7th – A♭

B♭7♭5

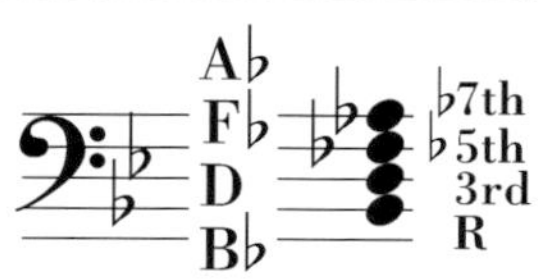

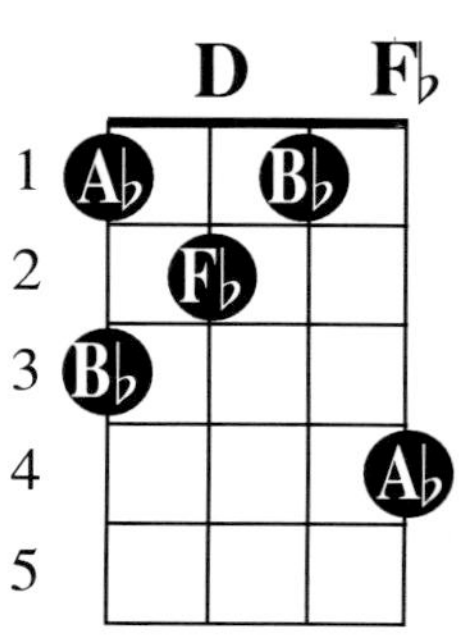

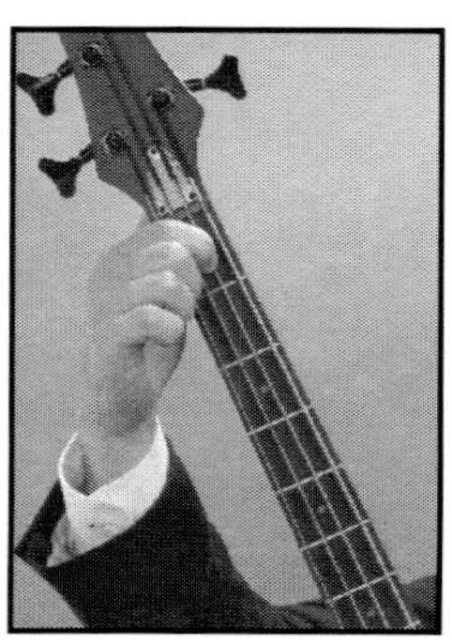
Root – B♭

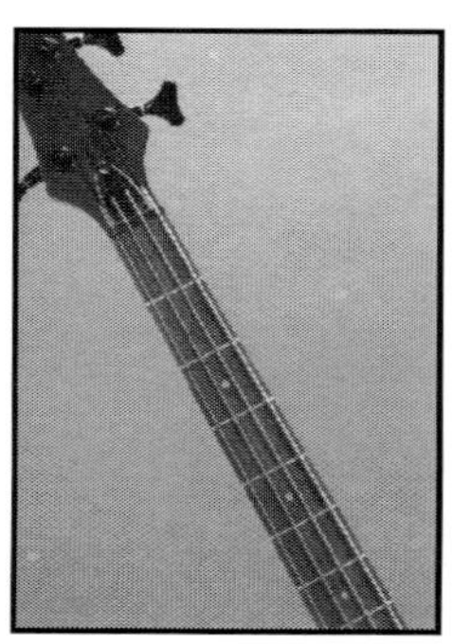
3rd – D

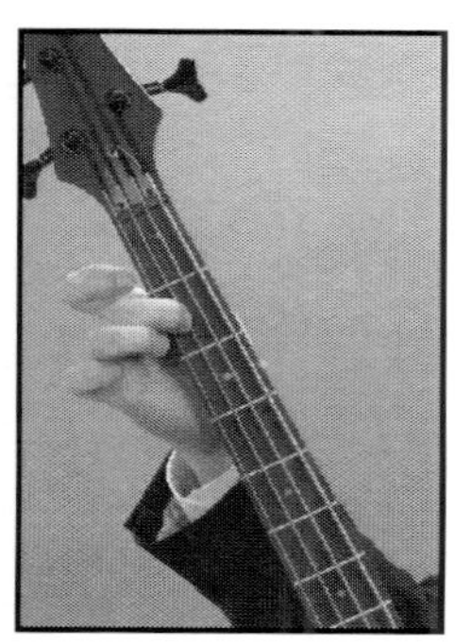
♭5th – F♭ or E

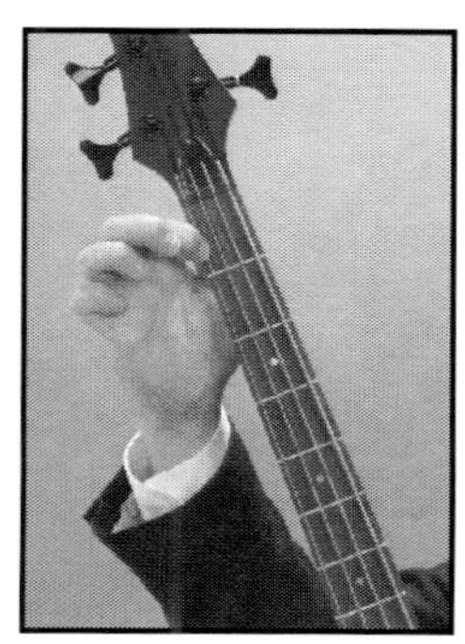
♭7th – A♭

Key of B

BMaj

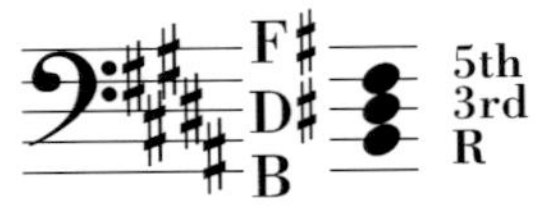

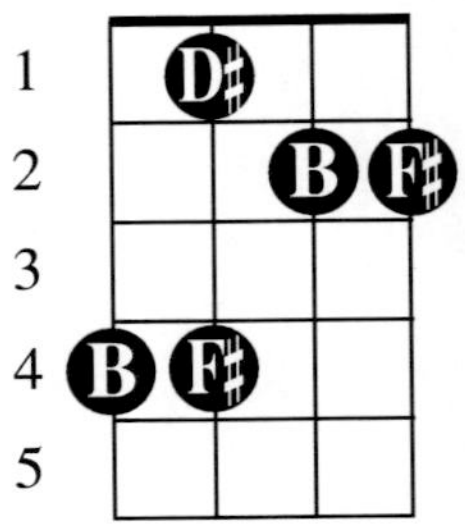

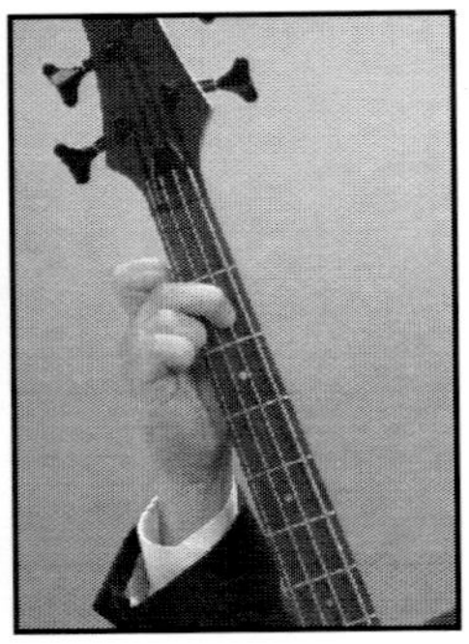
Root – B

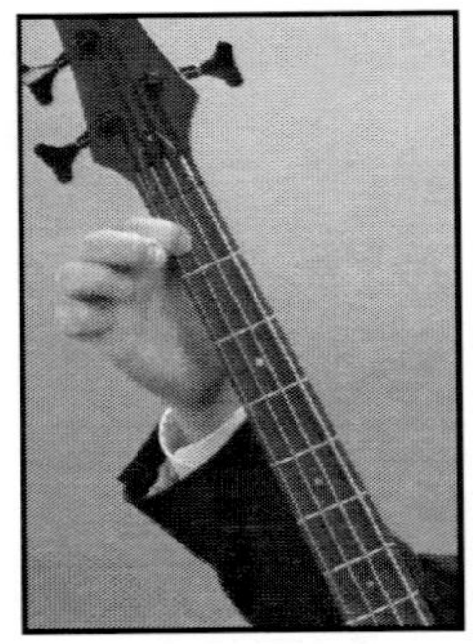
3rd – D♯

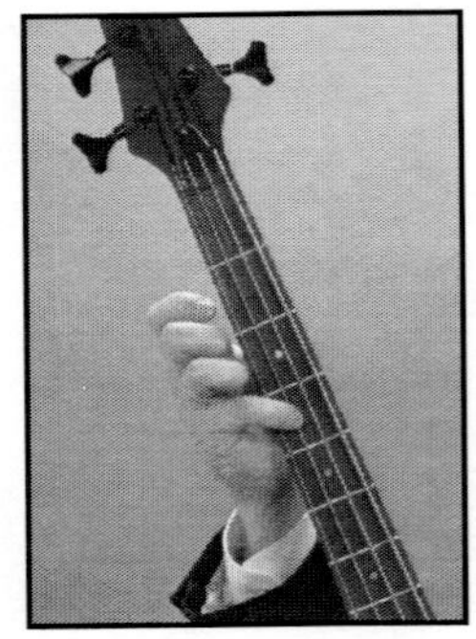
5th – F♯

Bmin

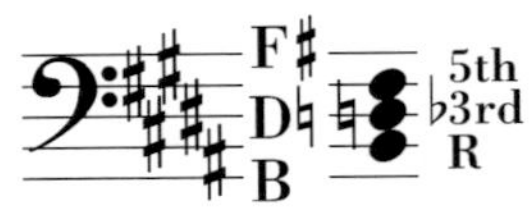

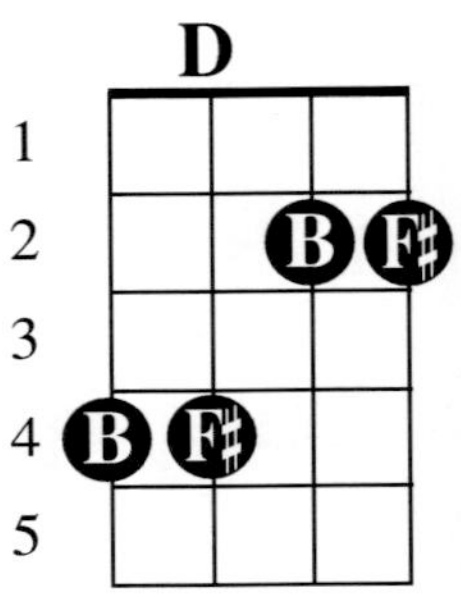

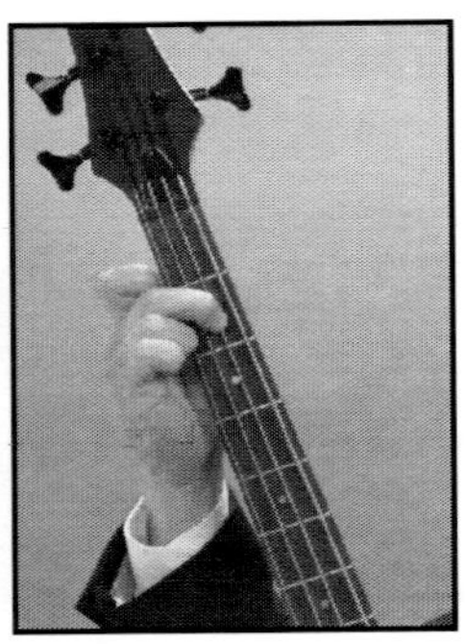
Root – B

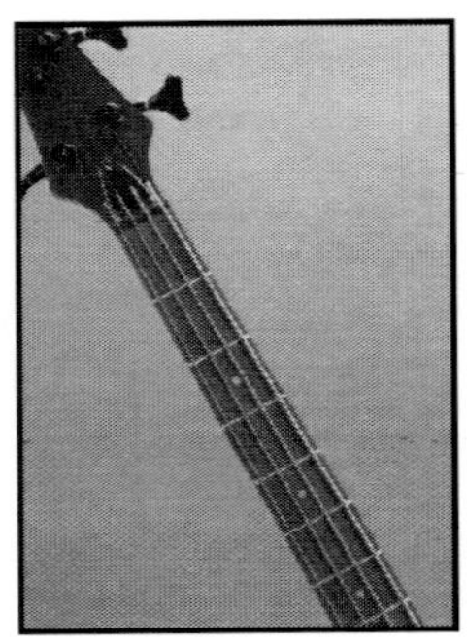
♭3rd – D♮

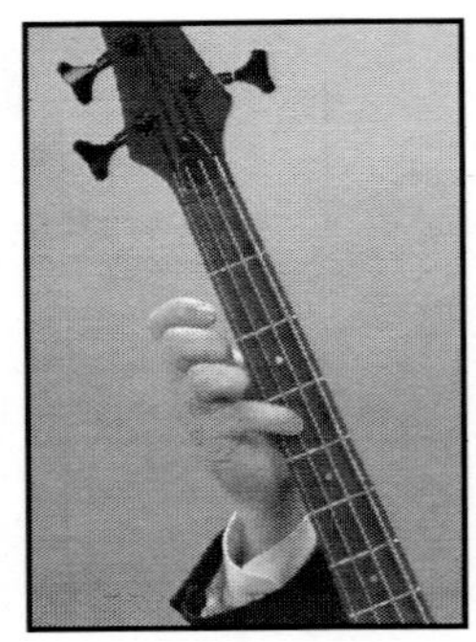
5th – F♯

B7

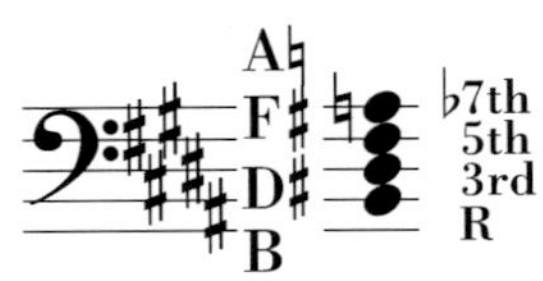

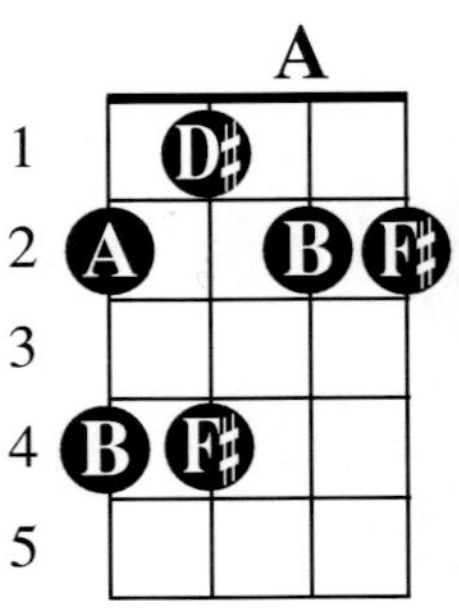

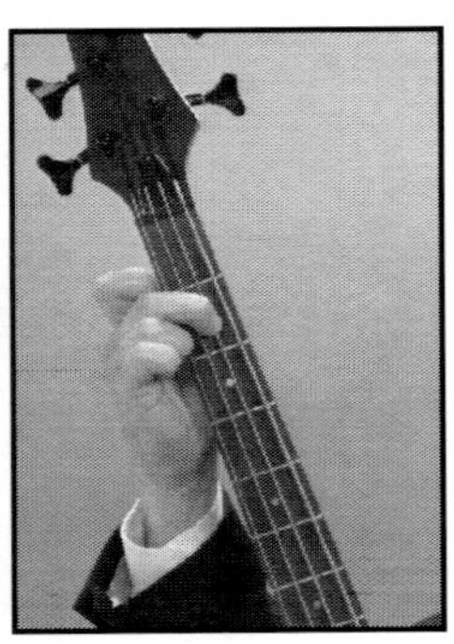
Root – B

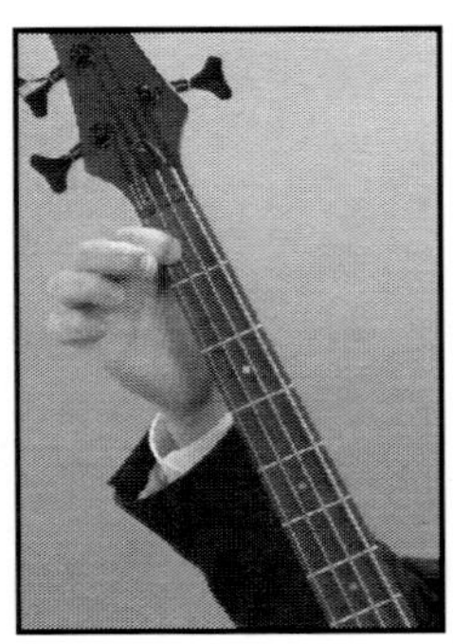
3rd – D♯

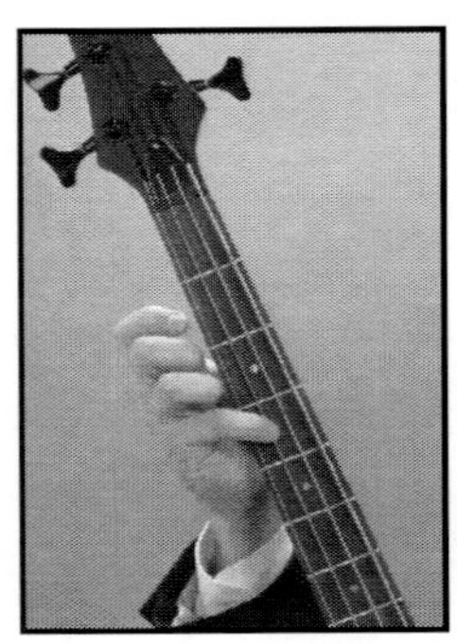
5th – F♯

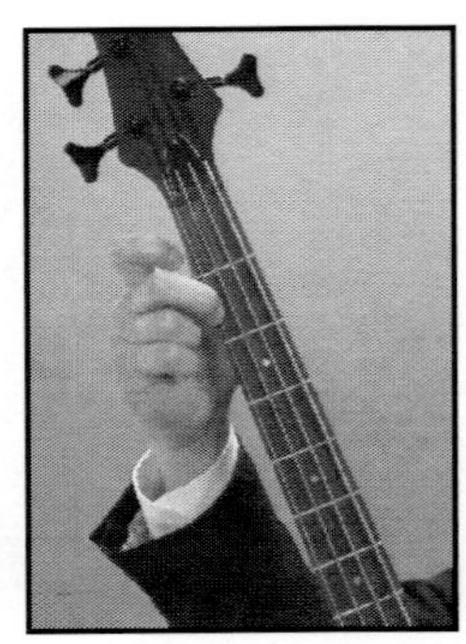
♭7th – A

Key of B (cont.)

B7sus

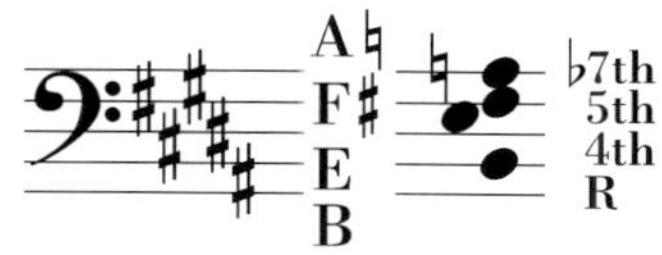

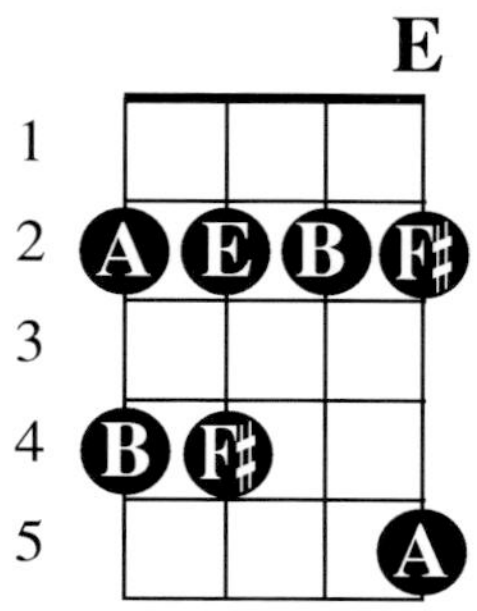

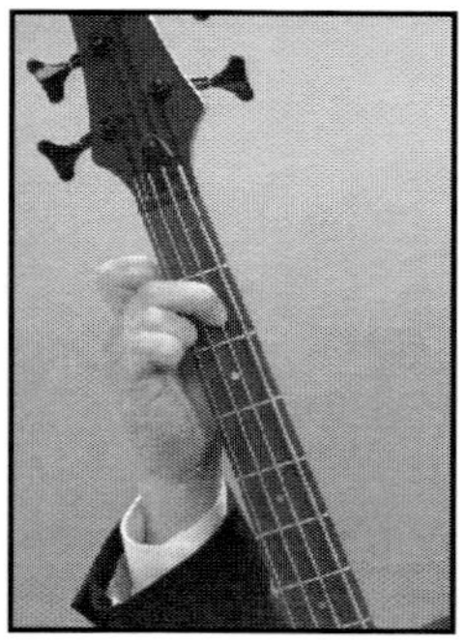

Root – B

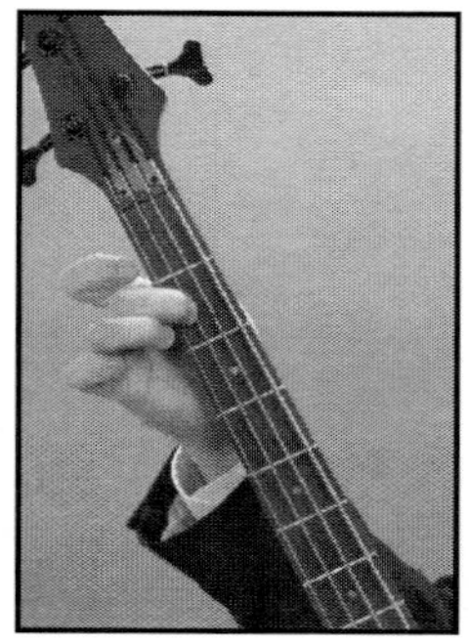

4th – E

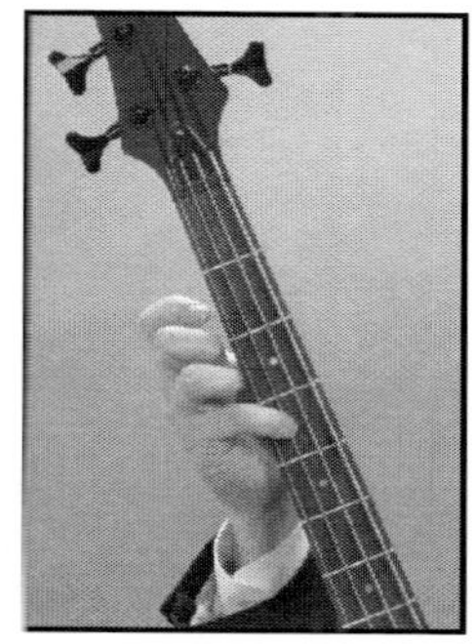

5th – F♯

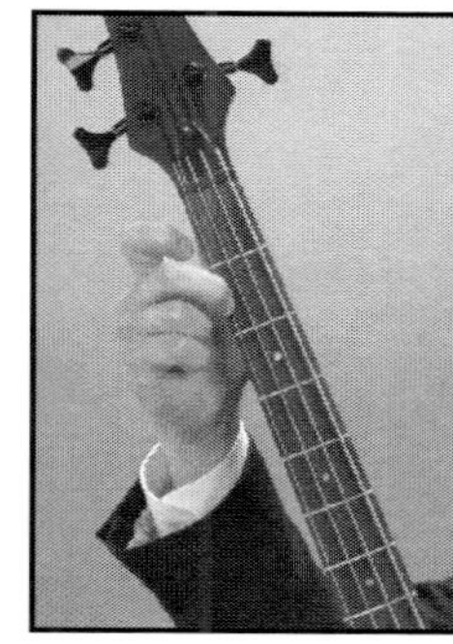

♭7th – A♮

Bm7

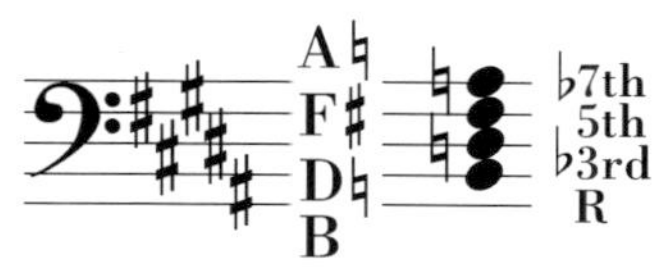

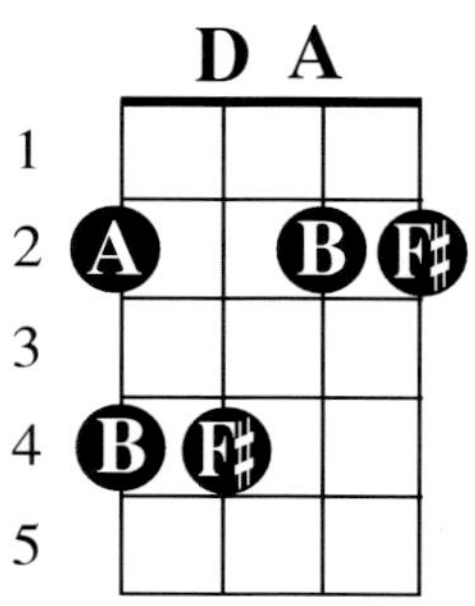

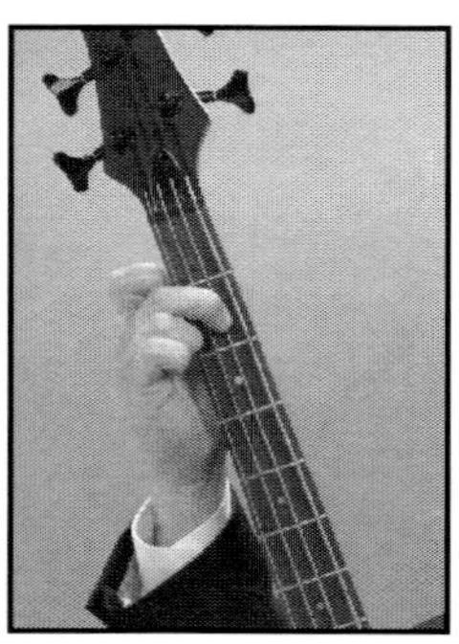

Root – B

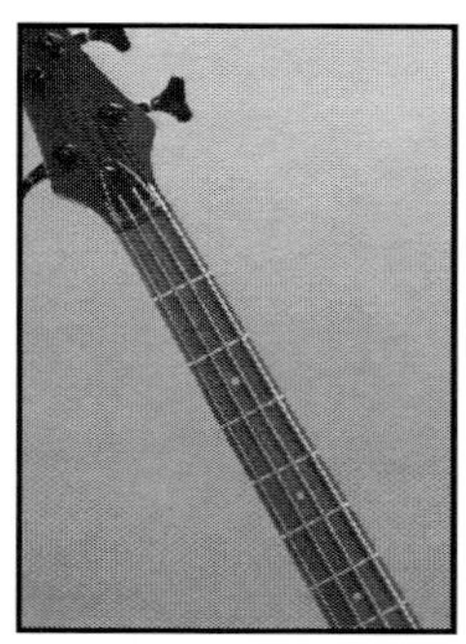

♭3rd – D♮

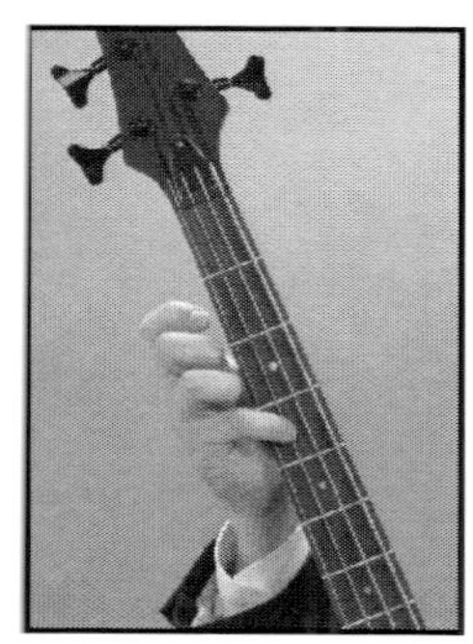

5th – F♯

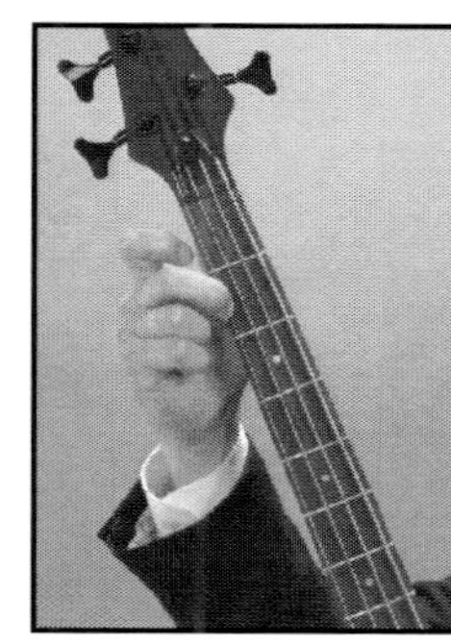

♭7th – A♮

BMa7

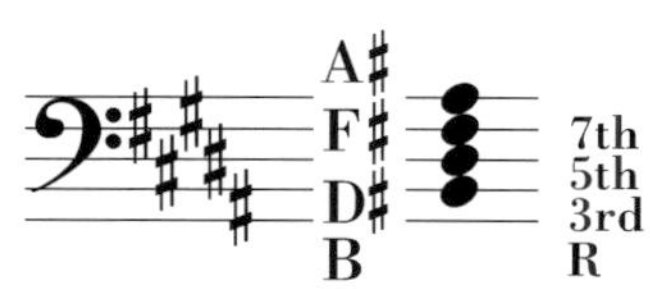

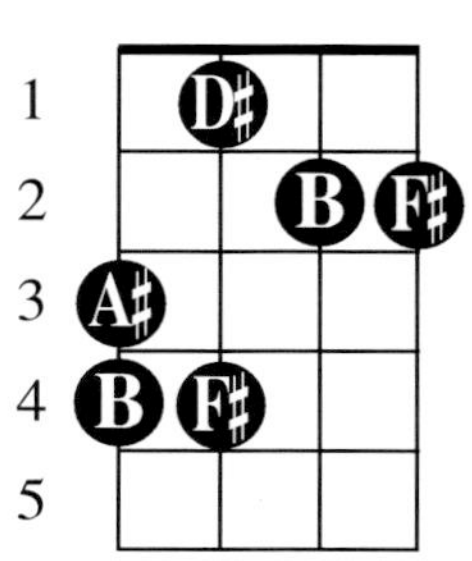

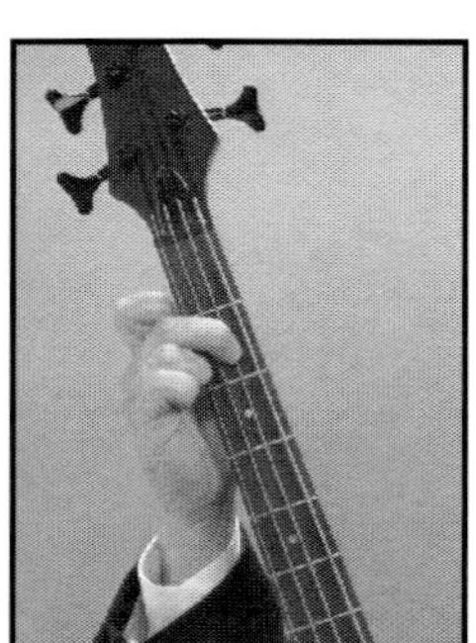

Root – B

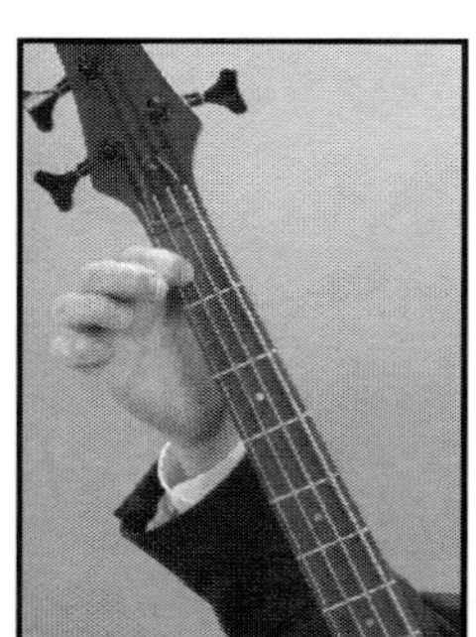

3rd – D♯

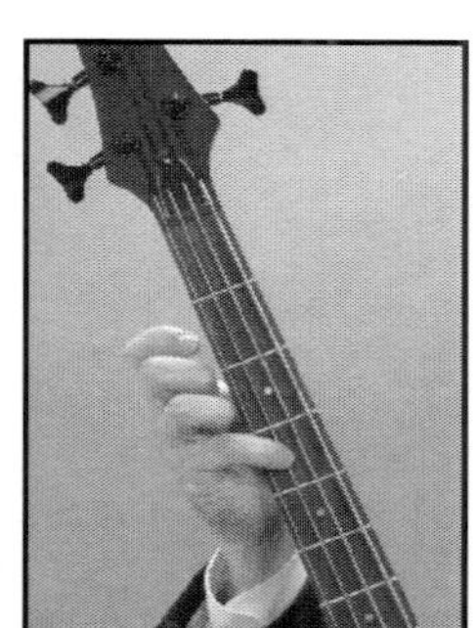

5th – F♯

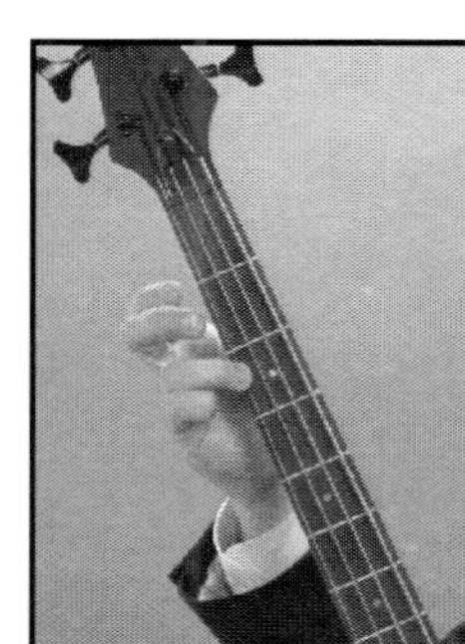

7th – A♯

Key of B (cont.)

Bdim

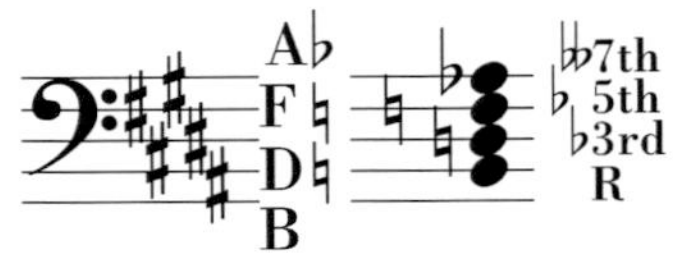

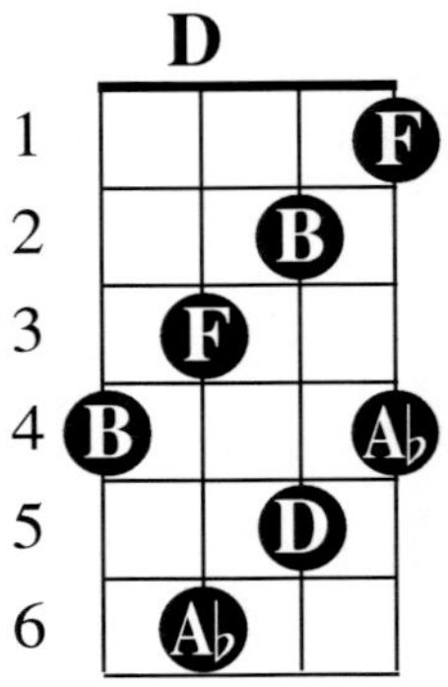

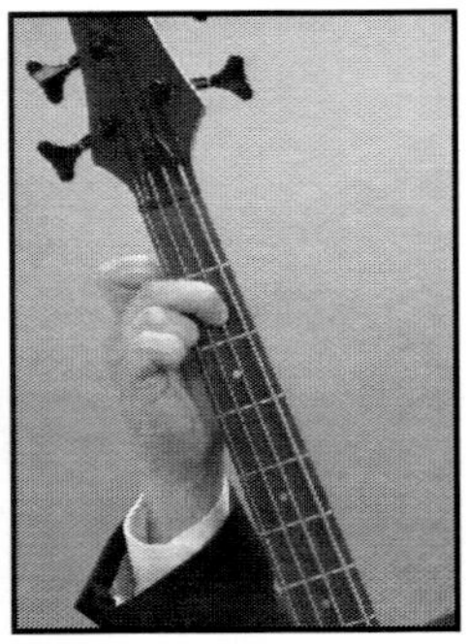

Root – B

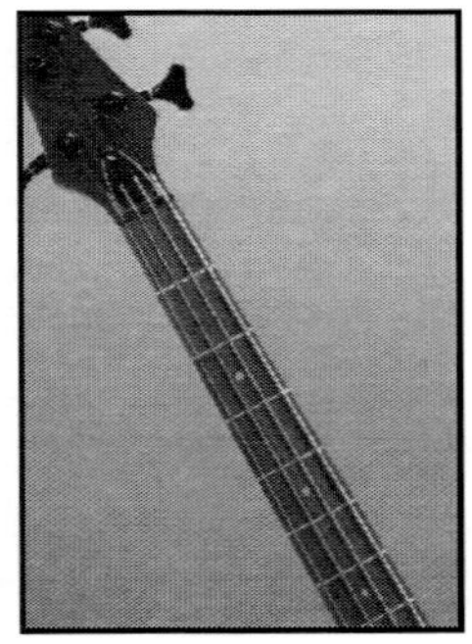

♭3rd – D

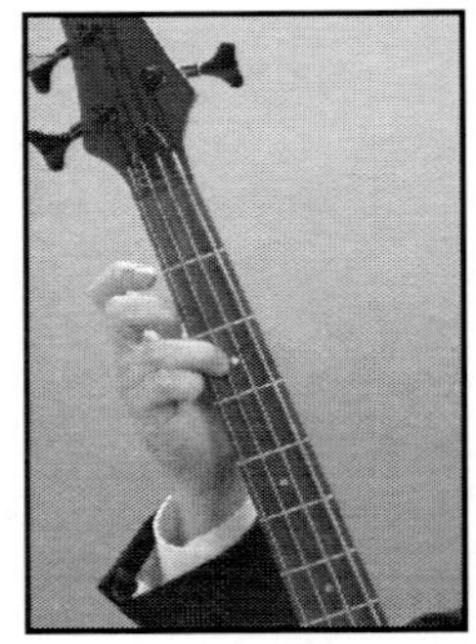

♭5th – F

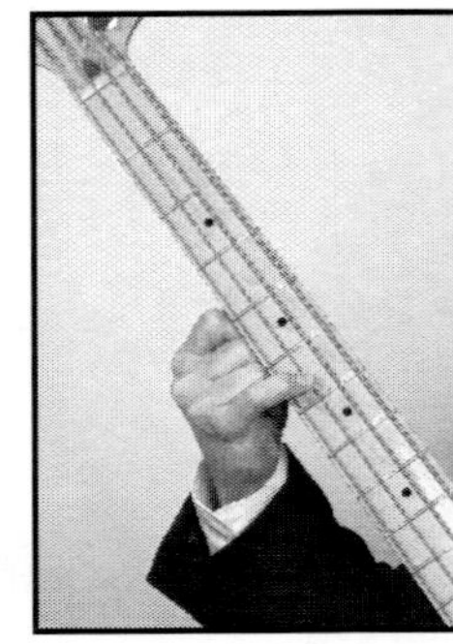

♭♭7th – A♭

Baug

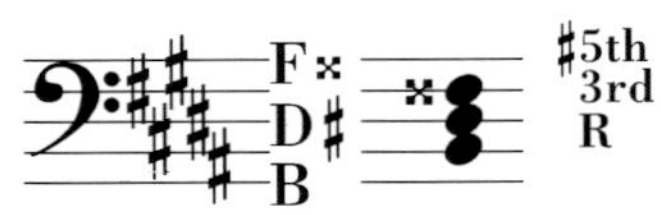

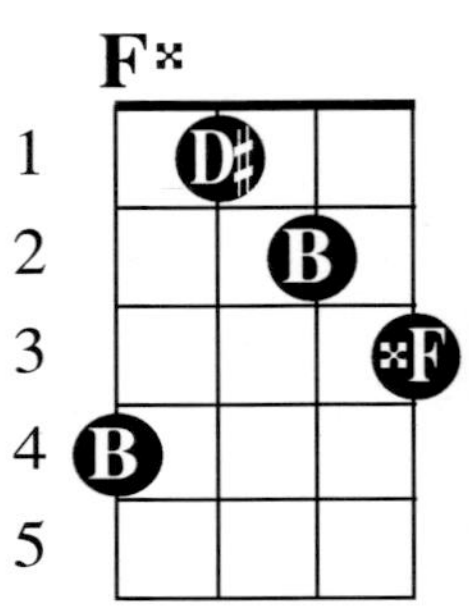

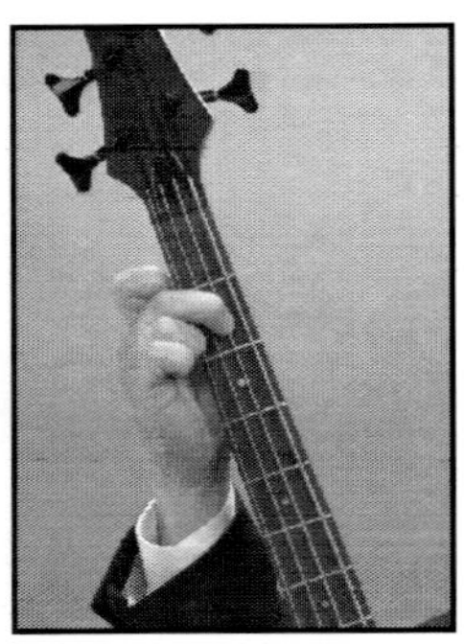

Root – B

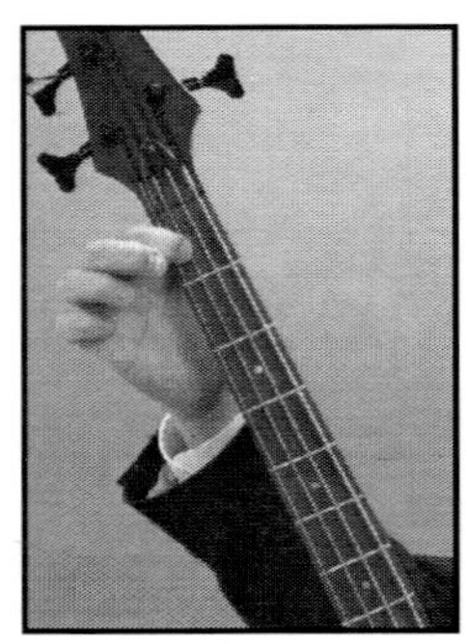

3rd – D♯

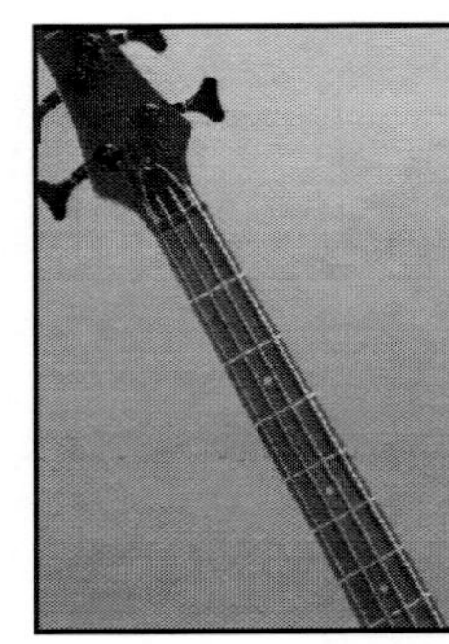

♯5th – F× or G

B6

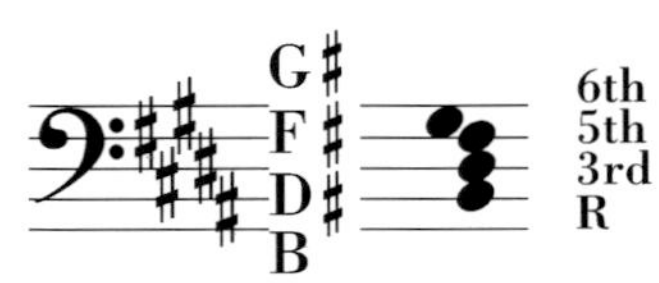

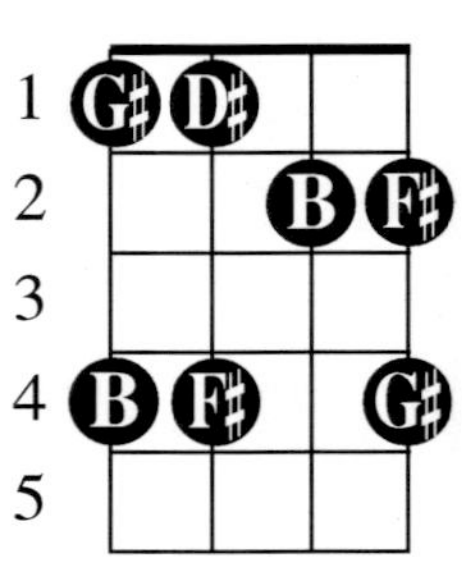

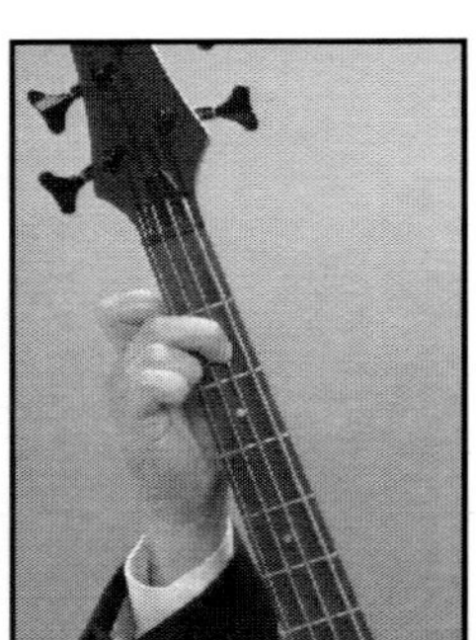

Root – B

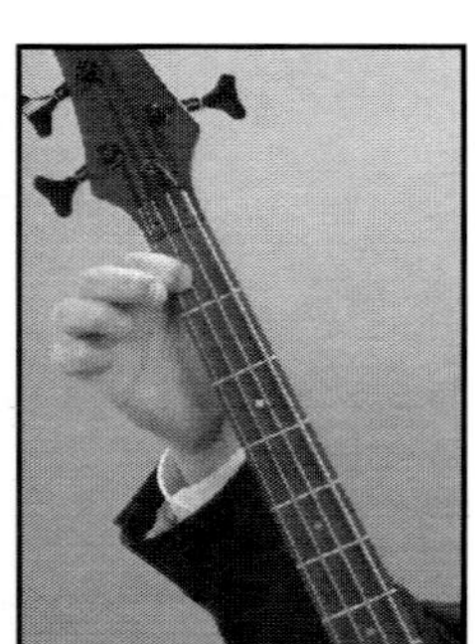

3rd – D♯

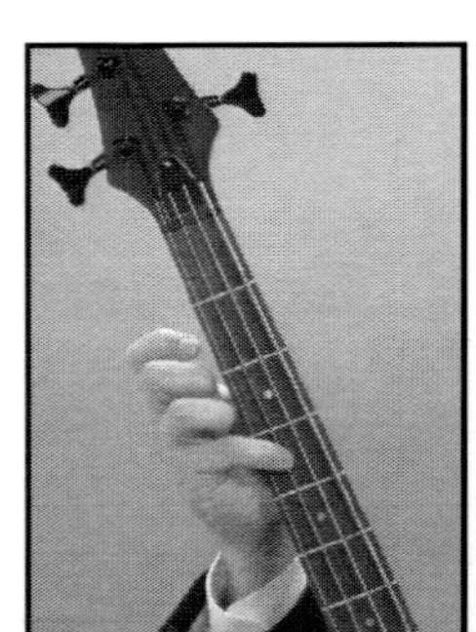

5th – F♯

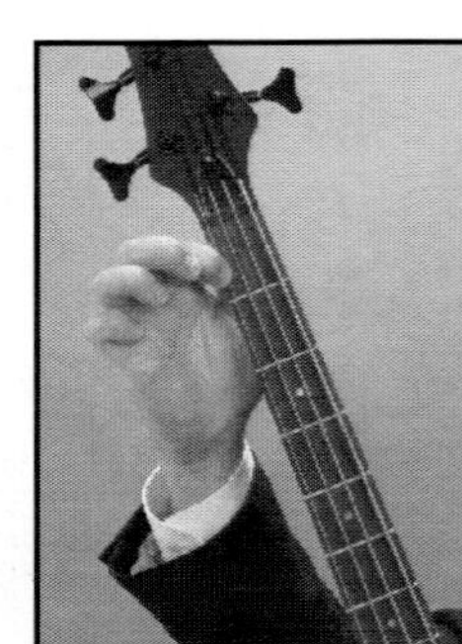

6th – G♯

Key of B (cont.)

Bm6

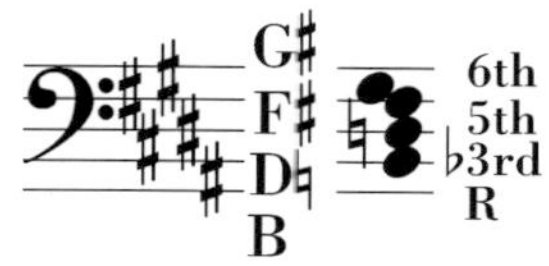

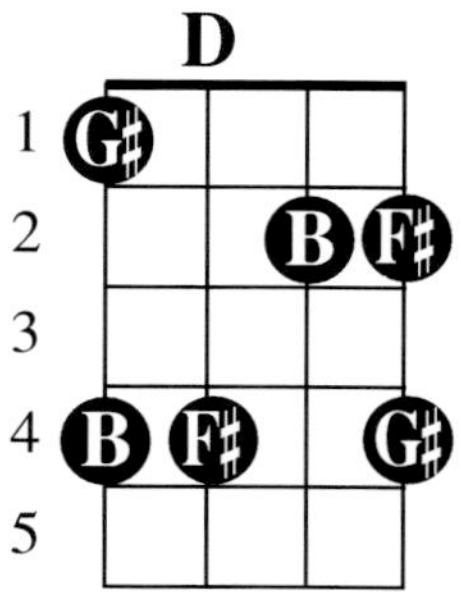

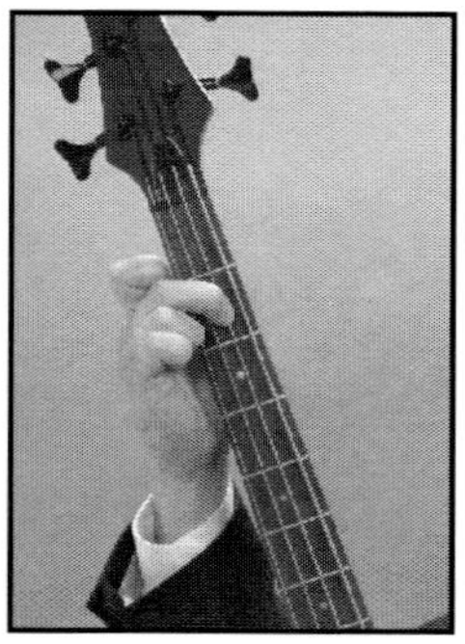

Root – B

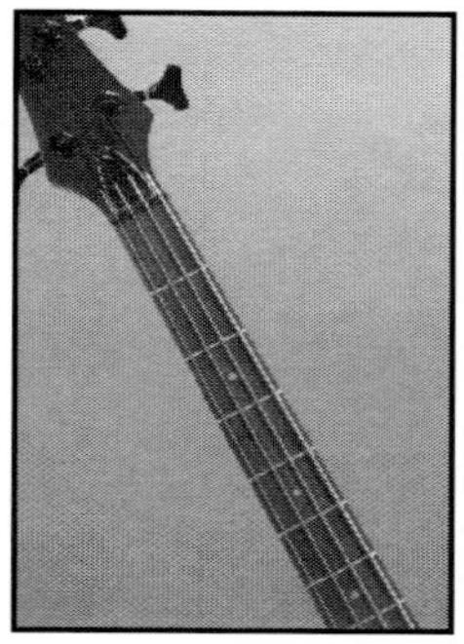

♭3rd – D

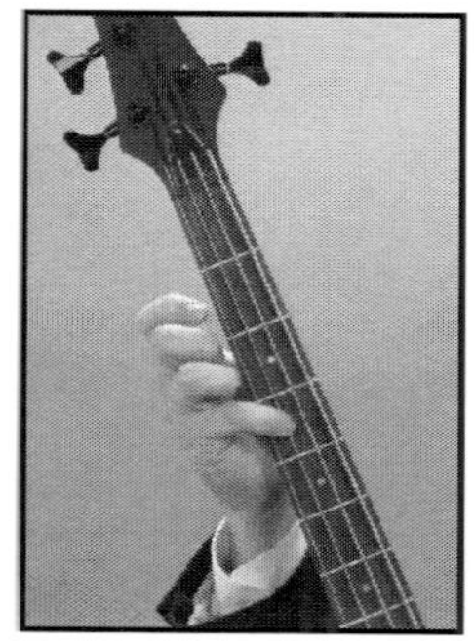

5th – F♯

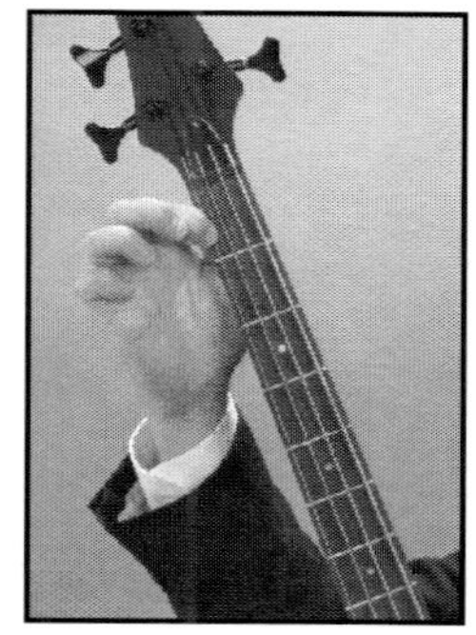

6th – G♯

B7♯5

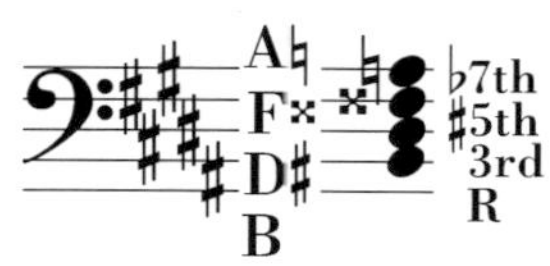

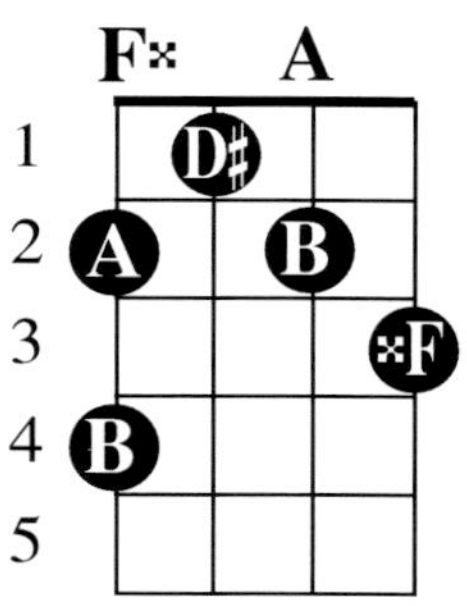

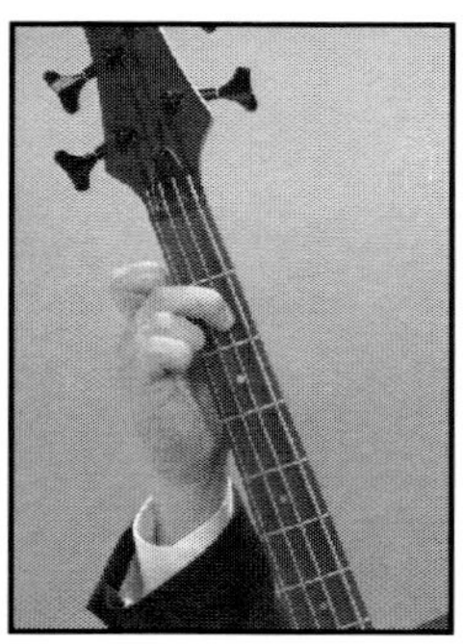

Root – B

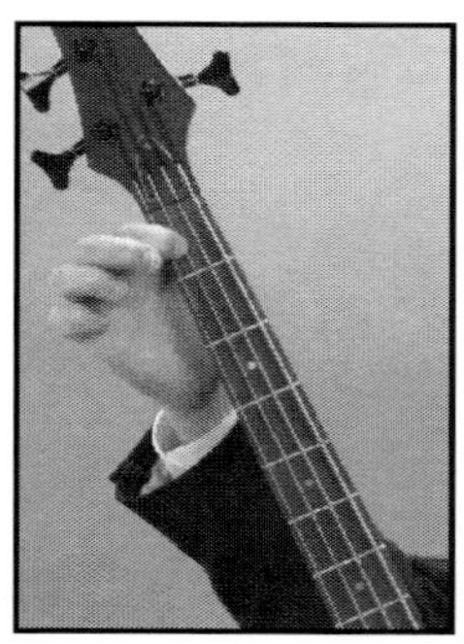

3rd – D♯

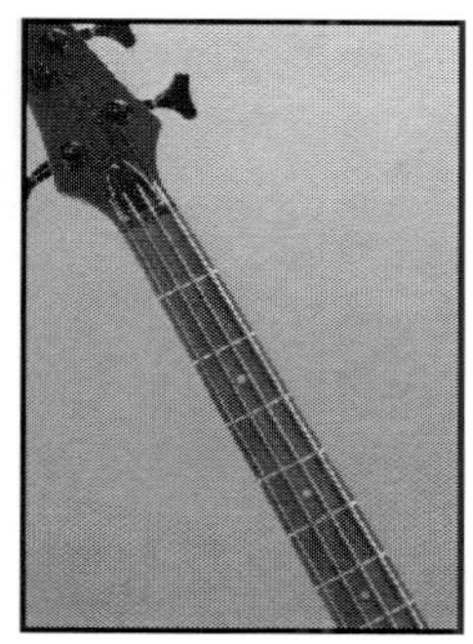

♯5th – F× or G

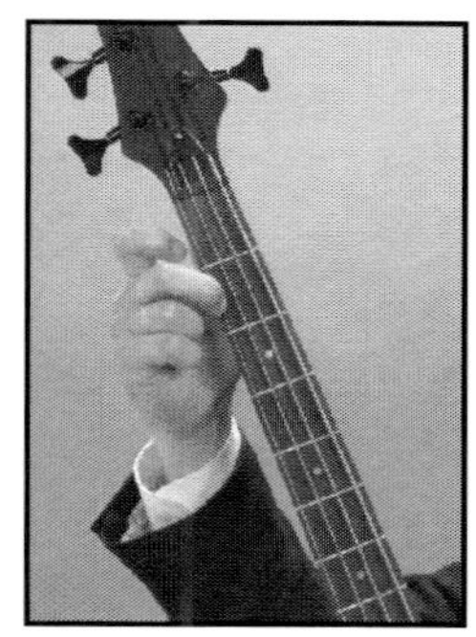

♭7th – A♮

B7♭5

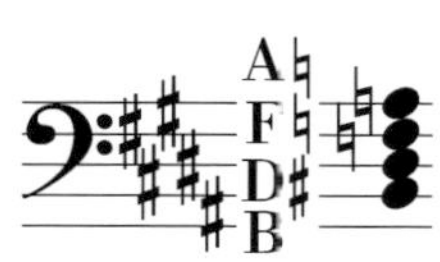

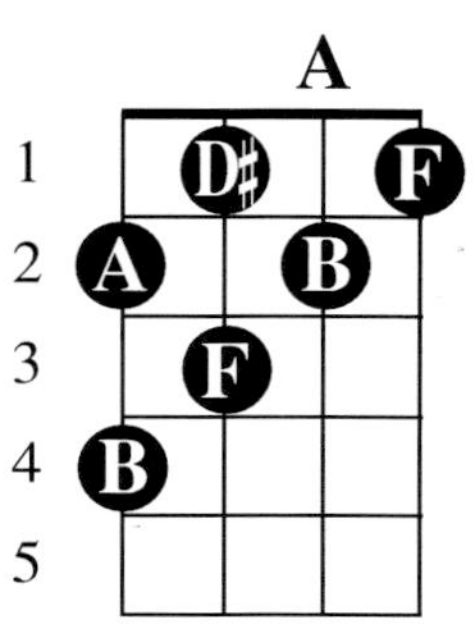

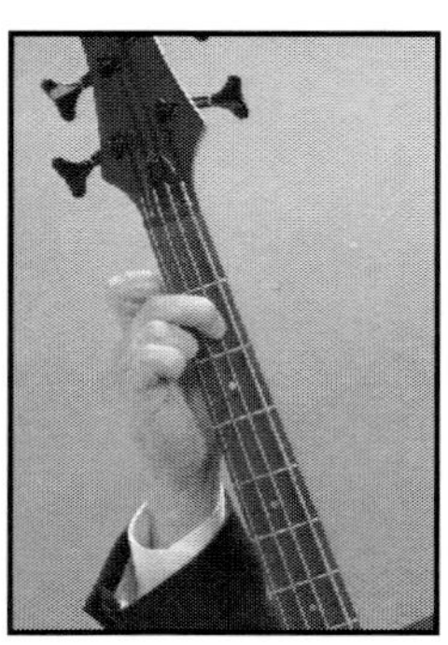

Root – B

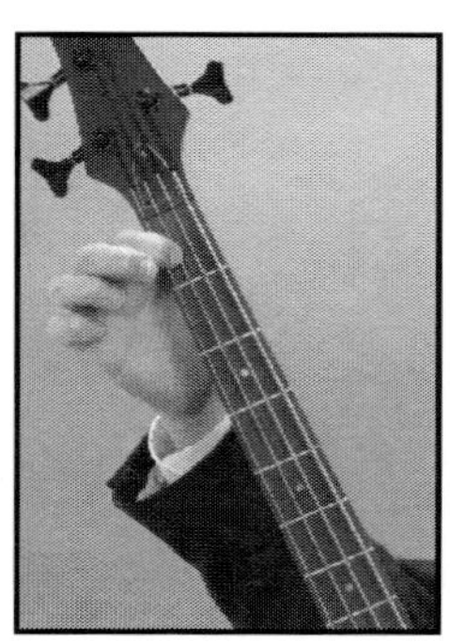

3rd – D♯

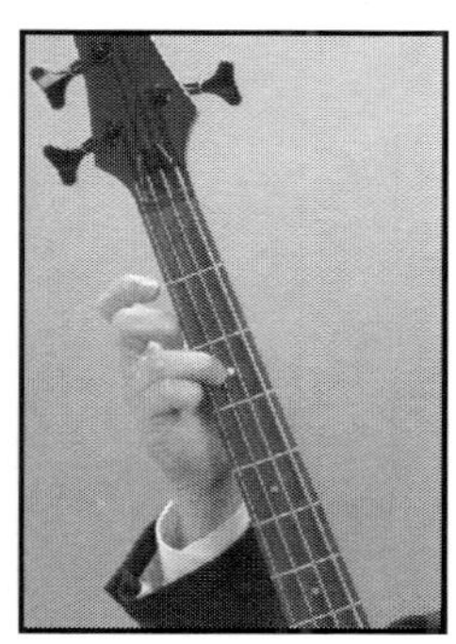

♭5th – F♮

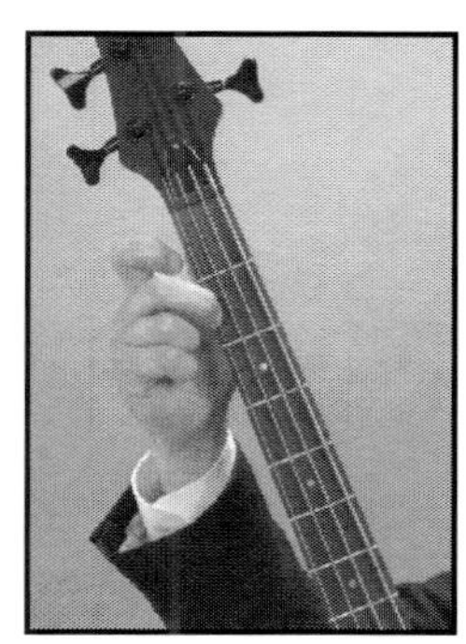

♭7th – A♮

Other Recommended Bass Books

Beginning Bass Solos (Gately)

Bass Styles Made Easy (Matheos)

Fun with the Electric Bass (Menke)

The Groove Book: A Study in Musical Styles for Bass (Ensign)

The Ultimate Heavy Metal Bass Book (Matheos)

The New Sound of Funk Bass (des Pres)

Encyclopedia of Bass Riffs (des Pres and Byrne)

Basic Bass Lines (Gately)

Reggae Grooves for Electric Bass (Matheos)

Percussive Slap Bass (Matheos)

Scale Studies for Bass (Monoxelos)

100 Rock & Roll Workouts for Bass (Matheos)

Learn to Burn: Electric Bass (Dozier)

New Passion of Playing Bass (Washburne)

WWW.MELBAY.COM